MARNY CLIFFORD'S
WASHINGTON COOKBOOK

Marny Clifford's Washington Cookbook

with illustrations by

John Falter

E. P. DUTTON & CO., INC. | New York | 1972

Copyright © 1972 by Marny Clifford
All rights reserved. Printed in the U.S.A.
First Edition

No part of this publication may be reproduced or transmitted in any form or by any means, electronic or mechanical, including photocopy, recording, or any information storage and retrieval system now known or to be invented, without permission in writing from the publisher, except by a reviewer who wishes to quote brief passages in connection with a review written for inclusion in a magazine, newspaper or broadcast.

Published simultaneously in Canada
by Clarke, Irwin & Company Limited, Toronto and Vancouver

SBN: 6-525-15300-4

Library of Congress Catalog Card Number: 72-82695

To Clark, Margery, Joyce and Randall
who have been my test pilots for many years

CONTENTS

Foreword by Mary Van Rensselaer Thayer   9

Introduction   17

Canapés and Quiches   21

Soups and Pasta   45

Egg Dishes and Cheese Dishes   73

Meat   87
   Beef
   Lamb
   Veal
   Pork
   Specialty Cuts

Poultry and Game   123

Fish and Seafood   161

Vegetables   203

Cereals (Rice and Barley)   241

Salads and Cold Mousses   249

Casseroles, Hot Mousses and Soufflés   299

Cold and Hot Sauces   329

Salad Dressings   361

Breads, Pancakes and Sandwiches   371

Desserts   395
    Fruits and Custards
    Cakes
    Ice Cream
    Dessert Mousses
    Pies
    Puddings
    Refrigerator Desserts
    Sherbets
    Dessert Soufflés

Frostings, Icings and Dessert Sauces   453

Cookies   465

Candy   477

Pickles, Relishes, Jams and Jellies   485

Beverages   497

Useful Information   509
    Herb Chart
    Equivalents
    Oven Heats
    Kitchen Equipment

Index   519

FOREWORD

This is not a cookbook in the usual sense, nor is it meant to be. Instead, it is a sharing of love of good food and the pleasure in creative cooking which Marny Clifford has enjoyed throughout the years. She started this book long ago, gathering for Margery, Joyce and Randall, her trio of daughters, generations-old recipes from a New England mother and grandmother. During twenty-five lively years in Washington, Marny has continued to coax recipes from her friends, the Capital's famous hostesses, and from the chatelaines of many foreign embassies where superlative food becomes a diplomatic asset in attracting high-ranking United States officials to dine.

Each recipe is a personal acquisition and its source is usually indicated. Marny comments gaily yet succinctly on her favorites, often fitting them into menus at her own parties where, through changing administrations, Presidents of the United States and top-ranking notables have been guests.

Some of the recipes are truly exotic, but most are deliciously different and imaginative ways of creating dishes whose ingredients may be purchased at most grocery stores. All of the recipes are intriguing and their diversity is impressive, from the tasty beef soup created by Mrs. Hubert Humphrey's father, to Mrs. Woodrow Wilson's elegant "Pears in Cointreau with Frozen Cream"; from Clark Clifford's favorite "Barbecued Mint Lamb" to Ambassador David Bruce's "Sauce Archiduc." There is Mrs. Richard Nixon's delicate "Pumpkin Pie"; Mrs. Lyndon B. Johnson's fiery "Enchiladas"; Mrs. Eisenhower's "Frosted Mint Delight"; Mrs. Truman's "Blarney Stones"; and, for sheer excitement, Nathaniel Benchley's "Nantucket Bluefish Broiled in Gin"! Even an "economy" dish with a new twist is included. It's "Chicken Gizzards in Sauce" which, Marny notes, are "very inexpensive and delicious. No one seems to know what they are eating which, for those who are 'anti-innards,' is a good thing!"

The seafood recipes are wonderfully varied. Some are family inheritances; others were acquired during summers the Cliffords spend in Nantucket, and many, of course, are from friends and Washington party-givers. The "Fish Chowder," which the late President John F. Kennedy doted on, comes from the former First Lady Jacqueline Kennedy Onassis. Here too are "My Grandmother's Clam Bouillon," which is flavored with unusual authority; "Indonesian Sole," a "subtle and superior" dish which Marny's doctor picked up in London; one of her easy-to-make, "never fail" dishes, "Filet of Sole Stuffed with Shrimp"; a dozen different ways to cook oysters and crabs; and an extravaganza called "My Special Party Scallops with Mushrooms and Wine," which requires eighteen pounds of the fluted bivalve and should serve forty lucky guests!

The recipes from distant lands are spectacular. Marny culled them without geographic favoritism from countries as far away as Malaysia and from nearby Mexico, but with a special emphasis on the delicious Polynesian dishes she has found so adaptable to party cooking. Surprisingly, one of her most intriguing foreign recipes, which she discovered in St. Louis, is of humble origin. Simply, "German Spaghetti"!

Marny's first gastronomic experience, which occurred when she was about ten, was reading her grandmother's personal recipe book. One favorite made an indelible impression. It read: "Plunge seven dozen lobsters into a wash boiler, two-thirds filled with boiling ocean water. When it boils again, cook for 18 to 20 minutes." The lobsters, cooked on a wood-burning stove, then kept steaming over a driftwood fire, were the *pièce de résistance* at the "rock" parties her grandmother gave during summers on the New Hampshire shore. Grandmother's ingredients were generous; the cooking directions simple and easily understandable. These two basic factors were to underscore the young girl's future approach to cooking. For throughout her cookbook the ingredients are grandly unstinted and the succeeding steps in preparation are precisely indicated and stripped of any diversionary patter.

Marny's mother, whose premarital culinary expertise was limited to fudge and popovers, became a very fine cook entirely by trial and error. Marny's father, too, was a self-taught expert. An ardent sportsman, he cooked the game he bagged and the fish he caught, and on summer Sundays relaxed, keeping open house for friends who dropped by to sample his blueberry pancakes, partnered with apple syrup and sluiced down with champagne. So, inevitably, by the time Marny was twelve, she was really learning to cook. Her mother taught her with patience and in her own imaginative way. Nevertheless, before Marny married and went off to live in St. Louis, her mother insisted that she learn the basics of cooking, properly, at a cooking school. Despite this conventional training, Marny remains a creative cook at heart. She cannot resist experimenting with every recipe she tests, adding a touch of this or a dash of that, in an effort to "pinpoint the result on the same wavelength as my taste buds."

Marny Kimball met Clark Clifford in Germany. With separate groups of vacationing young friends, they happened to sail along the Rhine in the same sight-seeing ship. He was a rising young lawyer from St. Louis. She came from Boston. Soon the Cliffords settled down in the bridegroom's home town where they remained twelve years before coming to Washington.

While in St. Louis, Marny burnished her cooking skill, collected recipes and, as a serious student of the piano over many years, turned her outside interests, naturally, toward music. She became one of the founders and first President of the St. Louis Opera Guild and in this role was associated with a wide cross-section of St. Louisans. Gradually Marny blossomed into a much-sought-after young hostess, famed for her delicious and often tantalizingly unusual food.

Her first really "important" party, though, hovered close to comic disaster. The after-the-show supper honored Giovanni Martinelli, veteran star of the New York Metropolitan Opera Company. An early arrival fell headlong down the front stairs; Marny's dog was untidily sick in the living room; and moments before the honored guest was due, the distracted hostess learned that the tenor preferred his beer warm. Bottles were hustled from the refrigerator and set atop radiators throughout the house. Martinelli arrived, was escorted to an uncomfortable chair originally owned by Daniel Webster and, when the stocky singer sat down, all four legs spread-eagled. That broke the ice and the party was a success.

In Washington, years later, entertaining an opera star, Marny coped with another nearly disastrous evening. A friend was bringing Mary Garden, the most glamorous diva of her era, to dine with the Cliffords. The menu, painstakingly planned, featured imported Cape Breton oysters, a gourmet treat provided by another friend, the Belgian Ambassador Baron Silvercruys. The dinner setup was very smart indeed, because the Ambassador sent his embassy chef to open the oysters just before they were served. But neither the hostess nor the diva's friend was aware of Miss Garden's unique dietary quirk. She refused both oysters and all other delicacies. All she wanted was her everyday dinner, chocolate ice cream and black coffee. And only ice cream and coffee. Since the Clifford freezer stocked, at the time, no chocolate ice cream, a member of the household was despatched to the nearest drugstore. Then, while the other guests sampled the delicious oysters, Mary Garden contentedly spooned her ice cream.

Marny was aware that if the chocolate ice cream had been unobtainable, this amusing incident might have turned into a minor calamity. So from then on, and well in advance of any party, she took pains to learn what her most special guests preferred to eat. Even if her dinner menu differed, she made sure that these friends were served the food they wanted, prepared the way they liked it. This attention, always warmly appreciated, added to her status as a thoughtful hostess.

The Clark Cliffords came to Washington in 1945. Harry S. Truman, a fellow Missourian, was the new President. Clifford, in the Navy during World War II, was appointed Naval Aide to Mr. Truman. Soon afterward he became Counsel to the President. Though he left the government in 1950 to form his own law firm, Clark Clifford, during the succeeding years, was seldom far from the White House. He served as Presidential Advisor to both Presidents Kennedy and Johnson. In 1960, he handled the governmental transition between the outgoing Republican and the incoming Democrat administrations and in 1968 he returned to government service as Secretary of Defense in Mr. Johnson's Cabinet.

In 1946, the Cliffords, with their three small daughters, had scarcely moved into an old-fashioned, wide-verandaed house in Chevy Chase, a comfortable Washington suburb, when Marny was caught up in the ceaseless round of official entertaining. The Cliffords were young, handsome, intelligent and refreshing. Besides, they possessed the added glamour of being within the magic White House circle and the initiative to return hospitality to even the most highly placed, with verve and lack of pretension. Before they outgrew the Chevy Chase house and acquired a rambling white 1700 farmhouse on Rockville Pike just outside the city line, both President and Mrs. Truman and the then General and Mrs. Eisenhower had honored them as guests.

In Washington, entertaining is a way of life, the *raison d'être* for the one hundred and sixteen foreign embassies and three legations currently established in the Capital, for the half dozen really influential social hostesses, and for several United States officials of important and even lesser rank. Unlike most major cities in the United States, Washington hospitality is usually offered in embassies or at home, rather than in restaurants. Most ranking United States officials live in pleasantly large houses or apartments; the great ladies in truly magnificent dwellings manned by superbly trained staffs; while the embassies, run by seemingly innumerable native domestics, maintain kitchens stocked with luxuries imported from home.

With so many eager to entertain, the competition for prominent guests is keen. And in a city with little night life and few fine restaurants, dining well takes on unusual importance. A reputation for serving superlative food, handsomely presented, becomes a notable diplomatic as well as social asset.

Marny soon realized that at many of the parties to which the Cliffords were invited, she was sampling some of the finest cooking in the world. So she began, at first timidly, then quite shamelessly, to ask her hostesses for the recipes of various delicious dishes she had fancied. She discovered, somewhat to her surprise, that a hostess was almost always flattered and happy to share her prized recipe. Occasionally, though, directions for making some especially famous dish, sauce or dressing, are jealously guarded. But Marny usually solved the mystery by guessing at the ingredients and testing until the consistency and taste were as she remembered them. "I sleep, dream and talk recipes," she sighs. "It's awful. . . ."

Marny met the wife of the Malaysian Ambassador at a luncheon party. Puan (Mrs.) Sri Ong, an enthusiastic cook, immediately invited her new friend to the embassy. There, the Malaysian menu proved so appealing that Marny asked her hostess to teach her guests how to prepare these delicious native dishes. Puan Sri Ong obligingly organized a cooking course and soon, notebooks in hand, pupils were trailing her around the embassy kitchen. Marny, besides learning the proper way to chop up the various fascinating ingredients essential to Malaysian cuisine, also learned how to use Oriental cooking utensils. In one of the many "tips" (instructive and often entertaining paragraphs of information which Marny has scattered among the recipes) she describes how to handle that indispensable Chinese pot, the wok, with its accessories.

Among the Malaysian creations Marny stars are a special way of making "Fried Rice" and "Monk's Dish," her most exotic recipe, which includes such components as tiger-lily flowers, dried mushrooms, cakes of bean-curd paste, dried lichens and gingko nuts.

Ambassadors and their ladies; visiting Chancellors and Ministers of foreign powers; Cabinet members; the most influential members of Congress; Associate Justices of the United States Supreme Court; multi-starred Generals and broadly striped Admirals; the shrewdest and most widely quoted oracles of the Fourth Estate; Vice-Presidents of the United States and, at a final farewell after the White House, the outgoing President and Mrs. Johnson; and many, many other friends of the three joyous Clifford daughters; Marny and Clark's friends of long standing—all have journeyed out Rockville Pike to the unpretentious historic white farmhouse which spreads haphazardly over wide lawns.

Except for the more expansive parties, catered by Clarence Ellis of "Ridgewells," dinners are prepared in a cosy, old-fashioned kitchen, devoid of chrome gadgetry, with two stoves, a brick-patterned linoleum floor and extra refrigerators on the back porch. The immense dining-room table can seat a score or more. The tree-shaded back lawn invites buffet tables and garden chairs for summer luncheons and suppers. But at the most famous of all Clifford parties, which "celebrated" eight successive New Year's Days when the Republicans were in the White House, the guests, who eventually numbered in the hundreds, sat on the floor to watch the brilliant, satirical-political wrapup of the year, talked, sung, extravagantly acted as well as authored by Clark and his three daughters. The guests downed oysters or clams from separate bars (a Clifford specialty) and demolished awesome quantities of other out-of-this-world eatables.

At another party, long remembered, Marny brightened the winter doldrums by inviting her guests to come dressed in summer clothes, gave them picnic baskets, and served a summer buffet in the bright warmth of her sunny house!

Marny Clifford's shining success as a hostess in Washington, where entertaining is so truly a fine art, lies not only in her ability to set a "good table" but also to serve food which is satisfying as well as delicious and sufficiently unexpected to arouse gastronomic curiosity. She puts immense personal effort into every menu she creates and she never relaxes in her search for new and wonderful recipes to please both herself and her myriad friends. *Marny Clifford's Washington Cookbook* is truly a sharing of her love for good food and the pleasure she takes in cooking.

Mary Van Rensselaer Thayer

INTRODUCTION

And so, now, my cookbook is in print and I am in trouble. After many months of testing my recipes, what I used to refer to as "my figure" is a thing of the past. My wardrobe, hopefully selected to last me a long time, is hanging, virtually untouched, much too small and relentlessly going out of style. But my husband, who has the strength of character of Richard the Lion-Hearted, has emerged from sampling my dishes thinner than ever.

Enough of this personal sorrow. Here are a few things you should know about my book.

As you will see, I always cook with butter, as I was taught to do by my mother and grandmother. However, I am sure that margarine or diet margarine may be substituted for butter in many of my recipes. Try it and see.

I remember, when I was very young, my grandmother remarking that she "liked her hot foods *piping* hot and her cold foods *icy* cold." This really makes a tremendous difference in the presentation of various dishes. Please take the time to heat the cups for soup and the plates and platters for hot dishes. Chill the plates and platters for cold salads and cold desserts.

When preparing the salads, soak the greens in ice water for at least an hour, and wipe each leaf very dry, for nothing is less attractive than water in the bottom of a salad bowl or platter. Use the various salad dressings with a very light hand. More, if needed, may always be added.

The day before the party, cook as much of the food as possible (many of my dishes improve in flavor if made ahead of time, as I have explained in the individual recipes).

Have the flowers arranged, the table set, the china, crystal and serving dishes selected, the cigarettes in their boxes, place cards written and plans for the seating arrangements made. I write "plans," for I always have a substitute plan in case a particular guest cannot be with us at the last moment. This often happens in Washington because of the long hours put in by Senators, Congressmen and government officials. I try to avoid that last-moment, harrowing experience of reseating the table.

You will observe, as you read my book, that there is very little reference to the proper wines to serve. There is a reason for this. My husband and I have always been allergic to wines and, therefore, have little real knowledge of them. We do, however, always serve wines at our dinners. They are selected with great care by our wine merchant, who is very knowledgeable.

Some of my foreign dishes have ingredients that must be purchased at a grocery store which carries the foods of that particular country. These stores are listed in the yellow pages of the telephone directory in any fair-sized city and are not difficult to find.

I shall be forever grateful to Mrs. Nixon, Mrs. Truman, Mrs. Eisenhower, Mrs. Onassis and Mrs. Johnson for graciously giving me one of their favorite recipes. Also to Puan Sri Ong of Malaysia, Mrs. de Besche of Sweden, Mrs. Lucet of France, Mrs. Gunneng of Norway, Mrs. Ortona of Italy, Mrs. Rabin of Israel, Mrs. Berckemeyer of Peru, Mrs. Vitsaxis of Greece, Mrs. Arguelles of Spain, Mrs. de Olloqui of Mexico, the Countess of Cromer of Great Britain, all wives of Ambassadors to the United States, Justice William O. Douglas, Mrs. Stuart Symington, Mrs. Edmund S. Muskie, Mrs. Edward M. Kennedy, Mrs. Hubert H. Humphrey, Mrs. Hale Boggs, Mrs. William C. Westmoreland, General John McConnell, Ambassador David K. E. Bruce, and many dear friends in Washington and around the country. Many recipes were inherited from my New England family and others I acquired from our children, all of whom are excellent cooks and genuinely interested in trying new as well as exotic recipes.

Mary Van Rensselaer Thayer, the author of *Jacqueline Bouvier Kennedy* and *Jacqueline Kennedy: The White House Years,* has interrupted a very busy schedule to write the Foreword. She has helped me edit the book and has made many valuable suggestions. Working with this fascinating, blithe spirit has been a constant joy. I can never thank her enough for her time, her interest and her help.

John Falter, the talented, busy and successful artist, created the cover and illustrations for my book with great charm and humor. John for many years did covers for the *Saturday Evening Post,* and he is a remarkably fine portrait artist as well.

My secretary, Mrs. Nancy Castle, has spent long, aching hours at the typewriter clearing the hundreds of recipes with me, always with renewed energy, good suggestions and a glorious disposition.

Josephine Alston, Mary Howard and John Lucas have cheerfully helped me test my recipes for many months. They have been indispensable.

I hope that everyone who has my book will derive as much pleasure from using it as I have had in writing it.

Please plunge into the calories and, like Scarlett O'Hara, "Think about them—tomorrow."

Marny Clifford

Large cocktail parties are disappearing from the Washington scene and I am enthusiastically in favor of this change. They are truly dreadful.

The parking problem is such that, when your husband finally parks and arrives at the party, and fights his way to your side, he looks as if he had gone three or four rounds with Joe Frazier. There is no place to sit down and one has to be an octopus or a born juggler to balance a canapé, cocktail and cigarette and still manage to have a free hand, or face, for the greeting of a friend.

I sympathize with the aged Yankee who somehow found himself, for the first time, at one of these huge, unwieldy cocktail parties. After a half hour of being jostled and stepped on, he allowed as how he wished he was "to home and the party was to hell"!

Cocktail parties now tend to be much smaller, as they should be. At the end of a hard working day, the guests may relax, comfortably, and enjoy their host and hostess and each other.

More and more dinner invitations are being sent with "Cocktails at eight—Dinner at eight forty-five" so that a guest may arrive a little later if he doesn't wish cocktails or is working late.

A trend in parties, because of the growing dearth of servants, is to have a "Cocktail Buffet" from six to nine thirty. This is taking the place of the formal seated dinner. These, too, are kept relatively small. We have them quite often with about sixteen to twenty guests and it is intriguing to serve a Malaysian, Italian or Swedish dinner, or any other national cuisine that lends itself to buffet service.

At many of the embassies and private dinners, no canapés are served at all; the hostess believes, and rightly so, that they detract from the dinner and too long a cocktail time only dulls the palate for the superb wines which are invariably served in Washington.

If you, as a hostess, plan to serve canapés, select one that you make best and have it the "specialty" of your house. Always have a tray of raw vegetables for your dieting friends and keep those cocktail parties small.

CAVIAR, SOUR CREAM AND ALMONDS

4 oz. fresh Beluga caviar
½ pt. sour cream
½ tsp. onion juice

¼ cup toasted, chopped almonds
12 small squares of white bread
6 tbsps. butter (softened)

1. Place caviar in center of round platter.
2. Mix sour cream with onion juice.
3. Completely frost caviar with sour cream.
4. In small skillet toast almonds in 2 tbsps. butter until golden.
5. Butter bread with remaining softened butter and toast under broiler until golden.
6. Scatter toasted, chopped almonds all over sour cream.
7. Refrigerate and serve very cold.
8. Arrange toasted bread squares around caviar mound.

SERVES 4.

If juice from the caviar runs out around the bottom of the sour cream, wipe it away with a paper towel before serving.

DOMESTIC CAVIAR WITH CREAM CHEESE

1 (3¾ oz.) jar lumpfish caviar
1 tsp. lemon juice
½ tsp. freshly ground black pepper
1 (8 oz.) pkg. cream cheese
¼ tsp. salt

¼ cup light cream
1 tsp. onion juice
6 tbsps. toasted chopped almonds
2 tbsps. finely chopped parsley
Melba toast rounds

Place lumpfish caviar on silver dish. Sprinkle with lemon juice and pepper. Frost with cream cheese mixed well with salt, cream, onion juice and toasted, chopped almonds. Sprinkle with chopped parsley. Serve very cold with hot Melba toast rounds.

SERVES 12.

HOT CHEESE WITH BACON

This is a specialty of our house and we always serve it with cocktails.

2 (4 oz.) pkgs. grated Cheddar cheese
1 egg, beaten well
1 tsp. onion juice
1 tsp. Worcestershire sauce

1 tsp. mustard dressing (I usually use Durkee's)
4 slices bread
2 strips bacon, cut in ½-in. pieces

Mix together cheese, egg, onion juice, Worcestershire sauce and mustard dressing, and spread on fresh bread (crusts removed). Cut each slice in four pieces. Top with piece of bacon. Put in preheated 375° oven until cheese is melted and bacon is done.

Makes 16 canapés.

HOT CHEESE HORS D'OEUVRES

2 cups grated sharp Cheddar cheese
1 cup flour

½ cup softened butter
⅛ tsp. salt

Thoroughly mix all together. Roll thin like pastry. Cut with 2-inch diameter cookie cutter or top of glass and bake 7 minutes on a (17 x 14 inch) cookie tin in preheated, hot oven (400°).

Makes 60 two-inch rounds.

HOT CHEESE AND CHUTNEY

16 small rounds of thin bread
4 tsps. chutney, finely minced

1 (4 oz.) pkg. of shredded Cheddar cheese

Place bread on a (15½ x 10¼ x ¾ inch) cookie tin, and toast on one side under preheated broiler.

Cover untoasted side with ¼ teaspoon chutney and cover with small amount of cheese.

Broil, six inches from broiler flame, until cheese is melted. Watch carefully! MAKES 16 canapés.

CHEESE PUFFS

24 "Puffs" ("Puff Paste," p. 425)
½ cup grated sharp Cheddar cheese
½ tsp. onion (scraped)
½ tsp. Worcestershire sauce
½ tsp. mustard sauce (I usually use Durkee's)

1. Make "Puffs," but bake them just 20 minutes. Cut "pocket" in center of each puff.
2. In a small bowl, mix cheese and seasonings well.
3. Stuff each pocket with 1 teaspoon of the cheese mixture.
4. Preheat oven to 375°.
5. Place "Puffs" on (17 x 14 inch) greased cookie sheet and bake for about 10 minutes—until cheese is melted.
6. Serve very hot.

MAKES 24 "Puffs."

HOT CHEESE CUBES

1 loaf unsliced bread
4 tsps. soft butter
2 cups grated sharp Cheddar cheese
1 egg, well beaten
1 tsp. lemon juice
1 tsp. onion juice
salt and pepper to taste

Cut bread into 1-inch cubes (no crusts). Place on (17 x 14 inch) cookie sheet. Cover tightly with refrigerator wrap and freeze overnight. Place butter and cheese (which has been at room temperature overnight) in a bowl. Add egg, lemon juice, onion juice, salt and pepper. Beat with a fork until soft and creamy.

Remove frozen bread cubes and frost (still frozen) each cube on all sides but the bottom. (Bread will not crumble by this method.) Let stand on same cookie sheet until cubes are thawed. Preheat oven to 350° and bake cubes for 10 minutes, or until they are browned a bit and the cheese is melted.

MAKES 30 cubes.

CHEESE WAFERS

½ cup soft butter or margarine
1 (4 oz.) pkg. crumbled blue cheese *or* 1 (4 oz.) pkg. sharp Cheddar cheese, shredded

1½ cups unsifted flour

Cream butter or margarine until light. Add cheese and beat until blended. Slowly blend in flour. Mix thoroughly. Form dough into a 12-inch roll. Wrap tightly with refrigerator wrap. Refrigerate until ready to slice. Dough may be frozen and thawed before slicing.

Using sharp knife, cut into crosswise slices ⅛ to ¼ inch thick. Place on ungreased baking sheets.

Bake in a preheated 400° oven for 8 to 10 minutes. Remove from baking sheets and place on wire racks to cool.

MAKES 48 wafers (¼ inch thick).

SMALL CHEESE HORS D'OEUVRES RESEMBLING POACHED EGGS

1 (8 oz.) pkg. cream cheese
¼ cup light cream
salt and pepper to taste

½ tsp. onion juice
4 slices bread, cut in rounds
⅛ lb. very sharp Cheddar cheese

1. Blend cream cheese with cream. Add salt, pepper and onion juice and beat until smooth.
2. Spread on rounds of bread.
3. In center of each round, place ¼-inch cube of sharp cheese.
4. Bake in preheated 375° oven until cheese cube is melted.

MAKES 12 canapés.

CHICKEN LIVERS IN A BLANKET

16 chicken livers

5⅓ slices bacon (partially cooked and cut in thirds)

Wrap each chicken liver in bacon and fasten with slightly dampened toothpicks. Broil until bacon is done. Serve hot.
SERVES 4.

WATERMELON PICKLE IN A BLANKET

16 pieces watermelon pickle

5⅓ slices bacon (partially cooked and cut in thirds)

Do as above, using watermelon pickle instead of livers.
SERVES 4.

STUFFED DATES IN A BLANKET

1 (4 oz.) pkg. cream cheese
2 tbsps. light cream
½ tsp. onion juice
salt and pepper to taste

16 dates (seeds removed)
5⅓ slices bacon (partially cooked and cut in thirds)

Soften cheese with cream, add onion juice, salt and pepper. Stuff dates with cream cheese mixture and finish as above.
SERVES 4.

HOT TAMALES IN A BLANKET

1 (14½ oz.) can hot tamales
6 slices bacon (partially cooked and cut in thirds)

Remove canned hot tamales from corn husks and cut in 18 pieces. Finish as above.
Serves 4 to 6.

HOT CRABMEAT CANAPÉ

This is another of our favorite canapés.

¾ cup commercial mayonnaise
1 tsp. onion juice
1 tsp. lemon juice
1 lb. fresh crabmeat, carefully deboned
½ (2¼ oz.) bottle capers, drained
seasoned salt to taste
10 slices bread (crusts cut off)

1. Mix mayonnaise, onion juice and lemon juice.
2. Mix well with crabmeat.
3. Add capers and seasoned salt.
4. Cut each slice of bread in four pieces and spread above mixture on each square.
5. Place on two (15½ x 10¼ x ¾ inch) cookie sheets and bake in preheated 350° oven until they are bubbly.

Makes 40 canapés.

STUFFED SESAME EGGS

6 hard-boiled eggs
1 tsp. prepared mustard
5 tbsps. mayonnaise
salt and pepper to taste
6 tsps. toasted sesame seeds
2 tbsps. butter

1. Cut hard-boiled eggs lengthwise down the center. Remove yolks to mixing bowl. Add mustard, mayonnaise, salt and pepper.
2. Cream with rotary beater until very smooth.
3. Blend in toasted sesame seeds. (To toast seeds sprinkle lightly with melted butter and put under broiler until golden.)
4. Place in pastry bag and squeeze back into whites of eggs or fill whites with fork. Chill.
SERVES 6.

RAW ENDIVE CANAPÉ

16 leaves of endive   2 tsps. Beau Monde seasoning

Separate leaves of endive and dust with Beau Monde seasoning. Serve *very* cold. Place in pattern on platter.
SERVES 4 to 6.

DEVILED HAM WITH CHUTNEY CANAPÉ

2 (4½ oz.) cans deviled ham   2 tsps. chutney, chopped fine
1 tsp. chutney juice   8 slices bread

Mix deviled ham with chutney juice. Mix chutney well with ham. Remove crusts from bread and cut each slice into 4 squares. Spread mixture on bread squares and broil in oven.
MAKES 32 canapés.

PICKLED SALT HERRING | Mrs. Hubert de Besche
(*Inlagd sill*)   The Royal Embassy of Sweden

This is a "must" on a true smorgasbord.

1 large salt herring

Dressing:
- ½ cup vinegar
- 2 tbsps. water
- ⅛ cup sugar
- 2 tbsps. chopped onions
- 5 peppercorns, crushed
- 10 whole allspice, crushed
- 2 sprigs fresh dill

Garnish:
- fresh dill sprigs
- onion rings

1. Clean herring, removing head. Rinse under cold running water. Soak in cold water 10 to 12 hours, changing water a few times so herring will not be too salty. You could start the soaking a few hours before going to bed, changing water a few times; then leave herring to soak overnight.

2. Cut herring along backbone. Remove big backbone and as many small bones as possible; pull off skin. The bones come out easily after the soaking. Drain filets on absorbent paper, then place filets one on top of the other, arranged so that they look like a whole fish. Cut into thin slices with sharp knife. Slide spatula under sliced fish and remove to a long narrow dish.

3. Mix all dressing ingredients together in a saucepan. Bring to boiling point and simmer for a few minutes. Cool and strain. Pour over herring.

4. Garnish with a few sprigs of fresh dill and some raw onion rings on top. Cover dish with aluminum foil and refrigerate a few hours before serving; better still, let stand in refrigerator overnight. The longer it stands the better the seasonings blend.

Serve with small boiled potatoes on the smorgasbord.

LOBSTER CANAPÉ WITH MUSTARD MAYONNAISE

1 lb. fresh lobster meat, cooked (p. 187)
1 cup "Mustard Mayonnaise" (p. 368)
inside leaves of 1 head Boston lettuce

Cut lobster meat in cubes and put toothpick in each piece. Place on crisp lettuce leaves around dish of "Mustard Mayonnaise."
SERVES 4 to 6.

SMALL MEATBALLS | *Mrs. Hubert de Besche*
(*Små köttbullar*) | The Royal Embassy of Sweden

We never get tired of these. Serve them on toothpicks with cocktails, cold on sandwiches, or as the Swedish people do, on the smorgasbord.

For the best meatballs select the meat yourself and have it ground. The fresher the ground meat, the better the meatballs.

¼ cup finely chopped onion
1 tbsp. shortening
¼ cup fine, dry bread crumbs
⅓ cup water
⅓ cup light cream
¾ lb. ground beef (round steak)
¼ lb. lean pork, ground
2 tsps. salt
¼ tsp. pepper
⅛ tsp. cloves
⅓ cup butter or margarine
¼ cup boiling water

Sauté onion in shortening until golden brown. Soak crumbs in water-cream mixture. Combine onion, crumb mixture, meats and seasonings. Mix thoroughly until smooth. Shape into small balls with your hands (wet your hands before handling meat so it won't stick), using a teaspoon dipped in cold water; or press through a pastry bag. Fry in butter or margarine until evenly brown, shaking pan continuously to make balls round; add boiling water, cover and simmer 5 to 10 minutes or until tender.

MAKES 70 small meatballs.

HOT MUSHROOM CANAPÉS

12 medium evenly matched mushrooms	salt and pepper to taste
2 tbsps. olive oil	⅛ tsp. nutmeg
1 medium onion	1 tsp. powdered consommé concentrate
⅛ lb. butter	½ tsp. lemon juice
1 tbsp. flour	½ cup crushed corn flakes
2 tbsps. heavy cream	

Remove mushroom stems. Brush caps with olive oil.

Finely chop mushroom stems and onions. Sauté in butter. Add flour. When thick, add heavy cream, salt, pepper, nutmeg, powdered consommé concentrate and lemon juice. This will make a thick paste. Stuff mushroom caps with this mixture and top with crushed corn flakes. Bake on cookie tin (17 x 14 inch) stuffing side up, in preheated 350° oven for 25 to 30 minutes. SERVES 4.

PATÉ EN GELÉE

1 lb. liverwurst	salt to taste
1 (8 oz.) pkg. cream cheese	1 envelope (1 tbsp.) plain gelatin
1 (6 oz.) can mushrooms (finely chopped)	1 (10½ oz.) can beef bouillon
1 tbsp. Worcestershire sauce	1 bunch watercress
⅛ tsp. Tabasco sauce	2 (4 oz.) boxes Melba toast rounds

1. Mix together first six ingredients until smooth. Shape into a mound and chill.
2. Dissolve gelatin in ½ can cold bouillon.
3. Heat rest of bouillon; pour over gelatin and stir to dissolve.
4. Line bottom of 1-quart buttered mold with ¼ inch of the bouillon-gelatin mixture and chill until set.
5. Place mound of liverwurst-cheese mixture on the above and pour the rest of the bouillon mixture around the sides (so that the mold is surrounded by the bouillon mixture except on the top). Chill overnight.

6. Unmold on a chilled platter and surround with watercress. Serve with toast rounds.

SERVES 10 to 12.

GIBLET PATÉ

This paté is one of our Christmas-morning canapés and is a favorite of our friends.

6 stalks celery, minced
3 medium onions, minced
3 oz. salt pork, minced
3 slices bacon, minced
4 garlic cloves, crushed or put through garlic press
½ lb. butter
3 tbsps. chicken fat
2½ cups chicken giblets (hearts and gizzards, cartilage removed), sliced fine
½ tsp. thyme
1½ tbsps. fresh chicken livers, cut in ½-in. pieces
3 eggs, hard cooked and sliced
1 cup dry sherry
2 tsps. salt
½ tsp. pepper
watercress

In heavy pot, simmer celery, onions, salt pork and bacon with garlic, butter, and chicken fat, until wilted. Add giblets and thyme and simmer slowly for 45 minutes (covered). Add livers, eggs and ½ cup sherry and simmer for 30 minutes more or until mixture is reduced and well blended. Cool. Put all this through food chopper. Add remaining sherry and season with salt and pepper. Pack into one (8½ x 4½ x 2½ inch) loaf pan and chill overnight. To serve, unmold on a chilled platter; garnish with watercress.

SERVES about 60 as a canapé spread, on crackers or Melba toast rounds.

LATVIAN PATÉ

1 lb. chicken livers
2 tbsps. water
½ lb. butter (sweet)
½ medium onion, scraped

salt and pepper to taste
2 tbsps. mayonnaise
½ tsp. mustard

Cook livers in small pan with 2 tablespoons water and ¼ pound butter until done (about 5 minutes). Put through potato ricer, food mill or meat grinder.

Soften the remaining butter and whip together with liver mixture. Add scraped onion, salt, pepper, mayonnaise and mustard. Pack in 2½-cup mold which has been rinsed in cold water. Refrigerate (covered). Unmold on chilled platter to serve.

SERVES about 16.

PATÉ WITH SCALLIONS AND BRANDY

8 (4¾ oz.) cans liver paté (I usually use Sells)
8 scallions, chopped very fine
8 tsps. soft sweet butter
8 tbsps. brandy

1 (10½ oz.) can beef bouillon
1 envelope (1 tbsp.) plain gelatin
¼ cup water to cover gelatin
watercress
3 (4 oz.) boxes Melba toast rounds

1. Thoroughly mix liver paté with scallions and butter and add brandy. Refrigerate.

2. Heat bouillon in a saucepan.

3. Sprinkle gelatin with cold water and dissolve in hot bouillon. Stir thoroughly.

4. In 1-quart wet mold place ¼ inch of bouillon and gelatin mixture. Refrigerate until thoroughly set.

5. Shape paté mixture into shape of mold. Place in mold on top of the set bouillon. Leave a ¼-inch space around sides and top. Pour remaining bouillon and gelatin into this space so that, when set, the gelée will cover the paté completely. Refrigerate overnight.

6. To unmold, set mold in hot water for a minute or two. Run a knife carefully around the sides; turn it over onto a platter. Garnish with watercress and serve with Melba toast rounds.

SERVES about 40.

BETTE KOVIN'S SMOKED SALMON WITH CAPERS

- 4 slices pumpernickel (crusts removed)
- ⅛ lb. sweet, soft butter
- 8 thin slices smoked salmon (cut in half the long way)
- 1 tbsp. onion juice
- 1 tbsp. lemon juice
- 2 tbsps. capers
- 1 small bunch parsley

Slice pumpernickel bread in long fingers and butter.

Place slice of smoked salmon on top and sprinkle with onion and lemon juice and capers. As you make the canapés, be sure to keep them moist by covering with a dampened dish towel. Refrigerate for one hour (covered). Decorate serving platter with parsley.

MAKES 16 canapés.

BROILED SARDINES

- 16 fingers of bread (crusts off)
- 2 tbsps. mustard dressing (I usually use Durkee's)
- 2 (3¾ oz.) cans sardines
- 1 tbsp. lemon juice

1. Spread bread fingers lightly with mustard dressing.
2. Place 1 sardine on top of each finger.
3. Sprinkle with lemon juice.
4. Put on cookie tin and broil until the bread is toasted.

Serve very hot.

MAKES 16 canapés.

SHAD ROE DIP

1 (7½ oz.) can shad roe
juice of 1 lemon
¼ cup "Never Fail Mayonnaise" (p. 368)
½ tsp. onion (freshly scraped)
salt and pepper to taste
1 (6 oz.) pkg. potato chips
1 sprig parsley

Mash shad roe and add lemon juice, mayonnaise, onion juice, salt and pepper.

Place in small chilled bowl in center of round platter and surround with potato chips. Garnish center of roe with parsley.

SERVES 4.

SMOKED TURKEY PATÉ

¾ lb. smoked turkey (put through grinder)
¼ cup sour cream
2 tbsps. mayonnaise (either homemade or commercial)
½ tsp. mustard
½ tsp. horseradish
½ onion, scraped
chopped tops of two scallions
1 pinch garlic powder (⅛ tsp.)
1 pinch sugar (⅛ tsp.)
½ garlic pickle, chopped fine
½ cucumber, peeled and chopped fine
8 sprigs watercress *or* 8 sprigs parsley

Mix first eleven ingredients together well. Chill overnight in buttered 1-pint mold. Unmold carefully. Place in center of round platter and garnish with sprigs of parsley or watercress.

SERVES 20.

STUFFED DILL PICKLE

1 medium dill pickle
1 (4½ oz.) can deviled ham
1 tbsp. mayonnaise *or* 1 tbsp. sour cream

1. Halve pickle (the long way).
2. Scoop out seeds with spoon.
3. Mix ham, in small bowl, with mayonnaise or sour cream.
4. Stuff each section of pickle with ham mixture.
5. Place halves together again.
6. Wrap in refrigerator wrap, tightly, and twist the ends of the wrap.
7. Chill overnight.
8. Just before serving, slice in ½-inch slices (the short way).

MAKES about 16 slices.

Variation:

1½ (3 oz.) pkgs. cream cheese
1 tbsp. cream
½ tsp. onion juice
salt and pepper to taste

Prepare pickle as above.
Mix cheese, cream, onion juice, salt and pepper to smooth consistency.
Stuff pickle and follow recipe above. Slice and serve.

MAKES about 16 slices.

STEAK TARTARE

2 lbs. lean sirloin steak, ground twice
2 egg yolks
4 tbsps. capers
2 tbsps. onion, scraped
¼ cup "Basic French Dressing" (p. 364)
¼ cup chili sauce
2 tbsps. Worcestershire sauce
1 tbsp. soy sauce (optional)
salt and pepper to taste
4 anchovies (optional) to decorate the mound of beef
10 whole slices rye bread
¼ cup sweet butter

Mix first nine ingredients in a wooden bowl with your hands and form into a mound on a platter.

Cover and chill. Add anchovies (optional).

Serve with buttered rye bread.

SERVES 8 to 10.

RAW VEGETABLE CANAPÉS

2 celery hearts, sliced thin
12 raw cauliflower buds
2 carrots, cut in half and sliced thin
8 radishes, pared halfway down
2 small zucchini, washed and sliced thin (¼ in.)
1 small yellow summer squash, washed and sliced thin (¼ in.)
12 stuffed green olives (with pimiento)
12 ripe olives
1 cup "Cold Curry Sauce" (p. 334)

Put celery hearts, cauliflower buds, carrot slices, radishes, zucchini, yellow summer squash in ice water to crisp.

Dry well and place in a pattern around edge of round platter with stuffed green and ripe olives.

In center have bowl of "Cold Curry Sauce."

SERVES 10 to 12.

ZAKUSKI | *Katya Burland*

In Russia this assortment of canapés is usually a "Men's Table." Before dinner, while the ladies sip sherry, men gather at a separate table laden with vodka, Zubrovka* and Zakuski (literal translation: "Bites"). They drink, select their "Bites," and talk. Each variety of "Bite" is placed in a separate serving dish on the table.

COLD ZAKUSKI

I. *The Vinaigrette*

8 cooked or canned beets, cut in ½-in. pieces
6 cooked potatoes, cut in ½-in. pieces
2 Polish dill pickles, cut in ½-in. pieces
2 or 3 sardines skinned, chopped or cut in small slices
4 tbsps. olive oil
1 tbsp. tarragon vinegar
salt and pepper to taste
1 tbsp. fresh dill *or* 1 tsp. dried dill

* Zubrovka is a Polish vodka. Its unusual flavor is due to several spears of buffalo grass which are in each bottle. Keep this vodka in your deep freeze and serve it in small liqueur glasses as it is *very* strong.

Prepare the first four ingredients above and mix (sparingly) with the oil, vinegar, salt and pepper. Place in a serving dish and sprinkle with the dill.

II. *The Salami Rolls*

12 very thin slices of *real* Italian salami	1 (3 oz.) pkg. cream cheese, softened 1 tsp. fresh chives

Mix cream cheese with chives. Spread lightly on the salami and roll. Hold with toothpick.

III. 12 (4 in.) slices smoked salmon

IV. 1 (4 oz.) jar "Giant Grain" Beluga caviar (served with small dishes of finely chopped onion and sour cream)

V. 12 stalks thick white French asparagus (This comes in glass jars from food specialty stores.)

VI. 36 (1½ in.) squares of black bread

FOR HOT ZAKUSKI

VII. *Pirogi*

These are small, baked pastries with meat or cabbage-egg stuffing.

2 cups sifted flour	4 tbsps. ice water
½ lb. butter, cut up	1 egg, beaten

1. Cover a bread board with wax paper and sift a bit of flour over it.
2. Make dough from the flour, butter and ice water (see "Pastry," p. 425).
3. Divide the dough in two parts.
4. Roll out one section to ⅛-inch thickness and keep the other cold in refrigerator (wrapped) to use another time unless needed.
5. Preheat oven to 350°.
6. With a 4-inch cookie cutter, or a glass, cut out the individual pastry rounds and fill each round with one of the following fillings.

Filling I

4 tbsps. butter	2 eggs, hard-boiled and chopped fine
4 tbsps. onion, chopped fine	
1 lb. sirloin (ground twice)	salt and pepper to taste

In a 10-inch skillet melt 2 tablespoons butter. Add onion and cook until golden. Stir in meat and the rest of the butter, and cook until meat is light brown. Add eggs and season. Pour off excess juices.

Filling II

Using method above, substitute 1 cup cabbage (chopped fine) for the meat.

1. Fill each Pirog round with about 2½ tbsps. of the meat or cabbage filling. Fold over and pinch the open edges together. Prick the top of each with a fork.
2. Brush each with the beaten egg.
3. Place on (17 x 14 inch) cookie tin covered with aluminum foil and bake about 30 to 35 minutes or until the top is brown. Watch them carefully!
4. Serve very hot on the Zakuski table.

Place plates, forks and cocktail napkins on the table and have your guests select the food they wish.

SERVES 6 to 8.

CRUST FOR QUICHE

1 cup flour	1 tsp. baking powder
1 tbsp. sugar	¼ lb. butter
⅛ tsp. salt	1 tsp. water (if needed)

Sift together flour, sugar, salt and baking powder. Blend in butter. Mix thoroughly with hands until sugar is dissolved. If necessary, add a few drops of water (not more than 1 tsp.) to get a rolling consistency. Roll between wax paper and line a 10-inch pie plate.

SERVES 8.

EASY QUICHE | *Bette Kovin*

1 pkg. (10 oz.) frozen patty shells, defrosted
1 cup diced ham
3 eggs
1½ cups milk
½ tsp. salt
½ tsp. Tabasco sauce
¼ tsp. mace
1 cup grated imported Swiss cheese

Press patty shells together and roll to fit 9-inch pie plate. Trim shell. Press ham into shell. Beat eggs, milk and seasonings until blended. Mix in **cheese**. Pour into shell. Place in preheated 450° oven and immediately reduce **heat** to 400°. Bake 30 to 45 minutes until puffed and brown.

SERVES 6 to 8 as first course. SERVES 4 for luncheon.

SHRIMP QUICHE

Use half of recipe for "Pastry (Double Crust)" (p. 425).

1½ cups cooked and shelled shrimp
4 tbsps. butter
salt and pepper to taste
⅛ tsp. oregano (optional)
⅓ cup dry white vermouth
1¼ to 1½ cups milk
3 eggs
½ tsp. salt
pinch each of pepper and nutmeg
1 tbsp. tomato paste
½ cup grated Swiss or Cheddar cheese

1. Make and partially bake an 8-inch pastry shell in a pie pan (about 5 minutes).
2. Toss shrimp in 2 tablespoons butter in a 10-inch skillet over moderately high heat.
3. Season lightly with salt, pepper and oregano. Add vermouth and boil rapidly until liquid has almost entirely evaporated. Spread shrimp in bottom of pastry shell.
4. Beat together the milk, eggs and seasonings. Add tomato paste and pour over shrimp, filling shell to within ⅛ inch of top. Spread grated cheese on top and dot with remaining butter.
5. Bake 35 to 40 minutes in a preheated 375° oven.

SERVES 4 to 6.

SEAFOOD QUICHE

1 "Crust for Quiche" (above)	1 tbsp. flour
½ lb. Swiss cheese, cut in slices ¼ in. thick	½ tsp. salt
	dash of pepper
1 cup crabmeat	dash of cayenne
½ cup small, cooked shrimp	½ tsp. nutmeg
1½ cups light cream	2 tbsps. melted butter
4 eggs, beaten	2 tbsps. dry sherry

Make pie crust. Put in 9-inch pie plate.

Line 9-inch shell with the cheese. Cover with layer of crabmeat and shrimp. In a bowl combine cream, eggs, flour, salt, pepper, cayenne and nutmeg. Stir in the butter and sherry. Beat well. Pour over seafood and bake in a preheated 375° oven for 35 to 40 minutes or until top is browned and custard is set.

SERVES 8.

AND PASTA

COLD ANDALUSIAN SOUP

- 3 hard-boiled eggs
- 2 tbsps. olive oil
- ⅛ tsp. finely chopped garlic
- 1½ tsps. Worcestershire sauce
- 1 tsp. dried mustard
- 1 dash Tabasco sauce
- ½ tsp. hand-ground pepper
- 1 tsp. lemon or lime juice
- 1 qt. canned tomatoes (strain out juice and reserve—about 1½ cups juice)
- 1 small cucumber, peeled and chopped
- 1 sweet green pepper, chopped fine
- 1 medium-sized onion, chopped very fine
- 2½ cups tomato juice
- 1 sweet green pepper, cut in strips
- 1 lime or lemon, sliced thin
- 1 cup beef consommé
- 8 ice cubes
- 24 garlic-flavored croutons (hot)

Work yolks of eggs and olive oil into a smooth paste in wooden salad bowl. Add garlic and seasonings. Add lemon or lime juice; then work in tomato pulp and add chopped cucumber, chopped green pepper, onion and all tomato juice. Stir briskly and chill on ice for 3 hours. Cut egg whites into strips. Put on bottom of soup bowl with strips of green pepper. Add thin slices of lemon or lime. Add refrigerated mixture and consommé (room temperature). Serve with 2 ice cubes and 6 croutons per cup, floating in it.

SERVES 4.

MRS. HUBERT H. HUMPHREY'S BEEF SOUP

1½ lbs. stew beef or chuck
1 soup bone
   cold water to cover
1 tsp. salt
½ tsp. pepper
2 bay leaves
1 cup chopped celery
½ cup chopped onion

4 or 5 medium-sized carrots, sliced
1 cup chopped cabbage
1 #2 can Italian style tomatoes
1 tbsp. Worcestershire sauce
1 beef bouillon cube
⅛ tsp. oregano *or* your preferred
   spice

Cover meat and bone with cold water in heavy 3-quart kettle. Add salt, pepper and bay leaves. Bring to bubbly stage while preparing vegetables. Turn heat low and add celery, onion, carrots and cabbage. Simmer, covered, at least 2½ hours or until meat is very tender. Remove bone and bay leaves. Cut meat into bite-sized pieces. Add tomatoes, Worcestershire sauce and bouillon cube. Simmer for ½ hour longer and serve.

SERVES 6 good, hearty bowls.

Mrs. Humphrey told me when she gave me this recipe that her father used to make this soup and it is Senator Humphrey's favorite. He likes to tell everyone that it gives him vim, vigor and vitality of which he has an astonishing amount. Mrs. Humphrey says that this recipe is especially good for a light supper meal with a fruit salad, a glass of milk, lots of crackers and dessert. It is low in calories, but high in food value.

COLD BLENDER BORSCH

3 cups beef bouillon, cold
1 (16 oz.) can whole medium beets
   (chilled, undrained)
4 tsps. lemon juice

1 tsp. salt
   pepper to taste
1 tbsp. minced lemon peel (optional)
8 tbsps. sour cream

Put all above, except sour cream, in a blender and blend for ½ minute until smooth. Chill and then serve in chilled bowls and top each bowl with 1 tbsp. sour cream.

SERVES 4 to 6.

ICED BORSCH

4 cups strong meat stock or beef bouillon
8 medium-sized canned beets, finely grated
⅓ cup red Burgundy wine
2 tbsps. tomato paste
2 crushed bay leaves
1 tbsp. lemon juice
4 egg whites
½ tsp. red vegetable food coloring
½ tsp. grated lemon rind
salt to taste
⅛ tsp. cayenne pepper
½ cup sour cream
4 new potatoes, cooked in jackets, then peeled and chilled

Put stock, beets, wine, tomato paste, bay leaves, lemon juice and stiffly beaten egg whites into heavy 4-quart earthenware pot on low heat. Start beating with an egg beater. Increase the heat; continue beating until soup is boiling fast. Set aside to cool for 30 minutes. Put through finest sieve and add food coloring. Put in refrigerator for 6 hours. Serve with a pinch of grated lemon rind, salt and cayenne pepper to taste. Add 1 tablespoon sour cream per cup. Drop one new potato into each cup at serving time.

SERVES 4.

LATVIAN BORSCH

3 bunches beets
water to cover
2 tbsps. vinegar
1 large soup bone with meat on (about 2 lbs. in all)
1 large Bermuda onion, cut in quarters
4 stalks celery, cut in half
2 qts. water
1 (10½ oz.) can beef bouillon (if needed)
salt and pepper to taste
½ tsp. red vegetable food coloring
8 tbsps. sour cream

Boil beets in plain water to cover until done. Drain and peel. Put through meat grinder. Add vinegar and put in dish, covered, in refrigerator overnight. Cook 1 large soup bone with onion and celery in 2 quarts water until meat is tender. Remove bone; strain and save the stock. Put meat from soup bone, onion and celery through meat grinder to get more stock. Combine

juice with original stock. If there is not 2 quarts of stock, add beef bouillon to obtain correct amount. Add beets and vinegar mixture and season with salt and pepper. Add red food coloring. Chill. Add 1 tablespoon sour cream per cup just before serving.
SERVES 8.

CHICKEN OR TURKEY SOUP

1 qt. fresh chicken or turkey stock or canned chicken broth
1 pt. light cream
4 cubes chicken concentrate dissolved in ¼ cup milk

1 tbsp. flour
½ cup milk
salt and pepper to taste
1½ cups diced cooked chicken or turkey, white meat

1. Heat together the stock, cream and chicken cubes.
2. Thicken with flour mixed with cold milk. Cook to desired consistency and season.
3. Pour into soup plates.
4. Stir into each serving ¼ cup of chicken or turkey meat.

SERVES 6.

MY GRANDMOTHER'S CLAM BOUILLON

1 qt. shucked clams (fresh)
3 pts. water
1 large onion, chopped fine
1 (16 oz.) bottle clam juice (if needed)
1 qt. milk
1 onion, cut in quarters

2 stalks celery (cut in half)
butter (1 rounded dessert spoon)
2 tbsps. flour (for thickening)
½ cup milk (for thickening)
salt and pepper to taste
½ cup heavy cream (whipped) mixed with ¼ tsp. salt

Put clams and water on to boil with onion, cut up fine. Let them boil for 15 minutes. Then simmer slowly for one hour. Let stand all night. Strain in the morning. Squeeze the juice out through cheesecloth. If there is not enough juice from the clams to make a solid quart, fill up with bottled clam juice.

Bring 1 quart milk, containing onion quarters and stalks of celery, to the boiling point. Strain and add butter. Then thicken with flour and milk mixed together well. Add clam juice and season with salt and pepper to taste. Serve with 1 tablespoon salted whipped cream to each cup.

SERVES 8.

MAINE CLAM CHOWDER | Mrs. Edmund S. Muskie

3 dozen shucked, raw soft-shell clams (Hen clams and quahogs ground up are a delicious substitute.)
liquid from the clams
2 cups cold water
½ lb. diced salt pork *or* 2 tbsps. butter or margarine
2 medium onions, sliced
2 tbsps. flour
¼ tsp. celery salt
¼ tsp. pepper
3½ tsps. salt
3 cups potatoes, pared and diced
3 cups milk (scalded)
1 tbsp. butter or margarine

1. Snip off necks of clams; cut fine with scissors. Leave soft parts whole.
2. In 2-quart saucepan place clams (necks and soft parts) with clam liquid.
3. Add water and bring to a boil. Drain and reserve liquid and clams, separately.
4. In 3-quart kettle, sauté salt pork until golden. Add onions and cook until tender.
5. Into this mixture stir flour, celery salt, pepper and 2 teaspoons salt, clam liquid and potatoes. Cook, covered, for 8 minutes or until potatoes are tender.
6. Add scalded milk, clams, the rest of the salt and butter or margarine.
7. Serve in large soup bowls or, for casual outdoor meals, in mugs.

SERVES 8.

NEW ENGLAND CORN CHOWDER

¼ lb. salt pork, cut in tiny cubes
2 medium onions, chopped fine
4 uncooked potatoes, diced
2 cups water
1 qt. milk
1 (1 lb. 1 oz.) can creamed corn
3 tbsps. butter
1 tbsp. flour

¼ cup milk
1 can (13 oz.) evaporated milk
salt and pepper to taste
1 tsp. paprika

Variation:
2 (7¾ oz.) cans salmon (for "Salmon Chowder")

Place salt pork in 10-inch skillet. Add onions and sauté until pork is crispy and onions are yellow. Dice potatoes and put in water in a saucepan. Let simmer for 10 minutes; then add to pork and onions and cook until potatoes are done but still firm. In another saucepan, heat 1 quart of milk with creamed corn and butter. When hot, combine with first mixture in top of double boiler. Thicken with flour and ¼ cup milk mixed. Stir until slightly thickened. Place over boiling water. Add evaporated milk. Season with salt and pepper to taste. Add paprika.
SERVES 6.
Salmon may be used in place of corn in order to make "Salmon Chowder."

FISH CHOWDER | Mrs. Aristotle Onassis

1 (2 lb.) haddock
2 cups water
2 oz. diced salt pork
2 onions, sliced
4 large potatoes, peeled and diced
1 cup celery, chopped
1 bay leaf, crumbled

1 tsp. salt
freshly ground pepper
boiling water (as needed)
3 cups milk
1 (13 oz.) can evaporated milk
2 tbsps. butter

1. Simmer haddock in a fish-poaching pan for 15 minutes. Drain. Reserve fish, broth and bones.
2. In a 10-inch skillet, sauté diced pork until crisp. Remove pork with a slotted spoon and reserve.
3. Sauté onion in the pork fat until golden brown.

4. Add fish (flaked), bones, potatoes, celery, bay leaf, salt and pepper.

5. Pour in fish broth plus enough boiling water to make 3 cups of liquid and simmer for 30 minutes.

6. Add milk and evaporated milk and simmer for 5 minutes. Correct seasonings and remove bay leaf and *all* the bones.

7. Add butter. Serve in a heated soup tureen and sprinkle top with salt pork.

SERVES 4 to 6.

MOTHER'S FISH CHOWDER

We serve chowders when a northeaster settles down for several days in the summer months, and again on cold snowy winter nights when spirits are low and a roaring fire is a must.

The chowder is the main course, accompanied by a hearty "Health Salad," "Corn Muffins" or "Old-fashioned New England Brown Bread," sliced, buttered and toasted.

For dessert there's "Portsmouth Brown Betty" or "Baked Indian Pudding" with "Café Brûlot."

Spirits revive, conversation flows and all is well.

1 (3 lb.) codfish
1 (2 in.) cube salt pork, cut into tiny cubes
2 onions, sliced
4 large potatoes, diced
1 cup celery, diced
1 bay leaf

1 tsp. salt
½ tsp. ground pepper
2 cups boiling water
1 qt. milk
1 (13 oz.) can evaporated milk
2 tbsps. butter

1. Simmer cod (in 4-qt. saucepan) in water to cover for 15 minutes. Drain and save the broth.

2. Remove fish meat from bones. Set meat aside.

3. Put broth back on stove with fish head, fish bones and tail and simmer for 15 minutes. Strain. Reserve stock.

4. Sauté pork in 10-inch skillet until it is golden and crisp. Save crisp pork cubes.

5. Add onion to pork fat and simmer until onion is transparent.

6. Add cod meat, diced raw potatoes, celery, bay leaf, salt and pepper. Add one cup of the cod broth, two cups boiling water and simmer for 30 minutes or until potatoes are done and still firm. Put in large 3-qt. double boiler over slightly boiling water.

7. Add hot milk, the evaporated milk, butter and the crisp pork cubes.

8. Correct seasonings and remove bay leaf.

SERVES 6 to 8.

COLD CONSOMMÉ WITH CAVIAR

3 (10½ oz.) cans beef consommé, chilled overnight to jell
4 tbsps. sour cream

1 (4 oz.) jar real Russian or Iranian caviar
1 tsp. scraped onion

To each cup jellied consommé add 1 tablespoon sour cream, 1 tablespoon caviar in center and top with ¼ teaspoon scraped onion.

SERVES 4.

COLD CURRY SOUP

3 tbsps. butter
3 tbsps. chopped apple
3 tbsps. chopped onion
2 tsps. curry powder
4 tbsps. flour
3 or 4 peppercorns
salt to taste

¼ tsp. chili powder
4 cups chicken broth (strong) in which 3 medium-sized potatoes have been cooked to a mush
¼ cup raisins
1 cup heavy cream, chilled

Melt butter in 2-qt. saucepan. Brown apple and onion slowly; add curry powder, flour, peppercorns, salt and chili powder. Stir in broth, slowly, to keep smooth. Let come to a boil. Put through a sieve. Add raisins. Chill. Stir in cream and serve.

SERVES 4 or 5.

CONSOMMÉ AND CREAM CURRY

3 cans (10½ oz.) beef consommé
2 onions, peeled and quartered
1 apple, peeled and quartered
1¼ cups light cream
salt and pepper to taste
1 tsp. curry powder
2 tsps. chopped parsley

Heat consommé with onions and apple and let stand for 1 hour. Just before serving, strain and add cream, salt, pepper and curry powder. Garnish with ½ teaspoon parsley per cup. Good hot or cold.
SERVES 4.

GASPACHO | *Mrs. Stephenson Mahoney*

½ cup onions, chopped fine
8 garlic cloves, minced
1 heaping tsp. coarse salt
5 green peppers, chopped fine
2 tbsps. paprika
½ lb. tomatoes, chopped fine
2 peppercorns
2 cloves
1 cup white vinegar
½ cup olive oil
salt and pepper to taste
1 qt. cold water
1 cucumber, peeled and chopped
1½ cups bread croutons

1. Mash onions, garlic, salt, green peppers, paprika, tomatoes, peppercorns, and cloves through a fine colander or, preferably, a food mill.
2. Put mixture in pottery bowl. Add vinegar and oil and heat.
3. Correct seasonings with salt and pepper.
4. Add water. Chill thoroughly.
5. Pass cucumbers and bread croutons in two separate bowls.

SERVES 6.

COLD MOCK GASPACHO I | *Kitty Warfield*

3 (10½ oz.) cans tomato soup
¾ cup heavy cream
¼ cup milk
3 tsps. chopped green pepper, seeded
¾ tsp. chopped cucumber
¾ tsp. chopped celery
3 tsps. chopped onion
3 tomatoes, peeled and cut up
¼ tsp. curry powder
salt, whole ground pepper, seasoned salt to taste

Put all ingredients in blender for 2 minutes. Then chill in refrigerator. SERVES 6.

COLD MOCK GASPACHO II | *Kitty Warfield*

5 (10½ oz.) cans tomato bisque
1 soup can milk
1 pt. heavy cream
1 pt. half and half
1 medium onion, diced
1½ tbsps. sugar
curry powder to taste

Blend all ingredients in blender. Chill and serve very cold with each cup topped by a heaping teaspoonful of the following mixture:

3 stalks finely chopped celery
½ green pepper, finely chopped
2 medium tomatoes *or* 1 large tomato, peeled and chopped
½ medium cucumber, peeled and chopped

SERVES 10.

TOM BLAKE'S COLD SOUP ORANGE MADRILENE

3 (13 oz.) cans consommé madrilene
1 can strained orange juice (use empty consommé madrilene can to measure)
2 limes, sliced thin
½ tsp. red food coloring (optional)

Stir consommé madrilene and orange juice together well. Chill overnight in bowl in refrigerator. Serve cold with a fresh lime slice in each cup. May also be served hot. Add food coloring (optional).
SERVES 6.

MUSHROOM SOUP

- 4 tbsps. butter
- 1 large onion, minced
- 1 tbsp. chopped parsley
- ½ lb. finely chopped mushrooms
- 3 tbsps. butter, melted
- 6 tbsps. flour
- 6 cups beef consommé
- salt and pepper to taste
- ½ pt. light cream

In a 10-inch skillet, melt butter and sauté onion and parsley until onion is transparent. Add finely chopped mushrooms and cook until mushrooms are done—about 3 or 4 minutes. Separately, in another 10-inch skillet, make a roux or paste of melted butter and flour. Stir in consommé, salt and pepper. Boil well, always stirring until smooth and thickened a bit. Remove from heat and add cream. Heat again and add slowly to first mixture. Simmer for 10 minutes. Correct seasoning.
SERVES 6 to 8.

COLD MUSHROOM SOUP

- ½ lb. mushrooms, stems and all
- 1 can (10½ oz.) chicken broth
- 3 cups whole milk *or* 1½ cups milk and 1½ cups light cream
- 1 heaping tbsp. minced onion
- salt and pepper to taste

1. Peel and cut up mushrooms.
2. Put chicken broth and milk in blender.
3. Add mushrooms and onion.
4. Blend at high speed for 1 minute.
5. Season to taste.
6. Chill thoroughly.

SERVES 4 to 6.
For a diet soup, use skim milk and no cream.

COLD HORS D'OEUVRE SOUP

- 2 small cloves of garlic, crushed
- 1 tsp. salt
- 2 small cucumbers (minced) with peel
- 6 ripe peeled tomatoes and their juice
- ¼ cup fresh bread crumbs
- ¼ cup olive oil
- ¼ cup sauterne wine
- ¼ cup wine vinegar
- 3 cups carrot juice (or water)
- 3 cups beef consommé
- ½ cup water
- ¼ cup sherry wine
- 1 cucumber, sliced very thin with the peel

Put in bowl crushed cloves of garlic and salt. Add cucumbers, peeled ripe tomatoes with juice and bread crumbs. Mix well. Add olive oil slowly. Add sauterne and wine vinegar. Work to paste through food mill and taste. Add carrot juice (or water) and consommé. Put ½ cup water over vegetable pulp remaining from food mill and squeeze all the juice out through cheesecloth. Correct seasoning and add sherry. Put in tightly closed jars in the refrigerator overnight. Serve with thin disks of unpeeled cucumber in each soup plate.

SERVES 6 to 8.

LOBSTER STEW

This is my family's most jealously guarded recipe and is one of the best in my book. I think it is high time to share it.

- 6 (1¼ lb.) lobsters
  boiling water to cover lobsters
- 1 cup salt
- ¾ cup butter
- 4 cups milk
- 1 can evaporated milk
- 2 cups light cream
- 1 Bermuda onion, peeled and quartered
- 4 stalks celery, broken in half
  salt and pepper to taste
- ¼ cup sweet sherry wine
- 2 tsps. Hungarian paprika to color (optional)

Place lobsters in well-salted water (boiling), preferably seawater. If you use ocean water, do *not* add the cup of salt. After water returns to a rolling boil, boil for 15 minutes. Remove all lobster meat from shells, cut in ½-inch cubes; with lobster "butter" (green in color) and roe (found in female lobsters—red in color) put in a 10-inch skillet over medium heat, and sauté in ½ cup butter, stirring constantly for 3 or 4 minutes. Remove from stove and reserve with the butter.

Take *inner* upper bodies of lobsters out of shells (do not use red outer shells or tail shells) and bring these inner membranes just to a boil in top of 3-qt. double boiler in milk, evaporated milk and cream to which the onion and celery have been added. Set back, off the heat, for one hour and strain. Add lobster-meat mixture and season with salt, pepper and add the remaining butter. Set top over bottom of double boiler over hot water (off heat) to blend for 2 hours. Just before serving, reheat and add sherry. Add paprika to color (optional).

SERVES 4 liberally.

If possible, I make this the day before I serve it, as it improves in flavor when set in the refrigerator overnight.

I usually serve this with:

"Hot Blueberry Muffins"
"Endive, Mushroom and Watercress Salad"
Sliced Fresh Peaches with Cream and Sugar
"Sponge Cake"

OYSTER STEW

1 qt. milk
8 celery tops
3 onions, quartered
1 qt. light cream
4 tbsps. butter

1 (13 oz.) can evaporated milk
3 qts. oysters and liquid
¼ cup sherry
salt and pepper to taste

Heat milk to boiling point with celery and onions in top of 3-qt. double boiler. Let stand 1 hour. Strain. Place again in top of double boiler and add cream, butter and evaporated milk.

Cook oysters in their liquor in 10-inch skillet just until the edges curl. Add oysters and their liquor to milk and cream. Place stew over hot water in bottom of double boiler off the heat. Let stand for 1 hour and reheat. Just before serving, add sherry and season with salt and pepper.

SERVES 8 to 10.

ECUADORIAN SALAD SOUP

3 green peppers, seeded
1 lb. tomatoes, peeled
1 cucumber, peeled
2 cloves garlic
1 large onion
4 hard rolls
½ cup vinegar
½ cup olive oil
1½ qts. water
1 pt. tomato juice
½ tsp. paprika
salt to taste
8 small ice cubes

Cut peppers, tomatoes, cucumber, garlic, onion and rolls into small pieces. Put in a glass or china bowl. Pour half of the vinegar, all of the olive oil and water over the mixture. Press down with a potato masher. Refrigerate for 2 hours.

Pass the mixture through a very fine sieve and add, little by little, the tomato juice and paprika. Season with salt. Add rest of vinegar. Serve in iced cups with a small cube of ice in each cup.

SERVES 8 to 10.

SCALLOP CHOWDER

3 big red onions, chopped
salt pork (1½- x 2-in. piece) cut in tiny cubes
2 small green peppers, chopped fine
1½ lbs. sea scallops cut in 1-in. squares
½ cup water
2 tsps. sugar
1½ tbsps. lime juice
1 tbsp. lemon juice
1 clove garlic, crushed
3 cups potatoes, boiled in their skins, peeled and diced
1 qt. milk *or* 1 pt. milk and 1 pt. light cream
1 (13 oz.) can evaporated milk (to bind the chowder)
2 tbsps. butter
2 tbsps. flour
¼ cup sherry, madeira or marsala wine
salt and freshly ground pepper to taste

Sauté pork in a 2-quart iron kettle until crisp. Lift out and reserve. Add onions and peppers to kettle and cook until tender. Put scallops in same pot with pork fat. Simmer with water just 3 minutes. Add the next seven ingredients. Stirring gently, add mixture of butter and flour to thicken. Add wine and pork cubes just before serving and season.

SERVES 6.

SHRIMP BISQUE

6 cups rich chicken broth or stock
¼ cup finely chopped celery
¼ cup minced green onion
2 tbsps. flour
2 tbsps. light cream

1 cup chopped, cooked shrimp
salt and pepper to taste
1 cup cream
4 tsps. fresh chopped dill *or* 2 tsps. powdered dry dillweed

Without allowing the celery to become mushy, slowly cook the vegetables in the stock in a 2-qt. saucepan. Strain and discard the vegetables.

Thicken the broth with flour mixed well with 2 tablespoons cream. Add the shrimp. Season with salt and pepper and add the cup of cream.

Serve with a sprinkling (½ teaspoon) of chopped, fresh dill or ¼ teaspoon powdered dry dillweed per cup.

SERVES 6 to 8.

SPLIT PEA SOUP

1 (16 oz.) pkg. quick split peas
1 ham bone
1 cup cooked ham scraps
5 carrots (scraped and cut up)
1 bunch celery (cut up)

½ tsp. powdered cloves
3 large onions, cut up
water to cover (about 9 cups)
salt and pepper to taste

Put first seven ingredients in 3-quart kettle and cover with water. Simmer slowly for 2 to 3 hours, adding more water if necessary. Season. Serve either as is or strain.

SERVES 6 liberally.

SENEGALESE SOUP

2 medium onions, chopped	2 qts. chicken stock or broth
3 stalks celery, chopped	1 bay leaf
4 tbsps. butter	2 apples, peeled and chopped
2 tbsps. flour	1 cup light cream
1 tbsp. curry powder	1¼ cups diced, cooked chicken

Sauté onion and celery in butter in 3-qt. saucepan until limp. Add flour and curry powder and cook, stirring, for 5 minutes.

Add stock or broth, bay leaf and apples and simmer 30 minutes. Strain and chill.

Before serving, add cream. Add 2 tablespoons chicken per cup.

SERVES 10.

(Cold!)

QUICK SENEGALESE SOUP

2 (10½ oz.) cans cream of celery soup	1 tsp. curry powder
2 cups milk	2 tbsps. soft butter
	¾ cup diced, cooked chicken

Heat soup and milk to boiling. Cream together curry powder and butter. Add to liquid and cook stirring constantly for 2 minutes. Strain and chill.

Garnish with chicken (2 tablespoons per cup).

SERVES 4 to 6. *Too thick + salty. Add ½ cup cold milk after chilling.*

HUBBARD OR BUTTERNUT SQUASH SOUP

4¼ cups milk	2 cubes chicken concentrate
2 onions, peeled and quartered	(dissolved in ¼ cup milk)
4 celery stalks, cut in half	2 tbsps. flour
2 cups cooked, mashed squash	½ cup milk
salt and pepper to taste	1 tsp. nutmeg for garnish
⅛ lb. butter	

1. Heat 4¼ cups of milk, onions and celery together. Do *not* boil. Strain and discard celery and onion.
2. Add squash and salt and pepper to taste. Add the butter and concentrated chicken cubes.
3. Let stand in top of double boiler over hot water to blend the flavors. Keep hot.
4. Add flour mixed with ½ cup of milk. Stir well until slightly thickened.
5. Sprinkle ¼ teaspoon nutmeg over each cup just before serving.
SERVES 4.

JELLIED TOMATO SOUP

3 cups tomato juice
1 (10½ oz.) can chicken broth
½ tsp. onion juice
salt, pepper and paprika to taste

1 envelope (1 tbsp.) plain gelatin
¼ cup water
½ tsp. red food coloring (optional)
4 lemon slices

Heat tomato juice and chicken broth with onion juice and spices. Dissolve gelatin in water. When tomato juice is very hot, fill a cup with the gelatin and tomato juice. Stir until dissolved and add to the soup. Put in a glass dish to cool. Chill covered overnight in refrigerator.

If desired, red coloring matter can be added while mixture is hot.

Serve with a slice of lemon on each cup.

SERVES 4.

VEGETABLE SOUP

1 large soup bone
1 large cabbage, cut up (about 3 lbs.)
1 lb. string beans, cut up
1 lb. lima beans
4 large onions, cut up
1 bunch celery, cut up
6 carrots, peeled and cut up

4 turnips, peeled and cut up
1 (28 oz.) can solid pack tomatoes
4 (10½ oz.) cans beef bouillon
1 lb. peas
2 zucchini, cut up
2 summer squash, cut up
salt and pepper to taste

1. In 8-quart iron pot, put all the above except peas, zucchini, summer squash and seasonings.
2. Just cover with water.
3. Bring to a boil and then simmer on low heat for 3 hours.
4. Add peas, summer squash and zucchini and simmer for 30 more minutes.
5. Season and remove soup bone, but keep the meat from the bone in the soup.

SERVES 12 to 14.

I try to save in the refrigerator all the juices from vegetables cooked during the week. I use this in place of some of the water needed to cover.

COLD WATERCRESS SOUP

1 (10½ oz.) can chicken broth
3 cups whole milk *or* 1½ cups milk and 1½ cups light cream (for diet soup, use 3 cups skim milk)
1 heaping tbsp. minced onion
1 bunch watercress (leaves only)
salt to taste

1. In blender place chicken broth, milk, onion and watercress.
2. Blend at high speed for 1 minute.
3. Season.
4. Chill thoroughly.

SERVES 4 to 6.

CRÈME VICHYSSOISE

4 leeks
1 small onion, thinly sliced
2 tbsps. butter
5 medium, raw potatoes (thinly sliced)
1 qt. chicken broth
½ tsp. salt
¼ tsp. cayenne
2 cups hot milk
3 cups light cream
6 tbsps. chopped chives

Cut white part of leeks into strips. Brown leeks and sliced onion lightly in butter in a 10-inch skillet. Add potatoes, broth and seasonings. Cover and simmer gently for 30 minutes. Force everything through fine strainer. Add 2 cups of hot milk and 2 cups hot cream. Bring to a boil. Cool and add 1 cup of cream. Chill and when ready to serve, garnish each cup with finely chopped chives.
SERVES 8 to 10.

QUICK ICED VICHYSSOISE

1 (10½ oz.) can chicken broth
2 (13 oz.) cans vichyssoise soup (I usually use Crosse and Blackwell's)
2 (13 oz.) cans light cream (use one of the soup cans to measure)

1 small onion, cut fine
½ tsp. cayenne
salt and pepper to taste

Put through blender and pour into milk bottles to chill overnight.
SERVES 8.

CANNELLONI | *Mrs. Egidio Ortona*
The Embassy of Italy

1½ lbs. flour
6 eggs
3 qts. water
1 tbsp. salt
2 (10 oz.) pkgs. frozen spinach
2 tbsps. butter
3 tbsps. flour
1 cup milk
salt and pepper to taste

1 lb. ricotta cheese
½ tsp. nutmeg
3 tbsps. grated Parmesan cheese
4 tbsps. butter (to grease baking dishes)
4 cups "White Sauce I" (p. 358)
1 cup grated Parmesan cheese

To make the pasta dough:

Place the flour in a bowl; add the eggs. Mix (sprinkling with a little water if necessary) until the dough can be made into a rough ball. Knead the dough, adding a little flour if it should become sticky. Let it rest for 10 to 15 minutes. Flatten the dough on a floured board and roll it until rather thin (when it reaches the consistency of a thick noodle). Cut the pasta into rectangles about 3 x 4 inches.

Bring water to boil in a large kettle, adding salt. Drop in the pieces of pasta gently, making sure they don't stick to one another. Cook for about 5 minutes. Drain and spread on a cotton or linen towel to dry.

To make the filling:

Boil frozen spinach according to directions. Drain well; chop fine. Make white sauce by stirring butter and flour over low flame and adding milk slowly (add salt and pepper if desired). Add sauce to the spinach, and mix with ricotta cheese (a special kind of cottage cheese available in Italian grocery stores). Add nutmeg to taste and 3 tablespoons grated Parmesan cheese. Mix well. Correct seasonings. Place a tablespoon or more of the filling in each rectangle of pasta and roll. Prepare two ovenproof baking dishes (13½ x 8¾ x 1¾ inches) spreading a thin film of melted butter at the bottom. Place the cannelloni in the baking dishes and cover with 4 cups white sauce. Sprinkle with 1 cup Parmesan cheese. Bake in a preheated 350° oven for about 15 to 20 minutes. Serve hot.

SERVES 18 (36 cannelloni).

Suggested Menu

Strained Minestrone Soup
Hot Italian Bread Sticks
"Cannelloni"
"Fennel Salad"
"Hot Fruit Dessert"
"Christmas Ginger Snaps"
Espresso Coffee
Liqueurs

GNOCCHI I

2 large eggs
¾ cup farina
¼ cup cornstarch
½ tsp. salt
1 qt. milk
¼ lb. butter

1 cup finely grated Parmesan cheese
¼ cup melted butter (for topping)
½ cup grated Parmesan cheese (for topping)

1. In a small bowl, beat the eggs until thickened and lemon colored.
2. In a 3-quart saucepan, stir together the farina, cornstarch and salt. Gradually stir in milk.
3. Stirring constantly, cook over moderately low heat until mixture comes to a boil. Boil 3 minutes and remove from heat.
4. Stir in ¼ lb. butter, 1 cup Parmesan cheese and beaten eggs, blending well after each addition.
5. Butter an oblong 3-quart glass baking dish (13½ x 8¾ x 1¾ inches). Turn the hot mixture into it, smoothing the top.
6. Chill until very firm (about one hour) or cover and refrigerate all night.
7. Slice (¼-inch thick) and cut out rounds with a 2-inch round cookie cutter.
8. In shallow (11¾ x 7½ x 1¾ inch) baking dish or large quiche round ovenproof dish arrange the rounds overlapping each other until dish is filled (go round and round, overlapping, to center of dish—just one layer deep).
9. Pour melted butter (¼ cup) on top.
10. Sprinkle lightly with extra Parmesan cheese.
11. Bake in preheated 400° oven until thoroughly hot (about 15 minutes).
12. Serve very hot.

SERVES 8.

This is good as a luncheon dish served with fresh asparagus and a "Crisp Salad" of mixed greens with a very tart French dressing.

GNOCCHI II | (From "Villa Papiano," Florence, Italy)

3 cups milk
1 tsp. salt
¾ cup Cream of Wheat
⅔ cup grated Parmesan cheese

½ tsp. dry mustard
1 egg, beaten well
2 tbsps. olive oil

Put milk and salt in top of a large double boiler and bring to a boil, stirring constantly. Add Cream of Wheat, gradually, and stir until thick. Place over hot water in bottom of double boiler. Add ⅛ cup cheese and stir until cheese is melted. Add mustard. Gradually add beaten egg and cook, stirring, for 3 to 4 minutes. Grease two (8 x 8 x 2 inch) pans with 1 tsp. of the oil. Divide mixture in half and place in the two pans. Smooth the top of each mixture. Cover with wax paper and refrigerate overnight.

Remove from refrigerator and cut out rounds of the cereal mixture with a 2-inch round cookie cutter. Arrange rounds, overlapping in a circle, on a greased 10-inch ovenproof pie plate or quiche pan, going round and round, clockwise, toward the center of the pan until it is completely covered. Cover with the rest of the cheese and sprinkle the oil over the top. Preheat oven to 400° and bake gnocchi for about 12 to 15 minutes or until top is golden brown.

SERVES 6.

LASAGNE | *Bette Kovin*

- 1 lb. ground round steak
- 1 large onion, chopped
- 1 clove garlic, minced
- 1 cup fresh, sliced mushrooms
- 3 tbsps. olive oil
- 1 (1 lb. 12 oz.) can tomatoes
- 2 (8 oz.) cans tomato sauce
- 1 tbsp. Worcestershire sauce
- 1 bay leaf
- 1 tsp. oregano
- 1 tsp. onion salt
- 1 tbsp. sugar
- salt and pepper to taste
- 2 eggs
- 1 (16 oz.) pkg. ricotta cheese
- 1 tbsp. chopped fresh parsley *or* 1 tsp. dried parsley
- ¼ tsp. nutmeg
- 1 (6 oz.) pkg. mozzarella cheese
- 1 cup grated Parmesan cheese
- 1 (16 oz.) pkg. lasagne noodles

1. In 2-quart heavy iron or enameled iron casserole, brown ground beef, onion, garlic and mushrooms in 2 tablespoons olive oil. When onion is transparent, skim off any excess fat and add tomatoes, tomato sauce and seasonings. Stir and simmer over low heat 2 to 2½ hours until thick. Correct seasonings and remove bay leaf.

2. In large bowl, beat eggs; then whip in ricotta cheese. Add parsley and nutmeg. Set aside. Have ready the mozzarella cheese, thinly sliced, and the grated Parmesan.

3. Cook lasagne noodles according to package directions; add 1 tbsp. olive oil to water to prevent boiling over. Drain.

4. In ovenproof 2-quart, glass casserole (11¾ x 7½ x 1¾ inches) place ingredients as follows:

cover bottom with meat sauce
top with layer of noodles
layer of ricotta mixture
layer of mozzarella
Parmesan

Repeat 4 (above) ending with meat sauce and topped with mozzarella and Parmesan.
Bake at 350° for 50 minutes to 1 hour.
SERVES 6 to 8.
This also makes a good meat sauce for spaghetti.

MACARONI AND CHEESE SUPREME | *Margery Clifford Lanagan*

1 large Bermuda onion, chopped fine
10 tbsps. butter
6 tbsps. flour
3 cups milk
1 tsp. salt
¼ tsp. white pepper
1 tsp. prepared mustard (optional)
½ tsp. Worcestershire sauce (optional)

2¼ (16 oz.) boxes elbow macaroni
8 qts. salted water (2 tbsps. salt)
1 lb. sharp Cheddar cheese, sliced
1 qt. sour cream
1 cup seasoned Italian bread crumbs
1 cup grated Parmesan cheese
½ cup sesame seeds
⅛ cup snipped, freeze-dried chives

1. Chop onion fine and sauté (in 10-inch skillet) in 4 tbsps. of butter until golden.

2. Remove onion from pan and reserve; add the remaining 6 tbsps. of butter. Remove from heat and add flour to make paste.

3. Heat milk (do not boil) and stir into the butter and flour to make white sauce. Stir until smooth. Add salt, pepper, mustard and Worcestershire sauce.

4. Boil macaroni in salted boiling water (12 to 15 minutes) until very soft. Drain and run cold water through macaroni. Drain again. Add to white sauce and mix in the reserved onion. Correct seasonings.

5. Butter 3-quart (13½ x 8¾ x 1¾ inch) ovenproof casserole.

6. Place a layer of macaroni mixture, then a layer of sliced cheese, and with a spatula spread ½ of sour cream on top. Repeat macaroni and cheese and add the rest of the sour cream.

7. Sprinkle liberally with seasoned Italian bread crumbs and Parmesan cheese.

8. Sprinkle with sesame seeds and chives.

9. Bake in preheated 350° oven until bubbly and lightly browned (about 35 minutes).

SERVES 24.

MANICOTTI | *Margery Clifford Lanagan*

4 strips bacon
⅛ lb. butter
⅛ cup olive oil
2 Bermuda onions, diced
1 garlic clove, crushed
1 tsp. allspice
½ cup medium sweet sherry wine
1 (1 lb. 12 oz.) can Italian tomatoes
2 (15 oz.) cans Italian tomato sauce
2 tbsps. sugar
1 tsp. oregano (optional)
1 tsp. basil
1 bay leaf
   salt and pepper to taste

2 lbs. ground round (lean)
1 tbsp. salt
2 (6 oz.) cans Italian tomato paste
1 cup Burgundy wine
2 (1 lb.) pkgs. manicotti pasta
6 qts. boiling water with 2 level
   tbsps. salt
3 lbs. ricotta cheese
4 eggs
1 tsp. cinnamon
2 tsps. nutmeg

1. In 8-quart heavy, covered kettle cook the bacon and pour off the grease. Add butter and oil, onions, garlic and allspice. Cover and cook until onions are golden. Add sherry and stir. Add tomatoes, tomato sauce, sugar and herbs. Add salt and pepper to taste.

2. In 10-inch skillet brown the beef in salt (until all the pink has gone) and discard the juice. Add to first mixture. Add tomato paste and Burgundy and stir well. Cover and simmer, stirring occasionally, for thirty minutes. Remove bay leaf.

3. Place manicotti in boiling salted water. Cook until tender, stirring often. Drain and place on a tea towel to dry. Do *not* overcook.

4. Place ricotta cheese in a bowl and add beaten whole eggs, cinnamon and nutmeg. Blend well with wire whisk. Season with salt and pepper.

5. Stuff the manicotti with the cheese mixture. (You will have 28 pasta tubes.)

6. In two (11½ x 7½ x 1¾ inch) ovenproof, greased, oblong casseroles pour 2 cups of the tomato-meat sauce mixture. Spread evenly over the bottom of the dish.

7. Cover this mixture with single layer of stuffed manicotti. Pour the remainder of the tomato-meat sauce to cover the manicotti completely in both casseroles.

8. Bake in a preheated 350° oven until it bubbles (about 30 minutes).

SERVES 14.

If you have some sauce left, freeze it to use over spaghetti.

"GERMAN" SPAGHETTI

Who ever heard of "German" spaghetti? The name stems from a fine German cook we had thirty years ago in St. Louis. She gave it this name and so it has remained, through the years. "German" or not, it has been a favorite dish in our family. Even our German friends, though slightly bewildered by its name, like it.

- 12 tbsps. butter
- 2 tbsps. bacon fat (*very important*)
- 2 large Bermuda onions, minced fine
- 2 lbs. ground chuck beef
- 1 lb. fresh mushrooms, sliced
- 4 (26½ oz.) cans spaghetti with sauce (I usually use Franco-American)
- 1 tsp. oregano
- 2 tbsps. sugar
- 2 tbsps. minced garlic
- salt and pepper to taste
- 1 (6 oz.) can tomato paste
- 1 cup grated Parmesan cheese

Melt 8 tablespoons butter and the bacon fat together in a 10-inch skillet and cook onions in this slowly until transparent. Add ground beef and cook, stirring constantly, until all the pink has gone. Set aside in large bowl.

In same skillet, cook mushrooms in remaining 4 tablespoons butter for about 5 minutes. Add to bowl. Add spaghetti and mix well. Add seasonings and tomato paste. Taste to see if you have enough salt.

Place in buttered, large 6-quart casserole (9½ × 4¼ inches, round). Cover with cheese and bake in preheated 350° oven until it bubbles and cheese is melted (about 35 to 40 minutes).

SERVES 24.

SPAGHETTI WITH SAUCE

In a large kettle boil 4 (16 oz.) boxes of spaghetti in 8 quarts salted water (to taste) until tender. Drain and keep warm.

Sauce:
- 2 (14½ oz.) cans tomatoes, juice and all
- 3 cups diced mushrooms
- 1 cup pimiento
- 1 green pepper, chopped
- 2 onions, chopped
- 2 garlic cloves put through garlic press
- 1½ lbs. ground round steak
- 1 bunch celery, chopped fine
- ¼ cup olive oil
- 1 cup tomato juice (if needed)
- ½ lb. bacon, cooked crisp and drained on paper towels, then chopped

Simmer first nine ingredients together, in a large saucepan, stirring occasionally, for 40 minutes or until thickened. Add tomato juice if too thick. Pour sauce over hot spaghetti and sprinkle with bacon.

SERVES 14 to 16.

EGG DISHES AND CHEESE DISHES

EGGS BENEDICT

8 slices ham *or* 8 slices Canadian bacon
2 tbsps. melted butter (measure after melting)
8 eggs
2 cups water
½ tsp. salt
4 English muffins, split with a fork
salt and pepper to taste
2 cups "Hollandaise Sauce" (p. 350)
8 truffles, 1 (2 oz.) can
8 tiny sprigs fresh parsley

1. Sauté or "frizzle" ham or bacon in butter in a 10-inch skillet until it curls at the edges.
2. Poach eggs in simmering, slightly salted hot water, in a 10-inch skillet. Remove from pan and keep warm.
3. Place hot ham on toasted English muffin (use two muffin halves for each serving); on the ham place a poached egg, being careful not to break it. Salt and pepper to taste.
4. Cover each egg with Hollandaise sauce.
5. Place truffles and parsley on top for decoration.
SERVES 4.

CHAFING DISH EGGS

1 pt. heavy cream (light cream may be used)
2 tbsps. Worcestershire sauce
2 tbsps. butter
salt and pepper to taste
8 eggs
4 English muffins, split with a fork and toasted
8 slices thin ham, sautéed in 2 tbsps. butter (melted)

In chafing dish put the cream, Worcestershire sauce, butter, salt and pepper. Heat over flame. When very hot, break eggs into this. When whites are set, remove, carefully, with slotted spoon and place each on top of English muffin and sautéed ham. Pour sauce from chafing dish over each one.
SERVES 4.

FLORENTINE EGGS EN CROUTE

1 loaf (1 lb.) unsliced white bread
¼ cup melted butter or margarine
2 (10 oz.) pkgs. frozen creamed spinach
4 eggs
2 cups water
½ tsp. salt
salt and pepper to taste

1. Slice crusts off loaf of bread. Cut trimmed loaf into four equal slices.
2. Scoop out the center of each slice, leaving a shell ½ inch thick. Brush inside and outside of shell with butter and bake in preheated 400° oven on a (17 x 14 inch) cookie tin 15 to 20 minutes or until golden brown and crusty.
3. Heat spinach according to package directions.
4. Break eggs into salted, simmering water to cover in an 8-inch skillet. Simmer gently until whites of eggs are set.
5. Place bread cases on serving plates; fill center hole with hot creamed spinach and top with hot poached egg.
6. Sprinkle with salt and pepper. Serve at once.
SERVES 4.

LUNCHEON EGG DISH FLORENTINE

4 cups spinach, cooked, drained well and finely chopped
1 tsp. onion, scraped
½ tsp. nutmeg
1 tsp. salt
1 tsp. pepper
2 cups "White Sauce I" (p. 358)
1 lb. fresh mushrooms, chopped
4 tbsps. butter
8 eggs
1 cup "Hollandaise Sauce" (p. 350)

1. Mix spinach with onion, nutmeg, salt and pepper, and add 1 cup "White Sauce I."

2. Sauté chopped mushrooms in butter in a skillet until golden. Mix with spinach mixture.

3. Partly fill 8 individual ovenproof (10 oz.) ramekins with mixture. Make well in center of each ramekin. In each well, carefully place a raw egg.

4. Bake in preheated 350° oven until yolk is set and egg white is done. Do not overcook.

5. Over all eight ramekins pour a heated sauce made by blending the remaining cup of white sauce with 1 cup of Hollandaise sauce (2 tablespoonfuls per ramekin). Put under broiler for 2 minutes. This may be baked in an (8 x 8 x 2 inch) baking dish instead of the individual ramekins.

SERVES 8.

EGGS EN GELÉE | Mrs. Stuart Symington

Eve Symington related to me that, once, when she and the Senator were living in a hotel apartment, she happily put about eight eggs on the stove to hard-boil. She was called away on an errand and completely forgot the eggs. Hours later she returned to find the hall saturated with a ghastly smell of sulphur. Anxious faces were peering from her neighbors' doors.

Horrified, she rushed to the kitchen and, for a moment, couldn't locate the eggs. She finally discovered them on the ceiling, for they had exploded and nested there.

2 cups beef consommé
½ tsp. tarragon
½ package (½ tbsp.) plain gelatin
2 tbsps. cold water
4 eggs
2 cups water
½ tsp. salt
4 slices bread

1 (2½ oz.) can imported pâté de foie gras
4 tbsps. mayonnaise
½ tsp. lemon juice
¼ tsp. dried tarragon
4 tsps. capers
1 bunch watercress

Heat consommé and tarragon, but do not boil. Put ½ package gelatin sprinkled with cold water in bowl. Dissolve gelatin with some of hot consommé mixture. Fill straight-sided cups with ½ inch of above mixture. Refrigerate until set. Poach eggs in salted water until cooked, but still very soft. When consommé is set, carefully put one chilled egg in each cup. (Must go in upside down, so turn out egg on plate and then put in the cup mold very carefully so as not to break the yolk). Cover with remainder of lukewarm consommé mixture and refrigerate again until set.

Toast rounds of bread exact size of the egg cups. Spread with ¼ inch of the imported pâté de foie gras, top with unmolded consommé and egg and add mayonnaise which has been seasoned with lemon juice and tarragon. Sprinkle capers over each egg on top of the mayonnaise. Garnish with watercress.

SERVES 4.

EGGS GOLDENROD

3 cups "White Sauce I" (p. 358)
16 hard-boiled eggs
   salt and pepper to taste
1 tsp. powdered ginger

8 slices buttered toast (crusts removed)
parsley

Make 3 cups white sauce. Cut up egg whites. Add whites to sauce in top of double boiler and season with salt, pepper and powdered ginger. Spoon over buttered toast and sprinkle top well with yolks forced through a sieve. Decorate with parsley.

SERVES 8.

EGGS GOLDENROD CURRY

3 cups "White Sauce I" (p. 358)
16 hard-boiled eggs
1 onion, peeled and cut up
1 apple, peeled and cut up
   salt and pepper to taste

3 tsps. curry powder
8 slices bread, toasted and buttered
1 cup Indian chutney

Make cream sauce as for "Eggs Goldenrod," but when heating milk for sauce, add cut-up onion and apple. Strain and season. Add curry powder.

Spoon over buttered toast or toast points and sprinkle on top egg yolks that have been put through a sieve. Serve with Indian chutney.

SERVES 8.

EGGS MORNAY

8 hard-cooked eggs, halved
4 tbsps. butter
4 tbsps. flour
1½ cups milk
½ cup heavy cream
salt and pepper to taste
nutmeg to taste

¾ cup grated Swiss or Gruyère cheese
⅓ cup finely grated Parmesan cheese

Preheat oven to 450°.

Arrange eggs, cut side down, in 2-quart (11¾ x 7½ x 1¾ inch) ovenproof, oblong buttered baking dish.

Melt butter, blend in flour, then milk (using whisk). Add cream and seasonings. Add Swiss cheese and when melted pour mixture over eggs. Sprinkle with Parmesan cheese. Bake until brown on top (about 10 to 12 minutes).

SERVES 4.

CAVIAR AND SOUR CREAM OMELETS

8 eggs
8 dessertspoons light cream
salt and pepper to taste
½ pt. sour cream

4 tbsps. red caviar
1 tsp. scraped onion
8 parsley sprigs

Make four (2 eggs each) "Fluffy Omelets" (see below). Place a band of sour cream across each omelet and place 1 tablespoonful of red caviar in the center. Scrape ¼ teaspoonful onion on caviar. Place parsley sprigs on top for garnish.

SERVES 4.

FLUFFY OMELET

8 egg yolks
8 dessertspoons cream (or water)
8 egg whites, beaten to soft peaks
salt and pepper to taste

2 tbsps. melted butter
2 sprigs parsley to garnish

1. Beat egg yolks. Add cream (or water).
2. Fold in beaten egg whites and seasonings.
3. Put butter in hot 10-inch ovenproof skillet. When butter is frothy (do not brown), tilt the skillet so the butter coats the bottom and sides.
4. Add the egg mixture and cook until, when you lift the side of the omelet, it is golden underneath.
5. Put pan under preheated broiler and finish the omelet. When it is golden on top, it is done.
6. Fold omelet over and slide onto a platter.
7. Garnish with parsley.

SERVES 4.

PLAIN FRENCH OMELET

8 eggs (room temperature)
8 tsps. cold water

salt and pepper to taste
2 tbsps. butter

1. In a bowl beat eggs thoroughly. Add the water and beat again. Season.
2. Place butter in a 9½-inch omelet pan over moderate heat and when butter bubbles, tilt the pan so that the butter coats the sides.
3. Pour in the egg mixture and, as it cooks, use a knife to pull the mixture away from the sides of the pan. Again tilt the pan so that the uncooked egg fills this space. Continue to do this until the omelet is cooked.
4. Using a spatula, loosen the omelet from the pan. Flip one half of the omelet over the other half (away from the handle) and slide it on to a platter. Garnish with parsley and serve.

SERVES 4.

To make "Omelet Fines Herbes," add 2 level teaspoonfuls finely powdered Fines Herbes to the original egg mixture. "Fines Herbes" is usually found in the spice section of any grocery store in ⅞-oz. glass jars.

PUFFY SOUFFLÉ OMELET WITH STRAWBERRIES

12 egg whites
½ tsp. salt
12 egg yolks
1 tsp. vanilla extract
2 tsps. grated lemon rind
¼ cup sugar
2 tbsps. flour
¼ cup butter
2 (10 oz.) pkgs. frozen strawberries, thawed, *or* 1 pt. fresh strawberries, sliced, with ¼ cup sugar

1. Beat egg whites and salt until peaks are stiff.
2. Beat yolks with vanilla, lemon rind, sugar and flour until smooth.
3. Fold egg yolk mixture into egg whites.
4. Heat butter in a 10-inch skillet until sizzling.
5. Pour in egg mixture, lower heat and cook slowly without stirring until omelet, when lifted gently at one side, looks golden brown underneath.
6. Place skillet under broiler until top surface is lightly browned.
7. Fold omelet in half in pan, then slide out onto platter.
8. Spoon strawberries and their juice over omelet. Serve at once.

SERVES 6.

SCRAMBLED EGGS

Water, in scrambled eggs or an omelet, is much better to use than the usual cream or milk. It makes the eggs much more delicate. I learned this many years ago in Paris from a French friend who was a superb cook. Scrambled eggs can be tricky to cook well, and the cold skillet has a great deal to do with their creamy consistency.

20 eggs
20 tsps. cold water
salt and fresh-ground pepper to taste
4 tbsps. butter (melted)
parsley

Break eggs into a large bowl. Add water and seasonings and beat well with wire whisk. Pour into a cold 12-inch skillet and place over medium heat. As the egg cooks, with a large spoon constantly scrape egg away from bottom of pan. When eggs are soft scrambled, remove from fire. Add melted butter. Taste to be sure seasonings are right. Place on heated platter and garnish with parsley.

SERVES 8 to 10.

SCRAMBLED EGGS WITH ONION AND SMOKED OYSTERS

4 tbsps. butter
1 medium onion, chopped fine
2 (3⅜ oz.) jars smoked oysters, chopped fine

8 eggs
8 tsps. cold water
salt and pepper to taste
parsley for garnish

1. Melt butter in a 10-inch skillet.
2. Add onion, cook until limp, and add chopped oysters. Set aside, covered, to keep warm.
3. Following method given above, make scrambled eggs in another 10-inch skillet.
4. When eggs are done, but still soft, add onion-oyster mixture and pan juices. Place on heated platter and garnish with parsley.

SERVES 4.

This is a simple brunch or luncheon dish served with "Endive, Mushroom and Watercress Salad," "Cheese Popovers" and "Lime Freeze," cookies, coffee and tea.

SHIRRED EGGS WITH CHICKEN LIVERS

1 cup light cream
½ tsp. Worcestershire sauce
4 tbsps. butter (melted)
salt and pepper to taste

4 eggs
1 lb. "Sautéed Chicken Livers" (p. 117)

In shallow, ovenproof 1-quart dish, place cream, Worcestershire sauce, butter, salt and pepper. Break into this 4 eggs. Place in preheated 350° oven for approximately 20 minutes (or until the whites of the eggs are set).

Top with "Sautéed Chicken Livers."

SERVES 4.

EGG ROLLS | *Puan Sri Ong*
The Embassy of Malaysia

Egg Roll Wrapping
- 5 eggs
- 20 tbsps. cornstarch
- 15 tbsps. flour
- 1 tsp. salt
- 2½ cups water
- 1 finger fresh ginger root (peel and slice one end diagonally)
- 4 tbsps. vegetable oil

Break eggs into large mixing bowl. Add cornstarch, flour and salt. Mix and stir into thick paste, then gradually add water, mixing and stirring thoroughly each time until it becomes a smooth thin batter. Water is added gradually to prevent lumping.

Heat 6-inch skillet or wok.

Dip cut end of ginger root into oil and smear skillet with it—just enough to coat surface. Then ladle 2 tablespoons of egg batter into skillet and spread to form a wafer-thin omelette. Cook over low flame for about 3 to 4 minutes. Remove from skillet, place egg wrapping in shallow container or on large piece of foil to cool. Repeat process until all egg batter is used.

MAKES 50 wrappings.

Egg Roll Filling
- *2 pieces mustard pickles (Wash and slice into thin strips.)
- 4 tbsps. vegetable oil (Set aside in dish for use in sautéing ingredients separately as instructed.)
- 1 clove garlic, peeled and minced
- *6 slices fresh ginger root (Peel and slice.)
- *1 lb. bean sprouts (Wash and remove roots—brown tails.)
- 1 medium-sized onion, peeled and shredded
- *1 lb. sweet roast pork (Slice into thin strips.)
- *2 oz. dried mushrooms (Soak in water for 2 hours, then cut off stems and slice into thin strips.)
- 1 tsp. sugar
- 2 tsps. thick soy sauce
- ½ lb. lean pork (Slice into thin strips.)
- 9 oz. fresh or frozen crabmeat, thawed and separated
- 1 pt. vegetable oil (to be used for deep-frying egg rolls)

* Available in Chinatown. Dried mushrooms are sold in 2- to 4-ounce packages. All other ingredients available at supermarkets.

1. Heat 10-inch skillet. Sauté mustard pickles, tossing rapidly, for 1 minute, then add 1 tablespoon oil and minced garlic. Mix thoroughly; sauté for another minute or two. Set aside in large mixing bowl. Heat 1 tablespoon vegetable oil; add ginger slices and sauté for about 1 minute. Then add bean sprouts and sauté for another minute or two. Pour into mixing bowl of mustard pickles.

2. Heat 1 tablespoon vegetable oil in skillet. Sauté onion for 3 minutes; then add sweet roast pork, mushrooms, sugar and soy sauce. Mix thoroughly and sauté for about 5 minutes. Pour contents into bowl of other cooked ingredients.

3. Heat 1 tablespoon vegetable oil in skillet. Sauté pork for 3 minutes.

4. Add all previously cooked ingredients (from large mixing bowl) into this skillet. Mix thoroughly, then add crabmeat and again mix thoroughly. Pour contents into large bowl.

5. This constitutes the filling for the egg rolls. Now we're ready to wrap.

Wrapping Procedure

6. Beat by hand 1 egg. This is to be used as sealant for closing fold of egg roll.

7. Place one egg roll wrapping on flat surface. Into it, spoon 7 heaping tablespoons of filling. Then fold one rounded end diagonally (diaper style) over the filling; roll over, then fold over the two sides. On edge of final fold, smear beaten egg with pastry brush or fingers. Fold to seal. Repeat until all wrappings are used.

Deep-frying Procedure

8. Heat 1 pint vegetable oil in deep-frying skillet over medium flame. Drop in several egg rolls at a time (as many as skillet will hold with ample room for them to float freely) and deep-fry until golden brown. (Be sure oil is heated to deep-frying temperature—375°.) To test without thermometer (marked for deep-frying), pinch a piece of bread and drop into heated oil, which should sizzle visibly and audibly the minute the bread is dropped into it. If it does not, test again a few minutes later.

SERVES 25.

EGGS IN TOMATOES

4 firm, ripe tomatoes
4 eggs
   salt and pepper to taste
4 tsps. butter
4 slices toasted bread made into rounds (no crust) and buttered
1 cup "Hollandaise Sauce" (p. 350)

Select firm, ripe tomatoes with skin. Remove stem end and enough of the pulp to hold an egg. Into each tomato drop a fresh egg, being careful not to break the yolk. Season each with salt and pepper and 1 teaspoon butter. Bake in a 350° oven until the tomatoes are tender and the eggs are set (approximately 20 minutes). Serve on rounds of buttered toast with Hollandaise sauce.

SERVES 4.

NEVER FAIL CHEESE DISH

12 slices bread (crusts removed and cut in 1½-in. cubes)
2 lbs. sharp Cheddar cheese, sliced ¼ in. thick and cut into 1-in. squares
4 eggs
4 cups milk
2 tbsps. Worcestershire sauce
½ medium onion, scraped for juice
⅛ tsp. cayenne pepper
2 tsps. mustard dressing (I usually use Durkee's)
   salt and pepper to taste

In 2-quart buttered ovenproof round glass baking dish, place layer of bread cubes, then layer of cheese, another layer of bread, then cheese, etc., ending with cheese. In bowl beat 4 eggs in 4 cups milk. Add Worcestershire sauce, onion juice, cayenne pepper and mustard dressing. Add salt and pepper to taste.

Heat oven to 375°. Pour milk mixture over bread and cheese and bake for 45 minutes.

SERVES 8.

TOMATO, TOAST, CHEESE DISH

2 (14½ oz.) cans tomatoes and their juice
2 tsps. sugar
1 tsp. salt
1 scant tsp. pepper
3 medium onions, minced
½ cup butter, melted (measure before melting)

12 slices bread
1 cup grated sharp cheese
1 tsp. paprika
2 tsps. fresh chopped parsley
1 cup hot tomato juice (if needed)

1. In a large saucepan place tomatoes, their juice, sugar, salt and pepper. Bring to a boil. Then turn down to simmer and cook until the mixture thickens (about 30 minutes).
2. Sauté onions in melted butter, in a 10-inch skillet, until onions are transparent and golden.
3. Add this to tomato mixture.
4. Toast the bread (crusts off) and cut in four squares to a slice.
5. Grease a 1½-quart round ovenproof glass baking dish.
6. Put layer of toast cubes first, then layer of tomato mixture, then another layer of toast, then a layer of tomato, etc., ending with tomato.
7. Scatter cheese all over the top, then sprinkle paprika and parsley over this.
8. Bake in 350° oven until mixture bubbles and cheese is melted. If this dries out too much, moisten with hot tomato juice.

SERVES 6 to 8.

This dish is good with fish served as a substitute for potatoes.

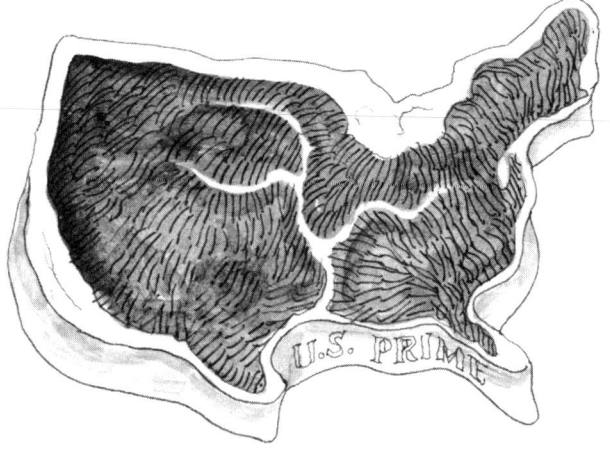

At many Washington dinners, the *pièce de résistance* is Filet of Beef or Saddle or Rack of Lamb, which are expensive, unimaginative and tiresome. I have not included such recipes, except for "Beef Wellington," as I believe that a completely different meat course can be infinitely better. Unhackneyed main meat dishes—such as a "Mixed Grill" or "Osso Buco," "Stuffed Lamb Chops" or "Mint Lamb," "Polynesian Chicken" or "Chinese Chicken with Vegetables"—are what I've tried to stress in the following sections.

My Washington friends will probably be amused by my claim of originality, for "Charcoal Steaks," done on an outside grill, have been served here dozens of times. Clark loves them and, somehow, they seem to be featured at most of our summer parties, try as I may to inject a new thought for the main course.

One of my friends, who has been with us for several traditional Thanksgiving and Christmas dinners, when she heard that I was writing a cookbook, murmured, "You—a cookbook? I thought all you could produce was turkey, boiled onions and squash!"

Perhaps one of the reasons I wrote this book was, hopefully, to enlighten her on this subject.

BETTY BRUCE BOWERSOCK'S BRISKET OF BEEF

1 (3 oz.) bottle liquid smoke
1 (6 lb.) fresh brisket of beef
½ tsp. celery salt
½ tsp. onion salt
½ tsp. garlic salt
½ tsp. pepper
1 tsp. salt
2 tbsps. Worcestershire sauce
1 (6 oz.) bottle barbecue sauce

1. Pour liquid smoke over beef in a roasting pan.
2. Sprinkle with celery, onion and garlic salts and refrigerate overnight.
3. In the morning sprinkle both sides of meat with pepper, salt and Worcestershire sauce.
4. Cover and bake in a preheated oven (275°) for 5 hours.
5. Uncover, pour on the barbecue sauce, and bake 1 more hour (uncovered).
6. Serve cold, sliced.

SERVES 14.

This may be reheated in the sauce. It will keep for months frozen.

FILET OF BEEF SHISH KABOB

20 (1 in.) tender cubes of filet of beef
3 cups red wine
1 crushed garlic clove
½ cup olive oil
1 tsp. black pepper
3 medium green peppers cut in cubes
18 medium mushrooms, washed and stemmed

4 firm tomatoes, quartered
¼ cup melted butter

Ingredients for Rice:
1 cup rice
2½ cups water
1 tsp. salt
2 tbsps. butter

Marinate for 4 hours, at room temperature, cubes of prime filet of beef in wine, crushed garlic, oil and pepper. Remove meat and arrange on 4 skewers, alternating each meat cube with piece of green pepper, a mushroom or a quartered tomato (with skin on). Brush generously with butter and broil, turning the skewers often until meat is done, but still rare. Cut open a cube while cooking to test rareness.

Serve with rice boiled until tender in salted water. Drain, add butter and keep hot. Cover rice with "Curry Sauce II" (p. 347). Allow 4 or 5 beef cubes per person.

SERVES 4.

BEEF STROGANOFF | *Margery Clifford Lanagan*

For many years this was the main supper dish at our annual New Year's Day Party. For cocktails we had an oyster bar and a clam bar. Two men tended each bar, opening the succulent Chincoteague oysters and the Cherrystone clams. The oysters and clams were placed, before opening, on a bed of chopped ice so they were very cold as they always should be. Bowls of lemon wedges and cocktail sauce were nearby. For the non-oyster and clam eaters we had chicken livers wrapped in bacon and small squares of buttered bread topped with rare filet of beef or chicken. On the supper buffet table, with the Stroganoff, we had steaming hot rice, various green salads, wheels of ripe Brie cheese and crackers, tiny French pastries for dessert and gallons of steaming hot coffee as our guests numbered over three hundred.

This annual party always gave us a great deal of pleasure. As I look back through years, I am still amazed at the patience and fortitude of our many guests who would arrive early in order to find a space to sit on the floor of our living room—packed together, waiting for the show which my husband and my family would produce in one corner of the room. We would remove all the furniture, except chairs around the walls and a piano in the corner.

The "review" started with Clark giving his annual "State of the Union" speech—lampooning various events of the past year. This was followed by various skits and songs from our daughters and their husbands accompanied by Howard Devron, a superb pianist. The preparation for these skits took many weeks of writing and polishing to make them entertaining, for this was a very sophisticated audience—and the skits *had* to be good!

The party grew each year until we had to enclose the porch and wire the entire downstairs for sound. It finally became so large that we discussed putting up a heated marquee on our lawn, which would have made our guests much more comfortable, but would also, we decided, spoil the entire flavor of the party. Then two of our daughters moved away and we could no longer have them here for the weeks of rehearsals—and so it ended. But, to this day, when New Year's Day comes around, Clark and I have a very "empty" feeling and yearn for all of our wonderful friends and the joy we had in planning and giving this party.

6 lbs. tenderloin of beef, sliced in ¼-in. slices
½ lb. butter
2 large Bermuda onions, chopped
2 lbs. fresh mushrooms, peeled, stemmed and sliced
2 cups consommé (optional)
4 cups sour cream
1 tsp. nutmeg
1 tsp. salt
pepper to taste
¼ cup sweet sherry (more if you want a stronger flavor)
4 cups rice
2 qts. boiling water
1 tsp. salt
4 tbsps. butter
½ cup finely minced parsley

1. Place strips of beef in a 10-inch skillet and brown slightly in the butter. Remove from skillet and reserve.
2. Add onions and simmer until they are limp.
3. Add mushrooms and cook for about 5 minutes.
4. Add consommé (optional—for a thinner sauce) and stir in the sour cream. Add seasonings and sherry. Set back on the stove off the heat.
5. Place rice in boiling, salted water, in a large saucepan and boil until tender. Drain rice in colander, then pour cold water through it. Separate

grains with a fork and place in the top of a large double boiler over hot water until ready to serve. Add butter and correct seasoning.

6. Just before serving reheat the mixture in the skillet. Add the beef and simmer for 4 or 5 minutes. Do not overcook; the beef should be rare.

7. To serve, place the Stroganoff in the center of a heated platter. Surround with the buttered rice. Sprinkle rice with parsley.

SERVES 14.

If you are making this recipe for a larger party (about 40 people) use the consommé.

QUICK BEEF STROGANOFF

1 medium onion, minced
¼ lb. butter
1 cup sliced fresh mushrooms
1 pt. sour cream
1 tsp. nutmeg
salt and pepper to taste

2 cups thin strips of leftover rare roast beef or steak (cut off fat)
¼ cup sherry (optional)

In a 10-inch skillet, sauté onion in butter until golden. Add sliced mushrooms and cook for 5 minutes. Stir in sour cream, nutmeg, salt and pepper to taste and sherry (optional). At last moment add beef and cook 2 minutes.
Serve at once.

SERVES 2 to 3 liberally.

BEEF WELLINGTON | *adapted from the Foxcroft cookbook*

8 to 10 lbs. filet of beef larded by the butcher with strips of salt pork
1½ lbs. finely chopped mushrooms
¼ lb. butter
salt and pepper to taste

5 pkgs. frozen patty shells
2 (8 oz.) tins pâté de foie gras
1 egg yolk
1 tsp. water
watercress

1. Roast filet in preheated 400° oven for 30 minutes. Remove salt-pork larding and cool beef for 45 minutes. *Save pan juices.*
2. Sauté mushrooms in butter for 5 minutes. Drain and *reserve juices.* Season with salt and pepper.
3. Defrost patty shells and roll out carefully between sheets of wax paper. Allow 5 inches extra all around to fold over filet.
4. Place filet in center of pastry.
5. Spread pâté over the filet.
6. Top with chopped mushrooms.
7. Carefully fold pastry to completely cover filet (as you would wrap a package).
8. With scraps left over from pastry, cut out flowers and leaves and decorate top of filet.
9. Beat egg yolk with water and brush over entire filet. This will further seal the pastry.
10. Place on cookie sheet with raised sides (15½ x 10¼ x ¾ inches).
11. Bake the filet in preheated 400° oven for 30 minutes; then reduce heat to 350° and continue baking for approximately 25 to 30 minutes more.
12. To ascertain rareness, use roasting thermometer in the thickest part of the filet or as a last resort, with a thin, very sharp knife, carefully make a slit in the filet, and look.

Garnish with watercress.

SERVES 10 to 12.

Beef Wellington Sauce
   pan juices from "Beef Wellington"
   mushroom juice, reserved in step 2
½ cup beef flavoring base
½ cup madeira wine

2 tsps. arrowroot
4 tbsps. cold water
1 (2 oz.) can truffles, chopped
   salt and pepper to taste

1. Put pan juices from original roasting and mushrooms in a 10-inch skillet.
2. Stir in beef flavoring base and wine.
3. Dissolve arrowroot in cold water and add to the above, stirring until slightly thickened.
4. Add chopped truffles and season to taste. Serve this sauce separately after filet has been sliced and served.

MEAT

Suggested Menu

Dry Sherry
Fresh Oysters on the Half Shell with Lemon Wedges
A Fine Beaujolais

"Beef Wellington"
Fresh Buttered Peas Surrounded by "Whiskey Carrots"
Tiny Croissants
Bibb Lettuce Salad with French Dressing
"Roquefort Mousse"
Hot Crackers

Champagne

"Apricot Soufflé"
with
"Chantilly Cream"
Coffee   Sanka
Liqueurs

CHILI CON CARNE

¼ lb. salt pork, diced
2 medium onions, diced
2 lbs. ground chuck beef
2 tsps. chili powder
1 tsp. crushed dried red peppers

2 large (1 lb. 12 oz.) cans tomatoes
2 stalks celery, cut fine
salt and pepper to taste
1 (16 oz.) can red kidney beans

Sauté salt pork with onion in a 10-inch skillet. Add and brown the ground chuck. Add chili powder. Sprinkle over this red peppers, tomatoes, celery, salt and pepper.

Cook over very low heat, covered, on top of stove for 4 to 5 hours.

Next day, add the red kidney beans. Cook, covered, on very low heat, for 2 to 3 hours.

SERVES 6.

GERMAN MEAT LOAF

1½ lbs. ground chuck and 1½ lbs. ground round *or* 3 lbs. ground venison	1 tsp. salt
2 medium-sized onions, chopped	½ cup of fresh parsley, chopped
1 cup finely chopped celery	½ cup "Basic French Dressing I" (p. 364)
½ tsp. garlic flakes	1 juicy apple, peeled and chopped fine
1 tsp. thyme	3 eggs, well beaten

Mix all ingredients in a large bowl with your hands. Place in ovenproof 2-quart (11¾ x 7½ x 1¾ inch) dish and bake in preheated 350° oven about 1½ hours.

Ground venison may be used instead of ground round and chuck. It gives an unusually delicious flavor.

SERVES 6 to 8.

CORNISH PASTRIES | *The Countess of Cromer*
The Embassy of Great Britain

8 oz. "Double Crust" pastry (p. 425; use ½ recipe)

Filling:

8 oz. lean beef steak	1 tsp. salt
2 medium-sized potatoes	freshly ground pepper
1 medium onion	1 to 2 tbsps. of stock to moisten
½ level tsp. dried mixed herbs (Fines Herbes)	1 egg beaten
1 tbsp. finely chopped parsley	2 tbsps. milk

Make the pastry and set aside while preparing filling.

Trim away any fat from meat, then shred meat finely. Peel potatoes and cut into small cubes; peel and chop onion. Mix meat, potatoes and onion together in bowl with mixed herbs, parsley, salt, pepper and enough stock to moisten. Divide pastry into 4 portions. Roll each portion out to a circle of about 5 or 6 inches in diameter.

Divide filling equally and place in center of each pastry circle. Dampen edges of pastry and draw two opposite sides together over filling. Brush with a little beaten egg and milk and place pasties on greased baking tray. Place in center of preheated hot oven (400°) and bake for 15 minutes. Then lower heat to 375° and bake for further 20 to 25 minutes. Serve hot.

MAKES 4 small pasties.

SAILORS' BEEF | Mrs. Hubert de Besche
(Sjömansbiff) The Royal Embassy of Sweden

A good hearty dish for cold days.

1½ lbs. chuck or round of beef	2 cups sliced onions
5 to 6 medium potatoes	¾ cup water
2 tbsps. butter or margarine	¾ cup beer
2 tsps. salt	chopped parsley
⅛ tsp. pepper	

Cut meat into ½-inch thick slices. Pound a little with meat hammer or edge of heavy saucer. Peel potatoes and cut into ½-inch thick slices (about 4 cups potato slices). Heat butter or margarine in 10-inch skillet. Add meat and brown quickly on both sides; sprinkle with 1 tsp. of the salt. Remove meat from skillet. Cook onions in the same skillet until brown. Remove from pan. Add water to pan, scrape and cook for 3 or 4 minutes.

Place meat, onions and potatoes in alternate layers in a 2-quart casserole, sprinkling each layer with remaining salt and pepper. Add pan liquid and beer. Cover and bake in moderate oven (375°) for 1¼ hours or until meat is tender. Sprinkle with chopped parsley before serving.

SERVES 4.

Suggested Menu

"Pickled Salt Herring"
"Sailors' Beef"
"Cabbage Baked with Consommé"
Swedish Flat Bread
"Swedish Apple Pudding"
Coffee   Sanka
Liqueurs

GERMAN SAUERBRATEN

4 lb. top round of beef with strip of fat on the bottom
red wine to cover
1 large Bermuda onion, peeled and cut up
8 peppercorns
2 bay leaves
2 tbsps. bacon fat
water to add to wine, if necessary, as it cooks down
1 tsp. sugar
salt to taste
outside crusts of a loaf of rye bread (dried, uncovered, for 24 hours)

1. Marinate meat in wine, onion, peppercorns and bay leaves in a large covered bowl in the refrigerator for 4 days. Turn the meat twice during this period.
2. Remove meat from marinade. Wipe dry, and brown on all sides in the bacon fat in a 10-inch iron skillet.
3. Transfer the meat to 10-quart iron pot with a tight cover.
4. Pour over the marinade and add enough water to just cover the meat. Add the sugar, salt and bread crusts.
5. Cover tightly, bring to a boil, then immediately turn burner down to simmer.
6. Simmer for 3½ to 4 hours, turning twice and adding enough water to keep meat covered. Do not cook too long or the meat will be difficult to slice. Remove bay leaves.
7. Serve hot with the juices from the pot or "Sauce for German Sauerbraten" (p. 357).
8. Serve with "Ruth Hayden's German Red Cabbage" (p. 214) and small, boiled potatoes (12) or 4 cups hot, buttered noodles (follow package directions). "Fruit Cup with Candied Ginger" and cookies are perfect for dessert.

SERVES 8 to 10.

CHARCOAL STEAKS | *Justice William O. Douglas*

¾ cup olive oil
¾ cup soy sauce
6 strip sirloin steaks (1½-in. thick)
1 cup salt
4 (6 oz.) cans tomato paste

¼ lb. butter
1 (10 oz.) bottle Worcestershire sauce
1 clove garlic, minced
juice of 1 lemon

Mix olive oil and soy sauce together and pour into (11½ x 7½ x 1¾ inch) pan. Place steaks in a row in this. Marinate, turning often, for half a day. Then remove from marinade and heavily salt the steaks on each side rubbing salt well into the meat. Place tomato paste, butter, Worcestershire sauce, garlic and lemon juice in a saucepan and bring to a boil. Keep hot.

In an outside grill, build an all-charcoal fire until the coals are at least four inches deep, uniformly across the bed. (Do *not* use Briquets—ever.) The steaks go *into* the charcoal, *not* on a rack over it. When the charcoal is "white," the steaks should be added, one at a time, turning each steak rather quickly so that it is seared and sealed. Thereafter, on each turning, add barbecue sauce with a spoon or a brush. If the coals are "white" when the steaks are added, it takes 8 minutes to produce a "rare" steak, 10 minutes for "medium rare" and 14 or 15 minutes for "well done."

SERVES 6.

If more steaks are used, the sauce should be increased proportionately.

MINT LAMB FOR BARBECUE | *Mrs. H. Bourne Pillsbury*

1 (6 lb.) leg of lamb
1 large bunch fresh mint leaves (chopped)
¼ cup dry mustard
2 tbsps. scraped onion
pepper to taste
salt to taste

Basting Sauce:
9 tbsps. butter
2 tbsps. scraped onion
1 clove garlic
¾ cup chopped fresh mint leaves

1. Have your butcher remove the bones from the leg of lamb and flatten it down so that it looks like a 2½-inch-thick steak.
2. Cut 4 or 5 slits across the top and fill with fresh chopped mint leaves.
3. Rub meat all over with mixture of mustard, onion juice and pepper.
4. Let stand for 2 hours. Meanwhile make sauce by melting 1 tablespoon

of the butter in a small heavy saucepan. Add the onion and garlic and cook quickly for a few minutes. Remove garlic clove. Add chopped fresh mint leaves and the remainder of the butter.

5. When your charcoal fire is very hot (gray in color) put lamb on to broil. Salt halfway through the cooking time (about 20 minutes on a side), and cut open to test the way you like it.

6. Baste with the sauce, turning the lamb every 10 minutes as you baste.

SERVES 12 to 14.

This may be done in your oven under a very hot preheated broiler. I have also seen this done most successfully on charcoal coals in a fireplace.

If you cook this in your fireplace, place the lamb in a double open-fire broiler with a long handle.

Serve this with:

"Spinach Squares"
Salad Greens with "Roquefort Dressing"
Hot French Bread
"Rum Cream Pie"
Coffee   Sanka
Liqueurs

STUFFED LAMB CHOPS

12 chicken livers, chopped
¼ lb. butter
1½ tbsps. finely chopped onion
¾ lb. fresh mushrooms, chopped fine

8 thick rib lamb chops
⅛ cup chopped parsley
salt and seasoned pepper to taste

1. Sauté livers in 2 tbsps. butter with onion and mushrooms until the pink has gone. Chop fine.
2. Make slit in each lamb chop.
3. Add parsley to livers and onion; season.
4. Stuff chops with above mixture. Secure with small skewers.
5. In rest of butter sear chops on each side.
6. Place in 2-quart (11¾ x 7½ x ¾ inch) ovenproof casserole and cover tightly with heavy foil. Bake in preheated 350° oven until tender (25 to 30 minutes).

SERVES 4.

Suggested Menu

"Consommé and Cream Curry"
"Stuffed Lamb Chops"
"Spinach Ring"
Filled with Tiny Buttered Beets
"Lancashire Stone Cream"
"Nut Lace Wafers"
Coffee   Sanka
Liqueurs

LAMB ROAST WITH LEMON PEPPER MARINADE

1 (6 lb.) leg of lamb
½ cup peanut oil

*¼ cup Lemon Pepper Marinade

Rub leg of lamb liberally with peanut oil. Cover completely with Lemon Pepper Marinade.

Roast in preheated 350° oven, 18 minutes per pound for pink lamb and 20 minutes per pound for more well-done lamb.
SERVES 8 to 10.

MIXED GRILL

16 large mushroom caps
½ cup madeira wine
8 double rib lamb chops
8 veal or lamb kidneys
16 link sausages

16 slices bacon
4 large, firm tomatoes, unpeeled
   salt, pepper and basil to taste
1 bunch watercress

1. Peel, cut off stems, and cook mushrooms (see "Mushrooms in Madeira Wine," p. 225).
2. Broil lamb chops 6 or 7 minutes on a side. Keep warm.
3. Broil kidneys following recipe "Broiled Veal or Lamb Kidneys" (p. 118) and cook sausages according to package directions.

* Lemon Pepper Marinade can be purchased in the spice section of the grocery store.

4. Broil bacon separately. Keep warm.
5. Cut tomatoes in half and broil with seasonings on top.
6. On large platter, place lamb chops in a row with kidneys and sausages in between each chop.
7. Around edge of platter alternate tomatoes and mushrooms.
8. Top chops with bacon and garnish each end of the platter with a small bunch of watercress. This dish takes time, but it is well worth it.

SERVES 8.

SASCHA BURLAND'S RUSSIAN SHASHLIK

1 (10 lb.) leg of lamb (cubed in 1-in. pieces)

Marinade:
enough liquid to cover lamb (⅓ water, ⅓ wine vinegar and ⅓ red wine for marinade)
1 tbsp. whole peppercorns
1 tbsp. dried chives
2 shakes of Worcestershire sauce
juice of ½ lemon
1 tsp. garlic salt
3 thick cucumber slices

6 large Bermuda onions
8 firm, slightly underripe tomatoes
6 green peppers, deseeded and quartered
2 lbs. unsliced bacon, cut in ½-in.-thick slices (cut about 1½ in. across)
3 cups rice
8 cups water with 1 tsp. salt
1 loaf black bread
½ lb. butter

1. Place meat in a 6-quart container.
2. Cover meat with the marinade and marinate overnight (turn once).
3. Continue to marinate all day.
4. Remove from marinade and save marinade for brushing on the skewers. (Keep it hot.)

Preparation:
5. Peel and quarter onions. Separate onion quarters by hand.
6. Quarter tomatoes (if small), or cut in eighths (if large).
7. Clean and quarter the green peppers.
8. Cut up bacon.

Method of threading on long skewers:
Follow directions closely as sections stay on skewers this way.
   a. first onion (skin side down)
   b. cube of lamb
   c. slice of bacon
   d. section of tomato (skin up)
   e. section of pepper (skin up)
   f. bacon again
   g. meat again
   h. onion (skin down)
   i. repeat above until skewer is filled
   j. fill other skewers by the same method until all are done

9. Have the coals in the grill piled low and white for 45 minutes. Add more coals as necessary.

10. Cook for 45 minutes turning every 15 minutes and basting with the hot marinade.

11. Leave last side 5 minutes. Cooking time will be 50 minutes in all.

12. Cook rice in water and add a little marinade for flavor. Drain, season and serve with the shashlik (removed from skewers).

13. Serve with hot black bread and butter.

SERVES 8 to 10.

LAMB CHOPS ORIENTALE

4 tsps. dark soy sauce
⅓ cup clover honey
½ cup lemon juice

8 lamb chops, cut thick
bunch of watercress

1. Make a mixture of soy sauce, honey and lemon juice.
2. Pour over lamb chops and marinate in refrigerator for one hour.
3. Take out chops and heat the marinade.
4. Broil chops, turning once, about 7 minutes on a side. Baste often with the marinade.
5. Serve with remaining marinade poured over chops. Season again to taste. Surround with watercress.

SERVES 4.

VEAL IN CONSOMMÉ

1 Bermuda onion, chopped fine
¼ cup butter
8 thin slices veal steak pounded to ¼-in. thickness by butcher
¼ cup flour
salt and pepper to taste
2 cans beef consommé
¼ cup madeira or sherry wine

Sauté onion in butter until golden. Remove onion with slotted spoon. Keep warm.

Lightly coat both sides of veal with flour mixed with salt and pepper. Brown veal in pan butter until golden brown. Do this quickly. Add onions, consommé and madeira or sherry. Cover skillet and simmer slowly for 1½ hours or until veal is tender. Taste and correct seasonings.

SERVES 4.

VEAL MILANESA

12 veal filets
½ cup lemon juice
½ cup all-purpose flour
1 egg, beaten
½ cup finely ground cracker crumbs
1 qt. cooking oil
12 slices Monterey *or* 12 slices mozzarella cheese
24 thin slices fresh peeled tomato
12 flat filets of anchovies
1 (1 lb.) box shell macaroni
salted water to cover
2 tbsps. "Garlic Butter" (p. 343)

Ask butcher to prepare thin filets of veal loin and to pound them paper thin. Cover both sides with lemon juice. Dredge them in a little all-purpose flour. Dip in beaten egg, then lightly in cracker crumbs. Deep-fry in cooking oil (380°) until golden. Place on paper toweling to drain.

Arrange the filets on a flat baking sheet (17 x 14 inches) and cover each with a thin slice of Monterey or mozzarella cheese. In the center place 2 small slices of tomato and a filet of anchovy. Bake quickly in an extremely hot preheated oven (500°) until the cheese begins to melt.

To serve, surround the veal (2 filets per person) with shell macaroni which has been cooked in salted, boiling water, drained and seasoned with garlic butter.

SERVES 6.

OSSO BUCO MILANESE

4 veal knuckles or shanks (cut in 2-in. pieces)	1 garlic clove, minced
1 cup flour	2 cups dry white wine
seasoned salt to taste	4 tbsps. tomato paste
½ lb. butter	3 cups beef bouillon (or more if needed)
1 medium onion, diced	4 cooked turnips, cut up
1 carrot, sliced	1 (10 oz.) box frozen peas (follow packaged directions)
1 bay leaf	
2 stalks celery, sliced	8 small, boiled onions

Dredge veal knuckles in seasoned flour (flour mixed with seasoned salt). Sauté in butter until well browned on each side. Place veal in 4-quart covered iron pot and add next seven ingredients with enough beef bouillon to cover veal halfway. Bring to a boil. Lower heat. Simmer, covered, 1½ hours or until tender.

Remove knuckles and keep hot. Simmer sauce until reduced by about ¼ its original volume. Remove bay leaf. Add freshly cooked turnips, peas and small onions. Bring to a boil and pour over knuckles. Serve very hot. (If too thin, thicken with some of the remaining flour and 4 tablespoons bouillon until gravy is medium thick). Correct seasoning.

SERVES 4.

Serve with 2 cups hot, buttered, cooked and seasoned rice (follow package directions), 24 stalks fresh asparagus, a tossed green salad with "Basic French Dressing," "Baking Powder Biscuits," and "Coffee Crème." Or:

Hot Consommé with Sherry
"Osso Buco Milanese"
Noodles
"Zucchini Parmesan"
Bibb Lettuce   "Basic French Dressing"
Fresh Sliced Peaches and Cream
"Grandmother's Angel Cake"
Espresso   Sanka
Liqueurs

I often substitute Italian Gorgonzola cheese, served with wedges of tart apples or fresh pears, for the peaches and angel cake. This is for hardy friends who love strong cheese.

VEAL STEW

1 tbsp. shortening
5 tbsps. butter
3 medium white onions, cut in thin slices
1 clove garlic, minced or put through garlic press
2 lbs. raw veal, diced and lightly floured
2 cups water (more if needed) *or* 2 cups beef bouillon (more if needed)
8 sweet red peppers, seeded and minced fine
3 tbsps. flour (as needed)
salt and pepper to taste
4 cups cooked rice (follow package directions) *or* 4 cups cooked noodles (follow package directions)

1. In a 10- or 12-inch heavy skillet (with a cover), melt shortening and 1 tablespoon of butter.
2. Add the onions and garlic and cook until the onions soften.
3. Stir in the veal and toss until it is brown.
4. Add the water (or bouillon) and the peppers.
5. Cover and simmer for 2 hours, stirring occasionally, until the veal is fork tender. Add more water or bouillon if liquid cooks away.
6. Lift out meat and keep warm in preheated 200° oven.
7. Add enough flour to pan sauce to thicken it a little, stirring until smooth. Season. Put meat back into skillet and stir into sauce.
8. Place this on heated platter and serve with rice or noodles mixed with the remaining 4 tablespoons of butter (melted).

SERVES 6 to 8.

BETTY BRUCE BOWERSOCK'S BAKED CANADIAN BACON

1 strip of Canadian bacon (5 lb.)
1 cup brown sugar
2 cups pineapple juice

1. Place bacon in a large piece of foil. Wrap completely but loosely.
2. Bake 1 hour in preheated 350° oven.
3. Unwrap and baste with the brown sugar melted in the pineapple juice. Cook, unwrapped, basting often, for another ½ hour.

4. Cool in the refrigerator overnight.
5. Slice and serve.

SERVES 10.

This may be reheated in the sauce and served hot.

Suggested Brunch Menu

Cold "Baked Canadian Bacon"
Cold "Brisket of Beef"
"Caesar Salad"
"Celery Root Remoulade"
"Corn Dodgers"
"Florentines I"
Coffee   Sanka

COUNTRY HAM | Mrs. William C. Westmoreland

"Kitsy" Westmoreland claims that after once preparing a ham in this incredible fashion, you will never cook one any other way. It also solves the problem of what to do with the Sunday *New York Times*, once read. As for the 50-lb. lard tin, I guess you have to marry into the United States Army (preferably a General)!

1. Place a country ham, unscrubbed, unwashed, unsoaked, in a large heavy kettle (or a 50-lb. lard tin) and cover with cold water.
2. Bring to a rolling boil and boil for 1 minute per pound (or 15 to 20 minutes).
3. Turn off heat and cover with a tight-fitting lid.
4. Take the Sunday *New York Times* and wrap around and over the kettle. Wrap an old blanket all around the kettle and the newspaper. In other words, insulate the kettle well.
5. Set aside and leave for 24 hours.
6. A dreadful sight is your ham, after 24 hours, but have faith.
7. Skin the ham, leaving about ¼ to ½ inch of fat or however much fat you prefer.
8. Glaze with your favorite glaze (or could be made with leftover jam mixed with dry mustard and brandy). Use your imagination here and taste until you like it.
9. Bake for 1 hour in a preheated 350° oven or until ham again looks as a ham should.
10. Let stand for 24 hours, then carve very, very thin.

TO COOK VIRGINIA OR COUNTRY HAMS

1 (15 lb.) ham
  cold water to cover
2 cups light brown sugar
1 cup cider

2 tsps. black pepper
1 box whole cloves
1 qt. pineapple juice

Soak the ham for 24 hours in cold water, then scrub thoroughly with a brush. Simmer for 20 to 25 minutes per lb. in *fresh* water to cover to which 2 tablespoons brown sugar have been added. When three-quarters cooked, add cup of cider. Cook until bone is loose. Cool ham in water in which it has been cooked. Before it is cold, remove skin carefully so as not to tear fat. When cold, trim fat. Sprinkle generously with black pepper, cover with a thick layer of brown sugar and stud with whole cloves. Bake in preheated 350° oven long enough to get a rich brown color, basting frequently with pineapple juice. This will take about 3 hours and 40 minutes.

Do not slice for 24 hours.

SERVES 40.

BONED COOKED HAM

1 (6 lb.) boned, cooked ham
1½ cups dark brown sugar
1 box whole cloves
1 qt. pineapple juice

¼ cup butter
4 pineapple slices
4 Maraschino cherries

1. Preheat oven to 350°.
2. Score ham diagonally across the top. Turn ham and score the other way (making a diamond pattern).
3. Cover top and sides of ham with brown sugar (1 cup).
4. Place a whole clove in each diamond pattern on top of ham.
5. Place in pan in oven and baste every 15 minutes with pineapple juice. Roast for 1 to 1½ hours.

To Decorate Ham:

6. Melt butter in 10-inch skillet. Add ½ cup brown sugar and heat till melted. Add pineapple slices and cook until golden. Place slices on top of the ham. Pour over any remaining pan juices. Place one Maraschino cherry

in center of each pineapple slice and secure with a toothpick. If ham is to be served cold and sliced thin, omit the decorating. Most stores will thin-slice the ham for you after it is cooked.

SERVES 24.

PIDCOCK HAM (GEORGIA HAM)

1 (15 lb.) Georgia ham
water to cover
3 cups light brown sugar
1 box cloves
1 large (1 lb. 14 oz.) can pineapple juice
8 slices pineapple
1 cup butter
8 Maraschino cherries

Soak ham in water to cover for 24 hours. Pour off this water, wash ham in warm water, and put in boiler, skin side down. Cover with cold water, again bring to a boil and let simmer until done. Allow 20 to 25 minutes to the pound. Ham is done when skin is slightly wrinkled. Take from boiler and skin while warm. Do not stick with fork while hot as the juices escape. Following directions for "Boned Cooked Ham" (above), bake for 3½ hours and decorate. Do not slice for 24 hours.

SERVES about 40.

HAM RING WITH TURNIPS

4 cups ground cooked ham
1½ cups soft bread crumbs
1 cup milk
2 egg yolks, beaten well
1 tbsp. chopped parsley
½ tsp. salt
⅛ tsp. pepper
2 tbsps. grated onion
2 egg whites, beaten stiff
8 medium turnips (cooked and mashed)
¼ cup butter (for turnips)
salt and pepper to taste (for turnips)

Mix ham with bread crumbs, milk, beaten egg yolks, chopped parsley, salt, pepper and grated onion. Fold in beaten egg whites. Fill well-greased

2-quart ring mold. Place mold in pan of hot water. Bake in moderately slow (325°) preheated oven until set (about 40 to 45 minutes). Serve filled with buttered, mashed turnips. Season to taste.

SERVES 8 to 10.

Your local market will grind the ham for you.

HAM SLICE | *Sally Dingwall*

- 2 (1 lb.) center cut slices precooked ham (¾-in. thick)
- ½ cup light brown sugar
- 2 tsps. mustard (wet)
- 4 tbsps. chutney
- 1 pt. sour cream

Cover one slice ham with ½ mixture of brown sugar, wet mustard and chutney. Top with the other slice of ham and rest of sugar mixture. Cover with sour cream. Bake 45 minutes in preheated 350° oven.

SERVES 4 to 6.

PINEAPPLE GLAZED LUAU PORK | *from Hawaii*

- 1 (6 rib) pork loin roast (about 3 lbs.)
- salt and pepper to taste
- ¾ cup syrup from canned sliced pineapple
- 2 tbsps. light brown sugar
- ½ tsp. ginger (fresh or powdered)
- ½ tsp. dry mustard
- 1 tsp. cornstarch
- 1 tsp. soy sauce
- 1 tsp. catsup
- 1 (1 lb. 4 oz.) can sliced pineapple
- watercress

Season roast with salt and pepper. Set in shallow (13½ x 8¾ x 1¾ inch) roasting pan. Insert meat thermometer into thick part of the roast (away from fat or bone).

Roast in preheated 325° oven until thermometer reaches 170° (or about 1½ hours). Meanwhile, drain syrup from pineapple and combine with brown sugar, ginger, mustard, cornstarch, soy sauce and catsup in small saucepan. Bring to a boil and simmer 1 minute to thicken slightly. Baste roast with sauce at 10-minute intervals after 1½ hours cooking. Cook and baste until thermometer reaches 185° (about ½ hour longer). Add drained pineapple slices last 5 minutes of cooking.

Lift roast to hot serving platter and arrange pineapple slices around the meat. Garnish with watercress.

SERVES 6.

SWEET-SOUR PORK

4 lbs. pork
1 tbsp. soy sauce
1 tsp. sugar
2 tsps. salt

3 eggs
½ lb. cornstarch
1½ qts. vegetable oil

Cut meat into (1½ x 1 x 1 inch) cubes. Marinate meat in soy sauce, sugar and salt. Let this mixture stand for about 2½ to 3 hours to absorb the seasonings. After this period, beat eggs, add to marinated meat and mix thoroughly. Dip each piece into cornstarch and deep-fry in vegetable oil heated to 375°. Garnish with "Cucumber Vinaigrette" (p. 265).

SERVES 8.

PORK ROAST

4 lb. pork roast (center cut of the loin)
1 tbsp. flour
1 tsp. salt
1 tsp. dry mustard
¼ tsp. pepper
2 cups water, more if needed
2 cups canned pears (1 lb. 4 oz. can), drained and sieved

¼ cup dark brown sugar, packed hard
½ tsp. powdered cinnamon
¼ tsp. powdered cloves
16 spiced crab apples for garnish
parsley

Place pork fat side up in an open roasting pan. Combine flour, salt, mustard and pepper and rub all over the roast. Do not sear; add water and cover. Insert oven meat thermometer in the thickest part of the roast and place roast in a preheated 325° oven. Cook for 2 hours and 40 minutes or until thermometer registers 185°. After 2 hours of roasting, pour over pork the pears and juice mixed with the sugar, cinnamon and cloves which have been melted together in a saucepan. Return to the oven and continue roasting, basting often with the pan juices. When roast is done, place it on a heated platter in a warm oven to rest for 15 to 20 minutes. Save roasting-pan juices. This gives you time to make the gravy (see "Pork Roast Gravy," p. 349). Before serving, surround meat with spiced crab apples and garnish with parsley.

SERVES 8.

As a guide if you use a larger or smaller roast, pork should be cooked 40 minutes per pound.

BARBECUED RIBS

10 lean and meaty spareribs (best cut)
water to cover
"Barbecue Sauce I" (p. 339)

1. Parboil ribs in 10-inch skillet in water to cover for 15 to 20 minutes. Drain and dry.
2. Preheat broiler.
3. Marinate ribs in sauce for 10 minutes.
4. Place ribs in ovenproof broiling pan.
5. Broil about 6 to 8 minutes on a side, basting often with the sauce.

SERVES 2.

SPARERIBS AND SAUERKRAUT

30 pork spareribs (cut into single ribs)
½ cup flour
1 cup butter
2 (1 lb. 11 oz.) jars sauerkraut
salt and pepper to taste

8 potatoes
¼ cup butter (for potatoes)
¼ cup cream
parsley

1. Wash spareribs. Flour and brown well in butter in a roasting pan.

2. Bring the sauerkraut to a boil (no longer) in fresh water. Drain, but save some of the juice for basting. Place layer of sauerkraut in roaster, then layer of ribs, salt and pepper. Alternate, ending with ribs on top. Sprinkle with 1 cup sauerkraut juice.

3. Cover and bake in a preheated 350° oven for 2 hours, basting with sauerkraut juice if too dry. For last ½ hour of cooking, take cover off and turn oven up to 375° to brown.

4. Boil potatoes until tender and mash until smooth and fluffy. Season with butter, salt and pepper and cream.

5. Serve large platter with mound of fluffy, mashed potatoes in center, ribs standing up around potatoes (like a crown roast) and piles of sauerkraut at each end of platter. Garnish with parsley.

SERVES 6 to 8.

"ANTICUCHOS" | Mrs. Fernando Berckemeyer
(Peruvian Barbecued Beef Heart) — The Embassy of Peru

1 large beef heart
wine vinegar to cover
1 tbsp. salt
1 tsp. freshly ground pepper
Sauce:
½ cup olive oil
¼ cup wine vinegar
½ large Bermuda onion, minced fine
1 clove garlic, minced (optional)
½ tsp. black pepper
¼ tsp. flaked hot peppers (more if you want the sauce hotter)
Tabasco sauce (optional)
chili sauce (optional)

1. Remove all membranes from the beef heart and cut into 1½-inch cubes.

2. Place in an earthenware or china bowl and cover with the vinegar, salt and pepper. Marinate in the refrigerator for 24 hours, turning once or twice.

3. Remove from marinade, pat dry and thread cubes on 10 long skewers (about 6 to 8 cubes per skewer). Discard marinade.

4. In a bowl, place olive oil, vinegar, minced onion, garlic (optional), pepper and hot pepper. Stir well to mix.

5. Place skewers with beef heart cubes over a very hot charcoal grill. Baste often with the sauce, turning skewers two or three times.

6. These cook quickly and must be served rather rare, so test one of the cubes to determine rareness.

7. Remove meat from skewers and place on heated platter.
8. Serve with Tabasco or chili sauce (both optional).

SERVES about 10.

This recipe may be cooked indoors under a *very* hot preheated broiler. If using this method, place the skewers on a (17 x 14 inch) cookie sheet. Broil for about 3 minutes on a side.

Suggested Menu

"Ecuadorian Salad Soup"
"Anticuchos"
"Crispy Green Salad"
"Sangría"
Hot French or Italian Bread, Buttered
Fresh Halves of Papaya with a Lime Wedge
"Rum Balls"
Coffee   Sanka

CALVES LIVER AND BACON

12 strips bacon
12 medium slices ½-in. thick calves liver
½ cup flour
salt and pepper to taste
bunch of parsley

2 Bermuda onions, sliced (for Variation I)
4 tbsps. butter
1 cup Indian chutney (for Variation II)

Broil bacon, drain, and save the fat. Set bacon aside and keep warm.

Dust liver with flour, mixed with salt and pepper, and cook liver slices in the bacon fat in electric frying pan or 10-inch skillet until pink in the center. Turn often and watch carefully.

Correct seasonings and garnish with bacon and parsley.

SERVES 6.

Variation I

Cover with sliced onions which have been sautéed in butter in a 10-inch skillet until they are golden.

Variation II

Instead of the sautéed onion, serve liver with chopped Indian chutney.

CHICKEN GIZZARDS IN SAUCE

This is a very inexpensive dish and it's delicious. No one seems to know what they are eating, which, for those who are "anti-innards," is a good thing. When the budget is low, and so are you, try it.

- 2½ lbs. chicken gizzards
- 1 onion, cut in quarters
- 4 stalks celery, cut up in large pieces
- water to cover
- 4 tbsps. butter
- 4 tbsps. flour
- salt and pepper to taste
- 1 tsp. curry powder (optional)
- 4 hard-boiled eggs, cut up
- 6 slices buttered toast (cut diagonally in triangles—crusts off)
- parsley for garnish
- 1 cup chutney (optional)

In a large saucepan, bring gizzards, onion, celery and water to a boil. Turn down heat and simmer until gizzards are fork tender. Remove gizzards from stock. Cook stock down until you have 2 cups left. Save and keep hot in top of double boiler over hot water. Slice gizzards thin and keep warm. Melt butter in small skillet. Remove from heat and add flour to make a paste. Stir gradually into stock until smooth and thickened. Season. (Add curry here if you are using it.) Add eggs. Make toast triangles. Serve gizzards on heated platter surrounded by the toast points. Garnish with parsley and if you use the curry powder, serve chutney in a side dish.

SERVES 6.

FRIED FRENCH BEANS WITH CHICKEN GIZZARDS | The Embassy of Malaysia

- ¾ to 1 lb. chicken gizzards (finely sliced)
- 1 tbsp. soy sauce
- ½ tsp. pepper
- 1 tbsp. cornstarch
- 6 tbsps. vegetable oil
- 4 to 5 cloves fresh garlic (chopped)
- 4 slices fresh ginger root
- 2 medium-sized onions (cut into eighths)
- 3 lbs. fresh green beans (sliced in whatever style desired)
- 1 tsp. salt
- 1 cup water

Season gizzards with soy sauce and pepper; mix in the cornstarch. Heat 12-inch skillet until warm, then add the oil. When oil is hot, add garlic and ginger and sauté until golden brown. Add onions and gizzards and fry slowly until gizzards are tender. Test with fork. Now add the beans and fry together with the gizzard mixture. Add salt. Keep stirring until beans have absorbed the oil and give the appearance of very fresh green color. Add the water and quickly cover the pan. The steam from the water will cook the beans. This is the basic method of frying vegetables in the Chinese style. Uncover the pan and test to see whether the beans are cooked or not. If not, cover pan again and continue cooking for another 1 or 2 minutes. Test again. The beans must be *just* cooked and give the appearance of fresh *green*.

Remove from pan and serve on a platter.

Please remember that Oriental meals consist of several courses. The above will serve 12, if two other dishes are included in the menu.

SAUTÉED CHICKEN LIVERS

2 lbs. chicken livers
½ cup flour
½ cup butter

salt and pepper to taste
watercress

1. Dip chicken livers in flour to coat them lightly.
2. Melt butter in 10-inch skillet and add the livers.
3. Stirring often over medium heat, cook the livers until they are done (when the pink inside has turned light brown).
4. Season to taste and garnish platter with watercress.

SERVES 4.

CHICKEN LIVERS WITH BRANDY

¼ cup flour
2 lbs. chicken livers
6 tbsps. butter, melted
4 tbsps. brandy

4 egg yolks
1 pt. light cream
salt and pepper to taste
watercress

Lightly flour and sauté chicken livers in the melted butter in a 10-inch skillet or chafing dish until they are tender and the inside is no longer pink. Sprinkle with brandy, light and burn.

Beat egg yolks in a bowl with cream. Add to above when brandy flame is out and stir constantly over very low flame until sauce is medium thick. Watch that eggs do not become scrambled. Season to taste. Garnish with watercress.
SERVES 4.

BROILED VEAL OR LAMB KIDNEYS WITH BROILED TOMATOES AND SCRAMBLED EGGS

4 veal kidneys or 12 lamb kidneys
4 firm tomatoes
   salt and pepper to taste
12 eggs
10 tsps. water or cream
4 tbsps. butter
   parsley

1. Have butcher trim all but ¼-inch fat from the kidneys. Slice in ¼-inch slices (across).
2. Place on (15½ x 10¼ x ¾ inch) cookie tin and broil under a preheated broiler for 2 or 3 minutes on a side. *Do not overcook.* Season, set aside and keep hot.
3. Place tomatoes cut in half on another pan the same size and broil until thoroughly hot, but not limp. Season and keep hot.
4. In cold 10-inch skillet, place eggs beaten with a whisk with the water or cream and seasoned. Place over medium heat and with a spoon scrape away the eggs from the bottom of the pan until they are done, but still soft. Add the butter.
5. Place eggs in center of heated platter. Surround with kidneys, tomatoes and parsley.
SERVES 6.

KIDNEY STEW

8 veal kidneys
   water to cover
1 onion, peeled and quartered
4 stalks celery, cut in large pieces
4 tbsps. butter
4 tbsps. flour
¼ cup sherry
   salt and pepper to taste

Place kidneys, covered with water, in a large saucepan. Add onion and celery. Bring to a boil and simmer until kidneys are tender. Take kidneys from pan, remove all their cartilage; cut into ½-inch cubes and reserve. Strain the stock and put back in the saucepan. Boil on high heat until stock is reduced to 2 cups. Keep hot.

Melt butter in small skillet. Remove from heat and stir in flour to make a paste. Gradually stir this into the stock until it is thickened and smooth. Add kidneys and sherry. Season.

SERVES 8.

This is our favorite winter Sunday breakfast. We serve it with fruit, "Cornbread," "Scrambled Eggs" and coffee. This menu is also good for a Sunday Brunch—but for brunch, I add a chafing dish of "Chicken Hash," a green salad and Brie cheese with toasted crackers and a good Beaujolais wine. The "Chicken Hash" is for our friends who don't like kidneys—so everyone is happy.

LIVER LOAF

1½ lbs. calves liver
hot water to cover
1 small onion, chopped
1½ lbs. fresh pork
1 cup dry bread crumbs
1 tsp. Worcestershire sauce
1 tbsp. lemon juice

1 tsp. salt
⅛ tsp. pepper
1 tsp. celery salt
2 beaten eggs
½ cup stock
4 slices bacon
watercress for garnish

Cover liver with hot water. Simmer for 5 minutes. Drain off liquid and reserve for stock. Force liver, onion and pork through meat chopper (medium blade). Add remaining ingredients except bacon and watercress. Form in a loaf in greased pan (9½ x 5¼ x 2¾ inches). Top with bacon strips. Set in pan of water to bake, but remove from water for last 20 minutes. Bake in preheated 350° oven 45 minutes. Unmold on oval hot platter and garnish with watercress.

SERVES 10.

HOW TO COOK SWEETBREADS

6 lbs. sweetbreads
  boiling water to cover
1 tsp. salt
1 tbsp. vinegar

Place sweetbreads in boiling salted water in a large saucepan. Add vinegar. Boil for 12 to 15 minutes and drain. Plunge into cold water to blanch. Remove skin and membranes and cut in 1-inch pieces. (If put in refrigerator, cover, as the sweetbreads pick up other flavors.)

BROILED SWEETBREADS

4 sweetbreads
½ cup butter (melted)
  salt and pepper to taste
4 slices toast, buttered (crusts off)
"Creamed Mushrooms" (p. 224)
watercress

1. Cook sweetbreads as directed above; remove outside membranes, but keep each one whole.
2. Brush well with melted butter and season.
3. Place in 1-quart (8 x 8 x 2 inch) buttered ovenproof baking dish in preheated broiler about 6 inches from the heat.
4. Broil until thoroughly hot.
5. Have buttered toast ready and hot and place a sweetbread on each slice on a heated platter.
6. Cover each with "Creamed Mushrooms" and garnish with watercress.

SERVES 4.

CREAMED SWEETBREADS WITH GINGER

3 lbs. sweetbreads
2 cups "White Sauce I" (p. 358)
1 tsp. powdered ginger
  salt and pepper to taste
3 slices toast (crusts off and each slice cut diagonally into four triangles)
watercress

Cook sweetbreads as directed under "Sweetbreads" (above) and cut in 1-inch pieces. Make white sauce. Keep sauce in top of double boiler over hot water. Add ginger. Add sweetbreads and correct seasonings. Serve garnished with toast triangles and watercress.

SERVES 6.

BEEF TONGUE

1 (3 to 4 lb.) smoked beef tongue
   cold water to cover completely
     (for soaking)
   cold water to cover completely
     (for boiling)
10 cloves
6 bay leaves
1 large Bermuda onion, quartered
4 stalks celery, cut up
1½ cups "Tomato Sauce" (p. 358) *or*
1½ cups "Horseradish Sauce" (p. 335)

Soak smoked tongue overnight in cold water. Place in new water in a 4-quart pot with cloves, bay leaves, onion and celery stalks. Bring to a boil, then turn down and simmer for 3 to 4 hours until very tender. Remove tongue from broth; discard broth. Cut skin long way of tongue on top and underneath, peel off and discard. Trim off the thick bottom end of tongue and save to cook for flavor with spinach later. Serve with tomato sauce or horseradish sauce.

SERVES 6 to 8.

POULTRY

AND GAME

Chicken is inexpensive and versatile. It is delicious hot or cold and the hostess spares herself a great deal of trauma by not having to worry whether it is rare or not, as with beef. I am always searching for new and different methods for cooking chicken as it is a great favorite in our household. Please try the "Chinese Chicken and Vegetables," the "Polynesian Chicken," the "Asian Style Broiled Chicken" and the "Iranian Shirin Polo." I know you will like them and they are not difficult to prepare.

The "Roast Duckling with Orange and Wine" and the "Crisp Chinese Style Duck" are fine for rather small dinners and may be prepared in advance.

If you are fortunate enough to have a hunter in your family, the recipes for game are great fun to prepare, but be sure that your guests like game. I may be the only woman in the world whose husband, after three days of hunting, limped home, beaming, and presented her with his loot—one half a rabbit. I have never been able to bring myself to inquire as to the whereabouts of the other half. Needless to say, when we have game it is given to us.

PUERTO RICAN ARROZ CON POLLO

- 3 lb. broiler-fryer cut in 8 pieces
- ½ cup olive oil
- 2 cups chopped onion
- 1 clove garlic, crushed
- ½ tsp. crushed red pepper
- 2½ tsps. salt
- ½ tsp. pepper
- 2 cups raw converted white rice
- ¼ tsp. saffron threads
- 1 (1 lb. 12 oz.) can tomatoes, undrained
- 1 canned green chili pepper, chopped
- 1 (10½ oz.) can condensed chicken broth, undiluted
- ½ cup water
- ½ (10 oz. pkg.) frozen peas
- 6 stuffed green olives, sliced
- 1 (4 oz.) can pimientos, drained and sliced

1. Wipe chicken pieces with damp paper towels.
2. In heavy 6-quart Dutch oven, heat the olive oil. Brown chicken, a few pieces at a time, until golden brown all over. Remove each piece as it browns.
3. Preheat oven to 325°.
4. Add chopped onion, garlic and red pepper to Dutch oven; sauté, stirring, over medium heat until golden—about 3 minutes.
5. Add salt, pepper, rice and saffron to Dutch oven. Cook, stirring, until rice is lightly browned (10 minutes).
6. Add tomatoes, chili pepper and chicken broth to rice mixture. Add chicken pieces. Bring just to boiling.
7. Bake, covered, 1 hour.
8. Add water. Sprinkle peas, olives and pimiento strips over the top. Do not stir. Bake, covered, 20 minutes longer, or until chicken is tender and peas are cooked.
9. Serve hot right from the Dutch oven.

SERVES 4.

ASIAN STYLE BROILED CHICKEN | *Puan Sri Ong*
The Embassy of Malaysia

- 1 bulb garlic, peeled and minced fine
- 2 onions, peeled and minced fine
- *1 root of fresh ginger (about size of palm), peeled and minced fine
- 4 tbsps. sugar
- *3 tbsps. thick soy sauce
- *1½ cups thin soy sauce
- 1 tsp. pepper
- 1 tsp. monosodium glutamate
- 8 lbs. chicken, cut into pieces of 3½- to 4-in. length
- 2 tbsps. dry sherry

Mix minced vegetables, spices and seasonings (except sherry) together in large mixing bowl and marinate pieces of chicken for 2 to 3 hours. (If you prefer a more pungent taste, marinate longer than 2 hours). Just before broiling chicken, add sherry to marinade and coat chicken thoroughly in marinade.

Broil over charcoal (preferably) or in cooking-range broiler. Broil pieces on each side for about 8 to 10 minutes. The cooking time is reduced for any meat that has been marinated for a long period.

SERVES 12.

Suggested Menu

"*Egg Rolls*"
"*Asian Style Broiled Chicken*"
"*Monk's Dish*"
"*Fried Rice*"
"*Cucumber Vinaigrette*"
Fresh Pineapple, Sliced
Fortune Cookies
Tea

This is an authentic Malaysian dinner.

* Available in Chinatown. All other ingredients are available at the grocery stores.

QUICK CHICKEN CACCIATORE

1 (2 lb.) chicken (broiler-fryer) cut up
2 tsps. seasoned salt
¼ cup salad oil
1 (1½ oz.) pkg. spaghetti sauce mix
1 (16 oz.) can tomatoes
¼ cup sauterne
2 cups cooked spaghetti *or* 2 cups cooked rice (follow package directions on either of these)

1. Sprinkle chicken with seasoned salt.
2. Brown in salad oil in a 10-inch skillet.
3. Remove chicken and pour off fat.
4. Blend spaghetti sauce mix and tomatoes in the skillet.
5. Add chicken, cover and simmer for 30 minutes.
6. Add sauterne.
7. Continue simmering (uncovered) for 15 minutes longer or until chicken is tender.
Serve over cooked spaghetti or rice.
SERVES 2 or 3.

CHICKEN WITH BURGUNDY | *Joyce Clifford Burland*

6 (2 lb.) broiling chickens, cut up
4 extra breasts, cut in half
4 extra thighs
2 cups flour
2 tsps. salt
1 tsp. seasoned salt
1 tsp. white pepper
1 lb. butter (to fry chicken)
8 bunches scallions
4 lbs. fresh mushrooms
4 garlic cloves (put through garlic press or minced)
3 cups Burgundy wine
½ tsp. thyme
½ tsp. rosemary
2 tbsps. chopped fresh parsley
1 lb. chicken livers
½ cup butter (to sauté livers)
1 (4 oz.) pkg. precooked ham slices (cut up)
1 bunch watercress

1. Wash and dry chicken pieces. Flour them lightly, in a bag, with the flour, salt, seasoned salt and pepper shaken up together.
2. Melt ½ lb. butter in each of two 10-inch skillets.

3. Brown chicken in butter, on all sides, lightly. Lift out of pan with slotted spoon and keep warm. *Save butter and pan juices* in the pans.

4. Chop scallions (white part only). Wash, peel and slice mushrooms (discard stems).

5. Cook scallions in the butter and juices from the browning of the chicken. Add garlic (half in each skillet). When scallions are clear or transparent, remove with slotted spoon and reserve. Add the mushrooms and cook over medium heat until they are golden. Remove mushrooms with slotted spoon and keep warm.

6. In two oblong (13½ x 8¾ x 1¾ inch) ovenproof dishes, place layers of chicken, then mushrooms, ending with chicken on top.

7. Put the butter and reserved scallions from the two skillets into one skillet. Mix together Burgundy wine, thyme, rosemary and chopped parsley. Pour two cups of this sauce over the chicken. Reserve *one* cup of the sauce (separately) and refrigerate this cup for 24 hours.

8. Bake chicken in a preheated 350° oven for 40 minutes. Cool and refrigerate, covered, for 24 hours.

9. On the next day, sauté the chicken livers in butter in a 10-inch skillet for 5 minutes, tossing occasionally with a spoon to cook evenly. Add the cut-up ham and then add the reserved cup of sauce.

10. Simmer together until very hot—about 3 or 4 minutes—and pour over the chicken. Place on heated platter and garnish with watercress.

SERVES 18 to 20.

I usually serve this chicken for a buffet supper with:

Noodles or Rice
"Mother's Baking Powder Biscuits"
"String Beans with Almonds"
"Mandarin Orange and White Grape Salad"
French Dressing
Brie Cheese with Toasted Crackers
Coffee   Sanka
Liqueurs

GRANDMOTHER'S CHICKEN, CELERY AND NOODLES

1 (6 lb.) fowl
tops from 1 large bunch celery
3 onions, quartered
water to cover
3 cups milk
½ pt. light cream
8 tbsps. butter

8 tbsps. flour
salt and pepper to taste
dash of Worcestershire sauce
1 (16 oz.) package noodles
1 tbsp. melted butter
1 cup finely chopped, raw celery
1 bunch parsley to garnish

1. Boil fowl slowly with celery tops and onions in water to cover, until fowl is tender (3 to 4 hours).
2. Strain and reserve broth.
3. Bone fowl, cut chicken meat in cubes and set aside.
4. Make sauce by heating milk and cream, then stirring in paste made by melting the butter and adding the flour. Stir until thickened and smooth.
5. Add salt, pepper and Worcestershire sauce to taste; then add the cubed fowl and keep warm.
6. Cook noodles in the boiling broth until tender. Drain and stir in 1 tablespoon melted butter.
7. Place noodles on heated platter. Cover with the fowl in cream sauce.
8. Scatter chopped, raw celery on top. Garnish with parsley.
SERVES 6 to 8.

CHICKEN CHAMBORD | Mrs. Alben Barkley

2 broilers (cut in pieces)
½ lb. sweet butter
¼ lb. salt pork, diced
1 cup chopped shallots
1 lb. mushrooms (washed, peeled, sliced)

2 cups chicken broth
½ cup Burgundy wine
1 tsp. cornstarch
1 tbsp. water
salt and pepper
bunch of watercress

Brown broilers in butter in a 10-inch skillet. Then bake in shallow (13½ x 8¾ x 1¾ inch) ovenproof glass dish in preheated slow oven (325°) for 45 minutes.

In another 10-inch skillet, sauté the diced salt pork; add shallots and mushrooms and brown gently. Add chicken broth with Burgundy wine. Add 1 tsp.

cornstarch (dissolved in water to clear the sauce). Season. Be careful not to use too much salt because of the salt pork in the sauce. Pour sauce over the chicken on a heated platter and garnish with watercress.

SERVES 6.

CHICKEN WITH COINTREAU OR GRAND MARNIER

- 2 (10½ oz.) cans cream of chicken soup
- 3 (4 oz.) cans sliced mushrooms, drained
- 1 pt. heavy cream
- 8 cups chopped, cooked chicken
- ½ cup slivered almonds
- salt and pepper to taste
- 2 tbsps. Cointreau *or* 4 tbsps. Grand Marnier
- ¼ cup chopped parsley (for garnish)
- 1 tsp. paprika (for garnish)
- 6 cups cooked noodles (follow package directions)
- 6 tbsps. butter

In the top of a large double boiler, place the chicken soup, mushrooms and cream. Add the chicken, almonds and season to taste. Heat over boiling water. Just before serving, add Cointreau or Grand Marnier. Place on a heated platter and garnish with parsley and paprika. Serve with noodles mixed with butter in a separate dish.

SERVES 12.

"Frozen Pear Salad" is good with this, plus "Mother's Baking Powder Biscuits" and hot "Swedish Cinnamon Cake" with whipped cream, coffee, Sanka and liqueurs.

CHICKEN CROQUETTES

- 4 chicken breasts
- 2 (10½ oz.) cans chicken broth
- 2 (2 oz.) pkgs. dehydrated mushroom soup
- 1 cup fresh bread crumbs
- 4 egg yolks
- 2¼ cups milk
- salt and pepper to taste
- 1 qt. shortening (if using electric skillet)
- 2 cups "White Sauce I" (p. 358)

1. Boil chicken breasts in a saucepan in chicken broth until tender. Remove bones and save the broth.
2. Drain breasts well, cut up and put through meat grinder.
3. Mix meat with the mushroom soup. Refrigerate overnight.
4. Shape mixture into croquettes and roll in bread crumbs; dip in eggs beaten with the milk and seasonings and roll again in the crumbs.
5. Heat shortening in skillet. To test, toss a cube of bread into the hot fat and when it is golden, the fat is ready for frying (360° with a deep-fat frying thermometer).
6. Deep-fry croquettes separately, and keep warm in low (200°) oven.
7. Serve a well-seasoned white sauce on the croquettes using the chicken broth as a base instead of milk in the "White Sauce I" recipe.

SERVES 4.

If using electric deep-fat fryer, use 2 (3 lb.) cans of shortening.

CHICKEN OR TURKEY HASHED IN CREAM

6 tbsps. butter
6 tbsps. minced, fresh onion
6 tbsps. flour
2 cups chicken stock or broth
4 cups light cream
2 tbsps. scraped apple
2 tsps. curry powder (or less if you want a light curry taste)
2 (10 oz.) cans water chestnuts, chopped fine
4 cups small cubes of white meat of turkey or chicken
salt and pepper to taste
8 slices buttered toast (crusts off)
1 (16 oz.) can cranberry sauce (sliced)
parsley or watercress

1. In a 10- or 12-inch skillet, melt the butter. Add onion and cook 5 minutes. Then, off the heat, add flour and stir until smooth. Put back on heat and add chicken stock gradually, until the sauce has thickened.
2. Add the cream, apple and curry mixed.
3. Stir again until this mixture thickens.
4. Add water chestnuts and the turkey or chicken.
5. Add salt and pepper.
6. Make toast points by cutting each slice of buttered toast diagonally in four pieces.

POULTRY AND GAME

Serve hot, surrounded by buttered toast points, on a heated platter. Place slices of cranberry sauce on a side platter. Garnish with parsley or watercress.
SERVES 10 to 12.

CHICKEN CURRY

1 (4 lb.) stewing chicken
water to cover
¼ lb. butter
3 small onions, chopped
1 lb. fresh mushrooms, sliced
  (discard stems)
½ cup flour
2 tsps. curry powder
2 tsps. salt
pepper to taste
1½ cups chicken stock from chicken

1 pt. light cream
1 green pear, peeled, cored and chopped
¼ lb. blanched, chopped almonds
½ cup chutney
½ cup chopped, hard-boiled eggs
½ cup toasted, chopped coconut
*½ cup fried raisins
2 tbsps. butter (for frying raisins)
½ cup chopped, cooked crisp bacon
½ cup chopped peanuts

1. Cook chicken in a 6-quart kettle in gently boiling water just to cover until tender.
2. Cool, remove bones and skin, and reserve. Cut up chicken meat.
3. Cook chicken broth down until only 1½ cups are left.
4. In large 10- or 12-inch skillet, melt butter and sauté onions until golden. Add sliced mushrooms and simmer for 5 minutes.
5. Combine flour, curry powder, salt and pepper and sprinkle over the onions and mushrooms.
6. Add chicken stock and cream and stir until thickened a bit.
7. Add the chicken, stir and set aside, covered, for a few hours (this improves the flavor). If it stands in the refrigerator overnight, so much the better.
8. Reheat just before serving, and add the chopped pear and almonds. Serve with chutney, chopped hard-boiled eggs, toasted coconut, fried raisins, chopped crisp bacon and chopped peanuts in separate small bowls.
SERVES 4 to 6.

* To fry raisins, place 2 tbsps. butter in small 4-inch skillet. Add raisins and fry for 5 minutes on medium heat, tossing often. Drain on paper towel and place in small bowl.

CHICKEN (OR SHRIMP, LOBSTER OR LAMB) CURRY WITH SAFFRON RICE

2 tsps. butter
1 tsp. chopped onion
1½ cups diced, cooked chicken (or shrimp, lobster or lamb)
1 tsp. curry powder
2 tbsps. tomato, chopped very fine
1 tsp. chopped coconut
1 tbsp. chopped chutney
1 tbsp. chopped apple
1 cup heavy cream
salt and pepper to taste
1½ cups cooked saffron rice (follow package directions)
½ cup finely chopped almonds (optional)

In a 10-inch skillet, melt the butter and sauté the onion until it is transparent. Add the next eight ingredients and cook for 5 minutes. Then serve on a small heated platter surrounded by saffron rice. Chopped almonds may be scattered over the top of the curry.

SERVES 2.

CURRY KAPITAN | *Puan Sri Ong*
The Embassy of Malaysia

3 lbs. shallots
2 bulbs garlic (the markets usually have 2 bulbs in each box)
1 finger ginger root (about 2-in. long)
⅛ lb. dried chilies (soak in hot water for 20 minutes to soften)
3 tsps. preground turmeric
1 pt. vegetable oil
6 lbs. chicken breasts and thighs (cut pieces into desired size)
juice of 10 lemons
5 tbsps. sugar
parsley

Clean and peel shallots, garlic and fresh ginger root. Drain chilies. Put shallots, garlic, ginger root, chilies and turmeric in electric blender and grind until fine. Heat oil in very large iron pot or large wok. Add ground ingredients and brown over very low flame until very aromatic (about 3 or 4 minutes). Add cut pieces of chicken and mix thoroughly with spices; add lemon juice and sugar. Increase flame, cover and simmer to thicken about 30 minutes or until chicken is cooked. Serve on platter garnished with parsley.

SERVES 12.

POULTRY AND GAME

Information on Buying a Wok

Almost all cooking in the Far East is done in a wok which is a large shallow pan shaped like a bowl. There they cook on a special stove that has holes to fit the bottom of the wok. In our country, it is necessary to buy a wok ring to set on our modern burners to hold the wok. Buy a wok cover to use while cooking. Also buy a Chinese long-handled stirrer and a sharp, heavy Chinese cutting knife. All may be purchased in a Chinese or Japanese grocery store in most cities.

CHICKEN (OR SHRIMP, LOBSTER OR LAMB) CURRY WITH RICE PILAF

- 2 tsps. chopped onion
- 4 tbsps. butter
- 3 cups diced, cooked chicken (or shrimp, lobster or lamb)
- 2 tsps. curry powder
- 4 tbsps. tomato, peeled and chopped fine
- 2 tsps. chopped coconut
- 2 tbsps. chopped chutney
- 2 tbsps. chopped apple
- 2 cups heavy cream
- salt and pepper to taste
- 2 tbsps. flour (optional)
- 2 cups cooked "Rice Pilaf" (p. 248)
- ¼ cup chopped almonds (optional)

Sauté chopped onion in butter in a 10-inch skillet. Mix it with diced, cooked chicken (or shrimp, lobster or lamb). Add curry powder, tomato, coconut, chutney, apple, cream and season to taste. Cook all ingredients for 5 minutes. If you want the sauce thicker, stir in the flour until the sauce is smooth. Serve on a heated platter around "Rice Pilaf." Chopped almonds may be added to this or served separately.

SERVES 4.

CHICKEN DIVAN

16 slices (8 servings) of cooked turkey or chicken
salt and pepper to taste
2 (10 oz.) pkgs. frozen broccoli spears (partially cooked)
2 (10½ oz.) cans condensed cream of chicken soup
½ cup mayonnaise
4 tbsps. milk
4 tbsps. sherry
2 tsps. lemon juice
2 tbsps. Parmesan cheese
paprika

1. In 2-quart, buttered ovenproof (11¾ x 7½ x 1¾ inch) casserole, place a layer of turkey or chicken. Season lightly with salt and pepper.
2. Cover with layer of broccoli spears.
3. Add another layer of turkey or chicken.
4. Place soup, mayonnaise, milk, sherry and lemon juice in blender at high speed until smooth. Correct seasonings.
5. Pour over chicken.
6. Sprinkle with Parmesan cheese.
7. Bake in preheated 350° oven for 20 to 25 minutes or until thoroughly hot.
8. Garnish with paprika.
SERVES 8.

FRICASSEE OF CHICKEN

1 (6 lb.) fowl, cut up
water to cover fowl
1 tsp. salt
½ cup flour (for flouring the fowl)
3 tbsps. butter
4 tbsps. flour (for the gravy)
2 cups stock from fowl
½ cup light cream
dash of powdered ginger
salt and pepper to taste

1. In a large kettle cook cut-up fowl gently in water until tender (about 1½ to 2 hours). Add salt last ½ hour of cooking.
2. Drain thoroughly saving the stock.
3. Flour the chicken pieces lightly, and brown delicately in the butter in a 10-inch skillet until golden. Remove from pan and keep warm.
4. Pour off excess fat leaving 3 tablespoons of the fat for the gravy.
5. Add 4 tablespoons flour and stir until thoroughly mixed.

6. Add 2 cups of the stock and the cream and stir constantly (over moderate heat) until it thickens a bit, then add seasonings.

7. Put chicken pieces in a 3-quart round ovenproof buttered casserole. Pour over the sauce.

8. In a 375° preheated oven, heat until it bubbles.

SERVES 6 to 8.

Serve with rice, peas with pearl onions, iceberg lettuce with Roquefort dressing, and "Lemon Chiffon Pie Supreme."

FRIED CHICKEN

3 frying chickens (cut up)
1 cup flour
½ tsp. salt
½ tsp. pepper
2 cups vegetable oil
2 cups bacon fat

Place chicken pieces in paper bag with flour, salt and pepper. Shake well. Fry in two 10-inch skillets in vegetable oil and bacon drippings until brown. Have oven hot (375°) with roaster pan on lowest shelf. As chicken pieces are browned, place them in the roaster in the oven. Cover and cook until tender (about ½ hour). Test with a fork. For last 20 to 30 minutes turn oven very hot (450°) and take off cover to crisp the chicken. Watch that it doesn't brown too much. Serve with "Country Gravy" (p. 348).

SERVES 8 to 10.

CHICKEN WITH GARLIC AND GINGER

2 (2 lb.) broilers (split)
½ cup butter
2 Bermuda onions, sliced
1 crushed garlic clove, soaked in ½ of (5 oz.) bottle soy sauce
1 can chicken broth
1 tsp. finely minced fresh ginger
salt and pepper
parsley or watercress

1. Place broilers (inside up) in shallow, ovenproof glass pan (11¾ x 7½ x 1¾ inches).

2. Dot with butter.

3. Sprinkle onions on top.

4. Remove garlic clove from soy sauce; mix soy sauce with chicken broth and ginger and pour over broilers. Season lightly.

5. Bake in preheated 375° oven for 30 minutes, basting often with the sauce.

6. Turn chickens and continue cooking for another 15 minutes or until tender.

7. Serve on warm platter and pour over the sauce. Garnish with parsley or watercress.

SERVES 4.

DELUXE CHICKEN OR TURKEY HASH

1 pt. fresh mushroom caps, cut up
½ cup butter, melted (for mushrooms)
1 cup "White Sauce I" (p. 358)
1 cup chicken or turkey stock
3 tbsps. butter (for the sauce)
1 tbsp. minced onion
1 clove
1 bay leaf
1 wineglass sauterne

3 egg yolks, slightly beaten
½ cup heavy cream
¼ cup sherry
2 cups diced, cooked chicken or turkey
½ cup chopped almonds
salt and pepper
2 (5 oz.) cans chow mein noodles

1. Sauté cut-up mushrooms in butter in a saucepan until golden.

2. In the top of a double boiler, over hot water, place 1 cup of white sauce. Add chicken or turkey stock, butter, onion, clove, bay leaf and sauterne. Heat thoroughly. Remove clove and bay leaf.

3. When hot, remove from the hot water and add the beaten egg yolks. Put back over the hot water and add cream and sherry.

4. Add the chicken or turkey, mushrooms and almonds. Season to taste with salt and pepper.

5. Serve this over hot, crispy chow mein noodles. Place these in an open pan in a preheated 350° oven to heat (about 10 to 15 minutes).

SERVES 6.

CHICKEN LOAF

4 cups diced white meat of cooked chicken
1½ cups chicken stock or broth (more if needed)
2 eggs, well beaten
¼ tsp. pepper
¼ tsp. salt
1 small onion, chopped fine
2 cups soft bread crumbs

Mix all together and place in greased loaf pan (8½ x 4½ x 2 inches) or 1½-quart ring mold set in larger pan of hot water ½ inch in depth.

Bake in a preheated 325° oven for 30 to 40 minutes.

SERVES 6 to 8.

CHINESE CHICKEN AND VEGETABLES

2 cups cooked chicken cut in (1 x 1½ in.) thick cubes
1½ cups green pepper, deseeded and coarsely chopped
¾ cup sweet onions, peeled and coarsely chopped
3 firm tomatoes, seeded and cut in 1-in. pieces
2 tbsps. cornstarch
2 cups chicken bouillon
3 tbsps. soy sauce
2 tbsps. peanut oil or vegetable oil
2 tsps. minced fresh ginger
2 cups cooked rice or "Fried Rice" (p. 245)
1 cup hot soy sauce

Place chicken and raw vegetables on wax paper sheets near stove. Mix cornstarch with chicken bouillon and soy sauce in bowl nearby.

Heat wok (or electric skillet) or heavy iron skillet over high heat. Add oil and when it is almost smoking, stir in green pepper and onions. Cook for 5 minutes, stirring constantly. Add bouillon mixture, stirring until the sauce is clear and thickened. Add tomatoes, chicken and ginger; simmer until just heated. Heat cup of soy sauce and serve, separately, in a small pitcher.

SERVES 4 liberally.

Serve over cooked or "Fried Rice." For calorie counters, serve with small amount of sauce and no rice.

FRENCH CHICKEN WITH WINE

¾ lb. butter (cut in small cubes)
4 large Bermuda onions, sliced thin
2 lbs. large, fresh mushrooms (whole, stems off)
12 chicken thighs
12 chicken legs
6 whole chicken breasts, cut in half

1 lb. chicken livers
1½ pts. light cream
½ cup madeira wine
salt and pepper to taste
24 thick rounds bread, toasted (buy unsliced bread)
parsley

In an 8-quart *earthenware* pot with a cover, place 6 to 8 cubes butter. Add a layer of sliced onions and 6 or 8 mushrooms. Place, over this, a layer of thighs and legs of chicken. Add another layer of butter, onions and mushrooms. Add layer of chicken breasts. Then repeat butter, onions and mushrooms. Add last layer of thighs and legs, last layer of butter, onions and mushrooms and last layer of breasts. Top with chicken livers and a few cubes of butter. Cover pot tightly. Place in a preheated 375° oven and bake for 1½ to 2 hours or until chicken is fork tender.

Heat cream in a saucepan but *do not boil*. Pour over the chicken in the pot. Remove from stove and add wine and seasonings. Cover again and let stand to blend with chicken juices for 20 minutes. Meanwhile, toast the 3-inch-wide, 1-inch-thick rounds of bread under the broiler. Turn oven to 200° and keep toast warm.

With a slotted spoon, remove chicken pieces to a large ovenproof pan. Turn oven up to 375° to keep chicken hot. Strain onions and mushrooms from the juice in the pot and put them over chicken in the oven. Correct seasonings in the remaining sauce. Reheat sauce in saucepan.

To serve, place toast rounds on a large heated platter. Place a piece of chicken on each one and cover all with the onion, mushrooms and livers. Pour over all 1½ cups of the sauce. Garnish with parsley and serve at once. Serve rest of sauce separately in a heated silver bowl.

SERVES 18.

I serve this dish with:

Green Beans or Fresh Asparagus
"Crispy Green Salad"
"Tart French Dressing with Tarragon"
"Hot Fruit Dessert"
"Vanilla Wafers"
Coffee   Sanka

POLYNESIAN CHICKEN

2 chicken breasts (split)
4 chicken thighs
1 (17 oz.) can fruit salad
1 clove minced garlic
1 tbsp. minced fresh ginger

⅓ (10 oz.) bottle soy sauce
1 (11½ oz.) bottle sweet and sour sauce
¼ cup sherry (optional)
watercress

1. Place chicken pieces in uncovered ovenproof (1¾ x 7½ x 1¾ inch) pan.
2. Pour over this the total contents of fruit salad can.
3. Over this sprinkle garlic and ginger and soy sauce.
4. Bake in preheated 325° oven until chicken is fork tender (about 1 hour).
5. Drain pan juices into saucepan and cook down for 6 minutes (boiling). Keep chicken warm in the oven in the pan in which it was baked.
6. Add to juices the sweet and sour sauce and the sherry (optional). Simmer for 3 to 4 minutes.
7. Place chicken on warm platter, pour sauce over, surround with watercress and serve.

SERVES 4.

This is one of my easiest and best recipes. For a dinner for eight, double the recipe and serve with rice, new peas with sweet butter, bibb lettuce salad with a tart French dressing and "Coffee Crème."

IRANIAN SHIRIN POLO

1½ cups long-grain rice (*do not* use quick rice)
3½ cups water
2¾ tsps. salt
18 tbsps. butter
2 broilers (cut up)
1 cup water
1 Bermuda onion (sliced)

skin from large orange
3 cups shredded carrots
¼ cup slivered almonds
⅛ tsp. saffron (dissolved in 1 tsp. water)
2 tbsps. sugar
2 tbsps. chopped pistachio nuts or parsley

1. Cover rice with about 2 inches of cold water and let stand overnight.
2. Place rice in saucepan and cover with 3½ cups boiling, salted water (1½ tsps. salt) and boil, covered, for 5 minutes. Drain well and reserve.

3. Melt 10 tablespoons butter in a 10-inch skillet or electric frying pan. Sprinkle chicken with 1¼ tsps. salt and brown lightly over medium heat. Do not crowd pan; remove pieces as they brown. When all are cooked, return the chicken pieces to the frying pan and add 1 cup water and the onion. Cover and simmer gently for 45 minutes or until chicken is tender when pierced. (Refrigerate, covered, if cooked ahead.)

4. Thinly pare the outer skin of the orange (no white) with a vegetable peeler. Cut it in slivers and cook, in boiling water to cover, for 3 minutes. Drain thoroughly. Reserve.

5. In a 10-inch skillet over medium heat, sauté the carrots, almonds, saffron and sugar in the remaining butter for 10 minutes, stirring well. Add rice and slivers of orange peel. Mix well and adjust salt.

6. Spoon the rice mixture into center of large buttered, ovenproof dish (13½ x 8¾ x 1¾ inches) and arrange chicken pieces around sides. Sprinkle with all the cooking juices from the skillets.

7. Bake immediately or cover and chill until ready to use. When ready to bake, cover casserole tightly with foil and bake in a preheated 375° oven for 15 to 20 minutes if ingredients are warm. Bake 35 to 40 minutes if any of the ingredients are cold.

8. Garnish with pistachio nuts or parsley and serve.

SERVES 6 (2 sections of chicken apiece).

LA POULE AU POT | *Mrs. Charles Lucet*
The Embassy of France

Henry IV, King of France (1589–1610), also known as Henry of Navarre, was called "Good King Henry" by his people as he was so greatly concerned with their welfare.

Returning from one of his voyages to his rich kingdom of Navarre, he was shocked by the dreadful poverty of the peasants and called upon his Minister "Sully" in order to discuss how the agriculture might be improved.

The traditional Sunday dish in Navarre was "La Poule au Pot" (Chicken in the pot) and Henry had enjoyed this meal throughout his childhood. He remarked to Sully that "Every citizen should have a chicken in the pot on Sunday."

From this memorable meeting between King Henry and Sully comes this famous recipe, renowned in France since the sixteenth century. A sumptuous family-style boiled dinner, it is brought to the table in its kettle or a reasonable facsimile, looking for all the world like a plain pot-au-feu with a stuffed chicken added.

This preparation provides two dishes: the soup, which should be delicious (toasted bread, various pasta products, rice and, in general, all garnishings suitable for clear soups, are added to it) and meat and vegetables. These two dishes, simple as they are, are always greatly appreciated. Serve with gherkins, samphire* pickled in vinegar, coarse salt and mustard for the boiled beef. Carrots, turnips, onions and leeks cook along with the meats. Boiled potatoes are prepared and served separately.

A nice simple red wine goes well: Beaujolais, Bordeaux or a chilled rosé.

This dinner is especially appreciated in winter time.

Beef:

(Cooking time 3½ to 4 hours): 4-lb. boneless rump roast or sirloin tip, bottom round, chuck pot roast or brisket, plus 3 oz. bone marrow.

Chicken:

(Cooking time 2½ to 3 hours): a 4-lb. ready-to-cook stewing hen of good quality.

Vegetable Garnish:

(Cooking time 1½ hours): 24 carrots, 24 small onions, 24 small turnips and 24 leeks.

Soup Vegetables and Herbs:

3 scraped carrots, 3 peeled onions, each stuck with a whole clove, 2 scraped parsnips, 2 celery stalks, 2 leeks, a large herb bouquet as follows: 6 parsley sprigs, 1 bay leaf, ½ tsp. thyme, 4 garlic cloves, 8 peppercorns tied in cheesecloth.

Cooking Stock:

Sufficient meat stock (or 3 cans of chicken broth plus enough water) to cover ingredients by 6 inches. Optional: raw beef or veal bones.

All the meats and vegetables are simmered together in the soup kettle, but are added at various times, depending on how long they take to cook. Start the cooking 5 hours before you expect to serve, to be sure the meats will be done. Trim excess fat off the beef. Tie piece so it will hold its shape during cooking. Truss the chicken. To piece of meat and to the chicken, tie a string long enough to fasten to the handle of the kettle, so that the meats may be removed easily for testing.

Prepare the vegetable garnish: Peel the carrots and turnips and quarter them lengthwise; peel the onions; trim and wash the leeks. Tie the vegetables in one or several bundles of washed cheesecloth so they may be removed easily from the kettle.

---

* Samphire is a seacoast plant in France.

Place the beef in the kettle with the soup vegetables, herb bouquet, the bone marrow (wrapped in a piece of muslin) and optional bones. Cover with cooking stock by 6 inches. More liquid may be added later if necessary. Set kettle over moderate heat, turn heat to simmer, skim. Partially cover the kettle and simmer slowly for 1 hour, skimming occasionally.

Stuff chicken with "Forcemeat" made of 1 cup fresh pork put through a grinder and 1 cup ground Bayonne or imported ham, mixed with 1 small chopped onion, 1 clove garlic (minced), 1 tablespoon parsley (minced) and 6 cooked chicken livers. Add chicken to kettle and bring quickly back to simmer. Taste for seasoning. Skim. Simmer 1½ hours more, skimming from time to time. Then add the vegetable garnish and quickly bring the kettle back to simmer. Taste cooking stock for seasoning and salt lightly. Simmer 1½ to 2 hours more. The meat and chicken are done when they are tender if pierced with a sharp pronged fork or skewer. If meat is tender before the rest is done, remove to a bowl and keep moist with several ladlefuls of cooking stock. Return to kettle to reheat before serving.

Serving:

Remove the meat, chicken and vegetable garnish. Discard trussing strings. Skim surplus fat from consommé or broth but bear in mind that it should have a few light circlets of fat on the surface. Remove the marrowbone, unwrap and put it back into the pot. Season if necessary. Serve the consommé. Arrange vegetables on a large hot platter and moisten them with a ladleful of cooking stock. Decorate with parsley. Either place the meat in a large casserole for presentation and carving at the table or carve in the kitchen and arrange on a platter.

SERVES 12.

Suggested Menu

Cups of "Poule au Pot" stock
"La Poule au Pot"
Hot French Bread
"Celery Root Remoulade"
"Chocolate Soufflé"
"Foamy Sauce"
"Café Brûlot"
Liqueurs

SOUR CREAM CHICKEN PAPRIKA

16 boned chicken breasts (cut in half)
8 tbsps. butter
8 large yellow onions, chopped
4 tbsps. Hungarian paprika
1 tsp. salt
3 tbsps. chicken bouillon (if needed)
2 tbsps. flour
3 pts. sour cream
½ cup chopped, toasted almonds
½ cup toasted bread crumbs
bunch fresh parsley
1 (2 lb. 10 oz.) pkg. rice (follow package directions)
6 to 8 tbsps. butter

1. Put chicken in bowl.
2. Melt butter in 4-quart iron pot with cover and sauté onions until transparent. Sprinkle in 2 tbsps. paprika until completely mixed. Remove this mixture with slotted spoon and reserve.
3. Drain, but do not dry chicken. Put into pot. Cover with onion and paprika mixture. Add salt and cover tightly. Simmer for ½ hour.
4. Check pot and add chicken bouillon only if chicken seems dry. Cook slowly for 1 more hour. Place chicken on warm ovenproof platter in 250° oven to keep warm.
5. Add flour to chicken cooking liquid in pot. Blend well. Let simmer so flour is thoroughly cooked.
6. Stir in sour cream mixed with the remaining paprika and correct seasonings to your taste. Pour over chicken on platter and sprinkle with almonds and bread crumbs. Garnish with parsley. Serve with buttered rice.

SERVES 32 (allowing ½ breast apiece).

MOTHER'S CHICKEN OR TURKEY RING

2 cups hot milk
2 cups fresh bread crumbs (not too fine—no crusts)
¼ cup butter, melted
1 tbsp. onion juice
1 tsp. salt
½ tsp. paprika
¼ tsp. nutmeg
3 eggs, slightly beaten with a fork
3 cups cooked chicken or turkey, cut in cubes
12 mushrooms, washed, peeled and minced
4½ cups "Mother's Chicken or Turkey Sauce" (p. 345)
3 (10 oz.) boxes frozen, tiny peas (follow package directions)
salt and pepper to taste (for peas)
3 tbsps. butter (for peas)
parsley or watercress for garnish

1. Pour hot milk over bread crumbs; add butter and seasonings and let stand in bowl for ten minutes.
2. Add beaten eggs; then add the chicken or turkey and mushrooms mixed together well.
3. Pour into a well-buttered 2-quart ring mold.
4. Set in larger pan of hot water (2½ inches deep) and bake in a preheated 300° oven for 20 minutes. Then turn oven up to 325° and bake for 20 to 30 minutes more.
5. Unmold on round, hot platter and serve with "Mother's Chicken or Turkey Sauce." Garnish with parsley or watercress. Fill center of ring mold with tiny, buttered peas.

SERVES 6 to 8.

SAUTÉED CHICKEN ROLLS

12 chicken thighs, boned and skinned
½ tsp. salt
1 (16 oz.) can chopped, broiled mushrooms *or* 1 lb. fresh, chopped mushrooms
¼ cup butter
1 tbsp. minced fresh chives
1 tbsp. minced fresh parsley
¼ tsp. dill weed
¼ tsp. thyme
2 tbsps. flour
½ cup butter
¼ cup water
1 cup sour cream
1½ cups rice (follow package directions)
4 tbsps. butter (for rice)
1 bunch watercress

1. Place chicken, cut side up, on a board.
2. Sprinkle with salt.
3. Drain canned mushrooms, reserving liquid, or sauté the fresh mushrooms in ¼ cup butter, reserving the butter and juice. Chop fine ½ of mushrooms; reserve the rest whole.
4. Combine chopped mushrooms and seasonings.
5. Place stuffing in chicken thighs; tie with string.
6. Dredge thighs in flour; brown on all sides in ½ cup butter in a heavy 10-inch skillet.
7. Add mushroom juice and water.
8. Cover and simmer for about 30 minutes or until cooked through.
9. Place chicken on heated platter. Keep warm.

10. Blend sour cream and remaining mushrooms with pan sauce. Heat, do not boil. Pour over chicken rolls.

11. Serve with rice (buttered well). Garnish with watercress.

SERVES 6.

CHICKEN AND VEGETABLES IN WINE

- 1 tbsp. olive oil
- bunch of parsley, chopped
- 2 large white onions, diced
- garlic salt to taste
- 9 fresh carrots, pared and sliced in strips
- pepper to taste
- ½ cup sherry
- 1 dozen chicken breasts, halved and boned
- 2 tsps. thyme
- 1 tsp. tarragon
- 1½ lbs. giant mushroom caps
- 1 cup Burgundy wine

In heavy 6-quart pot, warm olive oil. Add a carpet of parsley. Scatter ½ the onion on top and sprinkle with garlic salt. Place carrot strips over this, add pepper and pour sherry over all. Arrange chicken breasts on top, add herbs, and correct the seasonings. Scatter rest of diced onion over this and place mushroom caps over all. Add Burgundy wine and cover. Bake 2½ hours at 300°, taking lid off for last 20 minutes.

SERVES 12.

Serve with hot, buttered French or Italian bread, a tart "Crispy Green Salad" and mixed cheeses and crackers for dessert.

CRISP CHINESE STYLE DUCK | Mrs. Edward P. Morgan

- 2 (4–5 lb.) ducklings
- ½ cup soy sauce
- 2 tbsps. ground ginger
- ½ cup honey
- ½ cup dry sherry
- 1 clove garlic, coarsely chopped
- 1 bunch watercress

Sauce:
- ½ cup red currant jelly
- ½ cup strained orange juice
- ¼ cup red wine
- 1 tsp. arrowroot or cornstarch (with 1 tbsp. water)

1. Pull out and discard any loose fat from around the neck and cavity of the birds. Brush and pat dry inside and out. Prick skin all over to release the fat.

Mix 3 tablespoons of the soy sauce with 1 tablespoon ginger and brush over ducklings, inside and out. Leave at room temperature for 30 minutes to allow flavors to permeate.

2. Preheat oven to 325°. Place ducklings on roasting pan rack and cook for 1 hour.

3. Meanwhile, combine the remaining soy sauce and ginger with the honey, sherry and garlic. Mix well and simmer, stirring occasionally, for 10 minutes.

4. Prick surface of ducks all over a second time to ensure a crisp skin.

5. Remove garlic from soy-sauce mixture and discard, then brush sauce all over the ducklings. Continue cooking, brushing the skin with this mixture every 15 minutes until the ducklings are glazed and the juices run clear when the skin is pierced (about 1 hour more). For well done, cook 15 minutes longer.

6. Heat the currant jelly, orange juice and wine in a saucepan. Add the arrowroot or cornstarch mixed with 1 tablespoon cold water and cook until the sauce is slightly thickened. Place ducklings on heated platter and garnish with watercress. Serve sauce warm in separate heated bowl.

SERVES 6 to 8.

ROAST DUCKLING WITH ORANGE AND WINE

2 ducklings, quartered
2 cups orange juice
2 cups sauterne
2 cans (11 oz.) mandarin oranges

watercress for garnish
1½ cups wild rice (follow package directions)
3 cups applesauce

Marinate duckling, for 12 hours, in the juice and wine. Place in preheated oven (375°) in this marinade in an ovenproof pan (13½ x 8¾ x 1¾ inches). Cook, breast side down for ½ hour, then turn and cook breast side up for 45 minutes longer. Discard all pan juices. Serve on heated platter with mandarin oranges around the duckling. Garnish with watercress. Serve with wild rice and applesauce.

SERVES 4 to 6.

If ducklings are frozen, have your butcher saw them in quarters for you. Thaw them completely, then follow the above recipe.

HOW TO COOK A 22- TO 24-LB. TURKEY

When our whole family is together for Christmas, it is a very joyous time for us. Christmas is Clark's birthday and we start the festivities with an Open House for him at noon and serve cocktails with various platters of "Steak Tartare" with buttered rye bread, "Smoked Salmon Mousse," a paté, and cold "Georgia Ham" with hot biscuits.

Dinner is served late in the afternoon and the dining room is bursting with our twelve grandchildren and their parents and, usually, four or five friends.

We stagger from the table, much too full of food, gather around the piano for carols and talk in the evening before the fire, and at about eleven o'clock, Clark's birthday cake is brought in to end a very happy day.

1 (22 to 24 lb.) fresh-killed turkey
4 tbsps. salt.
about 8 to 10 cups "Cornbread and Herb Stuffing" (p. 158)
2 cups butter, melted
1 pkg. cheesecloth
2 (10½ oz.) cans chicken broth
7 navel oranges
2 (16 oz.) cans jellied cranberry sauce, chilled
1 bunch fresh watercress

Wash and dry the turkey. Rub it inside and out with salt, then stuff with "Cornbread and Herb Stuffing." Secure legs and wings to body with skewers. Seal the neck and bottom openings with small skewers, and place bird in roasting pan.

Melt butter in saucepan and dip cheesecloth (folded to size to cover the turkey) in butter until it is saturated. Place cheesecloth over the turkey. Pour chicken broth and remainder of butter in bottom of roaster.

Place turkey in cold oven and immediately turn oven to 325°. Roast, basting every ½ hour, for about 6 to 6½ hours or until the leg bone is loose and fork tender. Remove from roaster to heated platter. Cover with foil and let stand for ½ hour. Save all pan juices in roasting pan for "Turkey Giblet Gravy" (p. 349). Just before serving, remove all skewers.

To serve, cut oranges in ½-inch slices and place around turkey on the platter. Slice the cranberry sauce in ½-inch slices and place on top of the orange slices. Garnish with watercress.

SERVES 20 to 24.

Our Menu for Thanksgiving and Christmas Dinners

"Tomato Aspic" Filled with "Lobster Salad" with "Tarragon Sauce"
Turkey Garnished with Oranges and Cranberry Sauce and Watercress
Mashed Potatoes with Butter
"Butternut Squash"
"Onions Creamed with Slivered Almonds"
Hot Sauerkraut
Cold Pumpkin Pie with Whipped Cream (see "Mrs. Nixon's Pumpkin Pie")
Hot Mince Pie with "Hard Sauce"
"Christmas Plum Pudding"
Coffee   Liqueurs

I vary this by serving oyster stew with hot oyster crackers instead of the tomato aspic and lobster salad or, at other times, cold, cooked artichokes with tarragon sauce as a first course.

If we are entertaining Washingtonians, I serve hot sauerkraut as in this section of the country it is a *must* with turkey.

I also have vanilla ice cream on hand, for our grandchildren love it on their pumpkin pie.

TURKEY II

1 (22 to 24 lb.) fresh-killed turkey
about 8 to 10 cups "Cornbread and Herb Stuffing" (p. 158)
1 cup soft butter
2 tbsps. salt
1 tbsp. pepper

1. Stuff and truss turkey.
2. Smear entire turkey with soft butter, salt and pepper.
3. Using heavy foil, place turkey in center of foil in roaster. Fold foil loosely, so turkey is completely covered and sealed.
4. Bake in preheated 450° oven for about 3 to 3½ hours.
5. Unwrap and twist legs to see if they are loose or use oven thermometer inserted in thickest part of the breast until it registers 190°.
6. The turkey will brown while cooking in the foil and will be very moist. Remove from pan and keep warm. Save juices for gravy.

SERVES 20 to 24.

BREAST OF WILD DOVE

8 wild doves, cleaned, washed and dried
2 cups muscatel wine
4 cups "Mushroom Sauce" (p. 354)
¼ cup fresh-grated orange rind
8 slices hot buttered toast (crusts off)
8 tsps. butter (for toast)

1. Cook doves in preheated 350° oven in a small roasting pan (11¾ x 7½ x 1¾ inches) for 18 minutes, basting at intervals with muscatel wine (heated). Save the juices for the "Mushroom Sauce."
2. Remove the breasts from bones and keep warm, while preparing the sauce.
3. Reheat them in the sauce for 3 or 4 minutes.
4. To serve, sprinkle the breasts with orange rind and serve on slices of toast. Allow four breast halves per serving.

SERVES 4.

WILD DUCK IN FOIL I

2 mallard or canvasback ducks (cleaned, washed and dried)
4 prunes (seeded)
1 onion, peeled and quartered
¼ lb. butter, softened
salt and pepper to taste
½ cup fresh orange juice
½ cup red currant jelly
1 (12 oz.) box wild rice (follow package directions)
4 tbsps. butter (for rice)
salt and pepper to taste

Stuff ducks with prunes and onion. Rub butter on ducks with salt and pepper. Wrap loosely in foil. Seal edges. Roast in preheated 350° oven for 1½ hours or until fork tender. Discard prunes and onions.

Serve with sauce of orange juice and red currant jelly melted together in a saucepan, and wild rice with butter and seasonings.

SERVES 4.

WILD DUCK II (WITH SAUERKRAUT STUFFING)

2 large ducks *or* 4 smaller ducks, cleaned, washed and dried
⅛ cup salt
1 (1 lb. 11 oz.) can sauerkraut
8 strips bacon
½ cup fresh orange juice
½ cup red currant jelly
1 (12 oz.) box wild rice (follow package directions)
4 tbsps. butter (for rice)
salt and pepper to taste

1. Wash and rub ducks inside and out with salt.
2. Stuff loosely with sauerkraut.
3. Place strips of bacon across each duck.
4. Place on roasting pan and bake in a preheated 350° oven for about 1 hour for smaller ducks, 1½ hours for larger ducks, or until a leg is fork tender. Discard sauerkraut.
5. Serve with sauce of fresh orange juice and red currant jelly, melted and heated together, and with wild rice, buttered and seasoned.

SERVES 4.

PARTRIDGE WITH CROUTON DRESSING

This was my father's special dish. He would shoot the birds and hang them, uncleaned and with the feathers on, for two or three days in a covered area outside our kitchen door; then bring them in, dip them in boiling water for 2 or 3 minutes (to loosen the feathers), pluck off the feathers and clean the insides of the birds. This added to their "gamey" flavor and made them more tender. All game birds (fresh killed) are better if treated this way.

If you are using frozen birds, thaw them completely and cut them up.

2 cups fresh, toasted croutons *or* 2 cups packaged plain croutons
2 partridges (cut in sections as for fried chicken)
¼ cup flour
¼ lb. butter
3 to 4 cups light cream
¼ cup madeira *or* sherry wine
salt and pepper to taste
1 bunch watercress *or* parsley
1 jar red currant jelly

1. Make fresh croutons by toasting slices of bread (crusts off), cutting in small cubes and placing in a 200° oven to crisp.

2. Dust each section of partridge with flour.

3. Melt the butter in a 12-inch iron or electric skillet. (I prefer an electric skillet.)

4. Sauté partridge over moderate heat, turning until golden.

5. Add cream and turn heat to simmer. Cover and simmer for 1 hour and 20 minutes or until tender. Turn once or twice.

6. Add the wine, salt and pepper.

7. Just before serving, remove partridge to a warm platter, placing the pieces around the edge.

8. Remove half the sauce and place in a hot gravy boat to pass separately.

9. Quickly toss the croutons in the remaining sauce.

10. Place this crouton dressing in the center of the platter with the partridges around the edge. Garnish with watercress or parsley. Serve *at once* with a tart jelly.

SERVES 2 or 3.

ROAST PHEASANT

4 pheasants (cleaned, washed and patted dry)
juice of 2 lemons
2 tsps. salt
2 tsps. pepper
2 lbs. chuck beef, cut into ½-in. cubes
8 bacon strips

Sauce for Basting:
2 cups fresh orange juice
1½ cups red currant jelly
1 (12 oz.) pkg. wild rice (follow package directions)
1 bunch watercress

1. Rub pheasants, inside and out, with lemon juice, salt and pepper.

2. Stuff each pheasant with beef cubes and place 2 bacon strips across each bird.

3. Place in a shallow ovenproof pan (13½ x 8¾ x 1¾ inches), in a preheated 350° oven and roast for about 1½ hours or until fork tender.

4. Baste every 15 minutes with orange juice and jelly heated together in a saucepan. Discard stuffing.

5. Serve with wild rice covered with the sauce from the oven dish. Garnish with watercress.

SERVES 8.

PTARMIGAN | *Mrs. Arne Gunneng*
The Embassy of Norway

The ptarmigan, or snow grouse, is a delectable game bird. Served with a gravy made from its own juices, blended with heavy sour cream and a mixture of melted Norwegian goat cheese and Roquefort, it is a dish fit for the most discriminating gourmet. There are three basic requirements: a good cook, choice ingredients, and lots of time.

The ptarmigan is about the size of a pigeon, and half a bird per person is generally enough (for "Supreme of Ptarmigan," where only the breast is used, one bird per person is needed).

2 ptarmigans
4 strips unsmoked bacon or suet
6 tbsps. butter
6 tbsps. boiling water
1 cup sour cream
1 thin slice Norwegian goat cheese

1 tsp. Roquefort cheese
8 small Irish potatoes
1 cup small beets (cooked)
1 cup tiny peas (cooked)
1 cup tiny carrots (cooked)

Clean the birds well and tie strips of unsmoked bacon (or suet) around the breasts. Melt 2 to 3 tablespoons butter in heavy 4-quart casserole and brown birds well in the butter. Add 1 tablespoon boiling water and 1 teaspoon butter from time to time.

After 1 hour, pour ½ cup of sour cream over the birds and simmer (over burner) for 30 to 45 minutes more. Cover pot, but leave an opening for steam to escape, or the birds will be stewed rather than fried. When handling, use spoons only. When tender, remove birds from pot and keep them warm.

To prepare the gravy, stir remaining sour cream into juices in the casserole and simmer over low burner (uncovered) until fairly thick and smooth. Add Norwegian goat cheese and Roquefort, and stir until blended.

Cut ptarmigans in half and serve with the gravy, small, lightly browned Irish potatoes, a vegetable platter with 2 or 3 different vegetables, the salad of your choice, and "Coffee Charlotte Russe."

SERVES 4.

QUAIL AND DOVE WITH MUSHROOMS | *from Mexico*

10 quails and 10 doves (or 20 quails and 20 doves)
1 cup flour
½ tsp. salt
½ tsp. pepper
½ cup oil
6 onions, sliced

5 cups "Mushroom Sauce" (p. 354)
1 (4 oz.) can mushrooms
1 (15½ oz.) jar onions with juice
1 medium, minced green bell pepper
4 beef bouillon cubes, dissolved in 4 cups hot water
1 cup sherry or madeira wine

Have doves and quails cleaned. Roll lightly in flour mixed with salt and pepper and brown (turning) in hot oil.

Place a layer of birds in large turkey roaster with a cover. Place onion slices over birds. Alternate layers of dove, quail and onion. Then cover with mixture of remaining ingredients. Roast, covered, for four hours (or until tender) in preheated 300° oven.

Twenty birds will serve 10 people.

Serve with:

Wild Rice
French Bread
Red Currant Jelly
"Spinach Salad" with "Maria Blake's Mustard Sauce"
"Creamy Lime Sherbet" with Fresh Strawberries
"Sponge Cake II"

QUAIL OR PARTRIDGE WITH BRANDY SAUCE | *Mrs. Henry Buhl*

6 quails or partridges, split
¾ cup butter
½ cup brandy (more if needed)
1 pt. light cream
¼ cup horseradish (drained)

1 tsp. grated onion
fresh ground pepper to taste
½ tsp. salt (to taste)
2 tbsps. flour
½ bunch watercress

1. Brown the quail or partridge in a 12-inch iron skillet in ½ cup butter.
2. Pour over the brandy and flame.

3. Let flame die down and add the remaining butter and next five ingredients and simmer for 15 minutes, covered.

4. Preheat oven to 350°.

5. Put skillet with birds and sauce in the oven and bake for 45 minutes, covered.

6. Lift birds onto a warm platter and keep warm in oven turned to lowest heat.

7. Thicken gravy in the skillet with flour (back on stove burner) and add more brandy if desired. Pour over birds and serve garnished with watercress.

SERVES 4 to 6.

VENISON RIBS | *General J. P. McConnell (U.S.A.F. Ret.)*

20 venison ribs
   red wine to cover

salt and pepper

Marinate ribs in wine for 24 hours. Remove from marinade and rub with salt and pepper. Place under broiler in a roasting pan. Brown well on both sides. Heat oven to 350°. Cover ribs and cook until fork tender (about 8 minutes on a side).

SERVES 4.

This is good, as all venison recipes are, served with fluffy, mashed, buttered potatoes and "Ruth Hayden's German Red Cabbage." For dessert serve "Hot Fruit with Cointreau" and fresh, baked "Macaroons."

VENISON STEW

6 lbs. venison cut in 1-in. cubes
2 cups red wine (for marinade)
16 tbsps. flour (1 cup)
½ lb. butter
   water to cover venison
2 cups carrots, cut up

2 cups celery, cut up
2 cups onion, sliced
   salt and pepper to taste
4 to 6 tbsps. flour (for gravy)
2 tbsps. red wine (for gravy)

Marinate venison in wine for 48 hours. Drain. Dust with flour and brown in butter in 10- or 12-inch iron covered skillet. Cover venison with water and cook very slowly for about 1½ hours. Add carrots, celery, onion and seasonings for last 40 minutes of cooking. Remove venison and vegetables. Correct seasoning and keep warm. Thicken broth with 4 to 6 tablespoons of flour, stirring until smooth. Add 2 tablespoons wine. Pour over vegetables and meat and serve.

SERVES 10 to 12.

CORNBREAD AND HERB STUFFING
(FOR 24-LB. TURKEY)

4 cups cornbread
3 cups herb stuffing (commercial)
¾ cup butter
2 cups celery (chopped fine)
2 cups onion (chopped fine)
1 cup pecans (chopped fine)

2 tbsps. salt
1 tbsp. sugar
1 tbsp. white pepper
1½ tbsps. poultry seasoning
2 (10½ oz.) cans chicken broth

1. Make cornbread the day before you stuff the turkey. Break it into large crumbs and place in your largest bowl. Mix in the herb stuffing.
2. In an electric skillet or 10-inch skillet, melt the butter. Add the chopped celery and onions and cook over medium heat for 10 minutes, stirring. Add this mixture, plus the pecans, to the cornbread. Add the seasonings and mix well.
3. Heat the broth and add to the dressing. I use two large mixing spoons to toss the dressing.
4. Have turkey washed and dried. Stuff the neck and back cavities and secure with skewers.
5. Do not stuff turkey until the day it is cooked.

OYSTER STUFFING FOR TURKEY

1 (1 lb. 8 oz.) loaf stale bread (pulverized in blender, 2 or 3 slices at a time—makes 12 cups)
2 large Bermuda onions, cut fine
½ lb. butter
1 bunch celery, cut fine (with the tops)
1½ qts. oysters
1 (10½ oz.) can chicken broth (more, if necessary)
salt and pepper to taste

1. In large bowl place pulverized bread.
2. In 10-inch skillet sauté onions in butter until transparent.
3. Add the celery and cook for 3 or 4 minutes. Add to bread in the bowl with the pan juices.
4. In another 10-inch skillet cook the oysters in their own liquor for 2 minutes. Add to above mixture with their juice.
5. Add enough broth so mixture is moist but *not* wet. Toss to mix together.
6. Add salt and pepper.

MAKES enough to stuff a 16- to 18-lb. turkey.

SAUSAGE STUFFING FOR TURKEY

2 lbs. country sausage (in bulk)
2 tsps. sage

Follow the ingredients and directions for "Oyster Stuffing for Turkey" above, but substitute sausage for oysters and add the sage.

MAKES enough to stuff a 16- to 18-lb. turkey.

ONION DRESSING FOR DUCK

6 medium onions
   boiling water to cover
2 tsps. poultry seasoning
3 cups soft, stale bread crumbs
salt and pepper to taste
½ cup butter (soft)
1 egg, slightly beaten

Parboil onions in boiling water 10 minutes. Add poultry seasoning and cook 2 minutes longer. Drain off water. Finely chop onions. Add to crumbs with salt, pepper, butter and egg.

MAKES 3 cups.

AND SEAFOOD

Catching, cooking and eating fish is one of my greatest joys. As a child, I remember being coated with citronella and trudging along behind my father in search of trout streams; fishing with him off the reefs in New Hampshire with bamboo poles, sinkers and pretty primitive fish hooks; fishing for cod with a hand line, and later the exciting, but arduous, deep-sea fishing in the Bahamas.

My husband has always lived in mortal terror that I would catch the prize marlin of all time and insist on having it stuffed at $2.00 an inch or whatever the going rate is at the moment.

I remember one luncheon in Spain where we all ordered fried whitebait. They came to the table with each tiny, beady eye fixed upon us with such an accusing look that we hastily ordered filet of sole.

My publisher, John Macrae, Jr., is a great fisherman and, on Nantucket Island, caught and gave me a gigantic striped bass, uncleaned. I was taught, as a child, to clean and filet a fish and he knew it.

Wielding a fish scaler, I had the scales of the striper flying in all directions and, of course, sticking eternally to each surface they hit. Then, feeling like Bluebeard, I cut off the head, wrapped it carefully in a newspaper, and deposited it in the garbage can. Later, a little pigeonhole opened in my memory and I hastily retrieved the head and put it in the chowder pot, for I remembered that some of the most delicate meat for a fish chowder comes from the fish head.

I emerged, hours later, with twelve quarts of chowder and rode around dispensing it to hungry Nantucket Island friends, who ever since have called it "Garbage Can Chowder."

One time, on the Presidential yacht, President Truman, who loved to fish, caught a Schoolmaster. This is a very rare fish and he was jubilant at landing one. His military aide, General Harry Vaughan, hated fishing and ships in general as he was always terribly seasick. At this moment he was draped limply over the railing about to die. The President rushed over to him and said, "Look, Harry, I caught a Schoolmaster!"

The General didn't move an inch as he muttered, "Mr. President, I don't give a damn if you caught a Superintendent of Education!"

JANSSON'S TEMPTATION | Mrs. Hubert de Besche
(Baked Anchovies and Potato) | The Royal Embassy of Sweden

This dish is a real temptation when served on a smorgasbord or as an appetizer.

- 1 cup sliced onions
- ⅓ cup butter or margarine
- 4 cups raw potatoes, peeled and cut into thin strips
- 1 can (about 18) Swedish anchovy filets (Save the juice.)
- 1 cup light cream

Sauté onions in 2 tablespoons of butter or margarine. Butter a 1½-quart baking dish. Arrange layer of half the amount of potatoes; spread onions and anchovy filets over and top with remaining potatoes. Sprinkle 1 tablespoon of juice from anchovy can over potatoes and dot with remaining butter or margarine. Add cream and cover with aluminum foil. Bake in hot oven (400°) for 30 minutes. Remove aluminum foil and bake, uncovered, 20 to 30 minutes or until potatoes are tender and golden brown. Serve immediately from baking dish.

SERVES 4.

FISH MOLD

- 2 lbs. fresh halibut, boned
- 3 cups water
- 1 tsp. salt
- 1 cup milk
- 2 tbsps. butter
- 2 tbsps. flour
- 4 egg yolks, beaten
- 1 tbsp. grated onion
- 1 tbsp. lemon juice
- ½ tsp. paprika
- 4 egg whites, beaten

1. Boil boned fish in salted water in a large saucepan for 18 minutes. Drain completely and mash.
2. Heat milk in saucepan. Melt butter in 4-inch skillet and stir in flour to make a smooth paste. Stir this into hot milk until the sauce thickens. Remove from heat and stir in egg yolks. Add onion, lemon juice and paprika.
3. Add fish and fold in egg whites.
4. Place in 4½-cup buttered ring mold. Set mold in larger pan with about ½ inch of hot water.
5. Bake in preheated 300° oven for 30 minutes.
6. Unmold and serve with "Special Sauce for Fish Mold" (see p. 358).

SERVES 4 to 6.

FISH IN SOUR CREAM

2 lbs. haddock or halibut (fileted)
salt and pepper to taste
1½ tsps. basil *or* 1 tsp. minced parsley
1 pt. sour cream
½ cup fine bread crumbs (plain) *or* ½ cup herb-seasoned bread crumbs
watercress for garnish

Place fish in an ovenproof buttered dish (11¾ x 7½ x 1¾ inches) and season with salt and pepper, basil or parsley. Cover with sour cream and bread crumbs.

Bake in preheated 375° oven about 28 minutes or until fish flakes easily. Do not overcook.

Lift carefully and place on small, oval hot platter. Garnish with watercress.

SERVES 4.

NAT BENCHLEY'S NANTUCKET BLUEFISH BROILED WITH GIN

Being filled with culinary curiosity, I tried this recipe and it is superb! I must admit it is also different.

4 filets of bluefish
¼ lb. butter
4 tsps. onion flakes
salt and pepper to taste
3 jiggers gin
2 lemons, seeded and quartered
parsley for garnish

1. Preheat broiler.
2. Place fish in a row on an ovenproof (13½ x 8¾ x 1¾ inch) pan.
3. Melt butter in a saucepan and pour ½ of it all over the fish. Keep the rest of the butter warm.
4. Sprinkle onion flakes over the fish and season.
5. Place fish about 4 to 6 inches from the broiling coils and broil for about 7 or 8 minutes.
6. Remove from broiler, pour the remaining butter over the fish, then cover with the gin.
7. Put back under broiler. It will flare up with an explosive noise. Do not fear that your stove and house will soon be on fire; the flame will die down at once. Broil for 2 more minutes, then transfer to a heated platter. Pour the pan juices over the fish and garnish with lemon and parsley.

Serves 4 to 6.

SAUTÉED FROGS' LEGS IN LEMON BUTTER

8 large or 16 small to medium frogs' legs
salt and pepper to taste
½ cup flour
7 tbsps. butter
1 tsp. grated lemon rind
1 tbsp. lemon juice (fresh)
1 tbsp. finely minced onion
⅛ tsp. rosemary
1 bunch parsley
1 lemon, quartered

1. If legs are frozen, thaw completely and wipe dry.
2. Sprinkle with salt and pepper and coat evenly with flour.
3. Heat 4 tablespoons of butter in a 10-inch iron skillet.
4. Add the frogs' legs and sauté gently 5 or 6 minutes on a side.
5. In a 4-inch skillet, melt the remaining butter and stir in lemon rind and juice, onion and rosemary.
6. Spoon over frogs' legs.
7. Cover and simmer 6 to 8 minutes or until legs are tender.

8. Place on heated platter, garnish with parsley, and serve at once with lemon quarters.

SERVES 4 liberally.

BAKED FINNAN HADDIE

3 lbs. smoked finnan haddie in 1 piece
3 pts. milk
6 tbsps. butter
parsley

1. Soak finnan haddie for 1 hour in 1½ pints milk. Turn once. Discard milk.
2. Place fish in a buttered, shallow (11¾ x 7½ x 1¾ inch) ovenproof baking dish. Pour the rest of the milk over this and dot with 4 tablespoons butter.
3. Bake in preheated 375° oven for about 30 minutes or until the fish flakes easily when tested.
4. Remove from milk.
5. Place on heated platter and pour over the remaining butter, melted. Garnish with parsley.

SERVES 6 to 8.

CREAMED FINNAN HADDIE

2 lbs. cooked, flaked finnan haddie (follow recipe for "Baked Finnan Haddie" above)
2½ cups milk saved from the cooking of the fish
4 tbsps. butter
4 tbsps. flour
salt and pepper to taste (watch out for this as the fish is salty)
4 hard-boiled eggs, cut up
6 slices toast (crusts off), each cut diagonally into 4 triangles
parsley

1. Cook the fish. Keep warm.
2. Heat milk in top of double boiler. Place over hot water.
3. In 4-inch skillet, melt butter and stir in flour to make a paste.
4. Stir into hot milk until sauce thickens and is smooth. Season very carefully.

5. Add the fish and the eggs and mix carefully.
6. Have toast points ready and warm.
7. Place creamed finnan haddie and eggs on heated platter. Surround with toast points and place parsley on top.

SERVES 4 to 6.

HALIBUT "POINT SHIRLEY" WITH CLAMS

3 lbs. halibut filets
6 tbsps. butter
1 pt. clam juice
1 (8 oz.) can minced clams and juice
salt and pepper to taste
watercress
2 lemons cut into wedges

1. Place halibut filets in a 3-quart, ovenproof oblong (13½ x 8¾ x 1¾ inch) dish. Dot with butter and place in a preheated 375° oven.
2. Baste with hot clam juice mixed with the minced clams. Cook until fish flakes easily when tested with a fork—about 28 minutes. Season.
3. Pour the pan juices over the filets.
4. Garnish with watercress and lemon wedges.

SERVES 6 to 8.

BOILED SALMON WITH EGG SAUCE

This was always served by my grandmother on the Fourth of July in New Hampshire. It has remained a tradition in our family.

3 lbs. fresh salmon, center cut
1 pkg. cheesecloth
water to cover
2 tsps. salt
2 tbsps. white vinegar
2 cups "Egg Sauce for Boiled Salmon" (p. 347)
1 bunch watercress
18 small, new potatoes, boiled, skinned and buttered
3 cups buttered fresh green peas
parsley for garnish

1. Place salmon, wrapped in the cheesecloth, in a large 4-quart kettle with a cover.

2. Cover with boiling water. Add salt and vinegar and boil gently for about 20 to 25 minutes or until tender. Do *not* overcook. Drain well and remove the skin carefully. Place on a heated platter.

3. Have egg sauce ready and hot in top of double boiler over hot water. Pour over salmon and garnish with watercress.

4. Surround with alternate potatoes and peas and garnish with parsley.

SERVES 6.

BROILED SALMON

½ cup butter
2 garlic cloves, crushed
salt and pepper to taste
1 (3 lb.) slice of salmon

2 tsps. fresh dill
2 large cucumbers, sliced
3 lemons, quartered
parsley for garnish

Melt butter in skillet with garlic, salt and pepper. Let stand for 10 minutes. "Paint" the fish all over with this mixture, then place in an ovenproof (11¾ x 7½ x ¾ inch) pan under a preheated broiler. Measure accurately the thickest part of the fish and allow 10 minutes of cooking time for every inch. Thus, if the salmon is 3 inches thick, broil it 15 minutes on each side. Baste occasionally with the garlic butter. Serve hot or cold, skinned, or as is with crispy skin. Decorate with fresh dill, cucumbers, lemons and parsley.

SERVES 6.

COLD SALMON

1 (3 lb.) center cut fresh salmon
   (cooked and skinned)
4 small heads of bibb lettuce
8 strips pimiento for garnish
½ cup "Never Fail Mayonnaise"
   (p. 368)

1 tsp. fresh lemon juice
2 tsps. fresh chopped chives
2 tsps. small capers

1. Cook salmon as in recipe for "Boiled Salmon with Egg Sauce" (above), but omit sauce and chill overnight, covered.

2. Place in center of chilled platter and surround with washed, dried and chilled bibb lettuce leaves.

3. Garnish top of salmon in a design of your choice with thin strips of pimiento.

4. Serve with mayonnaise mixed with lemon juice, chives and capers.
SERVES 6.

BAKED SALMON STEAK | *General John McConnell (U.S.A.F. Ret.)*

2 salmon steaks, cut 1 in. thick
1 cup celery, chopped
2 small onions, chopped
½ lb. butter, melted

½ cup "Tarragon Sauce" (p. 338) *or*
½ cup "Hollandaise Sauce" (p. 350)

To prepare a moist steak, use a 2-quart (11¾ x 7½ x 1¾ inch) ovenproof glass dish (buttered). Place the salmon steak in the mixed celery and onion. Pour the butter over the steak. Broil for 2 minutes, then bake in preheated 325° oven for 27 minutes, basting 4 times or more. Just before serving sear under broiler for 2 more minutes. Serve with "Tarragon Sauce" or "Hollandaise Sauce."
SERVES 4 to 6.

FRESH SHAD AND ROE

12 slices bacon
6 filets boned shad
4 tbsps. butter
6 tsps. flour
4 pairs shad roe

salt and pepper to taste
8 lemon wedges
1 bunch parsley *or* 1 bunch watercress

1. Preheat broiler.

2. Place bacon on a tin pan (15½ x 10¼ x ¾ inches) and broil, turning once, until done. Drain and keep warm. Save the fat.

3. Place shad, dotted with butter, in tin baking pan (8 x 8 x 2 inches).

Broil 8 to 10 minutes. Examine center of a filet with a fork after 8 minutes. If done, remove from oven, cover and keep warm.

4. Lightly flour the roe and sauté in hot bacon fat, in a 10- or 12-inch skillet over medium heat. Turn once or twice until roe is golden outside and center is no longer pink. Do *not* overcook. Season both shad and roe.

5. To serve, place shad and roe, alternately, on a heated platter. Place bacon across the top and garnish with lemon wedges. Place parsley or watercress around the edge of the platter.

SERVES 8.

FILET OF SOLE FLORENTINE

5 lbs. filet of sole
1 tsp. butter (to grease baking dish)
8 standard size bags fresh spinach (cooked and drained) *or* 4 (10 oz.) boxes frozen spinach (follow directions on the box)
2 tbsps. butter
1 tsp. onion juice

½ tsp. nutmeg
½ tsp. salt
3 cups "White Sauce II" (p. 359)
1 lb. sharp Cheddar cheese, grated salt and pepper to taste
2 lbs. fresh mushrooms, sliced
½ cup butter
¼ cup sweet cooking sherry (optional)

1. Wash filets and wipe dry. Place in rows in a buttered ovenproof (13½ x 8¾ x 1¾ inch) baking pan.

2. Butter spinach and season with onion juice, nutmeg and salt. Cover filets completely with spinach.

3. Make white sauce in top of double boiler over boiling water. Add ½ the cheese and stir until it is melted. Correct seasonings and set sauce aside, covered, to keep warm.

4. Sauté the mushrooms in butter in a 10-inch skillet over moderate heat for 5 minutes. Toss several times and add to the cheese sauce. Add the sherry and stir well.

5. Pour the sauce over the sole and spinach and sprinkle the remainder of the cheese on top.

6. Place in preheated 350° oven and bake for about 30 minutes until it bubbles and the cheese has melted and become golden. If the cheese has not become golden in this period, put under broiler for 2 minutes.

SERVES 16 to 18.

INDONESIAN SOLE | *Dr. H. Arthur Grennan from London*

This recipe was given to me by my doctor. After listening to the ingredients, I was tempted to murmur that I understood now why he had so many patients—but I refrained from that rude comment and tried it. He was right—it is a subtle and superb dish.

2 lbs. (or 4 large filets) of sole
1 cup milk
6 oz. plain, soft peanut butter
   salt and pepper to taste
4 tbsps. Indian chutney juice
4 tbsps. chopped Indian chutney
1 firm banana (cut in long ¼-in.
   strips)
parsley or watercress

1. Place filets side by side in buttered, shallow (11¾ x 7½ x 1¾ inch) ovenproof glass baking dish.
2. Beat the milk and peanut butter together with egg beater in a bowl.
3. Pour this over the filets, and soak for one hour, turning twice.
4. Drain off the milk through a sieve, and coat the top of each filet with what remains of the peanut butter in the sieve. Season.
5. Bake in preheated 375° oven for 7 minutes.
6. Remove from oven and coat each filet with liquid chutney juice.
7. Surround the filets with chopped chutney.
8. Put back in oven for 3 minutes.
9. Place the long strips of banana on top of filets and put under broiler for 2 or 3 minutes more (4 inches from broiler flame).
10. Decorate with parsley or watercress and serve directly from baking dish.

SERVES 4.

POACHED FILET OF SOLE

2 cups milk *or* 2 cups white wine
½ tsp. salt
1 tsp. onion juice
2 lbs. filet of sole
   "Dill Sauce" (p. 348)

Place milk or wine with salt and onion juice in a 10-inch skillet. Over high heat, bring *almost* to a boil. Turn heat to simmer and add the filets. Simmer

gently until the filets flake when tested with a fork. Remove filets with a slotted spoon and keep warm. Reserve milk or wine broth for "Dill Sauce."
SERVES 4.

FILET OF SOLE STUFFED WITH SHRIMP

1 small onion, minced
¼ cup green pepper, minced
¾ cup butter
16 fresh shrimp, cooked (dice 12 and save 4 whole shrimp for garnish)
1 clove garlic, minced fine
¼ cup crumbled day-old bread
1 tbsp. parsley, snipped fine with scissors

½ tsp. salt
⅛ tsp. pepper
4 filets of sole (about 2 lbs.)
2 tbsps. flour
1 cup "Blender Hollandaise" sauce (p. 350)
parsley

1. Sauté onion and pepper in ¼ cup butter until golden.
2. Add the diced shrimp, garlic, bread crumbs, parsley, salt and pepper and blend together well.
3. Spread 2 tablespoons of this mixture on each filet and roll up. Secure with small skewer. Brush with ⅛ cup of melted butter.
4. Preheat oven to 350°.
5. Place filets on greased, ovenproof (8 x 8 x 2 inch) glass baking dish and bake for 25 to 30 minutes.
6. In 4-inch skillet, melt the last ⅛ cup of butter. Add the flour and whole shrimp, which you have reserved, and toss to brown a little.
7. Remove skewers from filets. Pour hot Hollandaise sauce over the filets. Top each filet with a whole shrimp. Garnish with parsley and serve.
SERVES 4.

FILET OF SOLE WITH SHRIMP MOUSSE
adapted from McCall's Cooking School

This is a delectable dish to serve as a main course for luncheons or a fish course for dinner.

8 filets of sole (2½ lbs.)
2 tbsps. lemon juice
1 tsp. salt
⅛ tsp. white pepper

1 tbsp. butter (soft)
"Shrimp Mousse"
"Shrimp Mousse Sauce"
watercress

Rinse filet of sole (if frozen, thaw completely) under cold water. Dry on paper towels. Brush both sides with lemon juice and sprinkle with salt and pepper. Lightly butter a 6-cup ring mold (8½ inches across, 2 inches deep). Line mold with sole filets, dark side up, narrow end to center and overhanging both rims. Make "Shrimp Mousse," as follows:

SHRIMP MOUSSE

1 lb. raw shrimp
2 egg whites
1 cup heavy cream
1 tsp. salt

1 tbsp. catsup
1 tbsp. chopped parsley
2 tbsps. sherry (sweet)
1 tbsp. butter (melted)

Shell and devein shrimp. Wash under cold water, drain well on paper towels and cut in small pieces. (If frozen, thaw completely and dry.) Place in electric blender with egg whites, cream, salt, catsup, parsley, sherry and melted butter. Blend at high speed, covered, for 2 minutes until smooth. Fill center of mold.

Preheat oven to 350°. Fold ends of filets, overlapping, over top of filling. Using spatula, spread top with butter. Cover top of mold, loosely, with a square of waxed paper. Place mold in ovenproof baking pan (14 x 10 inches) and pour boiling water around mold to depth of 1 inch. Bake for 30 to 35 minutes. *Do not overbake.*

Unmold on hot, round platter and top with "Shrimp Mousse Sauce," made as follows:

SHRIMP MOUSSE SAUCE

¼ cup butter or margarine
¼ cup flour
½ tsp. salt
1½ to 2 cups light cream
1 tbsp. catsup

2 egg yolks
½ cup dry sherry
¼ lb. mushrooms, sliced
2 tbsps. butter

In double boiler top over direct heat, melt ¼ cup butter; remove from heat. With a wire whisk blend in flour and salt. Gradually stir in 1½ cups cream and the catsup. Return to heat. Cook, over medium heat, stirring constantly, until mixture comes to a boil and thickens; simmer 1 minute. Remove from heat.

In small bowl, with wire whisk, beat egg yolks. Gradually beat in ½ cup of the hot sauce. Stir yolk mixture back into sauce and add sherry. If sauce is too thick, add ½ cup cream. Stir, over low heat, until hot. Keep warm over hot water in double boiler.

Sauté mushrooms in 2 tablespoons butter in a 10-inch skillet for 5 minutes over medium heat and add to above sauce. Pour over "Filet of Sole with Shrimp Mousse."

Garnish with watercress.

SERVES 6 to 8.

I serve this dish for luncheon with:

Hot Clam Broth
Toasted Crackers
"Endive, Olive and Bibb Lettuce Salad"
with French Dressing
"Mother's Baking Powder Biscuits"
Red Currant Jelly
Fresh Papayas or Crenshaw Melon
with a Wedge of Lime
"Nut Lace Cookies"
Coffee   Tea

FILET OF SOLE WITH SHRIMP SAUCE

This is a very easy recipe and good!

4 fresh filets of sole
1 (10 oz.) can frozen shrimp soup (undiluted)
salt and pepper to taste
½ cup grated Parmesan cheese
watercress for garnish

1. Place sole in ovenproof (8 x 8 x 2 inch) glass casserole.
2. Cover with *thawed* shrimp soup and add a little salt and pepper.
3. Sprinkle cheese over the top and bake in a preheated 350° oven for about 30 minutes.
4. Garnish with watercress.

SERVES 4.

FILET OF SOLE VÉRONIQUE

2 lbs. fresh sole filets (8 single filets)
1½ tsps. salt
¼ tsp. pepper
2 tbsps. butter or margarine
½ cup chopped fresh onion
2 cloves garlic
1 cup dry white wine *or* chicken broth
2 tsps. fresh lemon juice
½ cup light cream
2 egg yolks
2 tsps. flour
2 cups seedless white grapes
parsley

Sprinkle fish with salt and pepper. Roll up and fasten with toothpicks. Set aside. Melt butter or margarine in 10-inch skillet, add onion and cook until tender. Spear garlic on toothpick and add to skillet along with wine or chicken broth and lemon juice.

Arrange fish in skillet. Cover and simmer for 6 minutes or until fish flakes easily. Remove fish to a serving platter and keep warm. Discard garlic. Strain skillet liquid and pour back into skillet. Combine cream and egg yolks and stir gradually into liquid in skillet, off the heat. Return to heat; sprinkle flour over liquid and stir to blend. Cook over *medium* heat stirring constantly until thickened and smooth. Correct seasonings. Add white grapes.

Cook until just heated through. Remove toothpicks, pour sauce over fish filets, garnish with parsley and serve.

SERVES 8 (one rolled filet apiece).

To test or "flake" fish, take a fork and gently cut into center of the filet. If it is tender and has no "gray" look, it is done.

BROILED SWORDFISH NANTUCKET

Swordfish is often dry. Cooked by this method, it stays moist.

2 (3 lb.) slices swordfish cut 1½ in. thick
1 cup olive oil
seasoned salt to taste
2 cups "Tarragon Sauce" (p. 338)

Marinate swordfish in shallow pan for ½ hour in olive oil; turn and marinate for another ½ hour. Lift out of oil and sprinkle liberally with seasoned salt. Place under preheated broiler and broil for 8 minutes. Turn fish over and broil for another 8 minutes. (If you do this on an outside grill, have your coals very hot and gray). Do not overcook. Cut open while broiling and if fish is *just* cooked through, remove from fire. Serve with "Tarragon Sauce" in a separate bowl.

SERVES about 12.

I serve this with a platter of sliced beefsteak tomatoes and sliced, serrated cucumbers with French dressing, hot butter twist rolls, a large bowl of "Hot Fruit Dessert," cookies and iced coffee or iced tea.

BAKED TROUT

4 trout about ½ lb. each (fresh or frozen)
¼ cup water
juice of 2 lemons
salt and pepper to taste
3 tbsps. chives, minced fine
2 tsps. parsley, chopped fine (just leaves)
⅔ cup heavy cream
1 cup soft bread crumbs
¼ lb. butter
watercress or parsley

1. If using frozen trout, thaw. Dry trout carefully.
2. Place trout in greased 2-quart ovenproof baking dish (11¾ x 7½ x 1¾ inches) and add water, lemon juice, salt, pepper, chives and parsley.
3. Bake in preheated 400° oven for 15 to 20 minutes until the fish flakes easily.
4. Heat the cream but do not boil; then pour it over the fish.
5. Sprinkle with the bread crumbs, dot with butter and broil until golden in a preheated broiler. Garnish with watercress or parsley.

SERVES 4.

FRESH BROOK TROUT

½ lb. salt pork, diced
2 (1 lb.) trout, cleaned and washed
1 cup yellow cornmeal
watercress

1. Cut up the salt pork and place in a 10-inch skillet. Sauté, tossing often, until pork is crispy. Lift pork out with a slotted spoon and keep warm in a preheated 200° oven.
2. Roll trout in the cornmeal until they are completely covered.
3. Cover and sauté in the salt-pork fat over moderate heat, turning once. Cook until the trout are golden brown.
4. Place trout on heated platter and scatter diced pork on top.
5. Garnish with watercress.

SERVES 4.

TROUT BAKED WITH STUFFING

2 trout (about 1 lb. each) fresh or frozen
¼ cup chopped onion
12 tbsps. butter or margarine, melted
½ cup cracker crumbs
½ cup dry bread crumbs
¼ tsp. salt
½ tsp. sage
¼ cup light cream
½ cup dry white wine
½ lb. small mushrooms
4 lemon wedges
½ bunch parsley

1. If trout is frozen, thaw and dry carefully.
2. Sauté onion in 6 tablespoons butter until transparent.
3. Mix cracker crumbs, bread crumbs, salt and sage. Add the onion, pan butter and cream.
4. Stuff each fish with the mixture. Secure with skewers.
5. Make shallow gashes in top of each fish.
6. Bake, uncovered, in a preheated 400° oven for 10 minutes.
7. Brush with 2 tablespoons butter.
8. Add wine; continue baking (10 to 15 minutes or until fish flakes easily).
9. Remove fish; keep warm and save the drippings.
10. Sauté mushrooms in remaining butter in a 10-inch skillet over moderate heat until soft.
11. Add fish drippings to mushrooms and simmer for 4 minutes.
12. Sprinkle mushroom mixture and juices over fish. Remove skewers.
13. Garnish with lemon wedges and parsley.

SERVES 4, or 2 liberally.

As you can see by the number of recipes in this section, I am a true devotee of seafood. Being a New Englander, I attribute a great deal of our legendary health and hardiness to the iodine in fish or seafood—which for generations most New Englanders have had on Tuesdays and Fridays when the fishing fleet was in and the seafood was fresh in the market.

When faced with hot, boiled lobsters, my face lights up like a pinball machine. All conversation stops and I wade into the lobsters till the juice is running up my wrists.

One of the best parties we ever gave was a summer lobster dinner in February—complete with checkered tablecloth and for the shells, a huge old-fashioned tin baby bath surrounded by seaweed in the center of the table. The guests were asked to wear summer picnic clothes and we had piles of hot lobsters on platters at each end of the table, melted butter, blueberry muffins, corn on the cob, green salad, icy cold ale and "Deep Dish Blueberry Pie" for dessert.

Try an off-season party. They are always a surprise and create a real change of pace for a dinner.

STEAMED CLAMS

48 steamer clams
   cold water to cover
½ in. cold water for kettle or clam
   steamer

½ cup melted butter

1. Scrub clams with a brush, cover with cold water and soak for an hour.
2. Put ½ inch cold water in the bottom of a large kettle or steamer with a tight lid. Put in the clams and secure lid.
3. Place kettle over burner (moderate heat) until they are open. This takes about 5 to 10 minutes. Discard any clams which haven't opened. Place clams in two large chowder dishes or bowls.
4. Strain broth through 2 layers of cheesecloth and serve in cups.
5. Serve melted butter in side dishes.

If you have a lobster or clam steamer, follow the above recipe, but put the clams in the top of the steamer and the water in the bottom. Do not oversteam the clams as they become tough.

Two dozen clams generally serve one person.

SERVES 2.

BAKED CRABMEAT IN SCALLOP SHELLS | *Mrs. Eugene C. Carusi*

¼ lb. butter
4 tbsps. flour (sifted)
1 pt. heavy cream
2 egg yolks (beaten well)
1 lb. Jumbo lump crabmeat (the finest grade crabmeat)

1½ tsps. salt
½ tsp. Tabasco sauce
4 heaping tbsps. grated Parmesan cheese
4 sprigs parsley
4 lemon wedges

1. Melt butter in saucepan. Remove from heat and stir in flour to make a smooth paste.
2. Heat cream in another saucepan (do not boil) and stir in the above mixture until sauce thickens.
3. Remove from heat again and add beaten eggs. Stir until mixture is very smooth.
4. Preheat oven to 350°.
5. Jumbo crabmeat has very few bones and requires practically no cleaning. Just run your fingers over each large lump and if you feel a bone, carefully remove it. Add to the sauce, lightly, so that the crab lumps will remain large.
6. Add the seasonings.
7. Spoon into four large, buttered scallop shells and sprinkle top of each with Parmesan cheese.
8. Bake for 30 minutes.
9. Garnish each shell with a sprig of parsley and serve with lemon wedges.

SERVES 4.

A 1-quart ovenproof casserole dish may be used instead of the scallop shells.

HOT CRABMEAT WITH CAPERS

This is one of my favorite recipes to serve as the main course for luncheons or as a first course for dinners.

1 cup commercial mayonnaise
1 tsp. fresh onion juice (scraped)
juice from ½ lemon
seasoned salt to taste
½ (2¼ oz.) bottle capers
pepper to taste

1½ lbs. fresh Jumbo lump crabmeat (the finest grade crabmeat)
½ cup seasoned bread crumbs
2 tbsps. chives, minced (fresh, if possible)
1 tsp. tarragon (dry) optional

Mix mayonnaise, onion juice, lemon juice, salt, capers and pepper together in a large bowl. Pick over crabmeat very carefully to remove all bones. Carefully fold crabmeat into mayonnaise mixture and try not to break up the lumps. Preheat oven to 350°. Place crabmeat mixture in an ovenproof 1-quart lightly buttered baking dish. Top with bread crumbs and chives and bake for about 30 minutes or until bubbly.

SERVES 4.

If crabmeat is tasteless, as it sometimes is, add tarragon to the mayonnaise mixture.

Suggested Menu

"Cold Mushroom Soup"
"Hot Crabmeat with Capers"
"Egg and Swiss Cheese Salad"
"Icebox Rolls"
"Pineapple Sherbet with Black Bing Cherries in Brandy"
"Nut Lace Wafers"
Iced Coffee   Iced Tea

CRABCAKES CHESAPEAKE

1 lb. fresh crabmeat (boned well)
3 eggs, beaten whole
2 slices bread (crusts off) broken into large crumbs and dampened with 2 tbsps. milk
1 tbsp. mayonnaise
1 tbsp. mustard (dry)
1 tbsp. onion (finely minced)
salt and pepper to taste
½ cup melted butter (more if you need it)
1 cup tartar sauce
watercress

Mix first eight ingredients together well in a bowl. Refrigerate overnight and then form into eight round cakes. Melt butter in 10-inch skillet and when hot (but not brown), add the crabcakes and sauté, turning once, until they are golden brown on each side. Drain on brown paper, garnish with watercress and serve at once with tartar sauce.

SERVES 4.

HAWAIIAN CRAB CURRY

1 cup "White Sauce II" (p. 359)
1 cup commercial mayonnaise
1 tbsp. onion juice
1 tsp. curry powder
2 lbs. fresh crabmeat (carefully deboned)
salt and pepper to taste
1 cup light brown sugar
2 tbsps. butter
6 slices pineapple (canned or fresh)
2 tbsps. butter
1 cup toasted bread crumbs

Make white sauce in a 10-inch skillet. Stir in mayonnaise, onion juice, curry powder and the crabmeat. Season to taste. Keep warm.

In another 10- or 12-inch skillet, melt the sugar and butter. Add the pineapple slices and, over moderate heat, sauté until they are golden. Turn once. Place the slices in the bottom of an ovenproof (11¾ x 7½ x 1¾ inch) glass dish in rows. Spread crabmeat mixture on top.

In 8-inch skillet, melt butter, add bread crumbs and toss, over moderate heat, until golden. Sprinkle this over the crabmeat mixture. Bake in a preheated 350° oven for 30 minutes or until bubbly.

SERVES 6 to 8.

CRAB ROYALE

1 small onion, minced
½ green pepper, minced
¼ cup butter
⅛ tsp. Tabasco sauce
½ tsp. salt
½ tsp. freshly ground pepper
2 tbsps. flour
1½ cups milk
¾ cup commercial mayonnaise
1½ lbs. crabmeat, carefully picked over
3 tbsps. sherry wine
½ cup buttered bread crumbs
1 scant tsp. paprika
parsley

1. In a 10-inch skillet sauté onion and green pepper in butter until transparent.
2. Add seasoning and flour. Remove from heat.
3. Blend in milk slowly.
4. Return to stove and cook slowly until thickened, stirring often.
5. Remove from heat and blend in mayonnaise.
6. Mix crabmeat with sherry and add to above mixture.

7. Pour into buttered, 2-quart ovenproof casserole (11¾ x 7½ x 1¾ inches); top with buttered bread crumbs and paprika.

8. Bake in preheated 350° oven about 25 minutes or until bubbly. Garnish with parsley.

SERVES 6.

HOW TO BOIL LIVE LOBSTERS

4 (1½ lb.) live lobsters
water to fill a 16-qt. kettle two-thirds full (Use ocean water or add 1 cup salt to plain water.)

1 cup melted butter
2 lemons, cut in wedges
watercress

Heat water in covered kettle until it is boiling hard. Pick up lobsters just behind their eyes and drop into the water. Push them down so that they are all covered with water. Cover and bring to a hard boil again. Boil for exactly 16 minutes. Pour off all but ½ inch of water and replace lid. Turn off the burner. Lobsters will keep this way for quite a while. When ready to serve turn on burner to full heat and when water starts to boil, remove lobsters with tongs. Crack claws and joints (carefully) with lobster crackers or a hammer. Serve with side dishes of melted butter, lemon wedges and watercress.

SERVES 4.

Boiling Time:
1 lb. lobsters	—	12 minutes
1½ lb. lobsters	—	16 minutes
2 lb. lobsters	—	18 minutes
3 lb. lobsters	—	22 minutes

HOW TO STEAM LIVE LOBSTERS

Lobsters are more tender if done by this method, for they do not curl their tails as they do when they receive the shock of being plunged into boiling water. This is the more humane way to cook them for they are anesthetized slowly by the steam and drift off to the Happy Hunting Ground.

If you have a lobster steamer, place lobsters, alive, in the top and 4 inches of cold water in the bottom. Cover tightly. Place over high heat. When water is boiling, steam the lobsters for:

20 minutes for 1½ lb. lobsters
22 minutes for 2 lb. lobsters
25 minutes for 3 lb. lobsters

If you do not have a steamer, place the lobsters covered with cold water, in a 16-quart kettle and proceed as above.

With hot lobsters, I serve:

Corn on the Cob
Skinned Beefsteak Tomatoes, Sliced,
with Sugar and Vinegar
"Blueberry Muffins"
"Hot Swedish Apple Pudding"
Icy, Cold Ale

LOBSTER THERMIDOR

4 (1½ lb.) lobsters, boiled
¼ cup butter
1 small onion, minced
juice of 1 lemon
1 tbsp. flour
1½ cups light cream

salt to taste
2 tbsps. dry mustard
⅛ tsp. cayenne pepper
¼ cup Parmesan cheese
2 lemons, cut in wedges
parsley

Boil lobsters (see "Boiled Lobster" above). Split them with a heavy, sharp knife from head to tail (underneath). Remove meat and clean out the tail. Reserve tail shells for stuffing. Crack the claws and joints with a lobster cracker or hammer and remove meat. Throw these shells away. Cut all the lobster meat in ½-inch pieces.

Melt butter in 10-inch skillet, add onion and cook until golden. Add lemon juice and stir in flour. Add cream and stir until thickened. Season with salt, mustard and cayenne. Add lobster meat and mix well.

Stuff the lobster tails with this mixture and sprinkle cheese over each tail. Place the tails on a (17 x 14 inch) cookie sheet and bake in a preheated 375° oven until the filling bubbles and the cheese is melted. Serve with lemon wedges and parsley.

Serves 4.

Two tablespoons sherry may be substituted for the dry mustard. If so, substitute ¼ cup grated Cheddar cheese for the Parmesan cheese.

MOULES MARINIÈRE

½ cup butter
4 tbsps. minced onion
1 garlic clove, minced
3 tbsps. fresh parsley, minced
5 qts. mussels

1 cup dry white wine
1 tsp. salt
¾ tsp. pepper
1 cup light cream
8 tsps. flour

1. Place butter, onion, garlic and parsley in the bottom of a lobster or clam steamer and cook, slowly, until onion is transparent.

2. Place mussels, thoroughly cleaned and scraped (use a wire brush for this), in the top of the steamer and pour the wine and the seasonings over this. Cover tightly and simmer on low heat until mussels are open. (It will take 8 to 10 minutes.) Discard any shells which have not opened. Place mussels in chowder dishes.

3. Strain the liquid in the bottom through 2 thicknesses of cheesecloth into a saucepan to remove any sand.

4. Bring to a slow boil and add the cream. Turn down to simmer and stir in the flour. Continue stirring until smooth and thickened a bit. Correct seasoning.

5. Pour sauce over each dish of mussels and serve.

Serves 8.

NANTUCKET MUSSELS IN WINE

5 qts. fresh mussels
½ (⅕ qt.) bottle white wine
  (sauterne)
¼ lb. butter

salt and pepper to taste
2 loaves French or Portuguese bread
1 cup melted butter (for the bread)

In top of steamer or in a 10-quart kettle put freshly cleaned and scrubbed mussels. In bottom of steamer or in the kettle put wine, butter, salt and pepper. Steam until mussels open (about 8 minutes). Throw away ones that don't open. Strain the liquid in pot through cheesecloth.

Serve mussels in chowder dishes with bowl on the side of steaming juice for each person. Accompany with buttered slices of Portuguese bread cut 1 inch thick for dunking and toasted on both sides under the broiler.

SERVES 8.

FRIED OYSTERS

- 16 medium-sized fresh oysters
- 2 cups finely crushed crackers
- salt and pepper to taste
- 3 eggs, beaten until frothy
- 2 (1 lb.) cans shortening (if using electric skillet)
- watercress
- 1 cup tartar sauce

Roll damp oysters in cracker crumbs mixed with the seasonings. Dip in beaten egg and again in cracker crumbs. Heat shortening in frying pan to 380° (or test with a square of bread. When it is brown, the fat is hot enough). Place oysters in the frying basket and lower into the hot fat until completely covered. Fry for about 3 minutes. Lift out and place on brown paper to drain.

Garnish with watercress and serve on a heated platter with a side dish of tartar sauce.

SERVES 4.

If using electric deep-fat fryer, use 2 (3 lb.) cans of shortening.

SCALLOPED OYSTERS I

- 2 (3½ oz.) boxes crackers (unsalted) and coarsely chopped
- 1¼ qts. oysters
- ½ cup oyster juice (boiled for 2 minutes and skimmed)
- 2 tbsps. grated fresh onion
- salt and pepper to taste
- ¼ cup sherry (optional)
- ½ cup light cream
- ¼ cup butter
- 1 (2 oz.) jar pimientos, chopped
- 1 tsp. paprika
- 1 tsp. chives

Grease an ovenproof dish (11¾ x 7½ x 1¾ inches). Preheat oven to 375°. Divide crackers in thirds. Place one layer of crackers to cover bottom of dish. Add ½ the oysters and spread out in a layer. Add another layer of ⅓ the crackers and sprinkle over this ½ the oyster juice, onion, seasonings, sherry (optional) and cream, mixed together. Dot with ½ the butter. Add the remaining oysters in another layer and the remaining cracker crumbs. Sprinkle over this the rest of the cream mixture. Dot with remaining butter and sprinkle pimientos, paprika and chives over the top. Bake for 30 minutes or until sauce is bubbly and cracker crumbs are golden.

SERVES 6.

SCALLOPED OYSTERS II

½ cup butter
¾ cup flour
3 tsps. paprika
1 tsp. salt
½ tsp. black pepper
4 tbsps. green pepper (minced)
4 tbsps. onion (minced)

½ tsp. garlic (minced or put through a garlic press)
2 tbsps. lemon juice
1 tbsp. Worcestershire sauce
1 qt. oysters
½ cup cracker crumbs

Melt butter in a 10-inch skillet and add flour. Cook for 5 minutes or until dark brown, stirring constantly. Add paprika, salt and pepper. Cook for 3 minutes and add green pepper, onion and garlic. Cook slowly for 5 minutes. Remove from fire and add lemon juice, Worcestershire sauce and oysters which have been picked over and heated (in a separate skillet) in their own liquor.

Pour into an ovenproof (8 x 8 x 2 inch) baking dish. Sprinkle cracker crumbs over the top and bake in a preheated 375° oven for about 30 minutes.

SERVES 6.

OYSTERS ROCKEFELLER

½ lb. spinach
½ bunch celery
½ bunch shallots
½ bunch parsley
½ cup fine bread crumbs
½ lb. butter, melted
1 tbsp. Pernod

1 tbsp. Worcestershire sauce
salt, pepper and cayenne pepper to taste
8 cups rock salt (approximately)
2 doz. fresh oysters (with 2 doz. half shells)

Grind first five ingredients very fine and add to the butter in a bowl. Pour in the Pernod, Worcestershire sauce and add the seasonings.

Half fill four 9½-inch ovenproof pie pans with rock salt and set 6 oyster shells in each pan. Place 1 oyster in each shell. Cover each oyster with the spinach mixture. Place under a preheated broiler until the oysters are very hot.
SERVES 4.

SPANISH PAELLA

½ lb. Italian sausage, cut up
¼ cup flour
1 tsp. salt
⅛ tsp. pepper
4 lbs. frying chicken, cut in pieces and boned
2 tbsps. olive oil
2 cups chopped onion
2 cloves garlic, minced
3 tbsps. olive oil (for onion and garlic)
1 pt. oysters (optional)
1 lb. fresh-cooked lobster meat, cut up
1 large can (1 lb. 12 oz.) Italian tomatoes

2 cups water
3 beef bouillon cubes
1 tsp. oregano
2 tbsps. salt
¼ tbsp. pepper
2 cups long-grain rice (uncooked)
¼ tsp. saffron (powdered)
1 (10 oz.) pkg. frozen peas
1 (10 oz.) pkg. frozen artichoke hearts
1 (7 oz.) can pimiento strips
1 lb. shrimp (washed, shelled and deveined)
1 qt. mussels

Brown sausage in 10-inch skillet. Remove and place in heavy 10-quart kettle or Paella pan. Reserve drippings. Season flour with salt and pepper. Dust chicken pieces with flour. Add olive oil to sausage drippings. Brown chicken in this and add to sausages. Sauté onion and garlic in olive oil in another small (6 inch) skillet. Add to chicken and sausage.

Drain oysters (optional) which have been cleaned of any shells (save liquor). Add oysters, liquor, lobster meat, tomatoes, water, bouillon cubes, oregano, salt and pepper to other ingredients in kettle. Simmer 10 to 15 minutes. Stir in washed rice, saffron, and add peas, artichokes, pimientos, shrimp and mussels. Cover and simmer 15 to 20 minutes or until shrimps are tender and mussels are open. Discard any unopened mussels.

The Paella may be placed on a large heated platter or transferred to a Paella pan and served at the table.

SERVES 10 (very liberally).

I serve Paella with:

> "Cold Gaspacho Soup"
> "Crispy Green Salad" with
> "Tart French Dressing"
> "Mother's Parkerhouse Rolls"
> "Sangria"
> "Caramel Flan"
> Coffee   Sanka

SCALLOPS EN BROCHETTE

10 to 12 slices bacon (more if needed)
2 lbs. scallops (small bay scallops if possible; otherwise, sea scallops cut in half)
¼ cup butter
¼ tsp. garlic flakes
salt and pepper to taste
watercress
1 cup "Tarragon Sauce" (p. 338)

1. Broil bacon until it is half done. Cut in ¾-inch pieces.
2. Wash and dry scallops and thread on long skewers, alternating bacon, scallops, bacon, etc.
3. Place the filled skewers on a buttered (15 x 10 inch) cookie tin with raised sides.
4. Melt butter in a small saucepan with the garlic. *Do not brown.*
5. Brush scallops with this mixture. Turn skewers and brush the other side.
6. Place under preheated broiler and broil, turning over once, for about 4 minutes on each side. Do *not* overcook.
7. Remove from skewers and season.

8. Serve on heated platter garnished with watercress. Serve "Tarragon Sauce" in a side dish.

SERVES 4 to 6.

SCALLOPS IN CHEDDAR CREAM SAUCE

1 qt. bay scallops
2 cups water
1 tbsp. butter
1 tbsp. flour
1 cup chicken broth
juice of ½ lemon
salt to taste

⅛ tsp. cayenne pepper
4 egg yolks
1 cup heavy cream
¼ lb. Cheddar cheese, grated
chopped parsley
chopped pimientos

Simmer the scallops in water in a saucepan for about 3 minutes or until tender. Drain and put in buttered, ovenproof baking dish (11¾ x 7½ x 1¾ inches). In a 10-inch skillet melt butter and stir in flour to make a smooth paste. Mix in chicken broth and when well cooked and smooth, season with lemon juice, salt and cayenne. Cool a bit. Mix egg yolks and cream and add very slowly to sauce, stirring constantly. Cook over medium heat, stirring until thickened and smooth. Pour over scallops. Sprinkle cheese on top. Heat in a preheated 350° oven until hot and the cheese has melted. Garnish with parsley and pimientos and serve.

SERVES 8 to 10.

If you are using sea scallops, cut them in quarters.

CHINESE SCALLOPS AND MUSHROOMS

1½ lbs. bay scallops or sea scallops, fresh or thawed frozen
½ lb. fresh mushroom caps
1 tsp. peanut oil
2 scallions cut in 1-in. slivers (white part only)

½ tsp. ground ginger, minced (3 or 4 slices fresh ginger)
2 tsps. soy sauce
salt to taste
1 tsp. sugar

Wash scallops, drain, cut into pieces ¼ to ½ inch thick.

Cut mushrooms into ⅛-inch pieces. Place in small dish near stove. Set other ingredients nearby.

Heat a Chinese wok or a large 10-inch iron skillet or electric skillet to high heat. Add oil. When oil is almost smoking, add mushrooms. Cook for 2 to 3 minutes. Add scallions, ginger, soy sauce, salt and sugar and then the scallops and toss for 3 minutes.

SERVES 4 to 6.

Serve with "Quick Fried Rice."

CREAMED SCALLOPS

2½ lbs. scallops (cut up)	1 bay leaf
½ cup water	few whole black peppercorns
juice of 1 lemon (strained)	4 tbsps. butter
1 pt. milk	4 tbsps. flour
2 stalks celery (cut in quarters)	salt to taste
1 small onion, sliced	¼ cup sherry wine (or madeira)

1. Parboil scallops in own juice, adding water and lemon juice. Cook in saucepan for about 3 or 4 minutes over moderate heat.
2. Drain and place scallops in top of double boiler over hot water.
3. Scald milk with celery, onion, bay leaf and peppercorns.
4. Strain.
5. Melt butter in 10-inch skillet and stir in flour. Gradually, stir in the hot milk. Stir until mixture is thickened and smooth.
6. Season to taste.
7. Pour over scallops in double boiler and, just before serving, add wine.
8. Fill center of "Mushroom Ring" (p. 225).

SERVES 6 to 8.

QUICK SCALLOPS WITH SHRIMP

2 lbs. bay or sea scallops (if using sea scallops, cut in quarters)
1 cup water
1 tsp. salt
1 tsp. onion juice
1 tbsp. cider vinegar

2 (10 oz.) cans frozen shrimp soup
½ cup light cream
4 tbsps. sherry
4 slices bread (crusts off)
4 parsley sprigs

1. In a 10-inch skillet, cook scallops with their own juice, water, salt, onion juice and vinegar for 3 or 4 minutes. Drain and reserve scallops.
2. Defrost soup and heat in top of double boiler. Add cream, sherry and scallops. Correct seasonings.
3. Place over simmering water in bottom of double boiler until ready to serve.
4. Toast bread and place ¼ of scallop mixture on each slice. Place sprig of parsley on each serving.
SERVES 4.

MY SPECIAL PARTY SCALLOPS WITH MUSHROOMS AND WINE

16 lbs. bay scallops *or* 16 lbs. sea scallops, cut in quarters
1 cup water
juice from the scallops
2 large Bermuda onions, chopped fine
2¼ cups butter
6 lbs. fresh mushroom caps, washed and sliced

3½ qts. (or less) milk
1¾ cups flour
salt and freshly ground pepper to taste
1 tsp. garlic flakes
½ cup madeira wine (or more if you like a stronger flavor)
2 cups Parmesan cheese (grated)
½ cup fresh chopped chives

1. In 10-quart kettle, simmer scallops in water and their own juice for 5 to 6 minutes. Lift out scallops with slotted spoon and set aside.
2. Pour juice into 6-quart saucepan.
3. In 12-inch skillet, sauté onions in ¼ cup of butter until they are golden. Lift out onions and add to scallops. Keep the juices in the pan.

4. Add sliced mushrooms with 1 cup of butter and sauté 5 minutes, stirring. Lift out mushrooms and add them to scallops. Add these pan juices to the scallop juice.

5. Measure all the juices and add enough milk to make 3½ quarts. Heat all this to about scalding point. Do not boil.

6. Melt the remaining cup of butter in a 10-inch skillet. Remove from heat and blend in flour to make a paste.

7. Add this gradually to the hot milk and juices and stir until smooth and thickened. Add salt, pepper, garlic flakes and wine. Taste and correct seasonings.

8. Pour this sauce over the scallops and mix thoroughly.

9. Preheat oven to 375°.

10. Place scallop mixture in two buttered ovenproof dishes (13½ x 8¾ x 1¾ inches). Sprinkle each dish with 1 cup of cheese and bake until sauce bubbles and the cheese is melted.

11. Garnish each dish with chives and serve at once.

SERVES 40 liberally.

I serve this with 2 (4½ lb.) boned, cooked hams; 2 "Tomato Aspic" filled with 10 (10 oz.) packages frozen, mixed vegetables (undercooked so that they are crispy) mixed with 2 pints sour cream and flavored with salt and garlic flakes to taste; "Deep Dish Blueberry Pie" (triple the recipe), served hot with 5 large cream cheeses on a separate dish; coffee and liqueurs.

SEAFOOD CONTINENTAL

2 lbs. filet of sole
salt, pepper and paprika to taste
2 tbsps. flour
1 lb. fresh mushrooms (caps only)
2 tbsps. butter
2 cans (10½ oz.) cream of celery soup
¼ cup light cream
½ cup grated Parmesan cheese
2 tbsps. sherry
1 tbsp. minced parsley
½ tbsp. crushed dried basil
1 lb. shrimp, cooked and cleaned
1 tbsp. melted butter

Layer fish in buttered, ovenproof baking dish (11¾ x 7½ x 1¾ inches), sprinkling each layer with salt, pepper, paprika and flour. Reserve 8 mushroom caps for garnish. Slice remaining mushrooms and sauté in butter until tender. Spoon mushrooms over fish.

Combine soup, cream, cheese, sherry, parsley, basil and shrimp in a sauce-

pan and heat. Pour over fish. Garnish with mushroom caps. Brush with melted butter and bake in preheated 375° oven for 30 minutes or until sauce bubbles.
SERVES 8.

TO COOK SHRIMP

1 qt. water
3 tbsps. salt
2 bay leaves
1 Bermuda onion (quartered and peeled)

4 celery stalks and tops (broken up)
2 lbs. frozen, cleaned and shelled shrimp

Place water, salt, bay leaves, onion and celery in a 2-quart saucepan and bring to a rolling boil.
Add shrimp and when liquid starts to boil again, cook for 2 minutes.
Drain at once and discard all seasonings. Chill.
SERVES 4 to 6 as main dish, 12 as shrimp cocktail.

CHINESE SHRIMP WITH HOT SOY SAUCE

1 Bermuda onion, chopped fine
2 stalks celery, minced
4 tbsps. butter
½ cup crushed pineapple (optional)
3 lbs. fresh shrimp, shelled, cleaned and dried

1 (16 oz.) box wheat pilaf
salt and pepper to taste (use sparingly because of soy sauce)
1 (5 oz.) bottle dark soy sauce

1. Sauté onion and celery in butter in a 10-inch skillet until done and golden. (Pineapple may be added to this.)
2. Add uncooked shrimp to onion mixture and sauté for 2 minutes on each side.
3. Cook wheat pilaf according to the package directions and season.
4. Heat soy sauce.
5. Pile pilaf in center of hot platter, surround with the shrimp and pour the *hot* soy sauce over all.

SERVES 6 to 8.

I serve this with "Cold Mushroom Soup" and crackers, "Cucumber Vinaigrette," buttered snow peas, "Creamy Lime Sherbet" and fortune cookies. The cookies may be purchased at any Chinese grocery store and they are fun.

SHRIMP CREOLE

⅓ cup chopped onion
¼ cup chopped green pepper
⅓ cup chopped celery
4 tbsps. butter
1 tsp. salt
¼ tsp. paprika
⅛ tsp. garlic salt

1 bay leaf, crushed
3 tbsps. flour
2½ cups canned tomatoes
1 tbsp. minced parsley
1 cup cooked okra
2 cups shrimp, cooked
2 cups hot rice

Simmer onion, pepper and celery in butter in a 10-inch frying pan. Add seasonings and flour. Blend together and add tomatoes, parsley and okra. Cover and cook slowly for 30 minutes, stirring frequently. Add shrimp and cook 5 minutes. Remove bay leaf and correct seasonings. Serve on hot rice.
SERVES 4.

PUERTO RICAN SHRIMP ASOPAO

¼ cup olive oil
1½ cups finely chopped onion
1½ cups finely chopped green pepper
¼ lb. bacon, chopped
¼ lb. salt pork (cut in ½-in. cubes)
6 (10½ oz.) cans chicken broth
2 cups raw converted white rice

1 (10 oz.) pkg. frozen peas
½ cup capers, drained
½ cup sliced stuffed green olives (measured after slicing)
2 pimientos, sliced
4 lbs. cooked shrimp

1. Slowly heat oil in 6- to 8-quart kettle. Add onion, green pepper, bacon and salt pork. Cook covered over low heat for 10 minutes.
2. Add chicken broth. Bring to a boil; add rice, return to boiling and reduce heat. Cook covered, stirring occasionally, for 30 minutes.
3. Add peas, capers, olives and pimientos. Return to boiling, reduce heat

and cook 5 minutes or until peas are tender. Discard salt pork, add shrimp and cook for 3 or 4 more minutes over medium heat.

4. Serve in deep chowder plates.

SERVES 10 to 12.

SHRIMP SUKIYAKI

6 green onions, thinly sliced lengthwise
1 leek, thinly sliced lengthwise with 1 inch of stem
6 stalks celery hearts, thinly sliced lengthwise
1 cup crisp spinach leaves, washed and drained
1 cup thinly sliced fresh mushrooms
2 lbs. cooked shrimp, shelled, deveined and cut in half the long way

1 cup chicken stock
2 tbsps. soy sauce
1 tbsp. sugar
2 tsps. butter
3 cups cooked rice (follow package directions)
6 tbsps. butter (for rice)
salt and pepper to taste

Prepare vegetables.

In electric skillet or 10-inch iron skillet, heat shrimp, stock, soy sauce and sugar over medium heat for 5 minutes.

Add vegetables and 2 teaspoons butter and cook 5 or 6 minutes more. Stir occasionally.

Serve with buttered, seasoned rice.

SERVES 6 to 8.

SHRIMP WITH WILD RICE | *Lois Mack*

We served this, among other hot dishes, at the farewell buffet luncheon for President and Mrs. Johnson on January 20, 1969.

3 cups wild rice
4 qts. boiling water
1 tbsp. salt
1 green pepper, deseeded and cut up
3 Bermuda onions, peeled and cut up
½ cup butter
6 cups cooked shrimp
1 (12 oz.) bottle chili sauce
1½ cups light cream
½ cup sweet sherry
salt and pepper to taste
watercress

1. Wash rice in cold water 20 times, changing the water each time, until the water is clear.
2. Drop rice into boiling, salted water in a 5-quart kettle. Boil for 40 minutes, stirring occasionally. Drain completely. Set aside in your largest bowl.
3. Put green pepper and onions through a meat grinder with a pan underneath to catch the juice.
4. In a 10-inch skillet, melt the butter and add pepper, onions and their juice. Cook until they are transparent. When done, add to the rice in the bowl.
5. To the above, add shrimp, chili sauce, cream, sherry and seasonings. Mix together well and place in the top of 6- or 8-quart double boiler, over boiling water to keep hot. If you do not have this hotel-sized double boiler, use your largest kettle and reheat the shrimp-rice mixture just before serving, stirring constantly, so it will not burn.

SERVES 12 to 14.

This may be made the day before the party as the flavor is improved by standing overnight in the refrigerator. Any leftover may be frozen successfully.

For buffet suppers I serve this on a large, round heated platter garnished with watercress and accompanied by:

"Mandarin and Orange Salad"
"Green String Beans with Sliced Water Chestnuts"
Croissants
"Swedish Cinnamon Cake"
Coffee, Sanka and Liqueurs

VEGETABLES

I have found that friends, when they express an opinion of what they do or do not like, usually refer to vegetables. They are militantly for or against eggplant, squash, and, in my case, parsnips. Therefore, it is wise to have a platter of various vegetables. Not only is it attractive if you mix the colors in a pattern, but it gives your guests a choice. I have included some new ideas here such as "Endive with Cream" (p. 221), paper-thin "Zucchini Parmesan" (p. 239) and "Fennel Villa la Massa" (p. 222).

Fennel intrigues me for I love the flavor of anise or licorice. This vegetable is also very good, raw, in salads. It is well known to the Italians, but is seldom served in this country. This is a vegetable for those who, years ago, bought for a penny a long stick of black licorice and chewed on it for hours, emerging with a black mouth and, usually, an upset tummy.

METHODS FOR COOKING VEGETABLES

Vegetables may be cooked by boiling, steaming or baking. I usually boil my vegetables in a small amount of water and save the cooking water for soups. Boiling is much the fastest method. However, steaming or, in a few instances, baking (such as squash and cabbage) undoubtedly preserves vitamins and minerals and improves flavor.

HOW TO COOK ARTICHOKES

Artichokes are what I call "ritual food," beloved particularly by our grandchildren and an exciting treat for them. They are also entranced by other "ritual foods" such as steamed clams, lobsters, mussels, and escargots. They have to work with them in order to eat them, and that is half the fun.

4 artichokes
4 cups water
1½ tbsps. salt

1 tbsp. vinegar
1 tbsp. olive oil

1. Clean artichokes by forcing back the outside leaves carefully to reveal hair and tough leaves in the hearts.
2. Scrape all this away with the bowl of a teaspoon.
3. Push back in shape, clip ¼ inch off each leaf straight across at the top and tie a string around each artichoke. Cut the base so that it is level.
4. Place, standing upright, in boiling, salted water in a 3-quart saucepan with vinegar and oil added. The water should only come up to about a third of the height of the artichoke.
5. Boil until, when stuck with a fork, the heart is tender (about 25 minutes). Do not overcook as the artichokes must hold their shape.

6. Remove from water and drain, upside down, on a platter. Keep warm.

7. Serve hot with "Hollandaise Sauce" (p. 350) or melted butter or cold with "Tarragon Sauce" (p. 338).

SERVES 4.

ARTICHOKE BOTTOMS WITH CAPERS

1 (1 lb. 8 oz.) can fancy artichoke bottoms *or* 8 fresh artichoke bottoms
salt and pepper to taste
1 tbsp. onion juice
8 tbsps. capers
½ cup fresh juice from artichoke bottoms
1 bunch watercress

Cook artichokes (see method above) and just keep the bottoms. Keep warm. If using canned artichoke bottoms, heat quickly in a saucepan with ½ cup juice from the can. Drain.

Lightly salt and pepper, scrape a litttle onion juice over them and put 1 tablespoon capers over each bottom. Garnish with watercress.

SERVES 4.

ARTICHOKES SEVILLA | *Congress of the United States adapted from service in Hotel King Alfonso XIII, Sevilla, Spain*

6 artichokes
water
1 tbsp. olive oil
2 tbsps. salt
1 beef bouillon cube
½ tsp. garlic flakes
½ tsp. tarragon
½ tsp. summer savory
½ tsp. marjoram
juice and peel of one lemon

Marinade:
½ cup vegetable oil
½ cup lemon juice
4 tbsps. capers and juice from bottle
1 tbsp. prepared mustard dressing
1 tsp. imported prepared mustard
1 tsp. Worcestershire sauce
1 tsp. parsley flakes
1 tsp. dehydrated red and green bell peppers

Trim artichokes and clean (see "How to Cook Artichokes," above). Steam in tightly covered roasting pan in 2 inches of water, to which has been added olive oil, salt, bouillon cube, garlic flakes, tarragon, summer savory and marjoram. Add lemon juice and then throw in the twisted peels. Depending upon size and freshness, cook about 25 to 30 minutes. Drain the artichokes and while still hot, place on platter or dish with a lip.

Pour marinade over the artichokes, making sure lots of it gets between the leaves. Insert capers between leaves. Then chill.

The artichokes will keep for a week to ten days and the flavor will improve with cold storage. While under refrigeration, protect with refrigerator wrap.

SERVES 6.

CURRIED ASPARAGUS

2 eggs, beaten well
4 tbsps. water
1 tsp. salt
1 tsp. pepper
1 tsp. curry powder

24 equal-sized asparagus spears, cooked (see "Fresh Asparagus" below) and crisp (drain and keep warm)
1 cup fresh bread crumbs
¼ lb. butter, melted

1. Mix eggs and water well. Add seasonings.
2. Dip the spears in egg mixture.
3. Roll in crumbs.
4. Sauté the spears in butter in a 10-inch skillet over medium heat. Turn until the crumbs are brown all around.

SERVES 6.

FRESH ASPARAGUS

24 stalks fresh asparagus
cold water to cover

1 tbsp. salt

1. Wash carefully.
2. Trim stalks to about 6-inch length.
3. With string-bean slicer, peel the tough ends all around (about 1 inch).
4. Place asparagus (lying on its side) in cold, salted water just to cover. A roasting pan with a tight lid works well.
5. Cover tightly and bring to a rolling boil.
6. Boil just 3 minutes.
7. Remove from heat and (still covered) let stand exactly 15 minutes.
8. Drain and serve.

By this method the asparagus is always perfect. For cold asparagus, cool, cover and chill in refrigerator for 4 or 5 hours or overnight. For hot asparagus, serve at once or reheat in vegetable steamer until hot (no longer). Serve with "Egg Dressing Sauce" (p. 335) or "Sauce Archiduc" (p. 333).

SERVES 4.

An oval asparagus pan, with a lid and handles, is very handy to have in your kitchen. These pans measure 7 x 12¾ inches and come in heavy aluminum or copper. They can be purchased in the kitchenware section of any large department store.

FRESH STRING BEANS

3 cups fresh string beans
1 qt. boiling water
2 tsps. salt

2 tbsps. butter
salt and pepper to taste

Cut and cook string beans in boiling salted water in a 2-quart saucepan over medium heat. *Undercook* them so that they are crispy. Drain and add butter. Correct seasonings.

SERVES 6.

Variations:

1. To cooked, seasoned beans, add 1 cup sour cream and garlic powder to taste. SERVES 6.
2. To cooked, seasoned beans, add ½ cup pearl onions. SERVES 6.
3. To cooked, seasoned beans, add ½ lb. sliced mushrooms sautéed in butter until golden. SERVES 6 to 8.
4. To cooked, seasoned beans, add ½ cup toasted and chopped almonds. SERVES 6.

5. To cooked, seasoned beans, add 2 cups cooked, cut-up celery and ½ large finely chopped onion that has been sautéed in butter until golden. SERVES 10.

6. Put 3 cups fresh string beans in cold water with ½ cup light brown sugar, 1 teaspoon salt and 4 or 5 slices of bacon. Bring to a boil, lower heat, and cook very slowly (simmer) for 2 to 3 hours. Drain off the liquid, remove bacon and serve. SERVES 6.

LIMA BEANS SUPREME

1 (10 oz.) pkg. frozen large lima beans
1 can (10 oz.) mushroom soup
½ cup light cream
2 tbsps. finely minced onion
1 tsp. salt
¼ tsp. pepper
½ cup grated sharp Cheddar cheese

1. Defrost beans and put in buttered 1-quart shallow ovenproof casserole (8 x 8 x 2 inches).
2. Heat mushroom soup and thin with cream.
3. Stir in onion, salt and pepper and pour over the beans.
4. Cover with cheese.
5. Bake in preheated 350° oven for 35 to 40 minutes or until beans are tender and cheese is melted.
SERVES 4.

BEETS

Beets, although one of my favorite vegetables, have always been my mortal enemies. Because it takes such a long time to boil them until they are tender, I put them on the stove and go about my business. When I finally remember them, they have gobbled up all the water and are clustered, black and hideous, in the bottom of the pan like barnacles on the hull of a ship. I have at last developed a philosophy about this—namely, let someone else boil the beets. In other words, watch them or watch out!

8 medium-sized beets (unpeeled)	1 tsp. salt
water to cover	2 tbsps. sweet butter

Boil beets slowly in salted water in heavy saucepan until they are fork tender. Peel and slice or leave whole. Add butter.

SERVES 4.

Variation:
8 cooked beets
1 (4 oz.) jar horseradish or 4 tbsps. fresh-grated horseradish

Scoop out center of beets and fill with horseradish. Use as a garnish around a roast.

SERVES 4.

BROCCOLI

2 bunches broccoli	2 tsps. salt
1 qt. water	¼ cup melted butter

Trim off the tough stems and cut broccoli in half (the long way). Cook in a 4-quart saucepan in boiling, salted water or in a vegetable steamer until fork tender. Drain, correct seasoning, add butter and serve.

SERVES 4 to 6.

Variations:

1. Follow above directions, but serve with 1 cup "Hollandaise Sauce" (p. 350).

2. Follow above directions and serve with 1 cup cheese sauce. In a double boiler over hot water, melt ¼ lb. grated Cheddar cheese in "White Sauce I" (p. 358) until smooth.

3. When broccoli is cooked, purée in blender. Add pepper to taste. Pile on artichoke bottoms and top with 1 tsp. "Hollandaise Sauce."

CELERY CABBAGE WITH GINGER

1 celery cabbage
water to cover (boiling)
2 tsps. salt
4 tbsps. butter, melted

2 tsps. minced fresh ginger root *or*
1 tsp. powdered ginger
2 tbsps. soy sauce (optional)

1. Wash celery cabbage and cut in ¼-inch slices.
2. Place in large saucepan and pour over boiling water to cover. Add salt.
3. Cook until celery cabbage is tender but still crispy (about 10 minutes).
4. Drain completely.
5. Place in top of double boiler over boiling water.
6. Add melted butter, ginger and soy sauce (optional) and correct salt.
7. Cover and keep hot until ready to serve.

SERVES 4.

CABBAGE BAKED WITH CONSOMMÉ

1 head firm cabbage, cut in medium-sized wedges
2 (10 oz.) cans beef consommé

2 tbsps. melted butter
salt and pepper to taste

1. Place cabbage in covered 3-quart ovenproof baking dish.
2. Add consommé.
3. Bake in 350° oven until tender, basting occasionally with the consommé (about 1 hour).
4. When tender drain and add the melted butter, salt and pepper.

SERVES 4 to 6.

RED CABBAGE WITH APPLES

1 (4 lb.) head of red cabbage
2 tbsps. chicken fat or butter
2 tart, firm apples, peeled and chopped
1 medium-sized onion, sliced fine
2 cups water
½ cup red wine vinegar
½ cup sugar
½ tsp. salt
¼ tsp. pepper (white)
2 cloves
1 bay leaf
juice of 1 lemon
1½ tbsps. flour

1. Wash and shred cabbage.
2. Heat fat in 4-quart saucepan and cook onion and apples, gently, for 3 to 4 minutes.
3. Add water, vinegar, sugar, salt, pepper, cloves, bay leaf, and lemon juice.
4. Stir and bring to a boil for 3 minutes. Remove cloves and bay leaf and discard.
5. Add cabbage, mix well, cover and simmer for 3 hours or until tender.
6. Sprinkle flour over the top; mix well, cover again and cook for 5 more minutes.

SERVES 16.

RUTH HAYDEN'S GERMAN RED CABBAGE

1 (2 lb.) red cabbage, washed and chopped
6 tbsps. bacon fat
salt and pepper to taste
1 cup water (if needed)
4 large cooking apples, peeled and chopped fine
1 medium onion, chopped fine
½ tsp. powdered cloves
2½ tbsps. sugar
2½ tbsps. wine vinegar

1. Place cabbage in 5½-quart iron pot with bacon fat on the bottom.
2. Cook, stirring constantly, over a high flame for 10 minutes.
3. Add salt and pepper.
4. Cover and lower flame to simmer and add water.

5. Add, at once, apples and onion to cabbage (still over low flame).
6. Add powdered cloves.
7. Cook very slowly for 3 hours, adding more water if it gets too dry.
8. Add sugar and vinegar and let stand, covered, off the stove for as long as possible. Correct seasonings.
9. Reheat quickly to serve.
SERVES 16.

STUFFED GREEN CABBAGE ROLLS

6 cups water
1 large head green cabbage
1 lb. ground chuck beef
2 cups cooked white rice
½ cup chopped onion
1 egg
1 tsp. salt
1 tbsp. Worcestershire sauce
⅛ tsp. pepper

1 can (10½ oz.) beef consommé
2 tbsps. butter or margarine
2 tbsps. light brown sugar
2 tbsps. flour
1 medium onion, sliced (for sauce)
1 (1 lb.) can whole tomatoes, undrained
½ tsp. salt

1. In 4-quart saucepan, bring water to a boil. Remove 12 large outer leaves from cabbage. Trim thick rib of each leaf for easier rolling. (Use remaining cabbage another day.) Add leaves to boiling water and let stand for 2 minutes, just long enough to make leaves pliable. Drain well.
2. To make filling: In medium bowl, combine beef, rice, onion, egg, salt, Worcestershire, pepper and ½ cup of consommé. Preheat oven to 350°.
3. Place ⅓ cup of filling in center of each cabbage leaf. Fold ends and roll from sides over filling. Secure with wooden toothpicks.
4. Melt butter or margarine and brown sugar in 12-inch skillet. Add cabbage rolls and sauté until glazed on all sides (about 5 minutes).
5. Arrange rolls in a 3-quart ovenproof casserole (13½ x 8¾ x 1¾ inches). Combine flour with remaining consommé. Mix until smooth. Add to skillet with onion, tomatoes and salt. Bring to a boil, stirring. When mixture has thickened slightly, pour over cabbage rolls.
6. Bake, covered, for 1 hour and 15 minutes. Remove toothpicks.
SERVES 12 (one apiece) or 6 (two apiece).

CHINESE SWEET AND SOUR CABBAGE

1 lb. celery cabbage *or* plain
    cabbage (Celery cabbage
    is better.)
1½ cups water
½ tsp. salt

2 tbsps. sugar
1 tsp. soy sauce
2 tbsps. white vinegar
2 tbsps. cornstarch

Slice vegetable into 1-inch pieces, eliminating tough core. Place in a 2-quart kettle with water and salt, turn heat high and bring to a rapid boil. Boil hard, uncovered, 10 minutes.

In a small bowl, mix sugar, soy sauce, vinegar and cornstarch and stir into cooking vegetable. When juice becomes translucent, vegetable is done. Serve hot.

SERVES 4 to 6 as a vegetable with "Polynesian Chicken" and hot "Fried Rice."

CARROT RING

4 cups carrots, washed and
    scraped and finely shredded
2 cups water
1 tsp. salt
3 cups grated Cheddar cheese
⅔ cup carrot liquor *or* ⅔ cup from
    (12 oz.) can carrot juice
⅔ cup milk

2 cups bread crumbs (fresh)
onion salt to taste
celery salt to taste
garlic salt to taste
4 eggs, slightly beaten
4 cups "Creamed Mushrooms"
    (p. 224)
1 tbsp. Worcestershire sauce

1. Cook carrots in boiling, salted water until tender. Cool. Save the carrot liquid.
2. Mix the carrots with the next seven ingredients, then add the slightly beaten eggs.
3. Place mixture in a buttered 2-quart ring mold.
4. Set the mold in larger pan of hot water (about 3 inches deep).
5. Bake in preheated 325° oven for 1 hour and 15 minutes.
6. Unmold on heated round platter.

Place "Creamed Mushrooms" (with Worcestershire sauce added) in the center of the ring mold, and serve.

SERVES 10 to 12.

CARROTS WITH SOUR CREAM

2 cups carrots
4 cups water
1 tsp. salt
¼ cup onion, minced
4 tbsps. butter
½ cup sour cream
¼ cup light cream
salt and pepper to taste

1 (10 oz.) pkg. frozen tiny peas (cooked according to package directions)
salt and pepper to taste
2 tbsps. butter
1 (10 oz.) pkg. frozen artichoke hearts (follow package directions)
salt and pepper to taste
2 tbsps. butter

1. Scrape carrots, cut in strips, and cook in salted water until tender.
2. Sauté onion in butter until golden.
3. Combine with carrots and add sour cream, cream and seasonings.
4. Serve very hot in center of round platter surrounded by peas, seasoned with butter and artichoke hearts seasoned and buttered.

SERVES 4 to 6.

WHISKEY CARROTS LANSING

3 cups carrots, scraped and sliced
2 tbsps. butter, melted
2 jiggers Irish whiskey

2 tbsps. brown sugar
salt and pepper to taste

1. In a 1-quart, heatproof jar with a tight lid place the sliced carrots.
2. Pour in butter and whiskey. Add sugar, salt and pepper.
3. Cover jar tightly and shake well.
4. Place jar in a 5-quart kettle and fill with boiling water reaching the shoulders of the jar.

5. On medium to low heat, cook for 2 hours (more hot water must be added as it boils away).
SERVES 6.
Serve carrots with "Lansing Corn Soufflé."

HOW TO COOK CAULIFLOWER

1 large head cauliflower
2 tsps. salt (for soaking)
1 tsp. salt (for cooking)
4 tbsps. butter (melted)

salt and pepper to taste
1½ cups "Hollandaise Sauce"
(p. 350)

1. Remove leaves from the cauliflower.
2. Place cauliflower, upside down, in a 4- to 6-quart kettle or saucepan.
3. Cover with water and add 2 tsps. salt. Soak for 1 hour. Rinse.
4. Wash pan and replace cauliflower in it, right side up.
5. Cover with boiling, salted water and boil gently until the base of the cauliflower is fork tender. Do not cook too long or the head will fall apart.
6. Serve with butter and seasonings or topped with hot "Hollandaise Sauce."
SERVES 6 to 8.

CELERY

2 cups celery (cut in ½-in. pieces)
2 cups boiling water
1 tsp. salt

½ tsp. pepper
½ tsp. Beau Monde seasoning
4 tbsps. butter

Cover celery with boiling salted water and cook until tender, but not mushy.
Drain well and pepper. Add Beau Monde seasoning and butter.
SERVES 4.

SAUTERNE CELERY

6 cups celery, cut up
3 cups water
1 tsp. salt
3 tsps. fresh minced onion or shallots (minced)

4 tbsps. butter or margarine
1 cup heavy cream (whipped)
⅛ tsp. nutmeg
salt to taste
⅔ cup dry sauterne wine

1. Cook celery in boiling salted water in a 3-quart saucepan until fork tender.
2. Sauté onions (or shallots) in butter in a small skillet until transparent.
3. Drain celery completely. Place in top of double boiler over boiling water and add onions, cream, nutmeg and salt.
4. Just before serving, add the sauterne, off the heat, so cream won't separate.

SERVES 10.

CORN PUDDING

4 eggs, beaten well
3 cups milk
⅛ cup sugar
2 tsps. salt
4 tbsps. butter, melted

3 (10 oz.) pkgs. frozen corn kernels (cooked)
2 (17 oz.) cans cream corn
2 tbsps. flour
4 tbsps. butter

1. Beat eggs and add milk, sugar, salt and 4 tablespoons melted butter.
2. Mix all the corn with the flour.
3. Mix all the above together.
4. Place mixture in buttered ovenproof 3-quart round baking dish. Dot top with rest of butter.
5. Set in a larger pan of hot water (3 inches deep) and bake in preheated 350° oven for approximately 15 minutes.

SERVES 12.

EASY CORN PUDDING

1 scant tbsp. flour
2 tbsps. light cream
4 eggs, beaten well

2 (17 oz.) cans cream corn
2 tbsps. sugar
salt and pepper to taste

1. Mix flour well with the cream.
2. Add corn to beaten eggs.
3. Combine with the flour and cream.
4. Add sugar, salt and pepper.
5. Put in buttered 1½-quart ovenproof baking dish.
6. Set in a larger pan of hot water (2 inches deep) and bake in preheated 325° oven for about 45 minutes or until firm in the center.

SERVES 6.

EGGPLANT, SOUR CREAM AND RUSSIAN OR IRANIAN CAVIAR

8 (½-in. thick) slices eggplant
1 tbsp. salt
½ cup olive oil
8 dessertspoons of sour cream

1 (¼ lb.) jar *very best* caviar
1 small onion, scraped
1 bunch watercress or parsley

Place eggplant slices, salted, on cotton or linen towel; cover and place something heavy on top. Let stand for ½ hour to remove water. Sauté eggplant in hot olive oil in 10-inch skillet, turning often with spatula until each slice is golden. Drain on brown paper and keep warm in low oven (200°).

On each slice place one dessert spoon of sour cream in the center. Top each with 1 teaspoon caviar and ¼ teaspoon grated onion.

Surround with watercress or parsley. Use this as a first course.

SERVES 8.

GREEK STUFFED EGGPLANT

3 small eggplants
   boiling water to cover
1½ tbsps. lemon juice
½ cup chopped onion
1 clove garlic, crushed
1 lb. ground lamb
2 tbsps. olive oil
½ cup bread crumbs

1 egg, beaten
½ tsp. oregano
2 tbsps. chopped parsley
½ tsp. garlic salt
½ tsp. salt
¼ tsp. ground black pepper
1½ cups toasted bread crumbs

    Parboil whole eggplants 12 to 15 minutes. Drain, cut in half lengthwise and remove pulp to within ½ inch of skin. Chop pulp in small pieces. Reserve shells. Brush cut surface of eggplants with lemon juice.

    Add onion and garlic to ground lamb. In 10-inch skillet, sauté lamb in olive oil until pink color is gone. Add reserved eggplant pulp, bread crumbs, egg, oregano, parsley, garlic salt, salt and pepper. Mix well. Fill eggplant shells with this mixture. Top each with ¼ cup bread crumbs. Place in greased (15½ x 7½ x 1¾ inch) pan. Bake in preheated, moderate (350°) oven for 30 minutes. Serve hot as entrée.

SERVES 6.

ENDIVE WITH CREAM

6 large Belgian endive
   boiling water to cover
½ tsp. salt
1 cup heavy cream
4 tbsps. butter (dots)
   salt and pepper to taste

garlic salt to taste (optional) *or*
   1 tsp. Beau Monde seasoning
   (optional)
2 tbsps. chopped chives *or* 1 tbsp.
   dried chives

    Cut off root ends of endive, wash and place in large saucepan. Pour in boiling salted water. Boil until fork tender but still retaining original shape. Drain completely and cut each endive in half lengthwise.

    Butter a 2-quart (11¾ x 7½ x 1¾ inch) ovenproof dish. Preheat oven to 350°. Place endive in a row across the bottom of the dish. Pour cream over the endive. Dot with butter and sprinkle with salt and pepper and garlic salt or

Beau Monde (optional). Place in oven until thoroughly hot. Add chives 2 minutes before endive leaves the oven.

SERVES 6.

FENNEL VILLA LA MASSA

4 large bulbs fresh fennel
   boiling water to cover
½ tsp. salt
3 tbsps. olive oil

1 garlic bud, minced
1 tsp. salt
½ cup grated Parmesan-Romano
   cheese

1. Trim the fennel, leaving just bulb ends.
2. Boil in salted water until fennel is fork tender but still holding its shape.
3. Drain *well* and slice in ¼-inch slices.
4. Place in shallow, ovenproof (11¾ x 7½ x 1¾ inch) buttered baking dish.
5. Sprinkle with olive oil in which garlic has been soaking for 1 hour.
6. Salt sparingly.
7. Cover with thin layer of grated cheese.
8. Bake in preheated 350° oven until it is thoroughly hot and cheese is melted.

SERVES 6.

MONK'S DISH | *Puan Sri Ong*
The Embassy of Malaysia

*2 oz. (1 pkg.) dried tiger-lily flower
   (soak in water for 1 hour)
*2 oz. (1 pkg.) dried lichen (soak in
   water for 1 hour)
*2 oz. (1 pkg.) dried mushroom
   (soak in water for 1 hour)
*5 cakes chili bean-curd paste (sold
   in jars of about 10 cakes)
5 cloves garlic, peeled and chopped
   very fine

8 tbsps. vegetable oil
*1 (6½ oz.) can gingko nuts (drain
   water from can)
4 lbs. celery cabbage, washed and
   each stalk cut in 1-in. slices
2 tbsps. salt
4 tsps. sugar
1 tsp. monosodium glutamate

* Available in Chinatown and sold in packages as indicated.

Drain tiger-lily flower and cut off hard core from end of stems. Drain lichen. Remove crusty ends from core (center of lichen). Drain dried mushrooms, cut off stems and discard, then cut mushroom caps in halves or thirds. Blend chili bean-curd paste thoroughly with garlic. Heat oil in skillet, add chili bean-curd paste mixture. Stir for about 2 minutes.

Add all other ingredients, including seasonings. Mix thoroughly for about 5 minutes, then quickly cover skillet and let simmer for about 10 to 15 minutes. Serve on warm platter.

SERVES 12.

MUSHROOMS BENEDICT

6 thin slices of boiled ham	¼ cup sifted flour
¼ lb. butter	1 egg, well beaten
1 tbsp. instant minced onion *or* ¼ cup minced fresh onion	1 tbsp. fresh lemon juice
	½ tsp. salt
1 lb. fresh mushroom caps, washed and sliced	2 tsps. finely chopped parsley
	3 English muffins
1½ cups light cream	1 bunch watercress

1. Frizzle ham in 4 tablespoons butter. Remove ham and keep warm. Save pan juices. Add rest of butter to pan and sauté onion until golden.
2. Add mushrooms and cook for 5 minutes longer.
3. Add cream mixed well with the flour and stir until it thickens.
4. Slowly stir in egg (off the heat).
5. Add pan juices from the ham, the lemon juice and the salt and parsley.
6. Split muffins with a fork, toast and butter each half.
7. To serve, place a muffin half on each hot plate. Top each with slice of ham and cover with the mushroom and onion mixture.
8. Garnish with watercress.

SERVES 6.

MY GRANDMOTHER'S BAKED MUSHROOMS

1 lb. fresh mushrooms with stems cut off
4 tbsps. butter
¼ cup chopped celery hearts
¼ cup minced parsley
¾ cup heavy cream
salt and pepper to taste
4 slices hot buttered toast, crusts removed
4 sprigs fresh parsley

1. Place mushrooms flat (inside up) in large buttered, ovenproof pan (11¾ x 7½ x 1¾ inches).
2. Dot with butter.
3. Sprinkle with the celery and parsley.
4. Add cream and seasonings.
5. Bake in preheated 325° oven for 30 to 40 minutes.
6. Serve on hot buttered toast and garnish tops with sprig of parsley.

SERVES 4.

CREAMED MUSHROOMS

6 tbsps. butter
2 lbs. fresh mushrooms, sliced
3 tbsps. flour
¾ cup milk
¾ cup light cream (more if needed)
1 egg yolk (beaten well)
salt and pepper to taste

1. In a 10-inch skillet, melt 3 tablespoons butter.
2. Add mushrooms and sauté for 5 minutes. Reserve mushrooms and butter in top of double boiler over hot water.
3. In another 10-inch skillet melt remaining butter. Remove from heat and stir in flour to make a smooth paste.
4. Add milk and return to heat. Stir until thickened. Cool a little.
5. Place cream in bowl and stir in beaten egg yolk.
6. Gradually stir cream and egg mixture into the sauce off the burner. Return to low heat and stir until thickened. If too thick, add more cream.
7. Pour sauce over mushrooms. Stir and season and keep hot until ready to serve.

SERVES 8.

MUSHROOMS WITH MADEIRA WINE

24 large even-sized mushroom caps (washed)
½ lb. butter
1 cup madeira wine
salt and pepper to taste

1. Place mushrooms upside down in a covered pan. (I use a 2-quart aluminum pan with a glass ovenproof cover.) If mushrooms are smooth-skinned type, do not peel.
2. Dot mushrooms with butter.
3. Pour over madeira wine.
4. Cover tightly and simmer, very slowly, for 1 hour. (The mushrooms absorb most of the liquid and have a marvelous flavor.)
5. Season just before serving.

SERVES 4 to 6.

MUSHROOM RING

1 cut clove garlic (optional)
3 tbsps. flour
3 tbsps. butter, melted
1½ lbs. fresh mushrooms, peeled and chopped
4 egg yolks (beaten well)
3 egg whites (beaten stiff)
1½ cups heavy cream (whipped)
salt, pepper and paprika to taste
1 tbsp. minced parsley

1. Lightly rub 10- to 12-inch skillet with a cut clove of garlic (optional).
2. In skillet, lightly brown flour.
3. Add melted butter.
4. Add mushrooms and sauté for 10 minutes.
5. Cool. Place in bowl.
6. Add the beaten egg yolks.
7. Add the beaten egg whites.
8. Fold in the whipped cream. Mix well.
9. Season.
10. Add parsley.
11. Fill cold well-buttered 2-quart ring mold.
12. Set in pan of hot water (2 to 2½ inches deep) and bake in preheated 350° oven for about 1 hour. Do not let water in pan around mold boil.

13. Unmold.
SERVES 8.
Fill center with "Creamed Scallops."

ONIONS CREAMED WITH SLIVERED ALMONDS

1 (15½ oz.) jar of small white onions
1½ cups milk
½ cup onion liquid
4 or 5 celery tops
4 tbsps. butter

4 tbsps. flour
salt and pepper to taste
2 tbsps. butter (for almonds)
1 cup slivered almonds

1. Heat onions in own liquid and cook until they are tender. Drain and save liquid. Place onions in ovenproof (8 x 8 x 2 inch) glass dish.
2. Heat milk and onion liquid together with celery tops in top of double boiler. Do not boil. Strain out leaves; set aside, but keep hot over boiling water.
3. Make paste of 4 tablespoons melted butter and flour and gradually add to milk and onion liquid, stirring until smooth and thickened.
4. Season and pour over onions.
5. In a small skillet, melt 2 tablespoons butter and add the slivered almonds. Sauté, tossing often with a spoon, until almonds are golden brown.
6. Sprinkle almonds over onions and place in preheated 350° oven until sauce bubbles.
SERVES 4.

CHINESE FRIED PARSLEY

2 cups vegetable oil

1 bunch fresh parsley

Heat oil until it is gently bubbling (380° on deep-fat thermometer).
Place parsley in a strainer or use tongs and dip in the hot oil for a short while or until it crisps and turns a brighter shade of green.
Serve around "Hawaiian Chicken."

PARSNIPS

I don't even like to write that heading. I believe that the less said about this unfortunate vegetable, the better. I may be treading on the toes of parsnip addicts, but having had to eat them whenever they were served as I was growing up (my family adored them), nary a parsnip has crossed our threshold in forty years—nor will they in the future. Sorry.

PEAS

Basic Cooking:

2 cups fresh peas (shelled)
   boiling water to *just* cover
½ tsp. salt
½ tsp. sugar
1 tbsp. butter

Place peas in a saucepan; cover with boiling water and add salt and sugar. Boil for 25 to 30 minutes or until tender. Strain, add butter and correct seasonings.

Variations:

1. Follow basic recipe above but add, just before serving, 1 cup sliced fresh mushrooms which have been sautéed in 2 tablespoons butter.

2. Follow basic recipe above but add ½ cup chopped water chestnuts, ½ teaspoon ground ginger and 1 tablespoon soy sauce.

3. Follow basic recipe above but add 2 tablespoons chopped marrons in syrup (I use Raffeto's). Discard the syrup.

4. Follow basic recipe above but add 1 tablespoon chopped fresh mint leaves.

5. Follow basic recipe but add 2 tablespoons tiny pearl onions.

6. 2 tbsps. butter
   1 medium onion, peeled and diced
   8 lettuce leaves (large)
   2 cups fresh peas
   1 cup boiling water (more if needed)
   ½ tsp. salt

Melt butter in small skillet and sauté onion for 5 minutes. Line a 10-inch skillet with 4 lettuce leaves. Pour butter and onion mixture over this. Add the peas, water and the salt. Cover with 4 more lettuce leaves. Cover skillet and simmer for about ½ hour or until peas are tender; add more water if needed.

When done, remove from stove and tilt skillet over sink to discard water. With a knife, cut lettuce in fine strips (still in the skillet). Mix all together and serve.

All these variations SERVE 4.

PURÉED PEAS IN ONION SHELLS

4 large Bermuda onions
1 qt. boiling water
1 tsp. salt
2 (10 oz.) pkgs. frozen peas
½ cup beef consommé (from 10½ oz. can)

4 tbsps. sweet butter
salt and pepper to taste
2 tbsps. finely minced parsley

1. Boil onions in salted water until they are tender, but still retain their shape.
2. Scoop out centers of onions, leaving outer shells. Reserve centers.
3. Boil peas in consommé until done.
4. Purée peas, the consommé and the centers of the onions in the blender and season with butter, salt and pepper.
5. Fill onion shells with puréed peas.
6. Sprinkle each with parsley. Reheat in preheated 300° oven in a buttered ovenproof (8 x 8 x 2 inch) dish until hot.

SERVES 4.

DUCHESS POTATOES

4 cups freshly cooked, mashed potatoes
2 eggs, beaten
1 tbsp. fresh minced chives (or frozen)
4 tbsps. cooked crisp, diced bacon
salt and pepper to taste
2 tbsps. melted butter

1. Combine potatoes and eggs in a large bowl. Stir in chives, bacon and seasonings.
2. Form into 8 mounds and, with the blunt end of a knife, make spirals on top of each mound.
3. Brush with melted butter and place on greased (11½ x 7½ x 1¾ inch) ovenproof pan.
4. Bake in preheated 350° oven for 15 minutes.

SERVES 8.

HASHED BROWN POTATOES

3 cups cold, cooked, firm potatoes, cut in small cubes
1 medium onion, chopped fine
4 tbsps. butter or margarine
salt and pepper to taste
2 tbsps. bacon fat
fresh parsley

1. Cook and cube potatoes the day before serving. Undercook a bit. Cover and chill in the refrigerator.
2. Sauté onion in butter in a 10-inch skillet until golden.
3. Mix potatoes with onion and seasonings.
4. Add bacon fat to skillet, and when it is very hot, pack in the potato mixture. Push down with a fork to pack in solidly.
5. Turn heat to medium to low, cover and cook for at least 30 to 35 minutes or until crust forms on the bottom. Lift up with a knife to see if bottom of potatoes are brown.
6. Turn out on a platter by turning skillet upside down. Potatoes will look like pie with a crust on top. Garnish with parsley.

SERVES 6.

POTATOES O'BRIEN

4 cups raw potatoes peeled and cut in ½-in. cubes
2 qts. cold water
2 (3 lb.) cans shortening
2 slices onion, minced
½ cup diced green pepper
4 tbsps. butter
3 pimientos, chopped
salt to taste
1 tbsp. chopped parsley

1. Soak potatoes in cold water and drain *well*.
2. Put shortening in deep-fat fryer and when heat reaches 375° (use thermometer), put potatoes in a wire basket and fry until brown and tender. Lift out of fat and keep warm.
3. Sauté onion and green pepper in butter in 10-inch skillet until golden and tender.
4. Add pimientos, potatoes and salt. Stir carefully and when hot, remove to heated platter. Sprinkle parsley over the dish.

Serves 8 to 10.

GERMAN POTATO PANCAKES

4 Irish potatoes, grated with ¼ cup of finely minced onion
2 eggs, beaten a little
2 tbsps. flour
¼ tsp. nutmeg
½ tsp. salt
½ tsp. pepper
4 tbsps. butter or vegetable oil
3 cups applesauce
12 tbsps. sour cream (optional)

Pat potatoes and onion dry and measure 3 cups in all. Combine potato and onion with eggs, flour, nutmeg, salt and pepper.

In a 6½-inch skillet, slowly heat the butter or oil (⅛ inch depth) until it is very hot, but do not brown. Drop 2 tablespoons mixture at a time into the butter. Flatten with a spatula to make a pancake 3 or 4 inches across. Sauté 2 or 3 minutes on each side or until golden. Drain completely on paper towels. Keep warm in lowest degree oven until all are made. Turn up oven for a few minutes to 475° to crisp. Watch carefully!

Serves 6 (2 apiece).

Applesauce or sour cream are good with this. Serve them in separate bowls.

MOTHER'S SCALLOPED POTATOES

12 raw boiling potatoes, peeled and sliced thin
4 tbsps. flour
½ cup butter
salt and Java pepper to taste
2 Bermuda onions, sliced thin
1½ cups light cream *and* 1½ cups milk (or enough to just cover the potatoes)
1 tsp. paprika
2 tbsps. minced parsley
1 cup grated sharp Cheddar cheese (optional)

1. In a buttered ovenproof 2-quart round glass baking dish, place 1 layer of potatoes. Dust with flour, dot with butter, salt and pepper.
2. Add layer of onions.
3. Repeat above, in layers, until dish is full. End with onions.
4. Pour milk and cream over this, just covering the onions on top.
5. Bake in preheated 375° oven until potatoes are done—firm, but not soft.
6. Sprinkle with paprika and parsley and serve in the baking dish.
SERVES 8.
"Cheese Scalloped Potatoes" may be made by adding cheese between each layer and topping with cheese.

STRAW POTATOES

12 potatoes, peeled and cut in *very thin* ¼-in. strips, as evenly as possible
1½ qts. shortening or enough to make 6-inch depth in deep-fat frying pan
salt to taste

1. Put potatoes in bowl of water. Pat *dry* and wrap in wet dishcloth to keep from discoloring.
2. Place shortening in electric deep-fat fryer. When oil reaches 375° (on deep-fat thermometer), put potatoes in the frying basket, a cup at a time, and fry for 3 or 4 minutes or until they are golden.
3. Drain on brown paper and keep warm. Salt to taste.
4. Crisscross the strips on a platter and serve with steak or lamb chops.
SERVES 8 to 10.

GRANDMOTHER'S SWEET POTATO DELIGHT

12 sweet potatoes	½ tsp. nutmeg *or* cinnamon
2 qts. boiling water	2 eggs, beaten
1 tsp. salt	¼ cup sweet sherry
4 tbsps. butter, melted	salt and pepper to taste
4 tbsps. light cream	12 to 14 marshmallows *or* ½ cup
1 tbsp. scraped fresh onion	crushed corn flakes

1. Boil the potatoes, in their jackets, in salted water until tender.
2. Peel the potatoes and mash well with fork until very smooth or mash in an electric blender.
3. Stir in melted butter, cream, onion and spices.
4. Fold in beaten egg. Mix well.
5. Add sherry.
6. Correct seasonings.
7. Place mixture in buttered 2-quart ovenproof baking dish.
8. Heat in preheated 350° oven for 15 minutes or until very hot.
9. Place marshmallows or crushed corn flakes on top and continue baking until marshmallows melt or corn flakes are very crisp.

SERVES 8.

CLARK'S FAVORITE SAUTÉED SLIVERED POTATOES

6 medium Irish potatoes, peeled and cut into *very thin* slivers (about ⅛ in.)	1 tbsp. pure bacon fat salt and pepper to taste

1. Prepare potatoes in the morning. Soak in water.
2. Dry carefully between two dish towels.
3. Heat bacon fat in 8-inch skillet (iron, if possible) until very hot.
4. Pack potatoes down into skillet and turn heat to simmer.
5. Cover and simmer until the bottom potatoes are a rich, crispy brown (lift edge of potatoes up with a fork to see).
6. Season and turn skillet over on heated, round platter (This resembles a small pie.)

SERVES 4.

RATATOUILLE

- 12 tbsps. olive oil
- 2 small eggplants (peeled and sliced thin)
- 4 medium zucchinis (cut in 1-in. slices—ends cut off)
- 3 medium onions, chopped fine
- 4 medium green peppers, seeded and sliced in thin strips
- 4 cloves garlic, minced fine
- 1 tsp. basil
- ½ tsp. thyme
- 6 fresh, firm tomatoes, peeled, seeded and cut in large cubes
- 2 tbsps. cornstarch
- salt and pepper to taste

1. Heat 6 tablespoons of oil in a 10-inch skillet or an electric skillet. Either must have a lid.
2. When hot, add eggplant and zucchini and cook on high heat (covered), stirring often, for about 6 minutes. Remove vegetables from the skillet and reserve.
3. Add the remainder of the oil and when hot, add the onions, green peppers and garlic. Cover and cook for 12 minutes, stirring occasionally.
4. Place this mixture in layers with eggplant mixture in a 2-quart ovenproof baking dish with a tight cover.
5. Add basil and thyme and bake covered in a preheated 350° oven for 20 minutes.
6. Add tomatoes on top, cover again and bake for 10 more minutes.
7. Strain juice through a sieve into a small skillet. Stir in cornstarch with a wire whisk and cook until thickened a bit.
8. Strain this juice again through a sieve and add to the vegetables.
9. Add salt and pepper. Stir all together carefully to blend in juice and seasonings.
10. Serve either hot or cold.

SERVES 10.

EASY SPINACH DIVINE | *Katrine Savage*

- 2 (10 oz.) pkgs. frozen chopped spinach (thawed, but not drained)
- ½ cup sour cream
- 1 (2 oz.) pkg. dry onion soup mix
- salt and pepper to taste
- ½ cup bread crumbs

1. Mix spinach, sour cream and onion soup mix in a bowl. Season lightly.
2. Preheat oven to 350°.
3. Place spinach mixture in a buttered 1-quart ovenproof casserole.
4. Sprinkle with bread crumbs and bake for 30 minutes.

SERVES 4.

SPINACH WITH MUSHROOMS

1 onion, minced
¼ lb. butter
½ lb. sliced mushrooms
3 pkgs. fresh spinach, washed carefully
1 cup boiling water
salt and freshly ground pepper to taste
½ tsp. nutmeg

1. Sauté onion in butter in a 10-inch skillet until golden.
2. Add sliced mushrooms and cook for 5 minutes, stirring. Set aside.
3. Place spinach in deep saucepan. Pour in boiling water.
4. Cook very short time or until just tender (about 6 minutes).
5. Drain completely, discard spinach water, chop and add onion-mushroom mixture and pan juices.
6. Season with salt, pepper and nutmeg and serve.

SERVES 4.

SPINACH RING

1 onion, minced
¼ lb. butter
3 pkgs. fresh spinach
1 cup boiling water
½ pint sour cream
1 egg, beaten
½ tsp. nutmeg
salt and pepper to taste
2 (1 lb.) cans midget beets *or* 4 cups "Creamed Mushrooms" (p. 224)

1. Sauté onion in butter in a small skillet until transparent.
2. Place spinach in deep saucepan. Pour in boiling water. Cook about 6 or 7 minutes and drain thoroughly.

3. Mix cooked spinach and onion. Add sour cream and egg.
4. Stir well and pack into 1-quart buttered ring mold.
5. Set mold in larger pan of hot water (about 2-inch depth) and bake in preheated 350° oven for 30 minutes.
6. Unmold on round hot platter and fill center with tiny hot beets with butter or "Creamed Mushrooms."

SERVES 6 to 8.

SPINACH SQUARES | Mrs. Basil George Vitsaxis
(*Spanakopeta*) The Embassy of Greece

---

2 lbs. spinach
1 onion, finely chopped
4 tbsps. butter
1 cup "White Sauce I" (p. 358)
5 or 6 eggs, beaten
1 cup finely crumbled Feta cheese (goat's milk cheese)
salt and pepper to taste
dash of nutmeg
½ lb. phyllo pastry sheets
melted butter

Wash spinach and discard stems. Dry as thoroughly as possible on absorbent paper and cut in pieces. Sauté onion in butter until soft. Add spinach and sauté a few minutes longer. Cool. Add cream sauce, eggs, cheese, salt, pepper and nutmeg. Mix well.

Place 6 or 7 layers of phyllo pastry sheets in a (11 x 14 x 2 inch) pan, brushing each sheet well with melted butter. (While using phyllo sheets, keep them covered with damp tea towel as they dry out and crumble very quickly.) Let the excess phyllo hang over the edge of the pan. Fill the center with the spinach mixture and fold the phyllo back over it. Then place 7 or 8 layers of phyllo pastry sheets on top of filling, again buttering each sheet. Trim the excess phyllo with scissors to fit the pan. Bake in preheated 350° oven for about 30 minutes or until crust is golden brown. Cut into small squares before serving. Squares should be speared with a toothpick to keep phyllo pastry and filling together. This dish may be frozen.

MAKES 16 squares.

This may be made in an 8-inch or 9-inch pie pan using the same method and cut into wedges.

BUTTERNUT SQUASH

4 medium butternut squash (quartered)
boiling water to cover
1 tsp. salt
4 tbsps. butter
2 tbsps. cream
½ tsp. nutmeg
salt and pepper to taste
1 egg, beaten until frothy
½ cup crushed corn flakes

1. Place squash in salted boiling water. Boil (covered) until tender (about 30 minutes).
2. Drain *completely* and cool a bit.
3. Cut off outside shells and discard.
4. Put squash in bowl and, using potato masher, mash until all lumps are gone.
5. Add butter, cream and seasonings.
6. Fold in beaten egg.
7. Place mixture in buttered ovenproof baking dish (8 x 8 x 2 inches) and cover with crushed corn flakes.
8. Bake in preheated 350° oven until bubbly and corn flakes are golden.
SERVES 6 to 8.

YELLOW SUMMER SQUASH AND ZUCCHINI

4 sliced yellow summer squash
4 sliced zucchini
1 qt. boiling water
1 tsp. salt
2 tbsps. olive oil
½ tsp. garlic flakes
salt and pepper to taste
½ cup Parmesan or sharp Cheddar cheese

1. Boil squash and zucchini in boiling, salted water for 3 to 4 minutes. Keep very crisp.
2. Drain completely and pat dry with a tea towel. All the water should be out of the squash and zucchini.
3. In a shallow 2-qt. round ovenproof casserole coated with olive oil, arrange in clock fashion a row of yellow squash, then a row of zucchini and so forth until the casserole is covered.

4. Sprinkle squash and zucchini with the rest of the olive oil mixed with the garlic flakes.
5. Sprinkle with salt and pepper.
6. Top with cheese.
7. Bake in preheated 350° oven until it is very hot and cheese is melted.
SERVES 10 to 12.

BROILED TOMATOES I

4 large firm tomatoes (even size)
½ cup seasoned Italian bread crumbs
1 tsp. garlic salt
½ cup minced chives

1. Do not skin the tomatoes. Cut in half, horizontally, after cutting out the stem end.
2. Cover each half with bread crumbs mixed with garlic salt.
3. Top each with chives.
4. Place on (8 x 8 inch) ovenproof pan and broil about 6 inches from the broiler flame until the crumbs are golden brown and the tomatoes are hot.
SERVES 4.

BROILED TOMATOES II

4 large firm tomatoes (even size)
½ cup buttered bread crumbs
6 tbsps. grated sharp Cheddar cheese
2 slices bacon cut into 8 pieces
4 sprigs watercress

Prepare tomatoes as in "Broiled Tomatoes I" (above), but mix bread crumbs with 2 tablespoons cheese. Sprinkle tops with rest of cheese, add a square of bacon and broil until cheese is melted and golden and bacon is done. Top each with sprig of watercress.
SERVES 4.

TOMATO, ONION AND EGGPLANT

2 large eggplants
  boiling water to cover
1 tsp. salt
4 onions, chopped fine
¼ lb. butter
1 (1 lb. 12 oz.) can tomatoes

1 tsp. cornstarch
1 tbsp. water
salt to taste
½ tsp. oregano (optional)
1 cup grated sharp Cheddar cheese

1. Peel eggplants and cut in 1-inch cubes.
2. Cover with boiling, salted water and cook until *just* tender. *about 3 mins*
3. Drain completely and set aside.
4. In a 10-inch skillet sauté onions in butter until they are transparent.
5. Add tomatoes (juice and all) and cook down, over medium heat, until they thicken a bit (about 30 [20] minutes). Add cornstarch mixed with 1 tablespoon water to thicken further. Cook for 5 more minutes. *No. CS. — sugar to cut torms*
6. Combine all the above ingredients and place in buttered ovenproof casserole (11¾ x 7½ x 1¾ inches). Season with salt and oregano.
7. Cover with cheese.
8. Bake in preheated 350° oven until it bubbles and the cheese is melted.
SERVES 10. *about 15 mins for ½ recipe*

TURNIPS

Turnips, like beets, take a long time to cook, but unlike beets, are reasonable vegetables and emerge from their bath of boiling, salted water in a civilized manner.

12 fresh turnips (white or yellow)
  boiling water to cover
1 tsp. salt
4 tbsps. melted butter

salt and pepper to taste
½ pint sour cream (optional)
½ tsp. garlic flakes (optional)

Peel the turnips and boil, in salted water, in a medium-large saucepan until they are fork tender (about 25 minutes). Drain, then:

1. Serve them sliced with melted butter, salt and pepper.

2. Serve them, julienned, with sour cream and ½ teaspoon garlic flakes stirred in, over low flame just long enough to heat through.
3. Mash them, season with salt, pepper and butter and pile in the center of a "Ham Ring."

Each of these variations SERVES 4 to 6.

TURNIP, KALE, MUSTARD OR DANDELION GREENS

4 lbs. greens
2 cups boiling water
1 tsp. salt
 ham bone *or* a 2-in. piece of salt pork (cut up) *or* 8 slices of bacon
½ cup brown sugar
4 tbsps. apple cider vinegar (optional)

1. Wash greens very carefully.
2. Cover with salted boiling water and add ham bone, *or* salt pork, *or* bacon.
3. Add brown sugar.
4. Cook very slowly in covered deep saucepan for about 2 hours. Remove ham bone.
5. Drain completely, chop, correct seasonings and serve.

SERVES 8.

In New England, we always served vinegar, in a cruet, with greens.

ZUCCHINI PARMESAN

6 medium zucchini
 boiling water to cover
1 tsp. salt
2 tbsps. olive oil
1 garlic clove, minced
 salt to taste
½ cup grated Parmesan-Romano cheese

1. Wash zucchini thoroughly and boil, whole, in salted water for about 10 minutes.
2. Drain *well*.
3. Cut in half lengthwise. Dry with a towel.

4. Place side by side in shallow, buttered ovenproof baking dish (11¾ x 7½ x 1¾ inches).
5. Sprinkle with olive oil mixed with garlic.
6. Salt lightly.
7. Cover each half with cheese and bake in preheated 375° oven until zucchini is tender, but still rather crispy and the cheese is melted.

SERVES 6.

CEREALS
(RICE AND BARLEY)

BARLEY RING | *Baroness Silvercruys*

1 qt. chicken stock or broth
1½ cups pearl barley
1 tsp. salt
½ cup fresh mushrooms, chopped
¼ cup chopped onions
¼ cup minced green pepper

2 tbsps. butter
½ cup sharp Cheddar cheese (grated)
2 eggs, beaten
1 bunch watercress

1. Place chicken stock or broth in a large saucepan and bring to a boil.
2. Add barley and salt, turn heat to simmer and cook for 1 hour or until barley is tender. Stir occasionally to prevent barley from sticking to bottom of pan. Add water if needed.
3. Place mushrooms, onions and green pepper in a 10-inch skillet with the butter and sauté until tender.
4. Strain barley in a colander.
5. Mix barley with grated cheese, vegetables and add beaten eggs.
6. Turn into a greased 1½-quart ring mold.
7. Place in a larger pan of hot water (about 1½ inches deep) and bake in a preheated 350° oven until firm (30 minutes). Unmold to serve and garnish with watercress.

SERVES 6.

BAKED RICE IN CHICKEN CONSOMMÉ

1 cup long-grain rice
6 small white onions, chopped
6 tbsps. butter

2 cups chicken consommé
salt to taste

1. Wash rice thoroughly and drain.
2. In a deep 10-inch skillet with a cover, lightly sauté the onions in 4 tablespoons butter.
3. Add the consommé, rice and salt.
4. Cover, in the same skillet, and bake in a preheated 350° oven for about 35 to 40 minutes or until rice is tender.
5. Uncover and separate rice grains with a fork. Add the rest of the butter. Remove from oven.
6. Stir again with fork and serve.

SERVES 4.

If you wish to do this ahead of time, transfer cooked rice mixture to top of double boiler, cover and keep hot over low boiling water.

FRIED RICE | *Puan Sri Ong*
The Embassy of Malaysia

2 lbs. uncooked long-grain rice
5½ cups chicken broth
3 tbsps. vegetable oil
4 shallot buds, peeled and sliced thin
*1½ lbs. cooked sweet roast pork, diced
*2 tbsps. dark soy sauce

8 eggs, beaten
1 (1 lb.) package frozen Alaskan crabmeat (thawed and separated)
*2 tbsps. light soy sauce
1 tbsp. sugar
1 bunch spring onions, cut in ¼-in. slices

1. Place rice (washed until water is clear) and chicken broth in a 2-quart kettle and bring to a boil over medium-high flame. Lower flame and simmer until liquid is fully absorbed by the rice. Then let rice steam in the pot (covered) over very, very low flame for 15 or 20 minutes.

* Soy sauce, both dark and light, and cooked sweet roast pork are available in Chinese grocery stores. All other ingredients are available at supermarkets. A Chinese wok is by far the best utensil to use. This, also, may be purchased in a Chinese grocery store.

2. Empty rice into a shallow (11¾ x 7½ x 1¾ inch) pan. Separate the grains and fluff with a fork. Set aside to cool for 2 to 3 hours.

3. Heat oil in a 2-quart kettle or a wok, add shallots and brown. Add pork and dark soy sauce and stir for 5 minutes. Add rice.

4. Scramble eggs and add to above with crabmeat, light soy sauce and sugar. Mix thoroughly by tossing with a large spoon and continue cooking over a medium flame for 5 minutes. Then add the onions and mix again. Serve on a heated platter.

SERVES 10 to 12.

QUICK FRIED RICE

1 cup rice
2 cups water
½ tsp. salt
5 slices bacon

4 eggs
4 minced green onions, tops and all
soy sauce to taste

1. Cook rice in salted water (following package directions). Chill in refrigerator overnight.

2. In 10-inch iron skillet, brown the bacon until crisp. Do not pour off the drippings.

3. Chop bacon in small pieces, push to side of skillet and turn down the heat.

4. Scramble four eggs in bacon drippings.

5. Add rice, onion and onion tops.

6. Add soy sauce until mixture is as brown as you desire.

7. Stir well and cook on low heat for 15 to 20 minutes.

SERVES 4.

BAKED WILD RICE

2 cups wild rice
1 (16 oz.) can tomatoes
1 cup grated Cheddar cheese
1 (3 oz.) bottle olives stuffed with pimiento (sliced)

½ cup olive oil
1 cup boiling water
1 onion, sliced fine
salt and pepper to taste

Wash rice in fresh water (about 20 times) until the water is clear.

Put all the above ingredients in a bowl, mix and let stand for 2 hours.

Place in ovenproof 2-quart round, buttered covered casserole and bake for 1 hour and 15 minutes in a 350° oven.

SERVES 8.

GREEN RICE

1 cup white rice	salt and pepper to taste
1½ cups beef consommé	1 cup heavy cream (whipped)
½ cup water	4 egg whites, beaten stiff
¼ lb. butter	3 cups "Creamed Mushrooms" (p. 224)
1 medium onion, minced	
½ cup chopped green pepper	5 pimientos, thinly sliced
4 egg yolks	¼ cup grated Parmesan cheese
½ cup minced parsley	

1. Cook rice (following package directions) in boiling beef consommé and water until tender. Drain and separate grains with a fork.

2. Sauté in butter in a 10-inch skillet, the onion and green pepper until onion is golden and pepper is tender.

3. Beat egg yolks in a large bowl. Add rice, onion, green pepper, parsley and seasonings. Fold in whipped cream and the egg whites.

4. Place in buttered 2-quart ring mold; set in a larger pan with ½ inch hot water, and cook for 40 minutes in preheated 350° oven.

5. Unmold ring on ovenproof round platter. Fill the center with "Creamed Mushrooms." Top with pimiento and cheese. Place under preheated broiler just long enough to melt the cheese. Serve at once.

SERVES 8.

RICE PILAF

3 tbsps. finely chopped onion
4 tbsps. butter
1½ cups long-grain rice
3 cups chicken stock or broth (no fat)
1 tsp. curry powder

½ cup raisins
½ cup peanuts, chopped
salt and pepper to taste
*⅛ tsp. saffron (optional)
2 tbsps. boiling water (optional)

1. Sauté onion in 3 tablespoons butter in a heatproof casserole until soft.
2. Add rice and heat together for 1 minute.
3. Add stock or broth. Bring to a boil and cover tightly.
4. Transfer to preheated 350° oven and bake for 20 minutes.
5. Add curry powder, raisins and peanuts which have been browned a bit, in a small skillet, in the remaining tablespoon of butter. Season. Keep hot in low oven until ready to serve. Stir with a fork and serve.

SERVES 6.

* For "Saffron Rice Pilaf," soak saffron in 1 tsp. boiling water for 12 minutes and add to recipe above. Omit curry powder.

SALADS
and cold mousses

One of the best salads in this section is "Maurice." I have had this many times at a Washington hotel and I attempted, desperately, to get the recipe. Bribing the head waiter and, through him, the chef, did not work at all. I tried concocting the salad myself but it was not the same. Then, three or four years later, I mentioned to a friend that I was still searching for the recipe and, miraculously, she had it.

Usually it is not difficult to ascertain the ingredients of a salad, but in some, as in "Maurice," the dressing is the catalyst.

Another recipe which took me years to acquire was "Elizabeth Arden's Salad Dressing." I became pretty sneaky on this one, for I could *not* get it. Finally I cajoled my Chinese manicurist, who had worked at one time for Miss Arden, and who still had a friendly chef at court. She managed to procure the secret for me and it is a wondrous dressing. (Be sure to serve it at room temperature or it will be too thick.)

The "Hawaiian Shrimp Salad in Papaya" and "Polynesian Cantaloupe Salad" I had enjoyed in the Pacific. Once home, by trial and error, I reproduced them. These are two more of my favorites.

For luncheon, if the salad is a simple one, I generally serve a creamed soup as a first course. If it is a rich salad, I serve a consommé with sherry or another thin soup. Accompanied by crackers or toasted Arab or Greek bread* and a compatible dessert, the menu is complete.

---

* Arab or Greek bread may be purchased in most large grocery stores. It comes frozen in large discs. Defrost them completely and cut around the edge with a very sharp knife. Slowly pry them apart. Butter and bake them in a 250° oven, on a (17 × 14 inch) cookie sheet, for about 1 hour or until they are as crisp as Melba toast. Break them in 3-inch pieces and serve very hot.

This bread is marvelous with either soups or salads. I have yet to find anyone who doesn't rhapsodize over it when they have it for the first time. When six or eight guests are, earnestly, munching (even with mouths closed as taught by loving parents), the noise is deafening and conversation comes to a grinding halt. I have been assured that it is nonfattening—except for that butter!

AVOCADOS WITH CHUTNEY SALAD

4 small avocados
8 tsps. imported chutney
8 tsps. cider vinegar
1 head Boston lettuce

Peel and cut in half four small avocados. Fill each center with chutney mixed with vinegar. Place on crisp Boston lettuce cups. Serve *very* cold.
SERVES 4.

AVOCADO STUFFED WITH FRESH CRABMEAT SALAD

2 large avocados
1 tsp. salt
1 lb. fresh Jumbo crabmeat (boned)
1 tsp. scraped onion
1 cup "Never Fail Mayonnaise" (p. 368)
2 tbsps. light cream
2 hard-boiled eggs, chopped
4 tsps. fresh minced chives
1 large bunch watercress

Peel avocados. Cut in half. Salt each half with ¼ tsp. salt.
Mix crabmeat with onion juice and ½ cup mayonnaise. Correct seasoning. Fill avocado halves with crabmeat mixture. Top each half with some of remaining mayonnaise, thinned with cream.
Sprinkle chopped egg over each avocado. Top with chives. Serve on watercress.
SERVES 4.

AVOCADO AND GRAPEFRUIT SALAD

1 white grapefruit
1 pink grapefruit
2 ripe avocados
  juice of 1 lemon
1 head iceberg lettuce
8 tbsps. "Basic French Dressing I"
  (see p. 364)

1. Peel grapefruits and remove segments. Keep as whole as possible. Cut off all the white inner skin.
2. Peel and slice avocados ½ inch thick. Sprinkle with lemon juice.
3. Place in rows on bed of "shaved" iceberg lettuce, alternating with pink and white grapefruit segments.
4. Serve with "Basic French Dressing" on chilled salad plates.
SERVES 6 to 8.
To "shave" lettuce, cut across the head with a sharp knife in ¼-inch slices.

STUFFED AVOCADO SALAD WITH TOMATO ASPIC

2 large ripe avocados
2 tsps. lemon juice
1 cup "Tomato Aspic" (see p. 297)
  softened a bit
1 large bunch watercress *or* 4 heads
  bibb lettuce
4 tbsps. mayonnaise
4 tsps. minced chives

1. Peel avocados and cut in half.
2. Sprinkle with lemon juice inside and out.
3. Fill avocados with softened aspic.
4. Place halves together again, wrap tightly, twisting ends of wrap, and place in refrigerator.
5. Refrigerate for four hours or overnight.
6. Slice each avocado (the short way) in ½-inch slices.
7. Place slices on 4 individual nests of watercress or 3 or 4 lettuce hearts.
8. Serve with mayonnaise on each serving and garnish with chives.
SERVES 4.

STUFFED AVOCADO SALAD

- 3 ripe avocados, peeled and cut in half
- juice of 1 lemon
- 4 hard-boiled eggs, chopped *or* 1 cup finely chopped, cooked shrimp
- 2 hearts of celery, minced
- ½ cup chopped watercress leaves
- 1 tsp. imported mustard
- ½ cup mayonnaise
- 2 tbsps. light cream to thin the mayonnaise
- salt and pepper to taste
- 3 jumbo green, stuffed olives, sliced
- 3 large black olives, sliced
- 6 radishes, sliced
- 4 heads bibb lettuce

1. Peel and halve avocados (the long way); sprinkle inside and out with lemon juice.
2. In bowl, mix the rest of the ingredients except the olives, radishes and lettuce.
3. Stuff the avocados with this mixture.
4. Place each avocado half on a nest of bibb lettuce on a chilled salad plate and decorate with slices of olives and radishes.

SERVES 6.

MOTHER'S BAR-LE-DUC AND CREAM CHEESE SALAD

- 1 (8 oz.) pkg. cream cheese
- ¼ cup light cream
- ½ tsp. scraped onion
- salt and pepper to taste
- 3 heads Boston lettuce (use hearts only)
- 2 jars Bar-le-Duc jelly
- ½ cup "Basic French Dressing I" (see p. 364)

1. Soften cheese, stir in cream, onion juice, salt and pepper.
2. Chill 4 salad plates. On each plate place two or three hearts of lettuce to form a cup.
3. Sprinkle Bar-le-Duc jelly over the cups.
4. Place cheese mixture in a strainer and strain over the Bar-le-Duc, using spoon to force it through.
5. Serve with tart "Basic French Dressing I."

SERVES 4.

BAY RANCH SALAD

- 1 bunch romaine lettuce
- 2 (6½ oz.) jars marinated artichoke hearts (save marinade)
- *1 lb. fresh crabmeat, Fin Lump or Jumbo (boned)
- 2 green onions, chopped
- 2 hard-cooked eggs (1 chopped, 1 sliced)
- 2 heaping tbsps. mayonnaise
- salt and pepper to taste
- 1 head romaine lettuce
- 1 small head Boston lettuce, torn

Line salad bowl with romaine lettuce. Combine half of the artichoke hearts, half the crabmeat, the onions, chopped egg, mayonnaise mixed with marinade from both jars, salt and pepper. Toss lightly with torn lettuce. Turn into romaine-lined salad bowl. Top with remaining artichoke hearts, crabmeat and sliced egg.

SERVES 4 to 6.

NANTUCKET BLUEFISH SALAD

- 2½ cups cooked flakes of bluefish (chilled)
- 1½ cups "Never Fail Mayonnaise" (see p. 368)
- 1 tsp. lemon juice
- 1 tsp. onion juice
- seasoned salt to taste
- 1 head Boston lettuce
- 4 sprigs watercress
- 4 hard-boiled eggs
- 12 slices watermelon pickle
- 8 jumbo ripe olives

1. Place flakes of fish in a bowl.
2. Mix mayonnaise with lemon juice and onion juice in a smaller bowl.
3. Toss fish with ½ cup of this sauce and add salt. Try not to break up the flakes.
4. On a chilled platter, place the salad in the center surrounded by lettuce leaves and watercress. In a design, place, alternately, the eggs, cut in half the long way, the pickle and the olives. Serve with the rest of the mayonnaise mixture in a side dish.

SERVES 4.

* Jumbo crabmeat is the top grade of crabmeat, with larger pieces, fewer bones. Fin Lump crabmeat is next grade. Jumbo is sometimes difficult to find so use Fin Lump but be careful to remove all bones. I go through it twice to be sure.

BROCCOLI SALAD

2 bunches broccoli (trimmed and cooked)
1 head Boston lettuce
1 tsp. garlic flakes

½ cup "Basic French Dressing I" (see p. 364) *or* 8 tbsps. "Never Fail Mayonnaise" (see p. 368)
1 tsp. lemon juice

For each serving place ½ bunch broccoli on crisp lettuce leaves on a chilled plate. Sprinkle with ¼ tsp. garlic flakes. Top with ⅛ cup French dressing or 2 tablespoons mayonnaise thinned with lemon juice.
SERVES 4.

EAST INDIA CABBAGE SALAD

⅓ cup creamy peanut butter
⅓ cup sour cream
1½ tbsps. brown sugar
1 tsp. curry powder
2 tbsps. lime or lemon juice
1 tbsp. soy sauce
4 drops liquid hot pepper seasoning

4 cups finely shredded crisp cabbage
½ cup chopped celery
½ cup green onion, chopped fine
10 tsps. chopped, salted peanuts *or* 2 whole pimientos, sliced (optional)

For the dressing, combine peanut butter, sour cream, brown sugar, curry powder, lime or lemon juice, soy sauce and hot pepper seasoning in the electric blender or in a bowl. Mix until well blended. This may be done ahead of time and chilled.

In a bowl, combine the cabbage with the celery and onion. Add dressing and mix lightly. Garnish with peanuts or pimientos (optional). Serve at once.
SERVES 8 to 10.

RED CABBAGE SALAD

½ head red cabbage, sliced fine
1 red onion, sliced fine
2 cups ice water
4 heads bibb lettuce (use inside leaves)

¼ cup "Basic French Dressing I" (p. 364)
seasoned salt to taste

Soak cabbage and onion in ice water for 1 hour. Drain and dry thoroughly. In salad bowl place lettuce leaves. Add cabbage and onions mixed with French dressing in the center of the bowl. Season.

SERVES 6.

CAESAR SALAD

2 cups toasted croutons
¼ cup olive oil (for croutons)
1 minced garlic bud
3 qts. salad greens (escarole, bibb, romaine), torn
3 endive (sliced)
½ cup olive oil

juice of one lemon
1 tsp. dry mustard
1 tbsp. Worcestershire sauce
¼ cup Parmesan cheese (optional)
1 (2 oz.) can anchovies, chopped
2 eggs
salt and pepper to taste

1. Sauté croutons in a 10-inch skillet in olive oil with garlic.
2. Drain on brown paper and keep crisp.
3. Place salad greens in salad bowl with endive.
4. Just before serving add in this order (tossing constantly):
    a. olive oil
    b. lemon juice
    c. mustard
    d. Worcestershire sauce
    e. Parmesan cheese (optional)
    f. anchovies
    g. eggs (raw)
    h. croutons (at last moment just before serving)
    i. seasonings
5. Toss thoroughly.

SERVES 12.

CELERY AND MUSHROOM SALAD

4 hearts of celery
1 large onion, cut up
8 mushrooms
¼ cup "Basic French Dressing I" (p. 364)
2 heads Boston or bibb lettuce
4 tbsps. minced chives
8 thin slices pimiento (optional)
4 English muffins, split
8 tbsps. grated sharp Cheddar cheese

In boiling, salted water cook whole celery hearts (4 inches long) with the onion until celery is tender, but not limp when pierced with a fork. Drain and chill. Discard onion.

While this is cooking, peel and slice mushrooms. Marinate in the refrigerator in French dressing, turning several times.

Place sliced celery hearts (1 heart for each guest) on crisp cups of lettuce. Sprinkle mushrooms on top and over each salad pour marinade from the mushrooms. Add more French dressing if necessary. Sprinkle with cut fresh chives. Decorate (optional) with crossed strips of pimiento. Serve with buttered English muffins sprinkled with cheese and broiled until cheese melts.

SERVES 4.

CELERY ROOT REMOULADE

1½ cups "Never Fail Mayonnaise" (p. 368)
½ cup finely chopped sour pickle
2 tbsps. finely chopped capers, drained and dried
1 tbsp. imported mustard (I usually use Dijon)
1 tbsp. mixed chopped parsley, tarragon and chervil (dried may be used, but fresh is better); use ½ tbsp. if dried
salt and freshly ground pepper to taste
4 raw celery roots, peeled and julienned

Mix first six ingredients well and add celery root. Chill for 4 to 5 hours.
SERVES 6 to 8.

CHEF SALAD

- 1 celery cabbage, sliced thin
- 1 head iceberg lettuce cut in bite-size pieces
- ½ bunch watercress, leaves only
- 8 small spinach leaves torn in half
- 3 endive, sliced horizontally
- 2 avocados, skinned, deseeded and cut up
- ¼ cup French dressing
- 1 (8½ oz.) jar artichoke hearts, cut in half
- ¼ lb. Swiss cheese, julienned *or* ¼ lb. Roquefort cheese, crumbled (optional)
- ½ (2 oz.) can flat anchovy filets, cut up
- 2 hard-boiled eggs, chopped
- ¾ cup cooked tongue, julienned
- ¾ cup cooked chicken, julienned
- ½ cup French dressing
- salt and freshly ground pepper to taste
- ¼ cup fresh minced chives

1. In large wooden salad bowl, toss all the greens together.
2. Marinate avocados in ¼ cup French dressing for 1 hour.
3. On top of the nest of greens in the salad bowl, in design of pie-shaped wedges, put each of the rest of the ingredients (wedge of artichoke, then the cheese, anchovies, eggs, tongue, chicken, avocados, etc.). This looks pretty on a buffet table.
4. Just before serving and after guests have seen how nice it looks, add about ½ cup French dressing, salt, pepper and chives and toss all together.

SERVES 10 to 12.

CHICKEN SALAD I

- 2½ cups cooked white meat of chicken
- 1½ cups mayonnaise
- 1 tsp. lemon juice
- 1 tsp. onion juice
- 1 tsp. "Basic French Dressing I" (p. 364)
- seasoned salt to taste
- 1 head Boston lettuce
- watercress
- 12 medium, fresh, hot "Fried Oysters" (p. 190; optional)

1. Cut chicken in ½-inch or ¼-inch cubes and place in a bowl.
2. Mix mayonnaise with lemon, onion juice and French dressing and add ¾ cup mayonnaise to chicken.
3. Season.
4. Place in center of chilled platter and surround with lettuce and watercress. Serve remaining mayonnaise mixture in a separate bowl.

SERVES 4 to 6.

My mother often served this with "Fried Oysters." The cold salad and the hot, crispy oysters may seem like incongruous bedfellows, but tastewise they are compatible.

CHICKEN SALAD II

2 cups cooked, white meat of chicken, cut in cubes about the size of croutons
½ cup diced hearts of celery
¼ cup finely chopped almonds
1 cup "Never Fail Mayonnaise" (see p. 368)
1 tsp. onion juice
salt and freshly ground pepper to taste
16 crispy inside leaves of Boston lettuce
1 cup thinly sliced red onion (separate rings)
½ cup white seedless grapes (optional)

1. In bowl, place the chicken, celery and almonds. Refrigerate covered.
2. When it is time to serve salad, stir in ½ cup of the mayonnaise mixed with the onion juice.
3. Season to taste.
4. Place chicken salad in center of round platter and surround with lettuce leaves. Arrange the onion rings on the lettuce around the salad.
5. Serve with side dish of extra mayonnaise.

I usually soak the lettuce leaves and onion rings in ice water for 1 hour. Drain and dry completely with a towel.

SERVES 4.

Sometimes I add seedless white grapes and omit the almonds and red onion.

CHICKEN AND RICE SALAD

- 2 cups cooked rice
- 3 cups diced, cooked chicken or turkey
- 1 cup slivered almonds
- ½ cup minced onion
- 1½ cups mayonnaise
- 3 tbsps. curry powder
- ¼ cup soy sauce
- 2 tbsps. vinegar
- 2 heads Boston lettuce
- 1 (5 oz.) jar pimientos

Cook rice according to package directions. Rinse and refrigerate overnight. Add chicken, almonds and onion. Combine mayonnaise with the curry powder, soy sauce and vinegar. Mix the rice-chicken mixture with the dressing and chill. Place on chilled platter surrounded with lettuce leaves and decorated with pimientos.

SERVES 6 to 8.

HOT CHICKEN SALAD

- 2 (3½ oz.) pkgs. potato chips, crushed
- 2 cups diced white meat of chicken (large pieces)
- 1½ cups chopped celery
- 2 tbsps. minced onion
- 1 tbsp. lemon juice
- 1 (5 oz.) jar pimientos
- 1 (10½ oz.) can cream of mushroom soup
- ¾ cup commercial mayonnaise
- 1 cup grated American cheese

Place layer of potato chips on bottom of buttered (8 x 8 x 2 inch) ovenproof, square casserole. Combine next seven ingredients and place on potato chips. Combine remaining chips with cheese and place on top. Bake in a preheated oven at 450° for only 15 minutes.

SERVES 4.

GARDEN COLE SLAW

1 cup finely shredded green cabbage, loosely packed
1 cup finely grated carrots, loosely packed
½ cup finely chopped celery hearts
4 tbsps. finely chopped green pepper
½ cup finely chopped pared cucumber
½ tsp. salt
2 tbsps. mayonnaise
2 tsps. finely grated onion (pulp and juice)
3 tbsps. sweet pickle relish

Mix all the above thoroughly. Chill in refrigerator until very cold. SERVES 4 to 6.

NORA'S COLE SLAW

1 tsp. salt
¼ tsp. pepper
½ tsp. dry mustard
½ to 1 tsp. celery seed
2 tbsps. sugar
¼ cup chopped green pepper
½ tsp. grated onion
3 tbsps. vegetable oil
⅓ cup white vinegar
3 cups finely chopped cabbage
1 bunch watercress
6 stuffed green olives, sliced

Place all except watercress and olives in large bowl in above order. Mix, cover and chill.
Garnish with watercress and olives just before serving.
SERVES 4 to 6.

ALASKAN KING CRAB REMOULADE

1 (1 lb.) pkg. Alaskan king crab (frozen)
2 heads bibb lettuce
1 cup "Remoulade Sauce" (see p. 337)

Thaw crabmeat. Remove bones carefully. Pat *very* dry with paper towels. Keep in original "finger" shape.

Arrange on 4 chilled salad plates on a bed of lettuce leaves. Serve with side dish of "Remoulade Sauce."
SERVES 4 as a first course.

CRABMEAT OR SHRIMP SALAD

2½ lbs. fresh boned Jumbo or Fin Lump crabmeat *or* 2½ lbs. cooked shrimp
¼ cup "Never Fail Mayonnaise" (see p. 368)
juice of 1 lemon
1 tsp. scraped onion

seasoned salt to taste
2 heads Boston lettuce
10 black olives
5 tomatoes (skinned and sliced)
1 cup mayonnaise (for side dish)
juice of ½ lemon (for side dish)

Place crabmeat or shrimp in large bowl. Add mayonnaise mixed with lemon juice. Add onion juice and seasoned salt.

Place crabmeat or shrimp mixture in center of chilled round platter. Surround with lettuce, olives and tomatoes.

Serve mayonnaise mixed with the juice of ½ lemon in separate bowl.
SERVES 10.

CUCUMBER SALAD

4 tbsps. sour cream
2 tbsps. white wine vinegar
1 tsp. salt
¼ tsp. white pepper
2 large cucumbers, peeled and thinly sliced

1 medium red onion, thinly sliced
2 heads Boston lettuce
1 to 2 tbsps. chopped fresh dill

Blend together cream, vinegar, salt and pepper. Mix with cucumber and onion and chill for several hours in refrigerator. Just before serving on lettuce leaves, sprinkle with chopped dill.
SERVES 6 to 8.

CUCUMBER VINAIGRETTE | *Puan Sri Ong*
The Embassy of Malaysia

3 cucumbers
¼ tsp. salt
¼ lb. sugar
½ cup white vinegar

Wash cucumbers. Pare, but not completely. Leave on a few strips of skin. Cut cucumbers into halves (lengthwise); remove all seeds with a spoon, then cut again lengthwise. Slice cucumbers diagonally (about ⅛ inch thick). Add salt; mix thoroughly. Let stand for about 5 minutes. Then squeeze the water out of the cucumbers by placing in a towel and twisting it hard. Add sugar and vinegar. Mix thoroughly and let stand for 1 hour. Drain and save juice for use in sauce for "Sweet-Sour Pork."

SERVES 8 to 10.

EGG AND SWISS CHEESE SALAD

1 celery cabbage, sliced fine
1 head curly endive lettuce, cut up
4 hard-boiled eggs, chopped fine
4 slices imported Swiss cheese, chopped fine
¼ cup "Basic French Dressing I" (p. 364)
¼ cup "Never Fail Mayonnaise" (p. 368)
salt and pepper to taste
4 to 6 imported sardines, 1 (3¾ oz.) can

1. In wooden salad bowl, put the celery cabbage and lettuce.
2. Mix in the eggs and cheese.
3. Just before serving, mix the French dressing and mayonnaise together and toss into salad.
4. Season.
5. On top of the salad, place the sardines in a row.

SERVES 6.

ENDIVE, MUSHROOM AND WATERCRESS SALAD

8 Belgian endive
½ lb. fresh mushrooms, sliced
2 bunches watercress, leaves only
¼ to ½ cup "Basic French Dressing I" (p. 364)
salt and freshly ground pepper to taste

Wash and cut up endive and place in salad bowl. Add mushrooms and watercress. Toss, just before serving, with French dressing and seasoning.
SERVES 6 to 8.

FENNEL SALAD

4 large bulbs fennel (cut off long stems)
1 garlic clove (peeled and halved)
2 tbsps. olive oil
salt and pepper to taste
boiling water with 1 tsp. salt
3 heads bibb lettuce
6 tbsps. "Basic French Dressing I" (p. 364)
12 green, stuffed olives, finely chopped

1. In 4-quart saucepan, combine the fennel, garlic, olive oil, seasonings and boiling water to cover. Boil until the fennel is tender but still holds its shape.
2. Drain completely and pat dry with tea towel. Chill overnight.
3. Slice and serve on a bed of bibb lettuce (4 or 5 fennel slices per person).
4. Pour over French dressing.
5. Scatter olives on top.
SERVES 6.

EAST INDIAN FISH SALAD

- 2 cups cold rice (cooked according to pkg. directions)
- ¼ cup "Basic French Dressing I" (p. 364)
- 1½ cups boned, flaked, cooked fish (haddock or bluefish)
- 1 tbsp. lemon juice
- ¼ cup commercial mayonnaise
- ½ tsp. curry powder
- ½ cup chopped celery
- 1 tbsp. chopped chutney
- ½ cup cooked peas
- ½ tsp. salt
- 2 heads Boston lettuce

Fold together rice and French dressing. Chill 1 hour. Sprinkle fish with lemon juice. Chill. Mix mayonnaise and curry powder. Toss together rice, fish, mayonnaise, celery, chutney, peas and salt. Place in center of chilled platter surrounded by lettuce.

SERVES 6 to 8.

FRUIT SALAD

- 1 cup fresh pineapple cubes
- 1 cup fresh peaches, peeled, deseeded and sliced
- 1 cup fresh papaya, peeled, deseeded and sliced
- ½ cup fresh strawberries
- ½ cup fresh melon balls
- 2 heads Boston lettuce
- ¼ cup "Basic French Dressing I" (p. 364)
- 1 tsp. curry powder (optional)

Prepare fruits and place in center of chilled round platter. Surround with crisp lettuce hearts and serve with French dressing. Add curry (optional).

SERVES 8.

CRISPY GREEN SALAD

½ lb. mushrooms, sliced
1 cup "Basic French Dressing I" (p. 364)
8 heads bibb lettuce
½ cup chopped celery
8 green onions, sliced
1 (6½ oz.) jar of artichoke hearts with oil
4 endive, cut up
¼ cup cauliflower buds (raw)
1 small zucchini, sliced (unpeeled)
1 small yellow summer squash, sliced (unpeeled)
1 red onion, sliced thin
salt and pepper to taste

Marinate mushrooms in ½ cup French dressing for 1 hour. Toss well.
Chill next nine ingredients and place in large salad bowl. Add mushrooms and their marinade and season. Add the rest of the French dressing.
SERVES 12 to 14.

GUACAMOLE (MEXICAN)

2 large ripe avocados, peeled and mashed
2 tsps. lemon or lime juice
salt to taste
2 tomatoes, peeled, seeded and chopped
1 medium yellow onion, grated
1 small hot green or red chili pepper, minced *or* 1 sweet pepper (if less heat is desired)
1 tbsp. olive oil
watercress or lettuce

Add lemon juice and salt to avocado. Blend avocado, tomato, onion and chili (or sweet) pepper. Add olive oil. Correct seasonings. Serve in avocado shells or in a bowl. Garnish with watercress or crisp lettuce leaves.
SERVES 5 or 6.

HEALTH SALAD

- 8 raw mushrooms (sliced)
- 4 shredded carrots
- 1 small green cabbage (shredded)
- ½ cup chopped celery
- ¼ cup raisins
- 1 tsp. onion juice
- ½ cup sour cream
- ½ cup "Never Fail Mayonnaise" (p. 368)
- salt and pepper to taste
- garlic salt to taste
- 2 heads Boston lettuce

Put first six ingredients together in a bowl.
Add sour cream, mayonnaise, salt, pepper and garlic salt.
Serve in chilled, silver bowl on lettuce leaves.
SERVES 8 to 10.

LOBSTER SALAD

- 2 lbs. cooked, fresh lobster meat, cut up (save claws whole)
- 2 cups "Never Fail Mayonnaise" (p. 368)
- 1 tsp. lemon juice
- 1 tsp. scraped onion
- 2 tbsps. French dressing
- seasoned salt to taste
- 4 heads bibb lettuce
- 1 sprig watercress

In bowl place lobster meat. Add 1 cup mayonnaise, lemon juice, onion juice, French dressing and seasoned salt. Mix well.

Place lobster mixture in center of chilled round platter. Surround with lettuce leaves and garnish with lobster claws and watercress.

Serve rest of mayonnaise in side dish.
SERVES 6.

AFRICAN LOBSTER TAILS SALAD

4 (½ lb.) lobster tails (frozen)
water to cover
salt to taste
1 cup "Never Fail Mayonnaise" (p. 368)
½ tsp. tarragon
½ tsp. grated onion
juice of ½ lemon
seasoned salt to taste
1 head Boston lettuce
parsley

Defrost lobsters. Bring water to a rolling boil. Add salt. Drop in lobster tails and when water comes to a boil again, boil for 8 minutes. Drain and cool. Crack shells, remove meat and cut in ½-inch cubes. Chill, covered.

Mix mayonnaise with tarragon, onion and lemon juice and add seasoned salt. Mix, in a bowl, ½ the mayonnaise mixture with the lobster.

On 4 chilled salad plates, place dry, chilled lettuce leaves to form a cup. Place a fourth of the lobster mixture in center of each lettuce cup. Top with a sprig of parsley. Serve rest of mayonnaise in a side dish.

SERVES 4.

MAURICE SALAD

1 large head iceberg lettuce, cut in bite-sized pieces
1 cup julienned cooked white meat of chicken
1 cup julienned strips of cooked ham
1 firm medium tomato, peeled and cut in small pieces

Dressing:
½ cup olive oil
½ cup mayonnaise
2 tbsps. sweet pickle juice (from jar of candied dill strips)
¼ cup apple cider vinegar
1 tbsp. Worcestershire sauce
3 hard-boiled eggs, minced
1 tbsp. onion, minced
¼ cup candied dill strips, minced
1 tsp. Veg-e-sal

Beat first five dressing ingredients together well. Add egg, onion, dill strips and Veg-e-sal (from health store). Stir together and just before serving, toss with the salad.

SERVES 6.

With this hearty salad I serve:

> "Cold Mushroom Soup"
> "Cheese Popovers"
> Fresh Fruits (Cut-up) in a Chilled Bowl
> Cookies or "Daffodil Cake"
> Iced Tea or Iced Coffee

MANDARIN ORANGE AND WHITE GRAPE SALAD

- 2 heads Boston lettuce (torn)
- 2 (11 oz.) cans mandarin oranges (drained and chilled)
- 1 cup white seedless grapes cut in half
- salt and pepper to taste
- ½ cup "Basic French Dressing I" (p. 364)

Toss all ingredients together.

SERVES 6 to 8.

Good with seafood such as "Shrimp with Wild Rice" (p. 201).

SALADE NIÇOISE

- 6 Irish potatoes
- ¼ cup white wine
- salt and pepper to taste
- ¾ cup "Sauce Vinaigrette II" (p. 339)
- 4 tomatoes, cut in wedges
- 6 hard-boiled eggs, halved
- 1 shallot, minced
- 2 cups long string beans, cooked and chilled
- 1 head Boston lettuce (dried and chilled)
- ½ cup capers
- 16 Italian black olives
- 6 anchovies
- 1 (12½ oz.) can tunafish (flaked)

1. Steam potatoes in a vegetable steamer for 20 minutes and cool. Peel. Add ⅛ cup wine.
2. Combine salt and pepper with potatoes and slice. Add rest of wine.
3. Make "Sauce Vinaigrette II," and, sparingly, marinate tomatoes, eggs, shallot and beans separately in part of the sauce.
4. Place separated chilled leaves of lettuce on platter. Put potatoes in center. Make pattern of tomatoes and string beans with eggs in between. Place capers and olives in small mounds in between. Place anchovies on eggs and pile tuna-fish on potatoes. Sprinkle on rest of the sauce.

SERVES 8.

FROZEN PEAR SALAD

1 (1 lb. 4 oz.) can pear halves in heavy syrup
2 tbsps. sugar
½ cup water
1 tsp. lemon juice
whole peel of 1 lemon, spiraled

2 heads Boston lettuce
½ cup "Boiled Dressing II" (p. 364) *or* ½ cup commercial mayonnaise
½ cup heavy cream (whipped stiff)
½ tsp. curry powder (optional)

Cut pears in small to medium pieces and put pears in a 1-quart refrigerator tray. Heat pear syrup (from can) in a small saucepan and add sugar, water, lemon juice and lemon peel. When sugar is dissolved, and mixture has thickened a bit, remove peel, pour syrup over pears and place to freeze in refrigerator overnight. To serve, cut in 2-inch slices and place on lettuce nests. Serve with "Boiled Dressing II" beaten into whipped cream (½ tsp. curry powder may be added to the dressing).

SERVES 8 to 10.

Peaches or apricots may be substituted for pears.

STUFFED PEAR SALAD WITH CREAM CHEESE AND GRAPE JELLY

1 (8 oz.) pkg. cream cheese
¼ cup cream
 onion juice to taste
 salt and pepper to taste
8 pear halves (1 lb. 4 oz. can) *or* 4 fresh pears, peeled and halved

12 Boston lettuce hearts
8 tbsps. grape jelly
½ cup "Basic French Dressing I" (p. 364)

1. Soften cheese and blend with cream, onion juice and seasonings until smooth.
2. Stuff cheese mixture in 4 pear halves and top with another half.
3. Wrap each stuffed pear separately in refrigerator wrap and refrigerate for 1 hour.
4. Unwrap pears and place each whole pear on cup of three crispy lettuce leaves.
5. Dot each pear with small pieces of grape jelly (about six dots to each).
6. Serve with French dressing.

SERVES 4.

POLYNESIAN CHICKEN CANTALOUPE SALAD

This is an unusual, refreshing summer salad and one of my best.

2 ripe cantaloupes
2 cups cooked white meat of chicken, cut in ½-in. cubes
½ cup seedless green grapes, halved
½ cup finely cut celery
2 tbsps. toasted slivered almonds
¾ cup "Never Fail Mayonnaise" (see p. 368)

¾ cup sour cream
1 tsp. dark soy sauce
½ tsp. curry powder
1 tsp. salt or more to taste
1 bunch fresh mint or 1 bunch watercress

Halve melons. Remove pulp carefully and cut in ½-inch cubes. Sawtooth edges of melon shells. Combine melon cubes, chicken, grapes, celery and almonds. Mix together next five ingredients. Add ¾ cup of this sauce to melon mixture and toss. Serve in melon shells surrounded by fresh mint or watercress on chilled salad plates.

Serve rest of sauce in a separate dish.

SERVES 4.

EDNA ALTEMUS' POTATO SALAD

12 Irish potatoes
    boiling water to cover
¼ cup apple cider vinegar
2 medium onions, minced
1 cup minced celery
2 tbsps. celery leaves, minced
    salt and pepper to taste
3 tbsps. commercial mayonnaise

Boil potatoes in their skins until they are done. Be sure they are still firm. Peel, cool and cube. Place potatoes in large bowl.

Sprinkle with vinegar, folding from the bottom of the bowl up and over with your hands. This way the potatoes do not get mushy. Add onion, celery and celery leaves. Season and add the mayonnaise. Continue to fold over with your hands.

Let stand, covered, overnight if possible, in refrigerator.

SERVES 10.

POTATO AND EGG SALAD

12 medium Irish potatoes
4 hard-boiled eggs, cut up
1 tbsp. celery seed
1 cup finely cut celery
1 tbsp. scraped onion
½ cup "Never Fail Mayonnaise" (p. 368)
½ cup light cream
    salt and pepper to taste

Cook potatoes and place in refrigerator on the day before serving; leave the peel on. The next day, peel and cut them in ½-inch cubes or chunks. Mix with eggs, celery seed, celery, onion juice, mayonnaise, cream and salt and pepper.

SERVES 8 to 10.

CREOLE SHRIMP IN REMOULADE SAUCE

- 4 tbsps. olive oil
- 2 tbsps. tarragon vinegar
- 1 cup chopped celery
- ½ cup chopped green onions
- ¼ cup chopped parsley
- 2 tbsps. imported mustard (I usually use Dijon)
- 2 tsps. prepared horseradish
- 1 tsp. salt
- ⅛ tsp. seasoned pepper
- 1½ lbs. cooked shrimp, deveined and shelled
- 1 head Boston lettuce
- 4 hard-boiled eggs (sliced)

Combine first five ingredients in an electric blender (1 minute) or if not done in blender, chop onions, celery and parsley very fine and then blend in oil and vinegar. Stir in mustard, horseradish, salt and pepper.

Pour this sauce over shrimp in a large bowl and toss. Cover bowl. Chill 4 hours or overnight.

Place shrimp on inside leaves of lettuce in salad bowl and garnish with egg slices.

SERVES 6 to 8.

MARINATED SHRIMP SALAD

- 2 tbsps. wine vinegar
- 6 tbsps. olive oil
- 1 tbsp. paprika
- 4 tsps. prepared mustard
- ½ tsp. salt
- ½ celery heart, chopped fine
- ½ small white onion, chopped fine
- 1 tbsp. chopped parsley
- 1½ lbs. cold, boiled shrimp, shelled and deveined
- 2 heads Boston lettuce
- 4 stuffed olives, sliced
- 1 (2 oz.) jar whole pimientos, cut in ¼-in. strips

Mix vinegar, oil, paprika, mustard, salt, celery, onion and parsley in a bowl. Pour over shrimp. Cover and place in refrigerator for 2 hours or overnight to chill.

Serve in nests of crispy inside lettuce leaves and garnish with olives and pimiento strips.

SERVES 4 to 6.

HAWAIIAN SHRIMP SALAD IN PAPAYA

This is my best salad!

2 ripe papayas, peeled and cut in half	2 cups cooked shrimp, shelled, deveined and cut in half
juice from 1 lime	3 heads bibb lettuce
½ cup "Never Fail Mayonnaise" (p. 368)	4 whole cooked shrimp, shelled and deveined
1 tsp. lemon juice	4 sprigs watercress
½ tsp. curry powder	4 English muffins
½ tsp. onion juice	4 tsps. butter
salt and pepper to taste	½ cup grated sharp Cheddar cheese
1 tsp. apple juice	

1. Sprinkle papayas with lime juice on the inside.
2. Mix the mayonnaise with lemon juice, curry powder, onion juice, salt and pepper and thin a bit with apple juice. Put aside 4 teaspoons of this mixture.
3. Stir the shrimp halves with the rest of the mayonnaise mixture and fill the center of the papaya halves.
4. Place each half on a bed of crisp lettuce.
5. Top each with 1 teaspoon reserved mayonnaise, a whole shrimp and a tiny sprig of watercress.

Serve with fork-split English muffins, buttered, sprinkled with grated cheese and broiled.

SERVES 4.

With this I serve:

Hot Consommé Flavored with Sherry
Hot Crackers
Pineapple or Lime Sherbet
"Lace Cookies"
Iced Tea or Coffee

SHRIMP RING

1 envelope (1 tbsp.) plain gelatin
¼ cup cold water
2 (10½ oz.) cans tomato soup
1 cup milk
4 (3 oz.) pkgs. cream cheese
2 lbs. cooked shrimp, cut up
2½ cups "Never Fail Mayonnaise" (p. 368)
1 cup chopped celery
½ cup finely chopped white onion
1 cup chopped green pepper, very fine
salt and pepper to taste
2 bunches watercress
1 tbsp. lemon juice

1. Dissolve gelatin in cold water.
2. In saucepan, heat soup and milk. Add gelatin and stir to dissolve. Add cream cheese and mix together until smooth and cheese is melted.
3. Cool and add shrimp, 1½ cups mayonnaise, celery, onion, green pepper, salt and pepper.
4. Place in a 2-quart ring mold which has been rinsed in cold water. Cover with refrigerator wrap and chill overnight.
5. Unmold on round platter and surround with watercress.
6. Mix remaining mayonnaise with the lemon juice and serve in separate bowl.

SERVES 10.

SPINACH SALAD

6 cups spinach leaves torn in half (no stems)
8 slices crisp, cooked bacon (chopped)
1 tbsp. finely chopped onion (red or Bermuda)
salt and pepper to taste
1 cup "Maria Blake's Mustard Sauce" (p. 336)

Crisp spinach in ice water, dry carefully, add bacon and onion. Season. Mix with mustard sauce just before serving.

SERVES 4 to 6.

LORET HAYDEN'S SPECIAL SALAD

1 head iceberg lettuce, cut up
4 unskinned tomatoes, cut up
1 cucumber, peeled and cubed
3 endive, sliced
½ cup minced heart of celery

4 hearts of palm, sliced
10 stuffed olives, sliced
½ cup raw cauliflower buds, cut up
6 mushroom caps, raw and sliced

Mix all ingredients in salad bowl and toss with "Loret Hayden's Salad Dressing." It is the dressing that makes this salad special.
SERVES 8.

SWEETBREAD AND CUCUMBER SALAD

This is a delicious summer salad.

2 lbs. sweetbreads, cooked and cubed (p. 120)
2 cucumbers, pared and cubed
1 cup "Never Fail Mayonnaise (p. 368) with 1 tsp. lemon juice
salt and pepper to taste

½ tsp. tarragon (optional)
3 heads bibb lettuce
4 tomatoes, peeled and sliced
14 largest size black olives
14 green stuffed olives (with pimiento)

In large bowl, mix the first five ingredients.
SERVES 6 to 8.

I often serve this salad in the center of "Ham Mousse Ring II." If there is any left over, after the ring center is filled, pile at either end of the platter. Surround the ring with crisp lettuce, tomato slices, and black and green olives in a pattern. Serve extra mayonnaise in a side dish.

TOMATO STUFFED WITH PINEAPPLE, RED ONION AND CUCUMBER

- 4 large, firm tomatoes, peeled and chilled
- 1 tsp. salt
- ½ cup chopped cucumber, peeled
- 2 tbsps. red onion, chopped
- ½ cup crushed pineapple (drained)
- ¾ cup "Never Fail Mayonnaise" (p. 368)
- 1 head Boston lettuce
- 2 tbsps. cream

Scoop out tomato seeds and pulp. Turn upside down and then salt inside. Fill with cucumber, onion and pineapple, mixed with 4 tablespoons mayonnaise.

Serve in lettuce cups with remaining mayonnaise, thinned with the cream, in a separate side dish.

SERVES 4.

LEFTOVER VEGETABLE SALAD TOM BLAKE

- 1 cup string beans (cooked)
- 1 cup peas (cooked)
- ½ cup corn (cooked)
- 4 tbsps. red onion, chopped
- ½ cup finely chopped celery
- 4 tbsps. commercial mayonnaise
- 1 tbsp. dark soy sauce
- Crazy-Salt to taste
- 2 heads Boston lettuce

Mix first eight ingredients well and serve in lettuce cups.
SERVES 4 to 6.
Crazy-Salt is available in the spice section of specialty grocery stores.

One of the joys of a molded salad or salad mousse is the fact that it may be made the day before the luncheon. The next day all you need do is unmold it, garnish it attractively, and it's ready to serve.

MOLDED AVOCADO SALAD

1 (3 oz.) pkg. lime gelatin mix
1 cup boiling water
3 tbsps. lemon juice
½ tsp. salt
1 tbsp. green pepper
1 tbsp. onion, cut fine
½ cup heavy cream, whipped
¼ cup light cream and ¼ cup mayonnaise (mixed)
1 large avocado *or* 2 small avocados, cut in small cubes
1 bunch watercress
1 head iceberg lettuce
1 cup mayonnaise
juice of ½ lemon

Dissolve gelatin in boiling water, refrigerate, and when it begins to thicken, whip with egg beater and fold in all the other ingredients except lettuce, 1 cup mayonnaise and juice of ½ lemon.

Place in a wet 1-quart ring mold and refrigerate overnight. Carefully separate inside leaves of the lettuce, place on a round chilled platter and unmold avocado ring in the center. (To unmold, place hot, wet cloth over ring until the mold loosens). Garnish with watercress. Serve with 1 cup mayonnaise mixed with lemon juice.

SERVES 8.

AVOCADO MOUSSE

2 envelopes (2 tbsps.) gelatin
¼ cup cold water
1 cup chicken stock
1 tsp. (about) salt
2 cups mashed avocado
2 tbsps. lemon juice
1 cup mayonnaise (commercial)
1 cup heavy cream, stiffly beaten
few drops green vegetable coloring
1 large bunch watercress

Soften gelatin in cold water. Dissolve in boiling chicken stock. Add salt. Let stand until slightly thickened.

Stir avocado to smooth paste with lemon juice. Blend in gelatin mixture, then mayonnaise and lastly fold in whipped cream. Add coloring matter; place in 6-cup ring mold that has been greased with mayonnaise. Refrigerate overnight. Unmold and garnish around edge with watercress.

SERVES approximately 8.

Fill center of ring with 4 cups "Fruit Salad" or "Shrimp," "Crab" or "Lobster Salad."

RED CAVIAR MOUSSE

6 oz. red caviar
¼ cup finely chopped parsley
1 tbsp. grated onion
1 tsp. grated lemon peel
1 pt. sour cream
1 cup heavy cream, whipped

2 envelopes (2 tbsps.) plain gelatin
¼ cup water
freshly ground pepper to taste
1 bunch watercress
120 sliced party pumpernickel rounds
1 cup soft sweet butter

1. Combine caviar, parsley, onion and lemon rind in large bowl.
2. Stir in the sour cream.
3. In another bowl, whip heavy cream.
4. Sprinkle gelatin over the water in a saucepan over low heat, stirring until it is completely dissolved.
5. Stir gelatin into caviar and sour-cream mixture.
6. Fold in whipped cream and add pepper.
7. Pour into a 2-quart wet mold.
8. Cover with refrigerator wrap and chill in refrigerator overnight.
9. Unmold by running a sharp knife around the edge, turning upside down and shaking loose.
10. Surround with watercress and serve with small rounds of pumpernickel buttered lightly.

SERVES 35 to 40 as a canapé.

CHICKEN ASPIC

- 2 envelopes (2 tbsps.) gelatin
- 1 cup cold water
- 1 onion
- 1 stalk celery
- ½ tsp. dried tarragon
- salt and pepper to taste
- 2 cups chicken stock or broth
- ⅛ tsp. A-1 sauce
- 1 tsp. Worcestershire sauce
- 2 cups cooked (cold) chicken, cut in thin strips
- ⅓ cup pimiento
- ½ tbsp. finely chopped parsley
- 12 ripe olives, cut in half
- 1 bunch watercress
- ⅔ cup "Tarragon Sauce" (p. 338)

1. Sprinkle gelatin with cold water and let set for 5 minutes in a bowl.
2. Add onion, celery, tarragon, and seasoning to the stock in a saucepan and bring to the boiling point. Boil for 3 minutes, strain, pour over gelatin and stir until gelatin is dissolved.
3. Add A-1 sauce and Worcestershire sauce.
4. Rinse an (8½ x 4½ x 2 inch) glass loaf pan with cold water.
5. Pour ½ of the aspic in the bottom of the pan and chill. When the mixture begins to thicken, arrange ½ the chicken, ½ the pimiento, ½ the parsley and ½ the olives in a design and chill until set.
6. Then add another ½-inch layer of aspic and chill. When beginning to set, add another layer of chicken, pimientos, parsley and olives, and end with aspic.
7. Refrigerate, covered, overnight. Unmold on platter. Surround with watercress and serve with side dish of "Tarragon Sauce."

SERVES 8 to 10.

JELLIED CHICKEN SALAD MOLD

- 1 (5 lb.) roasting chicken
- cold water to cover
- 1 medium onion, peeled and quartered
- 2 stalks celery, broken up
- 1 carrot, peeled and quartered
- 2 sprigs parsley
- 5 whole peppercorns
- 1 tsp. dried tarragon
- 2 envelopes (2 tbsps.) plain gelatin
- ½ cup cold water
- salt to taste
- watercress
- 1 cup "Tarragon Sauce" (p. 338)

1. Place chicken in a deep 4-quart kettle. Add enough cold water to just cover the chicken. Bring slowly to a boil and add onion, celery, carrot, parsley

and peppercorns. Cover, turn heat down to simmer and cook about 50 minutes. Let chicken cool in the stock in the kettle.

2. Remove chicken, skin and remove meat from the bones. Cut meat in ½-inch cubes and set aside. Remove *all* fat from top of stock left in the kettle. Strain stock. Place in 2-quart saucepan and add tarragon. Boil hard until but 1 quart of stock is left (measure carefully). Strain stock again and keep hot.

3. Place gelatin in a large bowl and sprinkle with the cold water. Add the hot stock and stir until gelatin is dissolved. Add salt and set aside to cool in a wet (9½ x 5½ x 2½ inch) loaf pan. When cool and thickened a bit, add all the meat of the chicken, distributing it evenly in the pan. Cover with refrigerator wrap and chill overnight.

4. To serve: Unmold on a chilled oblong platter. Garnish with watercress and serve "Tarragon Sauce" in a separate bowl.

SERVES 8 to 10.

This is a mold which I serve, usually in the summer months, with:

"Cold Mushroom Soup" or "Gaspacho"
Hot Buttered Crackers
"Hot Buttered Fresh Asparagus"
"Popovers"
"Pineapple Sherbet with Black Bing Cherries in Brandy"
"Sponge Cake"
Iced Tea or Iced Coffee

CHICKEN AND CUCUMBER MOUSSE

2½ cups chicken stock or broth
3 envelopes (3 tbsps.) plain gelatin
¼ cup cold water
1½ cups cubed potatoes
1 bunch scallions, chopped (chop tops separately)
salt and pepper to taste
dash of cayenne
3 cups light cream

½ cup finely chopped cucumber (without seeds)
6 cups cooked chicken put through grinder
60 slices serrated cucumber
1 bunch watercress
2 cups "Never Fail Mayonnaise" (p. 368)
2 tsp. lemon juice

1. Heat chicken stock and add to gelatin which has been covered with cold water. Cool.

2. Cook potatoes and bottoms of scallions in a saucepan until soft. Press through a sieve (makes about 3 cups of purée). Add salt, pepper and cayenne.

3. Add cream, chopped tops of scallions, cucumber and chicken. Mix well and put in two (1½ quart) ring molds which have been rinsed in cold water. Refrigerate overnight.

4. Unmold and surround with cucumber slices and watercress. Serve with mayonnaise mixed with lemon juice.

SERVES 20.

CHICKEN MOUSSE SUPREME

1 envelope (1 tbsp.) plain gelatin
¼ cup cold water
2 cups chicken stock or broth
2 tsps. powdered chicken concentrate
2 cups mayonnaise
1 cup cooked, white meat of chicken, ground
1 small onion, grated with juice
½ cup finely chopped celery
½ cucumber, peeled and diced
1 (2 oz.) jar sliced pimientos, chopped

1 tsp. lemon juice
salt and pepper to taste
3 heads bibb lettuce
1 (1 lb. 4 oz.) can pineapple chunks (save juice)
1 cup papaya (fresh or in a 16-oz. jar), cut up
¼ cup fresh mint, chopped
*1 cucumber, serrated and sliced
1 bunch watercress
1 cup "Blender Mayonnaise" or "Never Fail" (pp. 367 and 368)
2 tbsps. pineapple juice

Dissolve gelatin in water in a large bowl. Heat chicken broth and add chicken concentrate. Pour over gelatin and mix mayonnaise in with a rotary beater. Add chicken to above mixture. Add onion, celery, cucumber, pimiento and lemon juice. Stir and season. Place in 6-cup wet ring mold and refrigerate overnight, covered. Unmold on a cold oval platter and surround with lettuce.

Put pineapple in a bowl and add papaya. Mix and fill center of ring. Sprinkle with chopped mint. Place cucumber slices around platter and garnish with watercress. Mix mayonnaise well with pineapple juice. Serve in separate bowl.

SERVES 10.

* To serrate cucumber, stand cucumber on its end and hold firm. With a fork, dig down the sides in stripes all the way around.

Suggested Menu

"Cold Consommé with Caviar"
Hot Buttered Crackers
"Chicken Mousse Supreme"
English Muffins Toasted with Sharp Cheese
Fresh Raspberries and Cream
"Macaroons"
Coffee   Tea

CHICKEN CURRY MOUSSE

6 tbsps. butter
1 Bermuda onion, minced
2 apples, cored and chopped
1½ cups cold water
3 cups chicken broth
1 tsp. cloves
2 sticks cinnamon
2 tbsps. curry powder

salt to taste
2½ envelopes (2½ tbsps.) plain gelatin
4 cups heavy cream, whipped
5 cups cooked, chopped chicken
2 cups mayonnaise *or* small bowls of chopped peanuts, chopped coconut and bowl of Indian chutney

1. In 10-inch iron skillet, melt the butter.
2. Add the onion, apple and 1 cup water.
3. Cook until onion and apple are tender.
4. Mix above in blender for ½ minute.
5. In saucepan, place the chicken broth, cloves, cinnamon, curry powder and salt.
6. Bring to a boil, then turn heat to simmer and cook for 30 minutes or more. After straining, you should have 2 cups. If more, continue to cook until you do have 2 cups.
7. Dissolve gelatin in ½ cup cold water. Then stir into the above broth until gelatin is dissolved.
8. Combine with the puréed apple and onion. Blend again in the blender until smooth and fold in the whipped cream.
9. Correct seasonings.
10. Chill in refrigerator until mixture is just starting to set.
11. Stir in the chicken and place mixture in two (2 quart) ring molds which have been rinsed in cold water.

12. Cover with refrigerator wrap and chill overnight.

13. Serve with mayonnaise or chopped peanuts, chopped coconut and Indian chutney.

SERVES 20.

CORNED BEEF MOUSSE

1 (12 oz.) can corned beef
1 (3 oz.) pkg. lemon gelatin
½ cup water, cold
1 (10½ oz.) can beef consommé
1 small onion, chopped fine
1 tbsp. green pepper, chopped fine
3 hard-boiled eggs, chopped fine

1 cup celery, chopped fine
2 cups mayonnaise
salt and pepper to taste
4 tomatoes, peeled and sliced
2 cucumbers, unpeeled and sliced thin
1 bunch watercress

1. Chop corned beef.
2. Sprinkle lemon gelatin over water in a bowl.
3. Heat consommé in saucepan and pour over gelatin until gelatin is thoroughly dissolved.
4. Cool a bit and add onion, green pepper, egg, celery, 1 cup mayonnaise and seasonings.
5. Add the chopped corned beef. Stir well.
6. Rinse loaf pan (9½ x 5¼ x 2¾ inches) with cold water and pour in above ingredients.
7. Refrigerate, covered, overnight.
8. Unmold on oval platter and garnish with tomatoes, cucumbers and watercress. Serve with the rest of the mayonnaise in a side dish with a little sprig of the watercress on top.

SERVES 8 to 10.

CRABMEAT MOUSSE

2 envelopes (2 tbsps.) plain gelatin
2 tsps. salt
½ cup cold water
1 cup boiling water
2 tbsps. lemon juice
1⅓ cups mayonnaise
½ tsp. dill weed
½ cup heavy cream
1 tbsp. finely chopped pimiento
1½ lbs. fresh crabmeat (boned carefully)
½ cup chopped celery
scraped onion juice
salt and pepper to taste
1 lemon, cut in wedges
1 bunch parsley
5 tomatoes, sliced
*1 cucumber, serrated
12 jumbo ripe olives
juice of ½ lemon

Dissolve gelatin and salt in cold water. Stir in boiling water, lemon juice, ⅓ cup mayonnaise and dill. Chill until thickened. Whip cream, fold in gelatin mixture, then fold in next five ingredients. Spoon into a wet 1½-quart mold. Chill overnight.

Unmold. Garnish with lemon, parsley, tomatoes, cucumbers and ripe olives. Mix lemon juice with rest of the mayonnaise and serve in separate side dish.
SERVES 10.

JELLIED CREAM CHEESE AND PINEAPPLE SALAD

2 (8 oz.) pkgs. cream cheese (softened)
1 (8¼ oz.) can crushed pineapple
½ (7 oz.) can pimientos (cut fine)
20 stuffed olives (cut fine)
1 tsp. salt
1 envelope plain gelatin (1 tbsp.)
¼ cup water (cold)
½ cup water (hot)
12 Boston lettuce hearts
1½ cups "Never Fail Mayonnaise" (p. 368)

Stir cheese in bowl. Add pineapple, juice and all. Add pimientos, olives and salt. Soak gelatin in ¼ cup cold water. Dissolve in hot water. Add cheese mixture.

* To serrate cucumber, stand cucumber on its end and hold firm. With a fork, dig down the sides in stripes all the way around.

Chill overnight in a wet 2-quart ring mold. Unmold and surround with lettuce hearts. Serve with mayonnaise in a side dish.

SERVES 10.

EGG CURRY MOUSSE

3 envelopes (3 tbsps.) plain gelatin
¼ cup cold water
2 cups hot chicken broth
1½ tsps. curry powder
1½ tsps. onion juice
    salt and pepper to taste
2 cups heavy cream, whipped

3 cups hard-boiled eggs, chopped
5 cups "Chicken Salad" (p. 260)
1 large bunch watercress
1 cup "Never Fail Mayonnaise" (p. 368)
juice of ½ lemon

Sprinkle gelatin over cold water. Dissolve this in hot chicken broth with curry powder, onion juice, salt and pepper. Cool and add whipped cream. Stir in chopped eggs. Fill a 2-quart ring mold which has been rinsed in cold water. Refrigerate overnight, covered.

Unmold, fill with "Chicken Salad" and garnish with watercress. Serve with mayonnaise mixed with lemon juice.

SERVES 10 to 12.

HAM MOUSSE I

1 envelope (1 tbsp.) plain gelatin
¼ cup cold water
1⅛ cups boiling chicken broth
2 egg yolks, lightly beaten
2 egg whites, stiffly beaten

1 cup heavy cream, whipped until stiff
3½ cups very finely ground cooked ham, chilled
¼ cup sherry

Soak gelatin in water, then stir in chicken broth. Stir to dissolve. Cool a little and add a little of the mixture to egg yolks. Then add yolks to broth, stirring constantly. Cook in a saucepan over low heat. Stir with a wooden spoon just until sauce coats the spoon. Do not overcook or it will curdle. Cool sauce but do not chill. Blend egg whites and cream. Then fold in the sauce, ham and sherry. Pour mixture into a 1½-quart wet ring mold and chill overnight, covered. Unmold and serve.

SERVES 8 to 10.

HAM MOUSSE II

- 1 pt. tomato juice
- 2 envelopes (2 tbsps.) gelatin
- ¼ cup cold water
- 2½ cups mayonnaise
- 2 cups cooked, ground ham
- 1 green pepper
- 1 small onion
- 2 heads bibb or Boston lettuce
- 1 tbsp. lemon juice

Heat tomato juice. Melt gelatin in cold water and dissolve in hot tomato juice. Beat in 1 cup mayonnaise. Add ham, green pepper and onion that have been put through the meat grinder. Place in 1½-quart ring mold (rinsed in cold water first) and refrigerate overnight. Unmold on cold platter. Surround with crisp lettuce leaves. Serve with side dish of the rest of the mayonnaise mixed with the lemon juice and fill center with "Sweetbread and Cucumber Salad" (p. 278).

SERVES 8 to 10.

LAMB MOUSSE WITH VEGETABLE SALAD

- 1 envelope (1 tbsp.) plain gelatin
- ¼ cup cold water
- 2 cups consommé
- 1 small onion, grated with juice
- 1½ cups ground cooked lamb
- ½ cup finely chopped celery
- 2 cups commercial mayonnaise
- 2 (10 oz.) pkgs. frozen mixed vegetables
- ½ pt. sour cream
- 1 tsp. garlic flakes
- salt and pepper to taste
- 2 heads bibb lettuce
- juice of ½ lemon

1. Dissolve gelatin in cold water. Heat consommé and pour over gelatin to completely dissolve.
2. Cool a bit and add onion, lamb, celery and 1 cup mayonnaise. Mix well.
3. Place in wet 1½-quart ring mold and refrigerate overnight.

4. Cook mixed vegetables (follow package directions). Drain and chill. Add sour cream, garlic flakes, salt and pepper.

5. After mousse is molded, fill center with vegetable salad mixture. Surround with lettuce and serve with a separate dish of 1 cup mayonnaise mixed with lemon juice.

SERVES 10.

MOLDED FRUIT SALAD

4 egg yolks
1 cup milk
½ tsp. dry mustard
1 pt. heavy cream
2 (8¾ oz.) cans sweet cherries (cut in half and pitted)
½ lb. almonds, chopped fine
½ (10 oz.) pkg. marshmallows (cut in half)
1 (1 lb. 14 oz.) can crushed pineapple, drained (save juice)
2 heads Boston lettuce
2 cups mayonnaise
2 tbsps. pineapple juice

To make custard, beat egg yolks, add milk and mustard. Put in small saucepan over medium heat, stirring constantly so as not to burn. Stir until custard is slightly thickened. Set aside and when cool, add the whipped heavy cream and fold in the cherries, almonds, marshmallows and pineapple which have been mixed together in a bowl.

Put in 3-quart ring mold which has been rinsed in cold water. Refrigerate overnight. Unmold on bed of lettuce leaves and serve with mayonnaise thinned with 2 tablespoons pineapple juice.

SERVES 18 to 20.

This is a very rich salad so be careful what you serve with it. I would suggest, as a first course, consommé madrilene (chilled in summer or hot in the winter) with a lemon slice in each cup, hot toasted crackers and either no dessert or several kinds of cookies (see pp. 469–476 for a choice) and coffee or tea.

MUSHROOM RING MOLD

1 (3 oz.) pkg. lemon- or
    lime-flavored gelatin
¼ cup cold water
1 cup boiling water
1 to 2 tbsps. chopped scallions
    (green onions)
1 tbsp. chopped parsley
2 tsps. wine vinegar
⅛ tsp. coarsely ground pepper
½ pt. sour cream
½ lb. fresh mushrooms, chopped
salt to taste
3 heads bibb lettuce
12 black, pitted olives
12 cherry tomatoes (stemmed)

1. Dissolve gelatin in cold water and add boiling water to completely dissolve.
2. Stir in scallions, parsley, vinegar and pepper. Chill until very thick, but not completely jelled.
3. Blend in sour cream and stir in mushrooms. Season.
4. Pour into 1-quart mold which has been rinsed in cold water.
5. Chill until firm (overnight) in refrigerator.
6. Unmold and garnish with bibb lettuce, olives and tomatoes.

SERVES 6.

PÂTÉ DE FOIE GRAS IN ASPIC WITH CHICKEN

3 envelopes (3 tbsps.) plain gelatin
¼ cup cold water
6 cups beef bouillon
8 tbsps. pâté de foie gras
8 rounds of cooked white meat of
    chicken (the size of the top of
    your 6-oz. molds)
1 bunch watercress
1 cup "Never Fail Mayonnaise" (p.
    368)
½ tsp. lemon juice
½ tsp. tarragon (optional)

1. Soften gelatin with water. Heat bouillon and add gelatin to dissolve.
2. Pour into 8 six-ounce greased molds and chill until firm.
3. With a hot spoon, remove 1 tablespoon aspic from center of each mold and fill center with pâté (1 tablespoon per mold). Chill again.
4. Unmold onto rounds of chicken, and garnish with watercress.

5. Serve with mayonnaise mixed with lemon juice and tarragon.
SERVES 8.
Serve as a first course.

ROQUEFORT MOUSSE

1½ cups heavy cream
2 (4 oz.) pkgs. Roquefort cheese, crumbled
2 tsps. Worcestershire sauce

1 tsp. grated fresh onion
½ envelope (½ tbsp.) plain gelatin
¼ cup cold water
2 tbsps. minced parsley

Place 1 cup cream in blender. Add the cheese mixed with Worcestershire sauce and onion. Turn to "blend" for just 3 seconds. Turn off blender. Stir mixture slightly with a rubber spatula. Turn blender on again for just 2 seconds. Watch carefully. (Any longer time will turn the cream to butter.) Remove from blender to bowl.

In a large bowl, place the gelatin and sprinkle with water. Heat remaining ½ cup cream in a small saucepan. Do not let boil. Pour over gelatin and stir until completely dissolved. Cool a bit and add to cheese mixture. Mix together carefully, for cream could still turn to butter. Place in a 2-cup mold which has been rinsed in cold water and refrigerate, covered, overnight.

Unmold on cold platter. Sprinkle entire surface with parsley and serve, surrounded by Melba toast rounds.

SERVES 20 to 30 as a canapé and 8 to 10 if served with a salad course (allowing 2 tablespoons per person).

SMOKED SALMON MOUSSE

1 lb. Nova Scotia smoked salmon
2 cups heavy cream
juice of 1 lemon, strained
3 tbsps. melted sweet butter
white pepper, freshly grated

salt to taste (optional)
60 sliced party pumpernickel rounds
½ cup sweet butter, softened
2 tbsps. capers, well drained

1. Cut salmon into small pieces, removing any discolored bits or bones.

2. In blender (purée speed) place the salmon and cream, small amounts at a time. Purée until smooth. Do not purée for over 4 or 5 seconds or the cream will turn to butter. If not completely puréed and cream is all right, turn on again for 1 or 2 seconds. Be careful!

3. Remove from blender to a bowl and carefully stir in lemon juice and melted butter.

4. Add several twists of pepper.

5. Add salt, if necessary.

6. Serve in chilled silver bowl surrounded by pumpernickel rounds, buttered lightly. Garnish the top with capers.

SERVES 20 to 30 as a canapé.

SHRIMP MOUSSE FOR SALAD

1 lb. cream cheese
1 cup mayonnaise
2 cups sour cream
½ cup chili sauce
⅛ tsp. hot pepper sauce
1½ tsps. salt
¼ tsp. rosemary
1 tbsp. Worcestershire sauce
2 envelopes (2 tbsps.) plain gelatin

juice of 2 lemons (strained)
¼ cup hot water
6 cups cooked, peeled, deveined shrimp, chopped fine
½ cup finely minced green onion
½ cup finely minced bell pepper
¼ cup finely minced pimiento
1 bunch watercress *or* parsley
2 cups mayonnaise

1. Cream together cream cheese, mayonnaise and sour cream. Add all seasonings. Beat with hand beater until smooth.

2. Sprinkle gelatin over lemon juice and stir in hot water until dissolved.

3. Gradually fold this into the cheese mixture.

4. Add shrimp, onion, pepper and pimiento and blend well.

5. Pour into a 3-quart ring mold which has been rinsed in cold water.

6. Refrigerate, covered, overnight.

7. Unmold on chilled platter and garnish with watercress or parsley. Serve with mayonnaise in separate bowl.

SERVES 20.

TOMATO ASPIC

6 cups tomato juice
   handful of celery tops
3 onions, quartered
14 whole cloves
1 tbsp. Worcestershire sauce (or more to taste)
   juice of ½ lemon
¼ cup sugar (optional)
½ tsp. garlic flakes (optional)
   salt and pepper to taste
3½ envelopes (3½ tbsps.) plain gelatin
⅓ cup cold water
2 bunches watercress
2 cups "Never Fail Mayonnaise" (p. 368)

1. Cook first nine ingredients together until mixture boils. Let stand, away from heat, for 1 hour. Strain.
2. Dissolve gelatin in cold water.
3. Reheat tomato mixture to very hot and add gelatin. Stir until gelatin is completely dissolved.
4. Pour into 2½-quart ring mold (which has been rinsed in cold water) and refrigerate overnight.
5. To unmold, dip mold in hot water just long enough to loosen aspic. Surround with watercress and serve with mayonnaise in a side dish.
SERVES 14 to 16.

Fill center with:
a. Fresh "Shrimp" or "Crabmeat Salad."
b. Cooked, frozen, mixed vegetables. Use 3 (10 oz.) boxes mixed with ½ pint sour cream and garlic salt to taste.
c. "Nora's Cole Slaw."
d. "Edna Altemus' Potato Salad."
e. Eight avocados cut up and immediately sprinkled with ½ cup French dressing. Soak 2 large sliced red onions in ice water for 1 hour to crisp. Drain, dry, chop fine and mix with avocados and dressing. Add more French dressing if needed.

TUNAFISH MOUSSE

2 envelopes (2 tbsps.) plain gelatin
½ cup cold water
1 (10½ oz.) can chicken broth
2 cups commercial mayonnaise
2 tbsps. catsup
2 tbsps. vinegar
salt and pepper to taste

6 hard-boiled eggs, cut up
1 (12½ oz.) can best white solid-pack tunafish, flaked
watercress
8 pimiento strips
2 cups "Sour Cream Sauce for Tunafish Mousse" (p. 337)

Cover gelatin in a large bowl with water. Heat broth and pour over gelatin. Stir until completely dissolved. Add mayonnaise and mix all together with a rotary egg beater or whisk. Add catsup, vinegar and seasonings. Fold in eggs and tunafish. Place mixture in a wet 4½-cup fish mold or ring mold rinsed in cold water. Stir so eggs and fish are evenly distributed in the mold. Cover with refrigerator wrap and chill overnight.

Unmold on chilled platter. Surround with watercress and place pimiento strips in a pattern on top of the mold. Serve with sauce dish of "Sour Cream Sauce for Tunafish Mousse."

SERVES 8.

HOT MOUSSES AND SOUFFLÉS

Casseroles have become, especially today, a very important ingredient in entertaining. What with the vanishing maid and the busy life of the modern woman, casseroles are a joy indeed. They may be made days ahead of a party and frozen. However, I would advise never freezing a casserole that contains crabmeat; something weird happens to that shellfish in the deep freeze. It assumes the consistency of shredded crepe paper and who wants that? Otherwise, most of the dishes in this section may be frozen, but I would not advise freezing the vegetable or egg casseroles. I try to keep several casseroles in the freezer for unexpected guests.

For buffet suppers casseroles are invaluable but must be made with loving care. "Moussaka" happens to be our favorite and freezes beautifully. It takes time to prepare, but it is a stalwart dish for the main course at a buffet supper. I always double the recipe, for most guests like it so much that they invariably return to the table for more. What is left, I freeze.

The seafood, vegetable and egg casseroles are better if made the day of the party. I usually make them in the morning and let them "marry" during the day.

Be sure that your casseroles are seasoned perfectly, then put them in the oven, relax and you will find that you have the lovely feeling that you are attending someone else's party.

STRING BEAN, MUSHROOM SOUP AND FRENCH FRIED ONION CASSEROLE

6 (10 oz.) pkgs. French-cut string beans
¼ lb. butter
salt and pepper to taste
2 (10½ oz.) cans cream of mushroom soup
½ pt. light cream
2 (3½ oz.) cans French fried onions
1 cup grated Parmesan *or* sharp Cheddar cheese

Cook beans according to package directions, but cut the cooking time in half to keep beans crispy. Drain well and season with butter and salt and pepper. Preheat oven to 350°. Heat soup in a saucepan with the cream and stir until smooth.

Place a layer of beans (½ the beans) in an ovenproof glass dish (11¾ x 7½ x 1¾ inches). Add a layer of onions. Top with the remainder of the beans and pour over the mushroom soup mixture. With a knife, cut this mixture into the beans. Sprinkle top with cheese and bake in oven until dish is bubbly and cheese is melted.

SERVES 10 to 12.

JOYCE CLIFFORD BURLAND'S BEEF, ZUCCHINI AND EGGPLANT CASSEROLE

This recipe is better if assembled the day before, refrigerated (covered) and cooked the next day.

304 | CASSEROLES, HOT MOUSSES, SOUFFLÉS

3 green peppers, deseeded and chopped	1 tsp. oregano
4 Bermuda onions, chopped	4 cups canned tomato sauce
6 tbsps. olive oil	1 cup sliced zucchini
6 lbs. ground beef	4 medium eggplants, peeled and sliced ½-inch thick
4 tsps. salt	salted water to cover
4 tbsps. flour	3 cups grated sharp Cheddar cheese
½ tsp. freshly ground black pepper	

1. Sauté green pepper and onion in 3 tablespoons olive oil until transparent.
2. Brown meat in rest of olive oil and the salt.
3. Drain meat in a colander and press out all accumulated grease.
4. Add to green pepper and onion.
5. Add flour, black pepper and oregano.
6. Add tomato sauce.
7. Cook over low flame until slightly thick.
8. Boil zucchini in salted water for 3 minutes. Drain *completely*.
9. Boil eggplant in salted water for 5 minutes. Drain *completely*.
10. In buttered, ovenproof 4-quart casserole with four-inch high sides, place eggplant and zucchini to completely cover bottom.
11. Add layer of meat, then cheese, then eggplant and zucchini, meat, cheese, etc. Top with cheese.
12. Bake in preheated 325° oven for 30 to 40 minutes until bubbly and cheese is melted.

SERVES 18 to 20.

LONDON BEEF AND KIDNEY PIE

2 lbs. bottom round, cut in 1-in. cubes	10 lamb kidneys, cleaned and cut in half (discard fat)
½ cup flour	salt and pepper to taste
½ cup butter	¼ cup madeira *or* sherry wine
2 cups cold water (or more if needed)	1 (8 oz.) can commercial buttermilk biscuits
2 onions, sliced	

Dip meat cubes in flour and sauté in butter in 10-inch skillet. Brown quickly, then cover with water, add onions, and bring to a boil. Reduce heat and simmer slowly for 2½ hours. If the water boils away, add more water to keep covered. The last ½ hour, add the kidneys and, about 20 minutes before taking off stove, season with salt and pepper. If you want thicker gravy, add more flour.

Put this mixture into a 2-quart ovenproof baking dish. Add the wine and put biscuits, uncooked, all over the top. Put in preheated 425° oven for 10 to 12 minutes or until biscuits have risen and are golden. This dish must be very hot when you put on the biscuits and must be put into the oven immediately and served immediately when biscuits are done.

SERVES 4 to 6.

CABBAGE CASSEROLE

4 cups cabbage, chopped fine
2 cups celery, cut up
1 tbsp. salt
    boiling water to cover
1 (10½ oz.) can cream of chicken
    soup
1 cup light cream
¼ lb. Cheddar cheese, coarsely
    grated
½ cup bread crumbs
1 (3½ oz.) can French fried onions

1. Place cabbage and celery in a 1½-quart kettle. Add salt and boiling water to cover. When it begins to boil again, cook for 10 minutes. Drain *well.*
2. In an ovenproof glass dish (11¾ x 7½ x 1¾ inches), spread a layer of ½ of the cabbage-celery mixture.
3. Cover this with ½ the soup mixed with the cream and heated. Top with ½ the cheese.
4. Add a second layer of vegetables, soup and the rest of the cheese.
5. Top with bread crumbs and the onions.
6. Bake in a preheated 350° oven for 45 minutes.

SERVES 8.

CARROT CASSEROLE

6 carrots, peeled and sliced
1 (10½ oz.) can beef consommé
1 (10½ oz.) can cream of mushroom soup
½ cup cream
½ cup slivered almonds
1 tsp. salt
½ tsp. pepper
½ tsp. dry mustard
½ cup bread crumbs
1 tbsp. butter (for crumbs)

Boil carrots in consommé in a saucepan until tender. Drain well.

Place in greased ovenproof baking dish (8 x 8 x 2 inches) or casserole. Cover with soup diluted with the cream and add the almonds. Season with salt, pepper and mustard. Mix well. Sprinkle with buttered bread crumbs.

Bake at 350° for 30 minutes, or until bubbly hot and crunchy on top.

SERVES 4 to 6.

CHICKEN CASSEROLE

2 (10½ oz.) cans mushroom soup
2 cups milk
salt to taste
½ tsp. poultry seasoning
1 cup creamed, large-curd cottage cheese
2 (3 oz.) pkgs. cream cheese (softened)
⅓ cup sliced stuffed olives
⅓ cup finely chopped onion
¼ cup chopped parsley
⅓ cup chopped, deseeded green pepper
8 oz. noodles, cooked
3 cups cut-up cooked chicken or turkey
½ cup bread crumbs
2 tbsps. butter

Mix soup and milk (heated together) with salt and poultry seasoning. Mix cheeses, olives, onion, parsley and green pepper together. In layers, starting with noodles, put chicken, cheese mixture, soup, more noodles, chicken, cheese mixture, and soup.

Cover with buttered bread crumbs and place in a buttered ovenproof casserole (11¾ x 7½ x 1¾ inches) and bake in a preheated 375° oven for 30 to 45 minutes or until bubbly.

SERVES 8 to 10.

CASSEROLE OF CHICKEN AND ALMONDS

6 cups cooked rice
4 cups diced chicken *or* turkey
2 chopped pimientos
1½ tbsps. scraped onion
½ lb. mushrooms (sliced)
1 cup slivered almonds
4 cups "White Sauce I" (p. 358, made with 2 cups chicken stock or broth instead of milk)
½ cup chicken stock or broth (to thin sauce)
¼ cup sherry
salt and pepper to taste
¾ cup bread crumbs
2 tbsps. chives

Combine first six ingredients and place in greased ovenproof 3-quart (13½ x 8⅔ x 1¾ inch) casserole. Make "White Sauce I" and thin with extra ½ cup of stock. Add sherry. Pour well-seasoned sauce over the top of casserole. Sprinkle with bread crumbs and chives. Bake about 1 hour in moderate, preheated 350° oven.

SERVES 14 to 16.

If you have stock from the cooking of the chicken or turkey, it is far superior to canned broth.

CASSEROLE OF CHICKEN OR TURKEY FLORENTINE

3 cups chicken *or* turkey stock *or* 3 cups chicken broth
6 tbsps. butter
6 tbsps. flour
salt and pepper to taste
4 cups cooked spinach, drained and chopped
⅛ tsp. seasoned salt
1 tsp. onion juice
½ tsp. nutmeg
4 tbsps. melted butter (for spinach)
1 (16 oz.) pkg. cooked noodles (follow package directions)
4 cups cooked chicken or turkey, cubed
½ cup Parmesan cheese

1. Preheat oven to 350°.
2. Heat stock or broth in the top of a 1-quart double boiler over direct heat. Melt 6 tablespoons butter in 6-inch skillet. Remove from stove and stir in flour until smooth. Add gradually to the hot stock and stir until thickened. Season.

3. Season cooked spinach with seasoned salt, onion juice, nutmeg and melted butter.

4. In buttered ovenproof casserole (11¾ x 7½ x 1¾ inches), place a layer of noodles, then a layer of spinach, then one of chicken and pour over ½ the sauce. Repeat this and end with the sauce.

5. Top with cheese and heat until bubbly and cheese is melted (about 28 to 30 minutes).

SERVES 8 to 10.

BRANDIED CHICKEN WITH GARLIC IN CASSEROLE

2 cloves garlic, peeled
⅔ cup olive oil
4 inside stalks of celery, cut in fine strips
6 sprigs of parsley
1 Bermuda onion, peeled and diced
1 tbsp. fresh or powdered tarragon
salt and pepper to taste
½ tsp. nutmeg
1 (2 lb.) broiler, cut up
⅓ cup Cognac (brandy)
½ bunch parsley

1. Soak garlic in olive oil for 1 hour.
2. Pour olive oil (garlic cloves removed) in bottom of covered 1½-quart ovenproof casserole.
3. Add celery, parsley, onion and tarragon and toss to mix well.
4. Sprinkle salt, pepper and nutmeg over chicken pieces.
5. Add chicken to casserole and toss to coat the chicken well.
6. Add the Cognac.
7. Cover the casserole and bake in preheated 375° oven for 1½ hours or until chicken is tender.
8. Garnish with parsley.

SERVES 2 or 3.

CHICKEN LIVER CASSEROLE

- 1 lb. chicken livers
- ¾ cup butter
- 1 small onion, finely chopped
- ½ lb. sliced fresh mushrooms
- 1½ cups diced cooked ham
- 1½ cups chopped green pepper
- ½ cup finely sliced celery
- 1 pkg. (10 oz.) frozen peas, uncooked
- 1 jar (2 oz.) pimientos, chopped
- 1 pkg. dry mushroom soup
- 2 cups milk
- 2 tsps. chicken stock base
- ½ cup sherry
- 1 pkg. (4 oz.) medium noodles, cooked

1. Sauté livers in ½ cup butter until livers are no longer pink inside. Do not overcook. Remove from pan and keep warm.
2. Cook onion and mushrooms in fat in pan until onion is golden.
3. Mix chicken livers, ham and vegetables together.
4. Prepare soup with milk and chicken stock base according to package directions.
5. Stir in sherry and pour over the livers and vegetables.
6. Mix well.
7. Place in buttered, ovenproof casserole (11¾ x 7½ x 1¾ inches) on bed of buttered (use rest of butter) noodles, cover with foil and bake in preheated 350° oven for 30 minutes.

SERVES 8.

CHICKEN NORMANDIE CASSEROLE

- livers, gizzards, legs, backs and wings from 4 broilers
- 2 tsps. salt
- 2½ cups water
- 4 cut-up broilers (breasts and thighs)
- ¾ lb. butter
- 4 tbsps. flour
- 1 cup carrots (salted water to cover)
- 1 cup peas (salted water to cover)
- 1 cup celery, diced (salted water to cover)
- 2 cups rice
- 4 cups chicken consommé
- 1 Bermuda onion, minced
- 1 apple, peeled and chopped
- 1 clove garlic, minced
- 2 tsps. curry powder
- salt to taste

1. Boil livers, gizzards, legs, backs and wings in a large saucepan in salted water over medium heat until tender. Reserve broth. Discard the rest.
2. Sauté chicken in ½ lb. butter and cook in covered pan on top of stove until tender in 2 cups of stock from gizzards and livers.
3. Remove chicken when done and keep warm. Thicken juices in pan with flour.
4. Cook carrots, peas and celery separately until tender. Drain.
5. Cook rice in consommé until tender. Drain.
6. Sauté the onion in ¼ lb. butter with the apple and garlic and add to the rice along with the curry powder. In a (13¾ x 8¾ x 1¾ inch) ovenproof casserole, place rice, then chicken. Then place a layer of mixed vegetables. Correct seasoning of thickened stock, pour over the mixture and heat until bubbly.

SERVES about 8 (2 chicken sections apiece).

CHOW MEIN CASSEROLE

1½ cups diced celery
2 medium onions, diced
¼ cup peanut oil (more if needed)
1 lb. ground beef
1 tsp. salt
¼ tsp. pepper
1 (10½ oz.) can cream of chicken soup
1 (10½ oz.) can cream of mushroom soup
1½ cups water,
3 tbsps. dark soy sauce
1½ cups or 1 (1 lb. 4 oz.) can pineapple chunks, drained
½ cup uncooked regular rice
1 (5½ oz.) can chow mein noodles

1. Preheat oven to 350°.
2. Sauté celery and onions in a 10-inch skillet in the oil and cook until vegetables are tender.
3. Add ground beef and sauté lightly, crumbling it as it cooks.
4. Add the rest of the ingredients (mixed together) except noodles and place in an ovenproof 2-quart casserole.
5. Bake, uncovered, for ½ hour.
6. Reduce heat to 300°.
7. Sprinkle chow mein noodles over the top and bake ½ hour longer.

SERVES 8 to 10.

CRABMEAT CASSEROLE

½ cup butter (1 stick)
⅔ cup flour
2⅔ cups milk (hot)
1 lb. fresh crabmeat *or* 1 lb. pkg. frozen king crabmeat
4 cups chopped celery
½ cup chopped green pepper (deseeded)
2 pimientos, chopped
⅓ cup blanched slivered almonds
4 hard-cooked eggs, diced
2 tsps. salt
1 tsp. scraped onion
1 cup grated American cheese
½ cup buttered bread crumbs

Melt butter in a large saucepan. Blend in flour. Add hot milk; cook and stir until smooth and thickened. Pick over crabmeat twice. To sauce add crabmeat, celery, green pepper, pimiento, almonds, eggs, salt and onion. Pour into a buttered 2-quart ovenproof casserole (11¾ x 7½ x 1¾ inches). Top with cheese and crumbs. Bake in a preheated 350° oven for 45 minutes or until bubbly.

SERVES 6 to 8.

BAKED EGGS AND SPINACH CASSEROLE

3 (10 oz.) pkgs. frozen, chopped spinach, thawed and drained
2 tsps. salt
3 tbsps. flour
3 tbsps. butter or margarine
1 cup milk
1 cup *or* 1 (4 oz.) pkg. shredded Cheddar cheese
6 eggs
⅛ tsp. pepper
6 slices toast (cut diagonally into triangles) crusts off
6 sprigs parsley

About one hour before serving:
Preheat oven to 325°. In buttered shallow ovenproof baking dish (8 x 8 x 2 inches), toss spinach with ½ tsp. salt and spread in an even layer; with spoon, make 6 indentations in spinach.

In small saucepan, over low heat, stir flour in melted butter or margarine until smooth; gradually stir in milk and cook stirring constantly, until sauce is thickened; stir in cheese and heat just until melted.

Break one egg into each indentation; sprinkle each egg with pepper and ¼ tsp. salt. Pour sauce over eggs. Bake 30 to 35 minutes or until eggs are of desired consistency. Serve on toast triangles (1 egg on spinach with sauce per person). Top each with sprig of parsley.

SERVES 6.

DEVILED CURRIED EGGS IN CASSEROLE

6 tbsps. butter	salt and pepper to taste
6 tbsps. flour	10 hard-boiled eggs
3 cups milk	½ cup mayonnaise
1 apple, peeled and quartered	1 tsp. onion juice
1 onion, quartered	½ cup finely minced celery
2 tsps. curry powder	½ cup buttered bread crumbs

1. Melt butter, remove from heat and stir in flour to make smooth paste.
2. Put back on medium heat and stir in milk (which has been heated with the apple and onion for flavoring and then strained).
3. When thickened add curry powder, salt and pepper. Keep warm in top of double boiler over hot water.
4. Cut the eggs (the long way) and remove the yolks. Put yolks in bowl and mash with a fork until smooth. Stir in the mayonnaise, onion juice, celery, salt and pepper.
5. Stuff the egg whites with egg yolk mixture.
6. Place the egg halves on the bottom of a buttered 2-quart (11¾ x 7½ x 1¾ inch) ovenproof glass baking dish.
7. Pour the sauce all over the eggs.
8. Sprinkle bread crumbs all over the top of the dish.
9. Bake in a 350° preheated oven until the sauce bubbles (about 25 to 30 minutes).
10. Serve right from the oven dish.

SERVES 10.

MRS. LYNDON B. JOHNSON'S ENCHILADAS

2 cups chili (see "Chili con Carne," p. 96) *or* use 1 (16 oz.) can chili con carne and the juice
12 tortillas
1 onion, chopped fine
2¼ cups grated American cheese
7 cups water

Take about 1 cup of the chili meat from the pot with a hand strainer. Save juice. Fill a 2-quart pot with water, let come to a boil. Place tortillas, one at a time, in the pot for 1 second. Drain. Keep water very hot.

Place ¼ teaspoon onion, 1 tablespoon chili con carne and 1 tablespoon cheese on each tortilla, and fold over (roll). Place filled tortillas side by side in a 2-quart (11¾ x 7½ x 1¾ inch) ovenproof glass dish. Pour remaining chili con carne and the juice over the enchiladas.

Bake 10 to 12 minutes in preheated 350° oven. Remove from stove and sprinkle with 1½ cups grated cheese. Return to oven for 5 more minutes or until cheese is melted. Serve immediately.

SERVES 6.

Tortillas may be purchased in your local store (frozen).

Suggested Menu

"Mrs. Lyndon B. Johnson's Enchiladas"
"Guacamole"
"Caramel Flan II"
"Sangría"

BARBECUED FISH CASSEROLE

1½ lbs. filet of sole
2 tbsps. Bermuda onion, chopped
1 tbsp. butter
¾ cup catsup
¼ cup vinegar
1 tbsp. Worcestershire sauce
2 tbsps. brown sugar
½ tsp. salt
6 lemon slices
parsley

Preheat oven to 375°.
Place fish filets in ovenproof, greased baking pan (8 x 8 x 2 inches).
Sauté onion in butter until golden in a 10-inch skillet. Add catsup, vinegar,

Worcestershire sauce, brown sugar and salt. Simmer 5 minutes. Pour over fish. Bake for 20 minutes in preheated 375° oven or until fish is tender. Serve with lemon slices and parsley.

SERVES 4.

YANKEE FRANKFURTER AND NOODLE CASSEROLE

1 lb. frankfurters
2 cups boiling water
4 tbsps. butter or margarine
½ cup chopped onion
1 can (10½ oz.) cream of celery soup
½ cup milk
½ cup chopped, canned tomatoes (solid pack)
2 cups cooked wide noodles (follow package directions)
2 tbsps. chopped parsley
½ tsp. basil or oregano, crushed
½ cup grated Parmesan or Cheddar cheese

1. Boil frankfurters in water for 5 minutes and drain.
2. In 10-inch skillet, brown boiled frankfurters in 2 tablespoons butter. Remove, cut in ½-inch slices and keep hot. In the same skillet add onion and cook in remaining butter until tender.
3. Stir in soup, milk and tomatoes. Add noodles and parsley. Add basil or oregano. Heat, stirring now and then. Add sliced frankfurters.
4. Place in ovenproof casserole (8 x 8 x 2 inches) and top with grated cheese. Bake in preheated 375° oven until cheese is melted and bubbly.

SERVES 4 to 6.

RUTH COBURN'S HOMINY GRITS WITH CHICKEN LIVERS

This is so good it is sinful!

1 qt. regular milk (not skim milk)
¾ cup hominy grits
⅛ tsp. salt
2 egg yolks, beaten
2 egg whites, beaten stiff
1½ lbs. chicken livers

3 tbsps. melted butter (for livers)
½ cup heavy cream
1 tbsp. flour
1 tbsp. butter (for gravy)
2 pkgs. chicken concentrate
salt and pepper to taste

1. Bring milk just to a boil.
2. Stir in hominy grits and salt.
3. Cook until thickened (about 30 minutes). Cool.
4. Break up grits in egg yolks.
5. Fold in egg whites.
6. Put in buttered, 2-quart round glass ovenproof casserole and bake in preheated 350° oven for 45 minutes.
7. Sauté chicken livers in butter until they are just done. Remove from pan and keep warm. Save pan juices.
8. Make gravy by heating the cream with the pan juices from the livers, thickening it with flour and butter and adding the chicken concentrate, salt and pepper.
9. Poke holes deep into the grits mixture and pour some of the chicken gravy in each hole.
10. Cover grits with the sautéed chicken livers. Serve in same casserole.
SERVES 4 to 6.

IRANIAN KHORAKE BADEMJAN

4 medium-sized eggplants, unpeeled	½ tsp. nutmeg
salt to taste	½ tsp. cinnamon
½ to 1 cup butter (more if needed)	¼ tsp. pepper
	1½ tsps. salt
2 large onions, thinly sliced	3 medium-sized tomatoes, peeled and sliced
1½ lbs. lean ground beef (ground twice)	1 tsp. Hungarian paprika
	1 cup beef bouillon (if needed)
2 small cloves garlic, finely minced	12 tbsps. yogurt or sour cream

1. Cut each eggplant in half lengthwise; then cut each section across in ½-inch thick slices. Sprinkle eggplant with salt generously and let stand for at least 30 minutes; rinse slices in clear water and dry *thoroughly*.

2. Melt enough butter in 10-inch frying pan to coat bottom. Cook eggplant slices, without crowding, over medium heat until lightly browned. Add more butter to pan as needed. Drain cooked slices on paper towels *completely*.

3. In the same pan, melt the balance of the butter (at least 4 tablespoons) and cook the onions, stirring, until soft.

4. Remove onions from the pan and put in the meat, garlic, nutmeg, cinnamon and pepper. Crumble meat and cook over high heat, stirring constantly, until it loses pink color and all the juices are evaporated. Add salt.

5. Arrange half the cooked eggplant slices over the bottom of an ungreased ovenproof (11½ x 7½ x 1¾ inch) casserole. Spoon the meat over the eggplant; then cover with tomato slices. Top with remaining eggplant and spread onions over all. Dust liberally with paprika. Bake immediately, or refrigerate, covered, until ready to heat.

6. Cover casserole and bake in a moderately hot preheated oven (375°) for 20 minutes if ingredients are warm or 30 to 40 minutes if casserole is cold. If the casserole becomes too dry add the bouillon as needed.

7. Top individual servings with cold yogurt or sour cream.
SERVES 10 to 12.

MOUSSAKA | *Mrs. Basil George Vitsaxis*
The Embassy of Greece

4 medium eggplants	2 to 3 eggs, beaten
salt to taste	½ cup grated Feta cheese
4 tbsps. butter	½ cup bread crumbs
2 lbs. ground beef	6 tbsps. butter
3 onions, chopped	6 tbsps. flour
2 tbsps. tomato paste	3 cups hot milk
¼ cup parsley, chopped	salt and pepper to taste
½ cup red wine	dash of nutmeg (⅛ tsp.)
salt and pepper to taste	4 egg yolks, lightly beaten
½ cup water	cooking oil
dash of cinnamon (⅛ tsp.)	grated Feta cheese

Remove ½-inch wide strips of peel lengthwise from eggplants, leaving ½-inch peel between strips. Cut into thick slices, sprinkle with salt, and let stand between two heavy plates while browning meat and making sauce. In frying pan melt the 4 tablespoons butter and sauté meat and onions until meat is browned. Add tomato paste, parsley, wine, salt, pepper and water. Simmer until liquid is absorbed. Cool. Stir in cinnamon, eggs, cheese and half the bread crumbs.

To make sauce: In saucepan melt the 6 tablespoons butter over low heat. Add flour and stir until well blended. Remove from heat. Gradually stir in milk. Return to heat and cook, stirring, until sauce is thick and smooth. Add salt, pepper and nutmeg. Combine egg yolks with a little of the hot sauce, then stir egg mixture into sauce and cook over very low heat for 2 minutes, stirring constantly.

Brown eggplant slices on both sides in hot oil in 10-inch skillet. Grease an ovenproof casserole (11½ x 7½ x 1¾ inches) and sprinkle bottom with remaining bread crumbs. Cover with layer of eggplant slices, then a layer of meat and continue until all eggplant and meat is used, finishing with a layer of eggplant. Cover with sauce, sprinkle with grated cheese and bake in a preheated 350° oven for 1 hour. Serve hot.

MAKES 10 to 12 servings.

Should be served with Greek "Ouzo" instead of wine.

Grated Swiss cheese may be substituted for Feta cheese.

PORK CASSEROLE

10 thick pork chops
½ lb. butter
6 tbsps. uncooked rice
1 can tomatoes
9 small onions, sliced thin

½ cup water
salt and pepper to taste
bay leaf
1 tsp. sugar

Brown chops lightly on both sides in butter in 10-inch skillet. Arrange in 2-quart (11¾ x 7½ x 1¾ inch) covered ovenproof casserole. Sprinkle with rice. Add tomatoes, onions, water and seasonings. Bake, covered, for 1½ hours in preheated 375° oven. Remove bay leaf.

SERVES 10.

QUAIL, RAIL OR WOODCOCK IN CASSEROLE

4 quail, rail or woodcock
salt and freshly ground pepper to taste
3 tbsps. flour
8 tbsps. butter
2 green onions, finely chopped
1 carrot, finely chopped
¼ tsp. basil

¼ tsp. tarragon
1 medium-sized apple, peeled and diced
½ cup chicken stock or broth
1 cup dry sauterne
½ bay leaf
1 cup sour cream

Rub the birds inside and out with salt and pepper and dust them with flour. In 10-inch skillet, melt butter, add onion, carrot, basil and tarragon. Stir and cook 5 minutes. Add birds and sauté until lightly browned. Place birds in 2-quart, ovenproof casserole with cover.

To skillet, add apple, stock, wine and bay leaf. Simmer 30 minutes; strain and pour over birds. Add sour cream, cover casserole and cook in a preheated 325° oven for 45 minutes. Remove cover and cook an additional 10 minutes. Correct seasonings. Serve right from the casserole.

SERVES 2 to 4.

An earthenware, covered casserole is best for this dish.

RICE CHICKEN OR PORK CASSEROLE

- 1 (10½ oz.) can cream of mushroom soup
- 1 (10½ oz.) can cream of chicken soup
- 1¼ cups uncooked white rice
- 8 to 10 pieces of chicken, uncooked *or* 8 to 10 pork chops (center cut)
- salt and pepper to taste
- 1 (4 oz.) pkg. dry onion soup
- 1½ cups water

Heat mushroom and chicken soup together in a saucepan.

In bottom of buttered, ovenproof (11¾ x 7½ x 1¾ inch) casserole, put in the rice; pour the two soups on top of this and add the chicken pieces or pork chops. Season and sprinkle top with the dry onion soup. Carefully add the water so as not to wash off the onion soup powder.

Cover and bake in a preheated oven (350°) for 2 hours.

SERVES 8.

WILD RICE CASSEROLE

- 1 cup wild rice
- 2 cups warm water
- 2 qts. boiling water
- ¼ lb. bacon
- ½ cup butter
- ½ cup finely chopped celery
- ½ cup finely chopped onion
- ¼ cup finely chopped green pepper
- ½ tsp. salt
- ½ tsp. pepper
- ½ cup chicken broth

Soak wild rice in warm water for 2 hours, then wash and drain it several times. Cook rice in boiling water for 20 minutes. Drain.

Chop bacon and fry until crisp in a 10-inch skillet. Drain well on paper towel.

In another 10-inch pan put butter. When butter is melted, add celery, onion, green pepper, salt and pepper. Sauté until partially done (about 5 minutes). Then mix with rice and bacon and chicken broth. Place in greased ovenproof 1½-quart baking dish and cover. Bake in a preheated 375° oven for 30 minutes.

SERVES 6 to 8.

CASSEROLE ST. JACQUES

1 cup dry white wine
1 small onion, sliced thin
1 tbsp. minced parsley
1 tsp. salt
1 lb. sea scallops (cut in quarters)
　　or 1 lb. bay scallops
1 can (3 oz.) broiled, sliced mushrooms
¼ cup butter
2 tsps. lemon juice
water as needed

4 tbsps. flour
1 cup light cream
crushed garlic bud (optional)
⅓ cup grated Gruyère cheese
few grains of pepper
1 can (5½ oz.) shrimp or ½ lb. fresh cooked shrimp
1 can (7 oz.) Alaskan king crabmeat or ½ lb. fresh crabmeat
1 cup buttered soft bread crumbs

Combine wine, onion, parsley and salt in saucepan. Bring to boil; add scallops and simmer 2 minutes. Add mushrooms with their broth, 2 tablespoons butter and lemon juice. Simmer until butter is melted. Drain scallops and mushrooms *saving liquid*. Measure liquid and add enough water to make 2 cups.

Melt remaining butter, blend in flour, add scallop liquid and cream. Cook over low heat (stirring) until thickened and smooth. Add garlic (optional). Add cheese and pepper. Stir until cheese melts. Stir in scallop-mushroom mixture, shrimp and crabmeat. Heat to serving temperature.

Turn into shallow, buttered ovenproof 2-quart casserole (11¾ x 7½ x 1¾ inches). Sprinkle with buttered bread crumbs. Brown under broiler.

SERVES 8 to 10.

BAKED SEAFOOD CASSEROLE

1 lb. crabmeat
1 lb. lobster (cooked and cut up)
1 lb. cooked deveined shrimp, cut in half
2 cups commercial mayonnaise
½ cup chopped green pepper

¼ cup minced onion
1½ cups finely chopped celery
½ tsp. salt
2 cups crushed potato chips
1 tsp. paprika

Mix first eight ingredients together as though making a seafood salad. Fill buttered ovenproof baking pan (11¾ x 7½ x 1¾ inches) and cover completely with crushed potato chips. Sprinkle with paprika and bake in a preheated 400° oven for 20 to 25 minutes or until bubbly.

SERVES 10 to 12.

SEAFOOD AU GRATIN WITH MADEIRA WINE

1½ lbs. bay or sea scallops (cut sea scallops in quarters)
6 tbsps. butter
2 cups "White Sauce I" (p. 358, but use ½ milk and ½ light cream)
¼ cup madeira wine
salt and pepper to taste
1½ lbs. fresh cooked lobster meat, cut up
1½ lbs. cooked, cleaned and shelled shrimp, cut up
⅓ cup grated Parmesan cheese

1. Sauté scallops in a 10-inch skillet in the butter, over moderate heat, for about 4 minutes.
2. Drain and reserve juice.
3. Add scallop juice and madeira wine to white sauce and season.
4. Place scallops, lobster and shrimp mixed with the sauce in an ovenproof (11¾ x 7½ x 1¾ inch) baking dish and sprinkle cheese all over the top.
5. Place in a 375° preheated oven and bake until it bubbles and the cheese is melted. (If the cheese melts before it bubbles, cover with foil.) Watch carefully!

SERVES 12.

I serve this dish right from the oven and usually have "Cold Mushroom" or "Watercress Soup"; "Popovers"; "Crispy Green Salad I" with a tart French dressing. For dessert, I have honeydew or Crenshaw melon, served with a wedge of fresh lime and garnished with fresh mint leaves.

SHRIMP CHEESE CASSEROLE

1 lb. sharp Cheddar cheese
6 slices bread
2 lbs. cooked shrimp
¼ cup melted butter
3 eggs
1 tsp. dry mustard
1 pt. milk

Break cheese and bread into bite-sized pieces. Put layers of bread, shrimp, cheese (in this order) into buttered, 1½-quart ovenproof round casserole. Pour butter over layers. Beat eggs and mustard together until blended. Add milk and mix thoroughly. Pour over ingredients in casserole. Cover and refrigerate for at least 3 hours (preferably overnight).

Remove from refrigerator and bring to room temperature. Bake in 350° preheated oven for about 1 hour.

SERVES 4.

EASY CHINESE SHRIMP AND ZUCCHINI CASSEROLE

3 or 4 medium zucchini, washed and cut in ½-in. thick round slices
boiling water to cover
1 tsp. salt
1 pkg. (15 oz.) shrimp chow mein

salt and pepper to taste
¼ cup melted butter
3 slices fresh bread, crumbed (1 cup)
¼ cup grated Parmesan cheese
½ cup slivered toasted almonds

1. Cook zucchini until tender in boiling salted water (about 4 minutes; have it tender but a little underdone).
2. Cook shrimp chow mein according to package directions.
3. Drain zucchini *well* and sprinkle with salt and pepper.
4. Place half of zucchini in bottom of ovenproof greased (8 x 8 x 2 inch) casserole. Add chow mein and top with remaining zucchini.
5. Combine butter and bread crumbs and sprinkle over top of casserole. Top with cheese and brown under the preheated broiler. Sprinkle with slivered almonds.

SERVES 6.

Serve with dish of hot "Fried Rice."

SWEETBREAD CHICKEN RAGOUT IN SCALLOP SHELLS OR RAMEKINS

- 1 lb. sweetbreads
- boiling salted water to cover (1 tsp. salt)
- 1 tsp. vinegar
- 1 (3 lb.) hen or frying chicken
- cold water to cover
- 2 tsps. salt
- 1 bunch parsley
- 4 stalks celery, cut in large pieces
- 1 carrot
- 6 peppercorns
- 1 onion, quartered
- 2½ tbsps. butter
- 2½ tbsps. flour
- 1½ cups chicken stock
- salt and pepper to taste
- 1 tsp. lemon juice
- 1 tbsp. madeira *or* port wine
- 2 egg yolks, beaten
- ½ cup light cream
- ½ lb. mushroom caps, chopped fine
- ¼ cup butter
- ½ cup freshly grated Parmesan cheese

1. Parboil sweetbreads in salted water with vinegar added in medium saucepan for 15 minutes. Drain sweetbreads and plunge into ice water. Drain, skin, dry and cut in small cubes.

2. Place chicken in cold salted water to cover in a medium kettle. Add parsley, celery, carrot, peppercorns and onion. Bring to a boil, then turn down to simmer and cook approximately 1 hour or until white meat starts to separate from the backbone. Remove chicken and reserve; strain stock and cook down to 1½ cups. Set aside.

3. Cut chicken in small cubes. Combine in bowl with sweetbreads.

4. Separately, in a 10-inch skillet, make a roux (white sauce) by melting 2½ tablespoons butter and stirring in flour (off the stove). Cook 2 minutes, then add reserved chicken stock, salt, pepper, lemon juice and wine. Cool a bit. Stir egg yolks into ½ cup of the sauce. Add cream and stir this mixture into white sauce. Stir until very thick. Add to chicken and sweetbreads.

5. Sauté mushrooms in an 8-inch skillet in ¼ cup butter until golden, about 4 to 5 minutes.

6. Put chicken-sweetbread mixture in six shells which have been greased with butter. Sprinkle mushrooms and cheese over the top. Put under preheated broiler until cheese is melted and golden.

This may also be put in a 1-quart (8 x 8 x 2 inch) ovenproof casserole.

SERVES 6.

Serve with rice seasoned with butter, salt and pepper, the salad of your choice and "Parfait Amandes."

CREAMED SWEETBREADS WITH SHERRY CASSEROLE

1½ to 2 cups "White Sauce I" (p. 358)
2 tsps. powdered ginger *or* 1 tsp. fresh, finely minced ginger
salt and pepper to taste

8 cooked sweetbreads (p. 120), cut up
2 tbsps. sherry wine (or more if you like it stronger)
1 cup toasted bread crumbs

Make white sauce, add the seasonings and the sweetbreads. Add wine. Use 2 cups sauce if not moist enough.

Place in a buttered 2-quart, round ovenproof casserole. Cover top with bread crumbs.

Bake in preheated 350° oven until crumbs are golden and casserole is bubbly.

SERVES 6 to 8.

PANDEMONIUM TUNA FISH WITH MUSHROOMS

This is *not* the most Epicurean dish in the world but when your husband phones at 6:30 P.M. and asks if he may bring to dinner two old friends who have just come to town, you can do this in a hurry from your storage shelf.

Said friends may no longer look on you as an expert chef, but they will not depart hungry.

Just be sure to keep all the ingredients on that shelf!

1 (12 oz.) bag potato chips (crushed)
2 (12½ oz.) cans best tuna fish, broken up

2 (10½ oz.) cans mushroom soup
1 cup light cream
salt and pepper to taste
¾ cup corn flakes (crushed)

Butter 1-quart ovenproof (8 x 8 x 2 inch) casserole. Place a layer of potato chips on bottom of the casserole, then add a layer of tuna fish, then layer of crushed potato chips, and so on, finishing with tuna fish.

Heat the mushroom soup in a saucepan. Add the cream and stir until hot and smooth. Season and pour over tuna fish just before it goes into the oven. Top with corn flakes. Bake in preheated 400° oven until it bubbles.

SERVES 4.

IMPERIAL CHICKEN MOUSSE

3 cups cooked chicken
1 small sweet onion
salt and pepper to taste
½ cup pitted ripe olives, cut up
1 cup heavy cream (more if needed)
6 egg whites, beaten stiff, but not dry

Force the chicken and onion through a fine food chopper. Season well. Add the olives and mix in the cream until the mixture resembles a very moist potato salad. Fold the egg whites into chicken mixture. Fill 6 well-buttered ovenproof glass molds two-thirds full. Place in an ovenproof glass baking dish (11¾ x 7½ x 1¾ inches). Fill dish with water to the same level as the chicken in the molds. Cover tightly with aluminum foil and bake in a very hot preheated 450° oven until set. Invert the molds onto a plate and cover with "Imperial Saffron Sauce."

SERVES 6.

FISH MOUSSE WITH LOBSTER SAUCE

2 lbs. raw halibut, sole or haddock
6 egg yolks
1 cup light cream or milk
1 tsp. scraped onion
salt and pepper to taste
½ cup finely minced parsley
6 egg whites

1. Put fish through meat grinder, then mash with a potato masher.
2. While mashing, add well-beaten egg yolks gradually.
3. Add cream or milk, onion juice, salt, pepper and parsley.
4. Add egg whites beaten stiff (fold in).
5. Mix well and pour into buttered 2-quart mold.
6. Set mold in pan of water (should come halfway up the mold).
7. Bake slowly in preheated 325° oven for about 1 hour or until firm.
8. Unmold and serve with "Lobster Sauce."

SERVES 8.

CHEESE SOUFFLÉ | Mrs. Edward P. Maffitt

8 tbsps. butter
4 tbsps. flour
2 cups milk
1½ cups grated sharp Cheddar cheese

1 tsp. salt (scant)
few grains cayenne pepper
8 egg yolks, lightly beaten
8 egg whites, beaten stiff

1. Melt butter in top of double boiler over direct heat.
2. Add flour (off the heat) and stir to make a paste.
3. Heat milk in a saucepan and add to above, stirring over direct heat until mixture thickens. Place over boiling water.
4. Add cheese, salt and cayenne and stir until cheese is melted. Stir in egg yolks, beating constantly. Remove from stove and cool a bit.
5. Preheat oven to 400°.
6. Place mixture in bowl and fold in egg whites until thoroughly mixed.
7. Pour into buttered 2½-quart soufflé dish. Add buttered collar* and bake for 30 to 32 minutes.
8. Serve *at once*.
SERVES 6.

CHEESE SOUFFLÉ RING

1 cup milk
2 tbsps. flour
2 tbsps. butter
1 (8 oz.) pkg. Old English Cheddar Cheese, sliced

4 eggs
1 tsp. salt
dash of cayenne pepper

1. Make "White Sauce I" (p. 358) with milk, flour and butter.
2. When thickened, add cheese. Stir until it is melted, then place sauce in top of double boiler over hot water.
3. Add eggs, one at a time, beating well after each is added.
4. Season.
5. Preheat oven to 350°.

* To make collar, see "Apricot Soufflé" (p. 448).

6. Pour into buttered 1-quart ring mold (set in a larger pan of hot water about 2 inches deep) and bake for about 35 to 40 minutes.
SERVES 4.
Serve with "Shrimp Creole" in center of ring.

CHICKEN SOUFFLÉ

1½ cups "White Sauce II" (p. 359)
½ cup fine white bread crumbs
1 tsp. lemon juice
salt and pepper to taste
1 tsp. finely chopped parsley

2 cups finely chopped cooked chicken (use meat grinder)
2 egg yolks, well beaten
2 egg whites, beaten stiff

Mix the white sauce, bread crumbs, lemon juice, seasonings, parsley and chicken together. Add egg yolks, then fold in egg whites. Pour into unbuttered soufflé dish (7½ x 3½ inches) and place dish in pan of hot water (about 1 inch up the side).
Bake in preheated 325° oven about 40 minutes.
Serve with "Mushroom Sauce."
SERVES 4.
Lamb or fish may be used instead of chicken.

COLD CHICKEN SOUFFLÉ

1 tbsp. sesame seeds
2 pkgs. (2 tbsps.) plain gelatin
½ cup cold water
2 (10½ oz.) cans cream of chicken soup
6 cups cooked chicken (put through meat grinder)

2 tbsps. curry powder
seasoned salt to taste
pepper (fresh ground) to taste
2 cups heavy cream, beaten stiff
½ cup slivered cooked chicken
2 cups chutney

1. Toast sesame seeds in preheated 350° oven until golden.
2. Dissolve gelatin in cold water.

3. Heat soup as directed on can.
4. Dissolve gelatin in the hot soup.
5. Add chicken to soup mixture. Add curry, seasoned salt and pepper.
6. Mix well and fold in the whipped cream.
7. Make a 3-inch collar* and tape it to a 1½-quart soufflé dish. Grease the dish and pour in the above mixture.
8. Refrigerate overnight.
9. Remove collar and top soufflé with toasted sesame seeds and slivered chicken.

Serve with chutney in a side dish.

SERVES 12.

LANSING CORN SOUFFLÉ

3 cups fresh *or* 1 (10 oz.) pkg. frozen corn kernels
4 tbsps. butter
1 tbsp. flour
¾ cup light cream (or milk)

1 tbsp. sugar
salt and pepper to taste
3 egg yolks, well beaten
3 egg whites, well beaten

1. Put corn through a grinder and then force through a sieve.
2. Make "White Sauce I" (p. 358) with 1 tablespoon of the butter, 1 tablespoon flour, and ¾ cup cream or milk. Stir until smooth.
3. Stir in corn pulp, the rest of the butter, melted, and season with sugar, salt and pepper.
4. Add egg yolks.
5. Fold in egg whites.
6. Place mixture in buttered ovenproof 2-quart baking dish.
7. Place in larger pan of hot water (2 inches deep).
8. Bake in preheated 350° oven until set (about 1 hour). Serve with "Whiskey Carrots."

SERVES 4 to 6.

---

* See "Apricot Soufflé" (p. 448).

COLD AND HOT

What's sauce for the goose is fat for the hips—but Ambassador Bruce's "Sauce Archiduc" and many of the other sauces given here are imperative for putting the final fillip on a particular dish. To omit them would be heresy. A "Benedict" without "Hollandaise" or an "Apricot Soufflé" without "Chantilly" would be like ashes in the mouth.

AMBASSADOR DAVID K. E. BRUCE'S SAUCE ARCHIDUC

1 cup olive oil
½ cup vinegar
1 tsp. fresh minced chives
1 tsp. fresh minced tarragon
1 tsp. fresh minced parsley
1 tsp. fresh minced chervil
1 tsp. dry mustard
3 hard-boiled eggs, chopped

Stir first seven ingredients together well.
Add hard-boiled eggs.
Stir well again before serving.
MAKES 1½ cups.
If you can't get fresh herbs, use powdered but cut the amounts in half. Fresh are so much better. Use this sauce on fresh, cooked, cold asparagus or cooked, cold broccoli spears.

AVOCADO SAUCE FOR TOMATO ASPIC

2 ripe avocados
juice of ½ lemon
1 cup mayonnaise *or* 1 cup sour cream
½ tsp. onion juice
salt and pepper to taste

Peel and mash avocados. Stir in lemon juice, mayonnaise or sour cream, onion juice and seasonings.
MAKES 1½ to 2 cups.

COLD CURRY SAUCE FOR VEGETABLE DIP

½ cup mayonnaise
½ cup sour cream
½ tsp. onion juice
½ tsp. lemon juice

¼ raw, tart apple (scraped) *or* 2 tsps. apple juice
1 tsp. curry powder

Place mayonnaise and sour cream in bowl and mix together well. Add onion and lemon juice, apple or apple juice and curry powder.
MAKES 1 cup.

DILL SAUCE I

1 pt. sour cream
¼ cup minced onion
¼ tsp. celery seed

¼ tsp. garlic powder
2 tbsps. chopped fresh dill *or* ½ tsp. dried dill

Mix all ingredients together in a bowl and chill. Let stand no longer than 2 hours.
MAKES 2 cups.

DILL SAUCE II FOR COLD SALMON

2 eggs
½ tsp. dry mustard
1 tsp. salt
½ tsp. pepper
juice of 1 lemon
1½ cups vegetable oil (cold)

½ cup sour cream *or* sour half-and-half
2 or 3 tbsps. fresh dill, chopped
2 cucumbers, peeled, seeded and chopped

In electric blender, on whip speed, place eggs, mustard, seasonings and lemon juice and blend for about 1 minute. Cover the blender jar with wax paper, secure with a rubber band and cut a small hole into the center of the paper. Blending at high speed, pour the oil through the hole in the paper as slowly as possible. When the blender clogs, sauce will be done. Mix the rest of the ingredients into the sauce by hand.

Makes 1½ to 2 cups.

EGG DRESSING SAUCE

1 cup commercial mayonnaise
½ cup white vinegar *or* ½ cup tarragon vinegar
salt and garlic flakes to taste
3 tsps. prepared mustard
4 hard-boiled eggs, minced
¼ cup finely minced chives

Place mayonnaise in a bowl. Beat in vinegar. Add salt and garlic flakes (use sparingly).

Add prepared mustard and stir in egg and chives.

Chill for an hour.

Makes about 2 cups.

Good on cold or hot asparagus. This will keep four or five days, covered, in the refrigerator.

HORSERADISH SAUCE

1 cup heavy cream, whipped
2 tsps. horseradish (or amount desired)
salt and freshly ground pepper to taste
2 tsps. sugar

Into the cream stir rest of ingredients until thoroughly blended.

Makes about 2 cups.

Good with "Boiled Smoked Beef Tongue."

LOUIS SAUCE

1 cup mayonnaise
¼ cup cocktail sauce
1 tsp. onion juice
1 tsp. lemon juice
4 tbsps. finely chopped sweet pickle
salt and pepper to taste

Stir mayonnaise and cocktail sauce together in a bowl. Add onion and lemon juice. Add pickle and seasoning.
MAKES 1¼ cups.
This sauce is particularly good with shrimp or crabmeat cocktail.

MARIA BLAKE'S MUSTARD SAUCE FOR "SPINACH SALAD"

1 pt. sour cream
1 tbsp. tarragon vinegar
1 tbsp. dry mustard
1 tsp. salt
2 eggs

Put all above ingredients in top of double boiler over hot water, stirring constantly for 10 minutes or until thickened. Cool and refrigerate, covered, until cold.
MAKES about 2 cups.

CREAMY MUSTARD SAUCE

2 tbsps. light cream
2 tsps. tarragon vinegar
⅛ tsp. salt
4 tbsps. mustard sauce (I usually use Durkee's)
2 tbsps. sugar
1½ tsps. minced onion flakes *or* 2 tsps. finely minced green onion

Mix all together and chill in the refrigerator.
MAKES ½ cup.
This is particularly good on cooked, crispy, long green beans, chilled. Just before serving, pour sauce over the beans and mix together. Serve on a nest of lettuce leaves in a salad bowl. Allow 3 cups of beans for four people.

PINK SAUCE FOR SHRIMP

1 cup mayonnaise
1 tsp. horseradish sauce
½ tsp. scraped onion

3 tbsps. cocktail sauce
1 tsp. lemon juice
seasoned salt to taste

Mix all ingredients together in a bowl.
Makes 1¼ cups.

REMOULADE SAUCE

1½ cups mayonnaise, home-made or commercial
1 generous tsp. Dijon mustard
2 tbsps. sour gherkins, chopped
2 tbsps. capers, drained
2 tsps. parsley, chopped fine

2 tsps. fresh tarragon, chopped fine, *or* 1 tsp. dried tarragon
1 tbsp. fresh chervil, chopped fine, *or* ½ tbsp. dried chervil
½ tsp. anchovy paste (optional)
salt and pepper to taste

Mix above together.
Makes 1½ cups.

SOUR CREAM SAUCE FOR "TUNA FISH MOUSSE"

1 cup sour cream
¼ cup chopped scallions
¼ cup chopped radishes
½ cup grated cucumber

2 tsps. lemon juice
1 tsp. horseradish
salt and pepper to taste

Mix all above ingredients thoroughly and chill for 2 to 3 hours in the refrigerator.
Makes about 2 cups.

TARRAGON SAUCE

1 cup mayonnaise
juice of ½ lemon
1 tsp. scraped onion

seasoned salt to taste
½ tsp. powdered tarragon (add more if you like it highly flavored)

Mix mayonnaise with remaining ingredients.
MAKES 1 cup.

TARTAR SAUCE

1 cup commercial mayonnaise
4 tbsps. India relish
½ tsp. onion juice

juice of ½ lemon
seasoned salt and pepper to taste

Mix mayonnaise thoroughly with remaining ingredients.
MAKES 1 cup.

SAUCE VINAIGRETTE I

1 cup olive oil (garlic clove may be soaked in this for 1 hour)
⅔ cup tarragon vinegar (*or* ½ cup if you prefer the sauce less tart)
2 tbsps. sweet pickle relish

¼ cup finely chopped chives
2 tbsps. mustard dressing (I usually use Durkee's)
salt and pepper to taste
4 hard-boiled eggs, finely minced

If garlic clove is used, remove from oil, then mix all the above together, adding egg last. Stir well before serving.
MAKES about 3 cups.
Good on crisp lettuce, asparagus, broccoli, fennel or zucchini salads.

SAUCE VINAIGRETTE II

¼ cup tarragon vinegar
1 tsp. dry mustard
1 tsp. salt
1 tsp. Java pepper

juice of ½ lemon
½ cup olive oil
1 clove garlic (put through garlic press or very finely minced)

In small bowl mix vinegar, mustard, salt, pepper and lemon juice. Stir in olive oil and add garlic. Shake well.

Makes ¾ cup.

Java pepper may be purchased in the spice section of your grocery store.

BACON AND PEA SAUCE

½ lb. sliced bacon
1 can (10½ oz.) green pea soup
½ cup consommé

¼ tsp. curry powder
2 tbsps. light cream
2 tbsps. sherry (sweet)

Broil bacon until crispy, drain, cut up and add to the other ingredients and heat with sliced leftover lamb.

Makes about 3 cups.

BARBECUE SAUCE I

½ cup brown sugar
2 tsps. salt
2 tsps. celery seed

4 tsps. chili powder
2 tsps. paprika

Melt sugar in small 6-inch skillet over medium heat, then add rest of ingredients. Simmer for 3 or 4 minutes.

Makes enough sauce for 8 spareribs or 2 servings.

BARBECUE SAUCE II

- 8 tbsps. minced onions
- 2 cups tomato paste
- 1½ cups water
- 6 tbsps. vinegar
- 4 tbsps. Worcestershire sauce
- 2 tbsps. salt
- 2 tsps. paprika
- 1 tsp. chili powder
- 1 tsp. pepper
- ½ tsp. powdered cinnamon
- ¼ cup sugar
- dash powdered clove
- 1 capful Liquid Smoke

Bring all ingredients except last to a boil in a 2-quart iron pot and simmer for 30 minutes.

Add Liquid Smoke.

MAKES about 4½ to 5 cups.

SPECIAL BARBECUE SAUCE

- ¼ cup cider vinegar
- 1 medium onion, chopped fine
- 1 clove garlic, crushed
- 1½ tsps. horseradish-flavored mustard
- ½ tsp. dried mixed herbs
- 1 can (4 oz.) mushrooms sliced, drained
- 1 tbsp. steak sauce
- ¼ cup butter or margarine
- ¼ cup chili sauce
- 1 tsp. sugar
- ½ tsp. salt
- dash pepper and cayenne
- ¼ cup whiskey
- water (if needed)

Combine all ingredients in a 10-inch skillet and simmer ½ hour. Add water if sauce gets too thick.

MAKES ¾ to 1 cup.

CHICKEN BARBECUE SAUCE I

¼ cup melted butter
2 tbsps. sugar
¼ tsp. Tabasco
½ tsp. dry mustard
½ cup olive oil

¼ cup catsup
1 tbsp. Worcestershire sauce
1 medium onion, chopped fine
2 tbsps. vinegar

Combine all above ingredients in 8-inch skillet and simmer for ½ hour. If too thick, add water to thin.

MAKES 1¼ cups.

CHICKEN BARBECUE SAUCE II

¼ cup olive oil
½ cup lemon juice
1 garlic clove, crushed
1 medium onion, chopped
2 tbsps. soy sauce

¼ tsp. pepper
1 tsp. each thyme, marjoram and rosemary
2 tsps. honey

Heat oil in 6-inch skillet. Add rest of ingredients and simmer for 15 minutes.
MAKES about ¾ cup.

BÉARNAISE SAUCE

2 tsps. minced shallots
1 tbsp. butter
1 tsp. minced fresh tarragon *or*
    ½ tsp. dried tarragon
1 tsp. minced fresh parsley

⅛ tsp. cayenne pepper
1 cup "Hollandaise Sauce" (p. 350)

1. Mince shallots and sauté in butter in your smallest saucepan for 2 minutes.
2. Add shallots and butter, tarragon, parsley and cayenne to "Hollandaise

Sauce" in top of double boiler over hot water.

3. Set entire double boiler back off the stove heat, covered.

4. Ten minutes before serving set double boiler back on stove heat to reheat. Stir once or twice and serve.

MAKES about 1 cup.

BÉCHAMEL SAUCE I

1 cup milk
1 cup chicken stock or broth
1 stalk celery, cut up
1 medium onion, peeled and quartered
6 tbsps. butter

6 tbsps. flour
⅛ cup whole milk, cool
2 egg yolks, slightly beaten
salt and pepper to taste
1 egg white, beaten stiff

Make a white sauce by combining milk, stock, celery and onion in top of double boiler. Heat to scalding point. Strain and put back in saucepan. Melt butter in a small skillet. Remove from heat, stir in flour to make smooth paste and gradually, over medium heat, stir into milk mixture until sauce is smooth and thickened.

Add ⅛ cup milk to egg yolks. Then add this to the white sauce, stirring constantly until smooth. Season. Keep warm over hot water in bottom of double boiler, over low heat, until ready to serve. Just before serving fold in egg white.

MAKES 2½ cups approximately.

BÉCHAMEL SAUCE II

4 cups "White Sauce I" (p. 358)
¼ cup cool milk
4 egg yolks, slightly beaten

½ cup grated Parmesan cheese
salt and pepper to taste
2 egg whites, beaten stiff

1. Make "White Sauce I."
2. Stir milk into egg yolks.

3. Add to "White Sauce I," stirring until smooth.
4. Add cheese and stir until melted.
5. Season and place in top of double boiler over hot water on low heat.
6. Fold egg whites into above mixture just before serving.

Makes about 4½ to 5 cups.

STEAK BUTTER

¼ garlic clove, peeled
½ cup butter
1 tsp. minced chives
1 tsp. finely minced tarragon (*or* basil, savory, dill or sage)
1 tsp. hickory salt (optional)
⅛ tsp. black pepper

Slash garlic and rub shallow bowl with slashed side; discard garlic.

Place the butter in the bowl and cream it until it is like mayonnaise in consistency. Work in remaining ingredients, blending thoroughly. Do not chill but keep cool. Spread on steaks immediately before serving.

Makes ½ cup or 8 tbsps.

I use 1 tbsp. per individual steak (filet mignon or strip sirloin). This may be made in advance and put in refrigerator, covered. Remove from refrigerator 2 hours before using and keep in cool spot. It will melt when it is placed on the hot steak.

GARLIC BUTTER FOR STEAK

1 clove of garlic put through garlic press
¼ lb. butter, softened

1. Stir garlic into butter.
2. Reshape into a stick.
3. Refrigerate for 2 hours or until solid again.
4. Cut stick in eight ¾-inch cubes (or 8 tbsps.).
5. Top each hot filet mignon with one cube. It will melt and give a fine flavor.

Enough for 8 filets.

TARRAGON BUTTER FOR STEAK OR BROILED FISH

Use above recipe, but instead of garlic, use ½ tsp. powdered tarragon (more if you like it stronger). If you have fresh minced tarragon, use about 1½ teaspoons.

CHEDDAR CHEESE SAUCE

1½ cups light cream
1½ cups milk
1 large onion, cut up
4 stalks celery, cut up

4 heaping tbsps. butter
4 heaping tbsps. flour
½ lb. sharp Cheddar cheese, grated
salt and pepper to taste

1. Heat cream and milk with onion and celery in top of double boiler. Strain and put back in top of double boiler over hot water.
2. In small skillet melt butter and stir in flour to make paste.
3. Gradually add paste to cream and milk, stirring until smooth and thickened.
4. Add cheese and stir until melted.
5. Season.

MAKES 3 cups.

This sauce may be frozen or kept in refrigerator, covered, for several days. Reheat over boiling water in top of double boiler until cheese has melted again. Stir well with wire whisk to smooth consistency. But the sauce is better if used the day it is made.

HOW TO MAKE CHICKEN OR TURKEY STOCK

all bones and skin from a large, cooked roasting chicken or turkey carcass (broken up)

6 stalks celery, broken up
1 large Bermuda onion, quartered
water just to cover

In very large saucepan or kettle place all the chicken bones and skin. Add celery, onion and water. Place over high heat and bring to a boil. Turn heat down to medium and cook for 2 hours. Strain, place stock back on stove and cook down to ½ the amount to concentrate the stock. Cool completely and remove the fat which settles on the top.

This may be frozen. In all chicken sauces, soup or mousse recipes, homemade stock is important to the taste. You may use canned chicken broth, but it lacks the strong flavor needed in these recipes. I always try to have this stock in my freezer. It will keep for several months.

MOTHER'S CHICKEN OR TURKEY SAUCE

¼ lb. butter
6 tbsps. flour
3 cups chicken or turkey stock or chicken broth
salt and pepper to taste
1 lb. fresh mushroom caps

1. Melt half of the butter in a 10-inch skillet.
2. Remove from heat and stir in flour to make a paste.
3. Put back on heat and add stock, stirring constantly, until it is thickened and smooth. Season.
4. Put in top of double boiler over hot water.
5. Sauté sliced mushrooms in the remaining butter, in a 10-inch skillet, over medium heat until golden.
6. Add to the sauce with the pan juices. Stir together well.

MAKES about 4 cups.

CREOLE SAUCE

1 cut clove garlic
4 medium onions, chopped
1 green pepper, chopped
⅛ tsp. red chili powder
1½ tbsps. butter
1 (1 lb. 12 oz.) can tomatoes
1 tsp. salt
½ tsp. each white pepper and paprika
1 tsp. thyme
2 cups tomato juice (as needed)

Rub a 10-inch skillet with garlic. Place onion and green pepper in the skillet. Add red chili powder, butter and tomatoes. Stir well. Add salt, pepper, paprika and thyme. Simmer for 2 hours, covered. Add tomato juice if sauce becomes too thick as it cooks.

MAKES 3 to 4 cups.

CUCUMBER SAUCE

2 cups "White Sauce I" (p. 358)
1 cup peeled and diced cucumber
¼ cup light cream
salt and pepper to taste
1 tsp. dill powder *or* 2 tsps. fresh, chopped dill

Make "White Sauce I" and stir in cucumber. Add cream. Season and add dill powder *or* fresh, chopped dill.

MAKES about 3 cups.

CURRY SAUCE I

1½ cups light cream
1½ cups milk
1 large onion, peeled and quartered
1 large apple, peeled and quartered
4 heaping tbsps. butter
4 heaping tbsps. flour
3 tsps. curry powder
salt and pepper to taste

Heat cream and milk with onion and apple in top of double boiler over direct heat. Bring to boiling point but *do not boil*. Strain and place top over boiling water below.

In a small skillet, melt the butter. Remove from heat and blend in the flour to make a smooth paste. Add this gradually to cream mixture, stirring until thick and smooth. Add curry powder, salt and pepper.

MAKES about 3 cups.

CURRY SAUCE II

3 cups beef bouillon
3 tbsps. flour

2 tsps. curry powder
¼ cup seedless raisins

Heat 2½ cups bouillon in 6- or 8-inch saucepan and add flour which has been blended with ½ cup cool bouillon. Stir until smooth. Add curry powder. Blend well and add raisins.

Makes 3 cups.

HOT CURRY SAUCE

3 cups rich beef stock or beef bouillon
6 tbsps. flour
2 tsps. curry powder to taste

2 tsps. sugar
1 tbsp. apple juice
1 tsp. onion juice
½ cup seedless raisins

Heat 2½ cups beef stock in top of 1-quart double boiler.

Stir flour, curry and sugar (mixed together) into remaining ½ cup cool stock in a bowl. Stir until very smooth. Add this mixture, apple and onion juice, slowly, to stock until thickened and smooth.

Stir in raisins. Place over hot water in bottom of double boiler on low heat until ready to serve.

Makes 3 cups.

This may be stored in refrigerator for several days.

EGG SAUCE FOR BOILED SALMON

2 cups "White Sauce II" (p. 359)
¼ cup light cream

6 hard-boiled eggs, cut up
salt and pepper (if needed)

Make "White Sauce II" in top of double boiler and stir in the cream. Add the eggs and fold them into the sauce carefully. Correct seasonings. Keep warm in top of double boiler over hot water.

Makes 2 to 3 cups.

DILL SAUCE FOR "POACHED FILET OF SOLE"

3 tbsps. butter	2 eggs, beaten well
3 tbsps. flour	5 tbsps. lemon juice
1 tsp. salt	1 tsp. onion juice
½ cup liquid in which fish has been poached	¼ tsp. hot red-pepper sauce
1 cup light cream	1 cup frozen peas (cooked according to pkg. directions)
1½ tbsps. dry dill *or* 3 tbsps. chopped fresh dill	

Melt butter in top of double boiler over boiling water. Blend in flour and salt. Add fish liquid and cream. Heat, stirring constantly, until thickened. Add dill. Remove sauce from heat and cool slightly.

In separate bowl, beat eggs. Stir eggs into sauce and return it to the heat. Stir for 1 minute and cool slightly. Season with lemon juice, onion juice and hot red-pepper sauce. For color, stir in cooked green peas.

MAKES about 2½ cups.

COUNTRY GRAVY FOR FRIED CHICKEN

1 pt. light cream	3 tbsps. flour
4 chicken concentrate cubes	salt and freshly ground pepper to taste

Pour all fat from skillet in which chicken has been fried, leaving only particles on bottom of the skillet. Scrape particles loose with a large spoon. Add ¾ pt. cream, heat, and add chicken concentrate cubes. Stir until they dissolve.

Add flour mixed with rest of cream to thicken, stirring constantly with spoon. Strain and keep warm in top of double boiler over hot water.

MAKES 2 cups.

PORK ROAST GRAVY

6 tbsps. juices from the roasting pan (see "Pork Roast," p. 112)
3 cups whole milk
4½ tbsps. flour
salt and pepper to taste

Pour fat and juices from roasting pan into a bowl. Refrigerate for 1 hour and skim off most of the fat. Measure out 6 tablespoons of remaining pan juices, put back in roasting pan and scrape with a large spoon to loosen the particles still in the pan.

Add 2½ cups milk and stir in flour mixed with remaining milk. Boil, on top of the stove, stirring constantly until gravy has thickened. Pour through a sieve into another saucepan. Season and keep hot over hot water until ready to serve.

Makes about 3 cups to serve 8.

TURKEY GIBLET GRAVY

neck, liver, heart and gizzard from 22- to 24-lb. turkey
½ lb. chicken gizzards
1 large Bermuda onion, peeled and quartered
3 stalks fresh celery, broken up
water to cover
2 cups chicken broth
½ cup flour
salt and pepper to taste
juice from roasting pan of turkey

Place turkey giblets and chicken gizzards in 2-quart saucepan with the onion and celery. Cover with cold water and bring to a boil; then reduce heat to simmer and cook until gizzards are fork tender. Remove giblets, cut up, including meat from turkey neck, and reserve. Discard onion and celery.

Place stock back on heat and boil to reduce amount to 2 cups. Add 1½ cups chicken broth and continue heating. In small saucepan, blend ½ cup cool chicken broth with flour until thoroughly mixed. Then stir, with a wire whisk, gradually into hot stock to thicken gravy. When smooth, add giblets and meat from turkey neck. Season to taste. After turkey is out of the roaster, add the roaster juices to this gravy. Correct seasonings.

Makes about 4½ cups gravy.

HOLLANDAISE SAUCE

4 egg yolks
juice of 2 lemons

½ lb. salt butter (cut in 6 pieces)
salt and pepper to taste

Beat egg yolks and lemon juice in top of double boiler over hot water. Add butter 2 pieces at a time. Beat hard with fork or a wire whisk. As you add fifth and sixth pieces of butter, hold pan up, away from hot water, so that sauce will not get too hot and separate. Stir well. Season. Put back over hot water (covered) off the heat until ready to serve. Reheat over medium heat for 10 minutes before serving.

MAKES about 1¼ cups.

This will keep covered in refrigerator for 3 or 4 days, and, tightly covered, in freezer for several months. But I prefer to use freshly made "Hollandaise Sauce."

JOYCE BURLAND'S BLENDER HOLLANDAISE SAUCE

1 cup butter
4 egg yolks
3 tbsps. lemon juice

¼ tsp. salt
¼ tsp. white pepper
⅛ tsp. cayenne pepper

1. Melt butter (do not brown).
2. In electric blender, place egg yolks, lemon juice, salt, white pepper and cayenne pepper.
3. Cover container and turn motor on high.
4. After one second, remove cover and, with the motor still running, start pouring the melted butter into the blender in a small steady stream.
5. When all the butter is in, the hollandaise should be ready to serve.

MAKES about 1½ cups to serve 6.

This, as in the other hollandaise recipes, may be stored for several days, covered, or frozen for several months.

FREEZER HOLLANDAISE SAUCE

1 cup butter
6 egg yolks
¼ cup lemon juice

½ tsp. salt
⅛ tsp. cayenne pepper

Melt butter. In electric blender, put egg yolks, lemon juice, salt and cayenne. Cover and blend a few minutes. Uncover, and add butter gradually, mixing until smooth and slightly thickened. Put in 2 small freezer containers and freeze.

MAKES about 2 cups.

To use, heat in top of double boiler over hot, not boiling, water until warm. Stir with wire whisk until smooth again. This will keep frozen for several months.

MOCK HOLLANDAISE SAUCE

2 tbsps. butter, melted
1 tbsp. flour
¾ cup boiling water
juice of 1 large lemon

2 egg yolks
salt and pepper to taste
2 egg whites, beaten stiff

In a saucepan, over medium heat, melt butter and stir in flour. Add boiling water. Cook until thick (like cream sauce). Remove from fire and add lemon juice. Into this beat the egg yolks, salt and pepper. Return to fire and cook until eggs set, stirring constantly. Remove from fire and place in top of double boiler over hot water to keep warm. Just before serving reheat in same double boiler over flame and fold in egg whites.

MAKES about 1 cup.

LOBSTER SAUCE

1 cup cooked lobster meat, cut in small pieces
¼ cup butter
2 generous tbsps. butter (for sauce)
1 tbsp. flour
1½ cups milk
salt and pepper to taste
1 cup finely chopped celery
2 tbsps. madeira wine *or* 2 tbsps. sherry wine

1. Sauté lobster meat in ¼ cup butter until yellow.
2. Make cream sauce by melting 2 tablespoons butter in skillet. Remove from heat and stir in flour to thick paste and then return to heat and stir in milk until sauce thickens and is smooth. Season with salt and pepper.
3. Add lobster meat, pan butter and chopped celery.
4. Add wine. This may be kept in top of double boiler over hot water set back on stove. Reheat before serving.

MAKES about 3 cups.

GOLDEN MARINADE

2 cloves garlic, crushed
½ tsp. freshly ground black pepper
½ tsp. ground ginger
2 cups beef bouillon (for spareribs) *or* chicken bouillon (for chicken)
½ cup soy sauce
½ cup gin
¼ cup honey
1 onion, chopped

Combine all ingredients. Pour over chicken or spareribs and marinate 24 hours. Use marinade as a basting sauce too.

MAKES 3¼ cups.

HONEY GINGER GLAZE MARINADE

1 (8 oz.) can crushed pineapple and juice
½ cup salad oil
⅛ cup white vinegar
⅓ cup honey
2 tbsps. soy sauce
1 tsp. freshly grated or crushed ginger root

Mix above well together.
MAKES 2½ cups.
This may be used as 4-hour marinade for one or two broilers, or to baste a roasting chicken.

ORIENTAL MARINADE

½ cup soy sauce
½ cup frozen orange juice concentrate
½ cup salad oil
⅛ cup honey
2 tbsps. lemon juice
2 tbsps. white vinegar
1 tbsp. grated orange rind
¼ tsp. ground ginger

Mix well. Serve hot or cold.
MAKES 2 cups.
This is a fine sauce for chicken, chops or seafood.

HOT SAUCE FOR AVOCADOS

6 tbsps. beef consommé
2 tbsps. chili sauce
2 tbsps. tart jelly
2 tbsps. tarragon vinegar

Mix ingredients together and heat in a saucepan. Serve over avocado halves.
MAKES ¾ of a cup or enough to serve 6.

MORNAY SAUCE

1 cup "White Sauce I" (p. 358)
⅛ cup grated Swiss cheese
⅛ cup grated Parmesan cheese

1 egg yolk, beaten
2 tbsps. butter (in dots)
salt, if necessary, to taste

Make "White Sauce I" and place in top of double boiler over hot water. Add cheeses and stir until they are melted.

Remove from heat, cool for 2 minutes and stir in the egg yolk. Add the dots of butter gradually just before serving. Correct seasoning.

MAKES 1¼ cups.

SAUCE MOUSSELINE

½ cup heavy cream (whipped stiff)
½ cup "Hollandaise Sauce" (p. 350)

Fold whipped cream into the "Hollandaise Sauce" just before serving.
MAKES 1 cup.

MUSHROOM SAUCE

2 cups sliced fresh mushroom caps
½ cup butter
4 tbsps. flour (use 6 tbsps. if you want a thicker sauce)

2 cups milk
salt and pepper to taste
2 to 4 tbsps. sherry wine *or* muscatel wine (optional)

Sauté mushrooms in the butter in a 10-inch skillet until they are golden. Remove mushrooms with a slotted spoon. Stir flour into mushroom juice and butter in the skillet and gradually add the milk, stirring constantly, until smooth. Add mushrooms and season. Stir in wine just before serving.

MAKES 2 to 3 cups.

When using this sauce with "Wild Doves," add the pan juices from the cooking of the doves to the mushroom sauce.

SWEET AND SOUR PINEAPPLE ORIENTAL SAUCE

1 tbsp. arrowroot *or* 3 tbsps. cornstarch
½ tsp. ginger
½ tsp. allspice
¼ cup brown sugar
1 can (13½ oz.) pineapple tidbits
¼ cup white vinegar
¼ cup soy sauce
2 tbsps. dried green bell pepper

Measure arrowroot, spices and brown sugar into a saucepan. Drain pineapple tidbits and reserve syrup. Add water to syrup to measure 1 cup. Gradually stir into spice mixture in saucepan, keeping mixture smooth. Add vinegar, soy sauce, bell pepper and pineapple. Cook, stirring, until mixture boils and thickens.

Makes 1½ to 2 cups.

Use as a flavorful sauce for seafood, meats or leftover roasts. Excellent also for appetizer meats and seafood.

POLYNESIAN SAUCE

2 tbsps. oil
1 medium onion, chopped
1 green bell pepper, diced (fresh or canned)
1 red bell pepper, diced (fresh or canned)
1 cup orange juice *or* beef bouillon
¼ cup brown sugar
½ tbsp. cornstarch
½ tsp. salt
¼ tsp. ginger
¼ cup vinegar
¼ cup gin
1 tbsp. soy sauce
1 (8¼ oz.) can mandarin oranges

Heat oil in 10-inch skillet; add onion and peppers and cook until onion is transparent. Stir orange juice (or bouillon) into vegetables and bring mixture to a quick boil. Lower heat. Combine next seven ingredients and add to vegetable-juice mixture, stirring constantly until thick. Serve hot over broiled meat, chicken or seafood, garnished with a few orange sections for color.

Makes about 2 cups.

RAISIN SAUCE

2¼ cups water
¾ cup raisins
2 tbsps. cornstarch
1 tbsp. dark brown sugar
⅛ tsp. salt

¼ tsp. powdered ginger
1 tbsp. butter or margarine
2 tbsps. port wine *or* red wine vinegar

In a 1½-quart saucepan, place 2 cups water and the raisins. Bring to a boil, reduce heat and simmer 10 minutes.

In a small bowl, stir together the cornstarch, sugar, salt and ginger. Gradually stir in the remaining ¼ cup of water. Keeping smooth, gradually stir into mixture in saucepan.

Bring to a boil, stirring constantly, and boil 1 minute. Remove from heat. Stir in butter and wine or vinegar. Serve warm over smoked tongue or ham.

MAKES 2 cups.

If sauce thickens on standing, add up to ¼ cup of water. Sauce may be reheated.

IMPERIAL SAFFRON SAUCE

2 cups rich chicken stock or broth
2 tbsps. butter (melted)
2 tbsps. flour

¼ cup diced sweet red pimientos
½ tsp. dried saffron
salt to taste

In top of 1-quart double boiler bring chicken stock to a boil. Stir in butter and flour, mixed to a paste in a 4-inch skillet, beating well with whisk to avoid lumps. When thickened, add the pimientos and saffron, blending to a creamy texture. Place over hot water in bottom of double boiler and remove from heat. Season. Reheat just before serving.

MAKES 2 cups.

Prepare sauce an hour before serving it with "Chicken Imperial Mousse" to improve the flavor.

SAUCE FOR "GERMAN SAUERBRATEN"

3 cups juice from the sauerbraten pot
1 cup sour cream
2 tbsps. flour
1 tbsp. sugar
salt and pepper to taste
½ cup onion, bread, etc., strained from the pot

1. Heat the juice in top of 1-quart double boiler.
2. In a bowl mix the sour cream thoroughly with the flour.
3. When juice is hot, stir in the sour cream mixture with a wire whisk. Stir until it thickens and is smooth. Add sugar, salt and pepper. Add the onion, bread, etc., from sauerbraten pot. Stir with a spoon to mix.
4. Place over hot water to keep hot.
5. Either pour this sauce over the sauerbraten on a heated platter or serve in a separate bowl.

MAKES 1 quart.

SAUCE FOR "SWEET-SOUR PORK" | *Puan Sri Ong*
The Embassy of Malaysia

1 tsp. vegetable oil
1 clove garlic, peeled and chopped fine
juice from "Cucumber Vinaigrette" (p. 265)
½ (14 oz.) bottle tomato catsup

Heat oil in saucepan and brown garlic. Add vinaigrette juice and catsup. Bring to boil and simmer for 1 to 2 minutes. Pour sauce over deep-fried "Sweet-Sour Pork." Garnish edge of platter with "Cucumber Vinaigrette."

MAKES about 2 cups.

Please remember that Oriental meals consist of several courses. The "Sweet-Sour Pork" recipe and this sauce will serve 12 if two other dishes are included in the menu.

SPECIAL SAUCE FOR FISH MOLD

1 cup "Never Fail Mayonnaise" (p. 368)
2 tsps. grated onion
8 green olives, chopped
8 ripe olives, chopped
2 tbsps. capers
½ cup boiling water
1 egg white, beaten stiff
1 tsp. chopped parsley
½ tsp. dill
salt to taste (optional)

Mix first five ingredients thoroughly and place in the top of a 1-quart double boiler, off the stove.

Add the boiling water. Stir well and place over hot water in the bottom of double boiler. Set back off the heat.

Just before serving, reheat and fold in beaten egg white, parsley, dill and salt (optional).

MAKES 2¼ cups.

TOMATO SAUCE

2 (10½ oz.) cans tomato soup
½ cup light cream
1 tbsp. butter
¼ tsp. powdered cloves
salt and pepper to taste

Heat all together in top of double boiler over boiling water until thoroughly hot. Keep warm on low heat until ready to serve.

MAKES 3 cups.

WHITE SAUCE I (thin)

1 cup milk
2 tbsps. butter
2 tbsps. flour
salt and pepper to taste

WHITE SAUCE II (thick)

1 cup milk
3 tbsps. butter
3 tbsps. flour
salt and pepper to taste

WHITE SAUCE III (thickest) for croquettes, etc.

1 cup milk
4 tbsps. butter
4 tbsps. flour
salt and pepper to taste

Heat milk in saucepan, but do not boil. Melt butter in medium-sized skillet. Remove from heat and stir in flour to make a smooth paste. Add this paste, gradually, to hot milk, stirring constantly until sauce is smooth and thickened. Season.

MAKES 1 cup.

SALAD DRESSINGS

ELIZABETH ARDEN'S SPECIAL DRESSING

1 tbsp. Worcestershire sauce
¼ cup tarragon vinegar
1 white onion, cut up fine
2 cups vegetable oil (fairly cold)
4 egg yolks
1¼ tbsps. Veg-e-sal

1 tsp. monosodium glutamate (optional)
1 tsp. horseradish
1 bunch parsley leaves
1 bunch watercress leaves

Mix together in electric blender. Veg-e-sal may be purchased in a health store. It is vital to the recipe. This delicious dressing is good on any green salad.

MAKES about 3 cups.

BOILED DRESSING I

1 cup sugar
2 tbsps. sifted flour
2 tbsps. dry mustard
1 tsp. salt

4 eggs
2 cups milk
2 tbsps. butter
½ cup heavy cream, beaten stiff

1. Mix dry ingredients.
2. Beat eggs in a bowl and add the dry ingredients. Add milk and stir well.
3. Put in top of double boiler over hot water and stir constantly until thick. Add butter.
4. When cool, fold in whipped cream.

MAKES about 1 quart.

BOILED DRESSING II

2 tbsps. flour
1 tbsp. sugar
4 eggs, beaten slightly
2 cups milk
juice of 2 limes

2 tbsps. butter
2 tbsps. mustard dressing (I usually use Durkee's)
½ pt. heavy cream, beaten stiff

Mix flour and sugar in top of double boiler. Add eggs. Slowly add milk and place over boiling water in bottom of double boiler. Beat with egg beater or whisk while cooking. Add juice of limes. When thick, pour in bowl, add butter and beat. Add mustard dressing and beat again. When cool, fold in whipped cream.

MAKES about 1 quart.

BASIC FRENCH DRESSING I

1 tsp. salt
1 tsp. sugar (optional)
1 scant tsp. pepper
½ tsp. dry mustard
½ tsp. paprika (to color)

6 tbsps. tarragon vinegar
1 cup olive oil
1 clove garlic (peeled and quartered)

Mix dry ingredients. Add vinegar and oil. Add garlic. Shake well and put in French dressing bottle.

Strain garlic from dressing after 24 hours.

MAKES about 1¼ cups.

BASIC FRENCH DRESSING II

1 tsp. salt
1 tsp. sugar
1 scant tsp. pepper
½ tsp. dry mustard
½ tsp. paprika

6 tbsps. cider vinegar
1 cup vegetable oil
1 small onion, minced fine
1 tsp. curry powder (optional)

Mix dry ingredients. Add vinegar, oil and onion. Add curry powder for fruit salads (optional).

Makes about 1¼ cups.

FRENCH DRESSING III | *Mrs. Alben Barkley*

1½ cups oil (olive or vegetable)
½ cup white vinegar
2 tsps. salt
1 tsp. sugar
1 tsp. dry mustard
½ tsp. coarse ground pepper
½ tsp. paprika
1 bud garlic minced very fine or put through garlic press

Makes 2 cups.

FRENCH DRESSING IV

1 garlic bud (put through garlic press)
½ onion, grated
1 green pepper, put through grinder
juice of 3 lemons
juice of 1 orange
small bunch parsley, chopped fine
2 tsps. sugar
1 tsp. salt
1 pt. olive oil

1. Mix garlic and onion.
2. Add green pepper.
3. Add lemon and orange juice.
4. Add parsley, sugar, salt and olive oil.

Makes about 3 cups.

PINK FRENCH DRESSING

1 (10½ oz.) can tomato soup
¾ cup vinegar
1 cup olive oil
1 tbsp. salt
1 tbsp. Worcestershire sauce

⅓ cup sugar
1 tsp. mustard (dry)
⅛ tsp. Tabasco sauce
1 garlic bud (peeled and cut in half)

Put all in 1-quart jar and shake well before using.
Will keep indefinitely in the refrigerator.
MAKES about 3½ cups.

DRESSING FOR FRUIT SALAD

1 cup "Basic French Dressing II" (p. 364)

2 tbsps. Indian chutney, minced
1 tsp. curry powder

Mix all above ingredients.
MAKES 1 cup.

LORET HAYDEN'S SALAD DRESSING

1 (8 oz.) pkg. cream cheese
¼ lb. imported Roquefort cheese
1 cup "Basic French Dressing I" (p. 364)

1 tbsp. Worcestershire sauce
salt and freshly ground pepper to taste

Soften cheese and mash together with French dressing and Worcestershire sauce. Season.

Toss, just before serving, with "Loret Hayden's Special Salad."
MAKES about 2½ cups.

MARSHMALLOW DRESSING FOR FRUIT SALAD

12 marshmallows, chopped (regular size—about 1 inch)	1 tsp. dry mustard
2 tbsps. cider vinegar	1 tsp. paprika
1 tbsp. sugar	2 eggs, well beaten
	¾ cup heavy cream, whipped stiff

In top of 1-quart double boiler, over boiling water, melt the marshmallows.
Add vinegar, sugar, mustard and paprika. Stir together well. Remove from stove and add beaten eggs.
Fold in whipped cream.
MAKES about 2 cups.

BLENDER MAYONNAISE

1 egg (room temperature)	2 tbsps. lemon juice, strained
¾ tsp. salt	1 cup olive *or* vegetable oil (chilled)
½ tsp. dry mustard	

Put egg, salt, mustard, lemon juice and ¼ cup oil in blender.
Place on "Whip," covered, for ½ minute. Uncover and pour in the rest of the oil in a fine stream.
If blender clogs a bit as dressing thickens, use a rubber spatula to stir, being careful not to touch blender blades. Takes about 3 or 4 minutes.
MAKES about 1½ cups.

BLENDER CURRIED MAYONNAISE

½ cup fresh lemon juice	2 cups olive oil (chilled)
½ tsp. dry mustard	2 tbsps. curry powder
2 tsps. salt	2 tsps. sugar
2 eggs	

In blender on whip speed, place lemon juice, mustard, salt and eggs. Whip for 2 or 3 seconds. Add ½ cup of oil, curry powder and the sugar. Whip again for 2 or 3 seconds.

At same speed, gradually pour in the remaining oil in a fine stream. Will take 3 or 4 minutes to make.

MAKES 3 cups.

MUSTARD MAYONNAISE

1 cup "Never Fail Mayonnaise" (p. 368)
1 tsp. mustard dressing (I usually use Durkee's)
½ tsp. onion juice
juice of ½ lemon
seasoned salt to taste

Mix together and serve.
MAKES 1 cup.

NEVER FAIL MAYONNAISE

1 whole egg *or* 2 yolks
¼ tsp. dry mustard
1 tbsp. vinegar (white wine or tarragon)
1 tsp. salt
¼ tsp. pepper
1 cup olive oil (chilled)
1 to 2 tbsps. lemon juice

Put first five ingredients in electric blender with ¼ cup oil and blend on "Whip" for 5 seconds. Then pour in remaining oil in a very fine, slow stream. Remove from blender when thick and add lemon juice.

MAKES 1½ cups.

If you wish a thinner mayonnaise, it may be thinned with more lemon juice, light cream or fruit juice (for fruit salads).

ROQUEFORT DRESSING I

1 cup mayonnaise
1 cup "Basic French Dressing I" (p. 364)

1 (4 oz.) pkg. imported Roquefort cheese, crumbled
juice of ½ lemon (optional)

In a bowl mix mayonnaise well with the French dressing and add the crumbled cheese. Stir in lemon juice (optional).

MAKES 2¼ cups.

If you like a smooth sauce, put the above in the electric blender for 1 minute.

ROQUEFORT DRESSING II

2 cups "Basic French Dressing I" (p. 364)
1 (4 oz.) pkg. imported Roquefort cheese

2 tsps. lemon juice (optional)

Follow directions for "Roquefort Dressing I."

MAKES 2¼ cups.

This, obviously, is not as thick as the recipe with mayonnaise. If you are serving a rich dinner, use this recipe.

SESAME DRESSING

¾ cup olive oil
½ cup tarragon wine vinegar
1 tbsp. lemon juice
1½ tbsps. brown sugar
1½ tbsps. catsup
1½ tbsps. prepared mustard

1½ tsps. onion powder
1½ tsps. seasoned salt
¾ tsp. tarragon flakes, finely crushed
¼ tsp. seasoned pepper
3 tbsps. toasted sesame seeds

Put all ingredients into a pint jar. Cover and shake vigorously until blended. Refrigerate for several hours before using to mellow flavors. Shake again before using.

Makes about 2 cups.

SOUR CREAM DRESSING

1 egg yolk
2 tbsps. vinegar
1 tbsp. lemon juice
1 tsp. salt
½ tsp. dry mustard
¼ tsp. pepper
⅛ tsp. sugar
1 cup sour cream, lightly beaten

Blend together egg yolk, vinegar, lemon juice, salt, mustard, pepper and sugar. Beat until well thickened. Add sour cream and beat until well mixed.

Makes 1¼ cups.

BREADS

PANCAKES AND SANDWICHES

Reaching for a loaf of bread on a grocery shelf is not nearly as fascinating as making your own bread, biscuits or muffins. It's just too easy and I, personally, always feel like a pioneer woman when I smell the breads cooking and when I remove them from the oven. A popover is still to me some kind of miracle and *so* easy to make, while "Icebox Rolls," although they take a long time, are like eiderdown and that extra time is well spent.

Pancakes or crepes lend themselves to many succulent dishes in various forms. Try them with lightly floured fresh blueberries mixed with the batter. Serve them with apple syrup and, as my father used to do on Sunday mornings when he held Open House in New Hampshire, with a fine champagne. Make them about four inches in diameter. Make plenty of batter—our friends used to eat six or eight apiece. They are that good!

MOTHER'S BAKING POWDER BISCUITS

2 cups sifted flour
1 tsp. salt
2 tsps. baking powder

½ cup shortening
⅔ cup buttermilk (scant)

Sift flour with salt and baking powder and add it to the shortening, working it in gradually with a pastry mixer or your fingers. Add buttermilk to make a light, soft dough. Handle as little as possible.

Place dough on a lightly floured pastry cloth or aluminum foil. Pat it out, evenly, to about ¼ inch thickness and cut with a 2-inch cookie cutter. Place biscuits on a buttered (17 x 14 inch) cookie tin.

Preheat oven to 400° and bake for 12 to 15 minutes or until the tops of the biscuits are a pale golden color. Serve, split across, buttered, and put together again.

MAKES 33 biscuits.

MOTHER'S BLUEBERRY MUFFINS

2 cups sifted flour
¾ tsp. salt
½ cup sugar
3 tsps. baking powder
2 eggs

1 cup milk
⅓ cup butter, melted
1 cup blueberries, hulled, washed and completely dried

1. Sift dry ingredients together in a large bowl.
2. Beat eggs well; add milk and melted butter.
3. Using a large spoon, mix with dry ingredients.

4. Lightly flour the blueberries. (This prevents them from settling to the bottom of the pan.)
5. Fold blueberries into the above mixture.
6. Fill 2 buttered 8-section muffin pans ½ full.
7. In preheated 350° oven, bake for 15 to 20 minutes.

MAKES about 16 muffins.

MY FATHER'S BRAN MUFFINS

¾ cup milk
2 eggs, well beaten
½ cup sugar
   butter the size of an egg (2 heaping tbsps.)

1 cup flour
2½ tsps. baking powder
½ tsp. salt
¾ cup bran

1. Add milk to beaten eggs.
2. Cream sugar and butter and add the above, stirring.
3. Sift the flour, baking powder and salt together and gradually add to the above.
4. Stir in the bran.
5. Pour into well-greased 12-section muffin pan (½ full) and bake in a preheated 350° oven for about 30 minutes.

MAKES about 12 muffins.

OLD-FASHIONED NEW ENGLAND BROWN BREAD

3 cups white bread crumbs soaked in ½ cup hot water
1 cup yellow cornmeal
1 cup dark molasses

1 cup sour milk
2 tsps. baking soda
pinch of salt

Mix all ingredients in a bowl and pour into a greased melon or round 2-quart mold with a cover. Tie wax paper over mold before putting cover on. Set in larger pan of water with water line around top of the mold. Cover and steam on top of the stove for 2¼ hours. Add boiling water if needed to keep water up to top of mold.

Makes 16 (1½ inch) slices.

MY MOTHER'S CINNAMON SUGAR LOAF FOR TEA

1 (1 lb.) loaf unsliced white bread
½ cup sugar
2 tsps. cinnamon
½ cup melted butter

1. Cut all crusts from bread except bottom crust.
2. With very sharp bread knife, slice in 1-inch slices, the long way of the loaf, leaving 1 inch at the bottom.
3. Slice across the short way of the loaf leaving an inch unsliced at the bottom.
4. Mix sugar with cinnamon.
5. Melt butter and, with a brush, cover the entire surface of the bread, inside and out.
6. Sprinkle sugar and cinnamon, covering all the buttered areas. (You may need to add more butter, sugar and cinnamon to cover outside and inside.) Place in ovenproof (11¾ x 7½ x 1¾ inch) pan.
7. Bake in preheated 375° oven until the sugar melts and becomes golden and the loaf is very hot (about 12 minutes). Watch carefully so as not to overcook. The loaf will unfold as it bakes.

Serve on oval platter. Be a proper hostess and let your guests break off all the spears. Then you may eat the bottom. (Don't tell anyone, but the bottom of the loaf is the best.) Everyone is happy and you are radiant!

Makes 1 loaf.

CORNBREAD MUFFINS

2 cups sifted flour
3 tsps. double-acting baking powder
½ tsp. salt
2 tbsps. sugar (optional)
⅔ cup yellow cornmeal
2 eggs, beaten until frothy
¾ cup whole milk
8 tbsps. butter, melted

Mix flour with baking powder, salt and sugar (optional). Add cornmeal. Stir. Add the eggs mixed with the milk. Stir slightly several times to mix. It will be a little lumpy. Stir in melted butter.

Preheat oven to 375°.

Fill greased 12-section muffin tins (iron, if possible) ½ to ⅔ full. Place in oven and bake for 25 minutes.

MAKES 12 muffins.

BETTY BRUCE BOWERSOCK'S CORN DODGERS

1 cup yellow cornmeal
1½ cups boiling water
⅛ tsp. salt
4 egg whites, whipped stiff

1. Scald the cornmeal with boiling, salted water to the consistency of oatmeal.
2. Cool slightly.
3. Fold in egg whites (the batter will be lumpy).
4. Bake in 2 iron cornstick pans, well greased, at 350° for 30 minutes if you like them moist—45 minutes if you like them dry.

MAKES 12 to 15, depending on the size of your cornstick pans.

When making the recipes for "Nut Bread," "Orange Bread" and "Lettuce Loaf," do not be unduly alarmed if the loaf seems heavy when it has cooked. It is supposed to be this way for they are "Tea Breads." Do not slice for 24 hours. Then cut off the crust end and spread soft butter lightly on the bread. Slice one very thin slice and butter again, slice, etc. This type of bread is very good buttered and toasted for tea.

LETTUCE LOAF

- 1½ cups sifted flour
- 2 tsps. baking powder
- ½ tsp. baking soda
- ½ tsp. salt
- ⅛ tsp. mace
- ⅛ tsp. powdered ginger
- 1 cup sugar
- ½ cup corn oil
- 1½ tsps. grated lemon rind
- 1 cup finely chopped lettuce
- 2 eggs
- ½ cup chopped walnuts

Sift flour with baking powder, soda, salt and spices. Combine sugar, oil and lemon rind. Mix in flour combination and chopped lettuce. Add eggs, one at a time, beating well after each addition. Stir in walnuts.

Turn into greased and floured (8½ x 4½ x 2½-inch) loaf pan. Let stand for 20 minutes.

Bake in preheated 350° oven for 50 to 55 minutes or until pick inserted in center comes out dry. Cool in pan for 15 minutes; then invert, remove from pan and cool on a wire rack. Keep at room temperature (covered) for 24 hours before slicing.

MAKES 1 loaf.

NUT BREAD

- 1 egg
- 1 cup sugar
- 4 cups flour
- 4 tsps. baking powder
- ½ tsp. salt
- 1½ cups milk
- 1 cup finely chopped walnuts

Beat egg in a large mixing bowl. Add sugar. Sift flour and sift again with baking powder and salt. Add to egg mixture alternately with the milk. Add chopped nuts. Place in two greased (8½ x 4½ x 2 inch) loaf pans. Let rise for 20 minutes in a warm place.

Bake in a preheated 325° oven for 55 minutes. Loosen bread from the pan with a knife and invert on a cake rack to cool. Keep at room temperature for 24 hours (covered).

MAKES 2 loaves.

ORANGE BREAD

3 cups flour
⅔ cup sugar
⅔ tsp. salt
3 tsps. baking powder

1 egg, beaten
1 cup milk
1 tbsp. melted butter
⅔ cup chopped candied orange peel

1. Mix dry ingredients and add egg and milk stirred together.
2. Add butter and orange peel. Pour into greased loaf pan (8½ x 4½ x 2 inches). Let stand 15 minutes.
3. Bake 1 hour in preheated 350° oven.
4. Turn out on rack to cool.
5. Let stand overnight at room temperature, covered, before slicing.

MAKES 1 loaf.

POPOVERS

2 eggs
1 cup milk
1 cup flour
⅛ tsp. salt

1 tbsp. melted butter
1 tbsp. shortening or butter for greasing

1. Preheat oven to 500°.
2. Beat eggs in bowl. Add milk alternately with flour mixed with the salt. Stir in butter and mix well.
3. Pour mixture into well-buttered hot iron popover pan, filling each cup ⅔ full.
4. Place in oven for *just* 20 minutes. Do not open oven during this time.
5. With a knife loosen popovers from the pan and serve at once.

MAKES 8 to 10 popovers.

I prefer to use 10 (8 oz.) hot custard cups, greased with shortening or butter, and filled ⅔ full. Place on a (15½ x 10¼ x ¾ inch) cookie sheet. I double the recipe for this. Bake as above. If you like your popovers crispier, bake for 25 minutes.

MAKES 10 large popovers.

CHEESE POPOVERS

1 cup flour
⅝ tsp. salt
1 cup milk
2 eggs, beaten well

¼ cup grated Cheddar cheese
1 tbsp. melted butter
1 tbsp. shortening for greasing

1. Combine, in a bowl, the flour, salt, milk, eggs, cheese and butter.
2. Preheat oven to 500°.
3. Fill each cup of a hot greased iron muffin pan ⅔ full of the above mixture.
4. Bake for *just* 20 minutes. Do not open the oven door until baking time is up. Loosen popovers with a knife and serve at once.
MAKES 8 or 9 medium popovers.

Again, I prefer to double this recipe and place the mixture in 10 greased hot (8 oz.) custard cups ⅔ full, set on a (15½ x 10¼ x ¾ inch) cookie tin. Bake in preheated 500° oven for 20 minutes. If you prefer drier, crispier popovers, bake for 25 minutes.
MAKES 10 large popovers.

ICE BOX ROLLS

3 tbsps. butter, melted
½ cup sugar
1 cup boiling water
1 yeast cake dissolved in ¼ cup lukewarm water

⅛ tsp. sugar
1 egg, beaten well
4 cups sifted flour
⅛ tsp. salt

1. In large bowl, place 2 tablespoons melted butter, ½ cup sugar and pour the boiling water over this. Cool until lukewarm.
2. Dissolve yeast cake in the lukewarm water.
3. Sprinkle ⅛ tsp. sugar over the yeast cake and add to the first mixture.
4. Add egg and, gradually, the flour sifted with the salt. (Be sure you measure the flour after it has been sifted.)
5. Put in the refrigerator, covered, for 24 hours before using.
6. Take out as much as you need and, on a lightly floured board, roll out with a floured rolling pin and cut with 2-inch cookie cutter (¼ inch thick).

Shape into rolls 4 hours before baking. (In hot weather, 3 hours is enough.)

7. Brush the rolls with the rest of the melted butter.
8. Bake in preheated 375° oven for 15 minutes.

MAKES 33 rolls (using a 2-inch round cookie cutter).

There are two methods for shaping rolls:

For Parkerhouse Rolls, butter roll and fold one edge almost halfway over.

For Cloverleaf Rolls, butter muffin tins and form 1-inch balls with the dough. Place in tins with butter in between. Use 4 balls in each section.

MOTHER'S PARKER HOUSE ROLLS

1 pt. milk
4 tbsps. butter, melted
2 tbsps. sugar
1 tsp. salt

½ yeast cake
¼ cup cold milk
4 cups sifted flour

1. Heat milk to boiling point.
2. Mix 2 teaspoons melted butter, sugar and salt and pour the hot milk over this.
3. Cool until lukewarm and add the yeast (which has been dissolved in cold milk). Stir well.
4. Add sifted flour.
5. Make dough about 9:00 A.M. Set in large buttered bowl, covered.
6. Knead dough down at 1:00 P.M.
7. Shake in a little flour and let the dough rise again until time to cut rolls out.
8. About 2½ hours before baking, on lightly floured wax paper, carefully knead dough down and roll out to about ½-inch thickness.
9. Cut with 2½-inch cookie cutter. The dough will be very soft and hard to handle, but that makes the rolls light.
10. Fold over once, not quite half way, and lightly butter inside the fold.
11. Place on buttered cookie tin (15½ x 10¼ x ¾ inches).
12. Bake in preheated 425° oven for about 12 to 15 minutes or until faintly brown.

MAKES about 33 to 36 rolls.

YORKSHIRE PUDDING

Follow ingredients in recipe for "Popovers" (p. 380) but omit shortening. When a roast of beef has finished cooking, remove to a platter, cover with foil and reserve. Turn oven to 500°. Pour the popover mixture into the pan juices in the roasting pan, return to the oven and bake for 20 minutes. Cut in squares, place around the roast beef and serve.

A roast of beef should stand for 20 minutes before it is served. This makes it easier to carve and gives time to bake the Yorkshire pudding.

If you have a large roast, double the recipe for "Popovers."

BLINTZES | *Mrs. Yitzhak Rabin*
The Embassy of Israel

Crepes:

4 eggs
2 cups flour
1 cup milk
1 cup water
4 tbsps. melted butter

Blend the above until mixture has a consistency of whipping cream and let stand for about 1 hour before using. (If mixture becomes too thick, add a little more water.)

Grease a heavy 6- or 7-inch skillet with butter. Pour in about half a soup ladle of the batter and spread evenly over the bottom of the skillet. Cook until the edges begin to leave the sides of the pan, then turn the crepe over with a spatula and brown lightly on the other side. As each crepe is cooked, slip it onto a plate until the whole batter is used up.

Filling:

1 (8 oz.) pkg. farmer cheese
1 (8 oz.) pkg. cream cheese
2 eggs
1 tsp. sugar
1 tsp. grated lemon peel

Mix the above thoroughly.

Place one heaping tablespoonful of the cheese mixture in the center of each crepe, fold the sides in to the center and then the top and bottom (like an envelope). Or, after the sides are folded in, the crepe may be rolled to a long and narrow form. Fry in butter until golden.

These may be placed in a buttered baking dish, dotted with butter or spread with sour cream, and baked until brown.

Serve hot with sour cream and/or applesauce, strawberries, etc.

MAKES about 30 blintzes.

In Israel the cheese filling is made with salt and not with sugar and lemon peel.

FRENCH CREPES OR PANCAKES

¾ cup flour, sifted before measuring
½ tsp. salt
1½ tsps. baking powder
2 tsps. sugar

3 eggs
½ cup milk
½ cup water
2 tbsps. cooking oil

Combine and sift all dry ingredients. Place in large mixing bowl and form a well in the center. Beat the eggs with the milk, water and oil. Pour in the well. Stir and mix with hand beater until smooth.

Heat a 6½-inch cast-iron skillet and add a few drops of cooking oil. Pour a small quantity of the batter into the skillet and tip from side to side to cover the bottom evenly (skillet must be very hot). Cook over high heat until brown and crisp on one side only. Add drops of oil before cooking each crepe. Remove each crepe when done and place it cooked side down on wax paper to cool.

MAKES about 14 (6½ inch) crepes.

SERVES 6 to 7 (2 apiece).

GERMAN PANCAKE

1 slice fat bacon
2 eggs
 salt to taste
1½ tbsps. powdered sugar
½ cup flour

½ cup milk
2 tbsps. butter (heated)
½ cup applesauce *or* 1 tbsp. sour cream

1. Wipe out 8-inch iron skillet with uncooked bacon (to grease it).
2. Beat eggs with wire whisk; add salt, sugar, flour and milk. Mix well.
3. Put butter in the pan and heat, but do not foam. Then pour in the batter. Score the top in the form of the letter N and lift around the edges.
4. Flip over while still soft. Score the top again.
5. Bake in same pan in preheated 325° oven for 6 minutes.

SERVES 1.

Serve with applesauce *or* sour cream.

THIN QUICK PANCAKES WITH BRANDY

1 cup commercial pancake mix
2 eggs
1 cup milk
2 tbsps. melted butter
1 tbsp. brandy
2 tbsps. shortening (for the skillet or griddle)

1. Place pancake mix in a large bowl.
2. In separate bowl, beat the eggs until frothy and light.
3. Add the eggs to pancake mix with the milk, melted butter and brandy.
4. Beat together with an electric mixer or hand beater until the batter is smooth.
5. Melt about 1 teaspoon shortening in a 6½-inch skillet over moderate heat.
6. After shortening begins to bubble, pour in 2 tablespoons of the batter and tilt the skillet to spread it evenly. Pancake should be about 5 inches in diameter, thin and delicate.
7. When pancake is light brown and begins to bubble, turn it over and lightly brown other side.
8. Continue this until all the batter is used. Place pancakes in a pan, cover with a clean cloth and put in a 200° oven to keep warm.

MAKES 12 pancakes.

Serve with "Chicken and Mushroom Filling" (below).

CHICKEN AND MUSHROOM FILLING

⅛ cup butter
⅛ cup flour
3 cups milk
1½ tsps. salt
¼ tsp. white pepper
2 tbsps. minced parsley
2 cups minced cooked chicken

½ lb. minced mushrooms
½ cup butter
½ cup shredded Swiss cheese
pinch of cayenne pepper
2 tbsps. heavy cream
2 sprigs parsley

1. Melt ⅛ cup butter in 10-inch saucepan over moderate heat and stir in flour.
2. Gradually add milk and cook, stirring constantly, until sauce is smooth and thick. Add salt and pepper. Cook over low heat for 5 minutes.
3. Set aside 1 cup of sauce in top of double boiler over hot water.
4. Add minced parsley, chicken and mushrooms (which have been sautéed in ½ cup butter for 3 minutes) to the remainder of the sauce.
5. To the 1 cup of sauce, add cheese and cayenne and cook until cheese is melted; then add cream.
6. Place ¼ cup chicken mixture on the end of each pancake and roll it up.
7. After pancakes are all filled and rolled, arrange them in a shallow buttered ovenproof (13½ x 8¾ x 1¾ inch) glass dish.
8. Spoon cheese sauce over pancakes.
9. Cook under the broiler (preheated) until sauce is brown and bubbly (about 3 minutes).
10. Garnish with sprigs of parsley and serve from the oven dish.

SERVES 6.

SANDWICHES

There are several basic rules for making sandwiches:
First—always buy the freshest, most thinly sliced bread.
Second—always lightly butter each slice.
Third—as you make the sandwiches be sure to cover them with a damp dish towel as you go to keep them moist.
Fourth—keep them completely covered in the refrigerator until they are to be served.
Fifth—always have a bowl of extra mayonnaise on the table.

I have discovered that most men like their sandwiches with crusts left on, but women prefer the crusts off. Whether it is considered more masculine to grasp a huge sandwich or whether dainty sandwiches are linked in men's minds with women's tea parties, I know not, but there it is, and my best advice is to serve "whoppers" for men. I have marked with a star the heartier sandwiches which men seem to like.

If both men and ladies are present make some with crusts, some with crusts off. On all the other sandwiches remove the crusts. Cut sandwiches in half before serving.

The following sandwich mixtures are enough for two servings. With each of the recipes use four slices of thinly sliced bread, lightly buttered. Cut off the crusts. All sandwiches are better using homemade mayonnaise (see "Never Fail Mayonnaise," p. 368).

1. *Celery and Nuts*

¼ cup finely chopped celery
¼ cup finely chopped pecans
4 tbsps. mayonnaise

½ tsp. onion juice
salt and pepper to taste

Mix mayonnaise with seasonings and add celery and pecans.

2. *Cream Cheese and Guava Jelly*

1 (3 oz.) pkg. cream cheese, softened
2 tbsps. light cream

2 tbsps. guava jelly

Mix together well and spread.

3. *Cream Cheese and Olive*

1 (3 oz.) pkg. cream cheese, softened
6 large green stuffed olives, chopped

4 tbsps. cream
pepper to taste

Mix together and spread.

4. *Sharp Cheese and Bacon*★

4 (4-in. square) slices sharp Cheddar cheese

6 slices crisp, cooked bacon

Use buttered bread (buttered side out). On bottom slice put cheese (2 slices per sandwich) and place 3 slices crisp bacon on top. Cover with top slice, place in a 10-inch skillet and sauté (turning once) until cheese melts. Serve at once.

5. *Chicken Salad Sandwich with Celery*★

¼ cup cooked, minced chicken
¼ cup finely chopped celery
4 tbsps. mayonnaise
½ tsp. lemon juice
½ tsp. onion juice
salt and pepper to taste

Mix all above together well and spread.

6. *Fresh or Canned Crabmeat*★

1 cup crabmeat, boned and chopped
¼ cup mayonnaise
½ tsp. lemon juice
¼ tsp. onion juice
2 tsps. small capers (optional)
salt and pepper to taste
4 crisp lettuce leaves

Prepare as "Lobster," no. 12 below.

7. *Cucumber*

½ cucumber, sliced thin and peeled
4 tbsps. mayonnaise
salt to taste
½ tsp. Java pepper (¼ tsp. per sandwich)

Place cucumber slices on bread. Top with mayonnaise, salt and pepper.

8. *Egg and Onion*★

4 hard-boiled eggs, mashed
1 very small onion, minced fine
4 tbsps. mayonnaise
salt and pepper to taste

Mix well in a bowl and spread on the buttered bread.

9. *Egg Salad with Stuffed Olives*

4 hard-boiled eggs, chopped
4 large green stuffed olives, chopped
4 tbsps. mayonnaise
pepper to taste
4 crisp lettuce leaves

Line bread with lettuce. Mix eggs, olives, mayonnaise and pepper and spread on lettuce leaves.

10. *Ham Salad★*

4 crisp lettuce leaves
¼ cup cooked ham, put through meat grinder
¼ cup minced celery
½ tsp. onion juice

4 tbsps. mayonnaise
2 tbsps. minced sweet pickle
½ tsp. Durkee's mustard sauce (optional)

Place lettuce on bread. Mix the rest of the ingredients together well and spread on the lettuce.

11. *Deviled Ham and Chutney*

1 (4½ oz. can) deviled ham
4 tbsps. mayonnaise

1 tsp. Indian chutney, cut fine

Prepare as "Egg and Onion," no. 8 above.

12. *Lobster★*

¼ cup mayonnaise
½ tsp. lemon juice
¼ tsp. onion juice

1 cup cooked lobster meat, cut fine
salt and pepper to taste
4 crisp lettuce leaves

Mix mayonnaise, lemon and onion juice. Add lobster meat and seasonings. Place two lettuce leaves on each sandwich and spread on lobster mixture.

13. *Peanut Butter and Bacon★*

4 slices crisp, cooked bacon, chopped

½ cup peanut butter

Mix together and spread on bread.

14. *Radish and Butter*

4 slices rye bread or pumpernickel
2 tsps. sweet butter

½ cup radishes, sliced very thin
salt to taste

Butter slices of rye bread. Add thinly sliced radishes. Salt. Top with other slice of rye bread.

15. *Sardine*

1 (3¾ oz.) can sardines, mashed (discard oil)	1 tsp. lemon juice 3 tbsps. mayonnaise

Mix together and spread on bread.

16. *Tunafish*

Make exactly as "Lobster" recipe, no. 12 above.

17. *Turkey or Chicken*★

4 crisp lettuce leaves 6 thin slices turkey or chicken (cooked white meat)	4 tbsps. mayonnaise *or* 2 tsps. mustard dressing salt and pepper to taste

Place lettuce on bread, add 3 slices turkey or chicken and top with mayonnaise or mustard sauce. Season.

18. *Turkey with Caviar*★

6 thin slices breast of turkey 4 tbsps. mayonnaise	½ tsp. lemon juice 1 (1 oz.) jar best caviar

Place slices of turkey on lightly buttered white bread. Mix mayonnaise with lemon juice and caviar and spread on the turkey slices. This is usually served as an open sandwich.

19. *Watercress*

1 bunch watercress leaves, chopped fine	4 tbsps. sweet butter ½ tsp. onion juice

Mix watercress, butter and onion juice together well and spread.

Before serving, garnish all the sandwiches with sprigs of fresh parsley or watercress.

HOT CHEESE, TOMATO AND BACON SANDWICH

2 lbs. grated sharp Cheddar cheese
2 eggs, beaten well
1 tbsp. onion juice
1 tsp. dry mustard
1 tsp. Worcestershire sauce
8 slices bread
4 tomatoes
16 slices bacon

1. Mix first five ingredients together well.
2. Cut crusts from bread.
3. Spread cheese mixture on the slices of bread until about ½ inch thick.
4. Make depression in center of each.
5. Cut tomatoes in half and place one half in each depression.
6. Cross two pieces of bacon over tomato.
7. Place sandwiches on cookie tin (17 x 14 inches).
8. Bake in preheated 375° oven until bacon is done and cheese is melted (15 to 20 minutes).

SERVES 4 (2 apiece).

LEFTOVER HOT CHICKEN, TURKEY, ROAST BEEF, PORK OR LAMB OPEN SANDWICHES WITH GRAVY

8 slices (½-in. thick) salt-rising bread *or* 8 slices (½-in. thick) white bread
16 thin slices leftover chicken, turkey, roast beef, roast pork or roast lamb, heated in own gravy, quickly, in a 10-inch skillet
salt and pepper to taste
2 cups chicken, turkey, roast beef, roast pork or roast lamb leftover gravy
8 sprigs parsley

Toast bread on both sides (crusts off).

Place two slices meat (one type only) on top of each slice of toast on a hot plate.

Correct seasonings in gravy. Pour *hot* gravy over each sandwich. Garnish with parsley.

SERVES 4 liberally.

TOASTED MUSHROOM SANDWICHES

1 lb. fresh mushroom caps chopped	salt to taste
6 tbsps. butter	16 slices bread (crusts off)
2 tbsps. flour	8 tbsps. butter (for bread)
1 cup light cream	1 bunch watercress

1. Sauté mushrooms in 4 tablespoons butter for 3 or 4 minutes in a 10-inch skillet over moderate heat. Add rest of butter.
2. Add flour and cream to thicken mixture and season. Spread on bread, make closed sandwiches. Butter the outside of each sandwich on both sides.
3. Preheat broiler and place sandwiches on (17 x 14 inch) cookie tin about 6 inches from the broiler flame. When one side is golden, turn and brown on the other side.
4. Garnish with watercress and serve at once.

SERVES 4 (2 apiece).

NANTUCKET SANDWICH

16 slices (½ in. thick) fresh Nantucket Portuguese bread, lightly buttered. Keep crusts on.	8 slices cooked ham
	8 long slices imported Swiss cheese
	8 tbsps. mayonnaise
	1 tbsp. wet mustard
24 lettuce leaves, crisp	

1. Place three lettuce leaves each on eight slices of bread.
2. Add ham slice and cheese.
3. Top with mayonnaise mixed with mustard and second slice of bread.
4. Cut each sandwich in half.

SERVES 4.

This sandwich may be made with French or Italian bread (very fresh), but Nantucket Portuguese is the best.

SHRIMP HOLLANDAISE OPEN SANDWICH ON TOAST

48 cooked shrimp, shelled and cleaned
½ cup butter
8 slices bread, toasted (crusts off)
16 thin slices tomato
2 cups "Hollandaise Sauce" (p. 350)
8 sprigs parsley

1. In 10-inch skillet, sauté shrimp in the butter just long enough to heat through. Keep warm.
2. On four heated plates, place two slices of toast apiece.
3. Place two slices tomato on each piece of toast.
4. Place six shrimp on top of the tomato.
5. Pour ¼ cup "Hollandaise Sauce" on each slice and put a sprig of parsley on top. Serve at once.

SERVES 4 (2 apiece).

The only time when a dessert, other than fruit, crosses our portals is for a party. Then it is a delight to me to create a soufflé with a thick and luscious sauce, a Brûlée, a Rum Pie or a hot pudding and let the calories fall where they may! My husband's look of utter horror when I dive into a large slice of "John's Pie" adds a zest to consuming it, for it is definitely a "No-No," but what then are your own "fancy" dinners for? I have even been known to have two servings with the excuse that it will encourage our guests to do the same—but my husband knows only too well what I am up to.

Once when testing "Rum Cream Pie" I took but one teaspoonful to taste it. I was just about to get a huge spoon and really attack it, when one of our daughters arrived, and, with a burst of will power, I thrust the pie into her hands, bid her a fond farewell, and retired to my boudoir, feeling properly self-righteous.

BAKED APPLES

4 large, red apples
4 tsps. honey
4 tsps. melted butter
4 tsps. chopped crystallized ginger
4 tbsps. butter (for topping)

8 finely chopped almonds
3 finely crushed dry macaroons (at least four days old)
"Chantilly Cream" (p. 459)

Core apples not quite through from stem end. Fill hollow with honey and melted butter, mixed. Preheat oven to 275°. Place apples in ovenproof (8 x 8 x 2 inch) pan and set this pan in a larger one with water an inch deep. Place in oven and bake, very gently, until apples are tender but still hold their shape.

Mix ginger, butter, almonds and macaroons and spread over top of each apple. Place under broiler and brown quickly. Serve hot with "Chantilly Cream."

SERVES 4.

CRÈME BRÛLÉE I | *Mrs. Edward M. Kennedy*

3 cups heavy cream
1 (1 in.) piece of vanilla bean
6 tbsps. sugar

6 egg yolks
¾ cup light brown sugar

1. In upper part of double boiler, heat cream with vanilla bean.
2. In a bowl beat sugar with egg yolks until light and creamy.
3. Take out the vanilla bean and stir the warm cream into the yolks very carefully. Then slowly return the mixture to the top of the double boiler, placing it over boiling water.

4. Stir constantly until the custard coats the spoon.

5. Put into a round 1½-quart soufflé dish and place in the refrigerator to set.

6. When ready to serve, cover the top of the custard completely with light brown sugar (¼ inch deep).

7. Place soufflé dish in a larger pan of crushed ice and place in broiler (about 6 inches from the flame) until sugar melts and caramelizes.

8. Keep watching it carefully so that the sugar will not burn.

9. Serve immediately or cool and place in refrigerator for 1 hour.

SERVES 6 to 8.

CRÈME BRÛLÉE II

1 qt. light cream
8 egg yolks
5 tbsps. granulated sugar
2 tsps. vanilla
¾ cup light brown sugar

In a saucepan, scald cream. In a bowl beat eggs and sugar together. Remove cream from heat and pour very slowly into egg mixture, stirring constantly. Add vanilla, set mixture in 2-quart ovenproof soufflé dish (3¾ x 7¼ inches) and place in larger pan of hot water (3-inch depth). Bake in moderate preheated oven (350°) about 1 hour or until silver knife comes out clean when inserted in center. When done, sprinkle with brown sugar ¼ inch thick. Place under broiler in larger pan of ice until sugar melts and forms a glaze. Cool and refrigerate for 2 hours and serve cold.

SERVES 8.

BAKED COFFEE CUSTARD

4 eggs
⅔ cup sugar
⅛ tsp. salt
2 cups milk
2 cups strong coffee

Beat eggs slightly in a bowl. Add sugar and salt, milk and coffee. Pour into four greased (8-ounce) custard cups. Place in pan of hot water about 1 inch deep. Bake in moderate, preheated oven (350°) about 1 hour or until firm.

MAKES 4 custards.

CHOCOLATE AND RICE KRISPIES RING

2 (6 oz.) pkgs. chocolate chips
4 cups Rice Krispies
2 qts. vanilla or chocolate ice cream
½ pt. heavy cream, whipped
3 tbsps. sugar
⅛ tsp. salt
½ (4 oz.) sweet chocolate bar

Melt chocolate chips in the top of a 1-pint double boiler over hot water. Place Rice Krispies in a large bowl. Stir in the melted chocolate until all the rice is coated. Butter a 1½-quart ring mold well and fill with the above mixture. Smooth the top with a spoon. Do not refrigerate. Keep at room temperature or it will be difficult to cut.

Unmold just before serving on chilled, round platter. Fill center with ice cream. Top with sweetened, salted, whipped cream and, with a sharp knife, shave the sweet chocolate bar all over the cream.

SERVES 10 to 12.

Coffee or peppermint ice cream or lime sherbet may be used to fill the center of the ring for variation. You may also press the chocolate-rice mixture into two 9-inch buttered pie pans. Top each with 1 quart of softened ice cream and freeze them (covered). Take out of the freezer for about ½ hour before serving, cover with whipped cream and shaved chocolate. If you do it this way, allow 1 pint of whipping cream mixed with 6 tablespoons sugar, ¼ teaspoon salt and the shaved sweet chocolate. It is difficult to cut, so use a knife dipped in very hot water.

COCONUT CARAMEL CRUNCH RING

¼ cup butter
1 cup light brown sugar
⅛ tsp. salt
4 cups corn flakes
1 cup shredded coconut
1 qt. vanilla ice cream

Melt butter in heavy 10-inch skillet. Add sugar and salt and place over a very low heat until sugar melts. Remove from stove and gently stir in corn flakes and coconut. Toss until well coated, keeping flakes whole. Pack into well-greased 2-quart ring mold for about 20 to 25 minutes.

Unmold on serving platter while still warm. Fill center with ice cream.

SERVES 10 to 12.

CARAMEL CUSTARD | Mrs. Basil George Vitsaxis
(*Krema Karamela*) The Embassy of Greece

1½ cups sugar
1 qt. milk
6 eggs
¼ tsp. salt

2 tsps. vanilla
½ cup blanched slivered almonds
    (optional)

Caramelize 1 cup sugar in a heavy 8-inch skillet over low heat, stirring constantly, until golden. Don't let it get too dark or it will become bitter. Pour into a 1½-quart mold, plain or fancy, coating all sides. Mold should be warm to prevent syrup from cracking. Scald milk in a 1½-quart saucepan and cool slightly. Beat eggs, add remaining ½ cup sugar, salt and vanilla and beat well. Slowly stir in milk. Strain mixture into coated mold. Place mold in a pan containing 1 inch hot water and bake in a preheated 325° oven for 1 to 1½ hours or until a knife inserted in center comes out clean.

Remove from oven, cool and refrigerate at least a few hours before serving. Invert on a chilled platter, let stand for 15 or 20 minutes and unmold, spooning any syrup from mold over custard. If desired, sprinkle almonds on top.

SERVES 8 to 10.

CARAMEL FLAN I

1¾ cups sugar
8 eggs
3⅓ cups evaporated milk

2 tsps. vanilla
"Caramel Sauce I" (p. 458)

1. Place 1 cup sugar in a small saucepan.
2. Cook, stirring constantly, over medium heat until the sugar melts and is light amber in color.
3. Pour into an (8 x 8 x 2 inch) ovenproof pan.
4. Tip the pan around until it is entirely coated with the caramel mixture. Let cool.
5. Put the eggs, evaporated milk, remaining ¾ cup sugar and vanilla into the blender container. Cover and turn blender on low speed until the mixture is blended.

6. Pour into the caramel-coated pan.

7. Cover and place in a larger pan containing about 1 inch of hot water.

8. Place in preheated 350° oven and bake 1 hour or until knife inserted in center of custard comes out clean.

9. Chill for 3 hours.

10. To unmold, loosen edges with a knife. Cover with a serving plate and turn upside down. Let stand for 10 minutes until syrup runs down over custard. Gently lift off mold. Serve with "Caramel Sauce."

SERVES 8 to 10.

CARAMEL FLAN II | *Mrs. de Olliqui*
The Embassy of Mexico

1¼ cups sugar
2 tbsps. water
6 eggs

2 (13 oz.) cans evaporated milk
2 tsps. vanilla

1. Combine ½ cup sugar and the water in small pan. Cook over medium heat, stirring constantly until sugar dissolves. Continue cooking until syrup turns golden brown. Pour into an 8-cup ring mold; quickly tip and turn mold to coat bottom and sides with syrup, which will harden quickly.

2. Beat eggs slightly in a medium-sized bowl; stir in remaining ¾ cup sugar, evaporated milk and vanilla. Strain into prepared mold.

3. Set mold in a larger baking pan, place on oven shelf, pour boiling water into pan to 2 inch depth.

4. Bake in preheated 350° oven for 1 hour or until custard is set. Remove at once from pan of water. Cool and chill for 3 hours.

5. When ready to serve, loosen custard around edge and center of ring with a knife. Cover with a serving plate; turn upside down. Let stand for 10 minutes until syrup runs down over custard then gently lift off mold. Spoon custard into serving dishes. Spoon some of the caramel syrup over each.

SERVES 8 to 10.

FRUIT CUP WITH CANDIED GINGER

2 fresh peaches, sliced and peeled
2 apples, peeled and sliced
8 strawberries, cut in half
8 (1 in.) chunks fresh pineapple
8 melon balls
8 orange sections
8 grapefruit sections
½ cup white seedless grapes
6 tsps. chopped candied ginger

In a bowl place fresh sliced peaches, apples, strawberries, pineapple chunks, melon balls, orange and grapefruit sections, grapes or any other kind of fruit. Place in refrigerator for 1 hour to chill. Just before serving, scatter chopped candied ginger on each serving.

Variation: After fruit is cut up, sprinkle with ½ cup Cointreau and chill. Omit ginger. Sprinkle top with 4 tablespoons chopped fresh mint leaves.

Allow one cup of fruit per person.

SERVES 4 to 6.

HOT FRUIT DESSERT

3 oranges, peeled (reserve rind)
3 lemons, peeled (reserve rind)
1½ cups light brown sugar
2 cans (8¾ oz.) apricots, drained
2 cans (8¾ oz.) pineapple chunks, drained
1 (1 lb.) can pitted Bing cherries, drained
2 tsps. nutmeg
¼ cup Cointreau (optional)
12 tbsps. sour cream

Grate rind of oranges and lemons into sugar. Slice fruits very thin and spread, layer by layer, in ovenproof (11¾ x 7½ x 1¾ inch) baking dish. Sprinkle each layer with brown sugar mixture, nutmeg, and Cointreau (optional). Heat all until very hot and serve topped with 1 tablespoon sour cream per person.

SERVES 6 to 8.

FRUITS WITH KIRSCH LIQUEUR

I. 3 cups fresh fruit (of your choice)   1 tbsp. Kirsch
   2 tbsps. good orange marmalade   ½ cup slivered almonds

Cut up fresh fruit, add orange marmalade, blend with Kirsch and add slivered almonds. Mix and serve.
SERVES 4.

II. 2 pt. boxes frozen strawberries   ½ pt. sour cream
    2 tbsps. Kirsch

Partially thaw strawberries and add Kirsch. Blend with sour cream. This comes out a lovely shade of pink. (This may be done in electric blender for 1 minute at Blend speed.)
SERVES 6.

III. 4 fresh pineapples   1 pt. box strawberries, washed and sliced
     ½ cup powdered sugar
     ¼ cup Kirsch

Remove fruit from pineapples, leaving just the husk (½ inch thick) and the top (trimmed). Cut pineapple fruit into cubes. Add powdered sugar and strawberries which have been soaked with the Kirsch for ½ hour. Put back in pineapple husks and cover with pineapple tops.
SERVES 4.

LANCASHIRE STONE CREAM | *The Countess of Cromer*
The Embassy of Great Britain

1 pt. heavy cream *or* 1 pt. light cream   1 tsp. vanilla
2 tbsps. sugar   6 tbsps. apricot jam
¼ oz. gelatin (or ½ oz. if cream is light)   1 wineglass dry sherry
   juice of 1 lemon

Heat cream in a saucepan with sugar, gelatin which has been dissolved in ⅛ cup cold water, and vanilla just to boiling point. Cover bottom of 1-quart glass dish with a mixture of apricot jam, sherry and lemon juice. Cool cream mixture a little and pour into dish slowly and carefully from a height (best to put dish on floor on paper for this). Cool for 4 hours or more in refrigerator.

SERVES 6.

LEMON SNOW | Mrs. Michael de V. Flinn

1 pkg. (1 tbsp.) unflavored gelatin
⅔ cup sugar
1½ cups boiling water
¼ tsp. grated lemon peel
½ cup lemon juice
3 egg whites
"Sauce for Lemon Snow" (p. 463)

1. Mix gelatin and sugar. Add boiling water. Stir until gelatin is dissolved. Add peel and juice. Chill until mixture is syrupy (about 1 hour).
2. Beat egg whites until stiff.
3. Add to lemon mixture and beat until it thickens.
4. Chill overnight in 1-quart mold (covered) which has been rinsed in cold water.

SERVES 4 to 6.
Serve with "Sauce for Lemon Snow."

MACAROON RING WITH ICE CREAM AND CARAMEL SAUCE

½ cup pecans
14 square soda crackers
1 tsp. baking powder
4 egg whites
1 cup granulated sugar
2 tsps. almond extract
1 qt. coffee ice cream (homemade or commercial)
1½ cups hot "Caramel Sauce" (p. 458)

Grind pecans and soda crackers in meat grinder. Mix with baking powder. Whip egg whites in a large bowl until very stiff. Beat in, slowly, sugar and almond extract. Fold in cracker mixture. Place in a 1½-quart buttered ring mold and bake in a preheated 300° oven for 30 minutes. Cool and unmold and serve with ice cream in the center of the mold. Serve hot sauce separately.

SERVES 10.

MUSCATEL MARSHMALLOW FLUFF | *Mrs. Joseph Charyk*

22 marshmallows (regular size—about 1¼ inches)
½ pt. heavy cream, whipped stiff
¼ cup muscatel wine

Melt marshmallows in the top of a 2-quart double boiler over boiling water. Add melted marshmallows to whipped cream.

Stir in the wine. Cool and refrigerate for an hour in bowl in which it is to be served.

SERVES 4 to 6.

FROSTED ORANGES COINTREAU | *Ruth Coburn*

8 large navel oranges
1 cup sugar
1 cup water
1 cup pure orange juice (strained)
1 tbsp. Cointreau or brandy
½ cup chopped pistachio nuts

Peel oranges completely with a sharp knife. Boil together sugar and water. Add orange juice and Cointreau or brandy. Chill. Pour over oranges in a (11¾ x 7½ x 1¾ inch) glass dish and put in deep freeze until frosted.

Serve one to a person on a platter with chopped pistachio nuts on top of each.

SERVES 8.

FRESH PEACH BRÛLÉE

4 cups sliced fresh peeled peaches
2 tbsps. sugar
juice of ½ lemon
1 pt. sour cream
1 cup light brown sugar

1. Fill 10-inch glass pie pan with sliced peaches.
2. Sprinkle with sugar and lemon juice.
3. Frost, immediately, with sour cream (to completely cover the peaches).
4. Add ¼ inch of light brown sugar to completely cover the sour cream.
5. Broil (6 inches from the flame) until the sugar melts. Watch this carefully!

6. Place in refrigerator to chill again.
7. Before serving, tilt pie pan to drain off excess juice into the sink.
SERVES 8.

This may be made with 4 cups white seedless grapes or sliced strawberries or blueberries instead of peaches.

PEACHES AND STRAWBERRIES FLAMBÉ

⅔ cup quick or old-fashioned oats, uncooked
⅓ cup flaked or shredded coconut
¼ cup firmly packed light brown sugar
¼ cup butter or margarine, melted
2 cups fresh or frozen sliced strawberries
1 cup fresh or frozen sliced peaches, drained
⅓ cup Curaçao liqueur, warmed
1 cup heavy cream, whipped

Combine oats, coconut, sugar and butter in a 9½-inch pie pan. Heat in preheated 350° oven for 10 minutes. Cool; break into pieces. Place pieces in 6 individual serving dishes. Combine strawberries and peaches in shallow flameproof dish (8 x 8 x 2 inches). Pour liqueur over fruit and light. When flame has gone out, spoon fruit over the coconut pieces. Garnish with whipped cream.
SERVES 6.

MRS. WOODROW WILSON'S PEARS IN COINTREAU WITH FROZEN CREAM

12 perfect firm Bartlett pears
  enough water to cover pears
½ tsp. lemon juice
4 cups light brown sugar
6 cups water
1 teacup Cointreau
1 pt. heavy cream

1. Peel the pears, leaving them whole with the stems.
2. Put immediately in cold water to cover with a few drops of lemon juice. This prevents them from turning brown.

3. Melt sugar and water in a 10-inch skillet and boil for 5 minutes, stirring.

4. Add the pears (which have been wiped dry with a cloth) and cook until they are transparent and tender, but not mushy.

5. Fill a teacup with Cointreau and when the pears are done, lift each, separately, and dip in the Cointreau until well saturated.

6. Put them in a big glass dish, piling them in a pyramid if possible.

7. Continue to boil the syrup until it is moderately thick.

8. Add the Cointreau in which the pears were dipped. Stir and pour this mixture gradually over the pears.

9. Place in refrigerator to chill.

10. One and a half hours before dinner is announced, empty the cream into a refrigerator tray. When ready to serve the pears, this cream should be crystallized and not quite stiff.

11. Put the cream in a very cold silver bowl and pass with the pears.

SERVES 12.

STRAWBERRY BAVARIAN | *Ruth Coburn*

1 qt. vanilla ice cream
1 pt. heavy cream, whipped stiff
1 pt. fresh strawberries
2 jiggers of brandy

To slightly softened vanilla ice cream, add the whipped cream. To serve, top with fresh strawberries that have soaked for 1 hour in brandy.

SERVES 6.

STRAWBERRIES WITH CREAM CHEESE

1 large (8 oz.) pkg. cream cheese, softened
¼ cup sour cream
1 pt. fresh strawberries, with stems
4 tbsps. powdered sugar

Mix cream cheese in a bowl with sour cream until smooth. Pack in 10-oz. custard cup and set in refrigerator. (Rinse mold first in cold water.) Unmold in center of small tray and surround with fresh strawberries dipped in powdered sugar.

SERVES 4.

To soften cream cheese remove from refrigerator and keep at room temperature overnight.

STRAWBERRY, KUMQUAT AND ALMOND SUPREME

2 pt. boxes strawberries
1 (12½ oz.) jar kumquats in syrup
2 tbsps. sugar
1 spiral lemon peel from 1 lemon

1 (2⅜ oz.) pkg. blanched slivered almonds
4 tbsps. Cointreau
12 to 16 macaroons

1. Wash, hull and slice strawberries and place in a silver bowl.
2. Deseed and slice kumquats in fine slivers.
3. Place kumquats in pan on top of stove and add all the juice from the jar. Then add sugar and lemon peel.
4. Cook for 3 or 4 minutes, stirring at high heat to slightly thicken.
5. Remove from stove, add almonds and Cointreau and remove lemon peel.
6. Pour this over the strawberries and chill in refrigerator.

SERVES 6 to 8.

Serve with fresh macaroons.

ALSATIAN CAKE

½ cup butter
1¼ cups powdered sugar
4 egg yolks
¼ cup very strong coffee, cold

2 dozen ladyfingers
1 cup rum
½ pt. heavy cream

Cream butter in a large bowl until soft. Add sugar, beat until the mixture is very light and fluffy. Add yolks beating hard. Beat in coffee slowly. Line a 1½-quart loaf tin with wax paper. Dip ladyfingers in the rum; then put in bottom of pan. Next add half of egg mixture, rest of ladyfingers and remaining egg mixture on top. Can be kept in refrigerator 24 hours. To serve, cover with whipped cream, whipped stiff.

SERVES 8.

GRANDMOTHER'S ANGEL CAKE

12 egg whites
1 tsp. cream of tartar
⅔ tsp. salt
1 tsp. almond extract

1½ cups sugar
1 cup cake flour, sifted before measuring

1. In a large bowl, beat egg whites until they are foamy.
2. Add cream of tartar, salt and almond extract.
3. Beat this mixture until it stands in peaks, but not dry. (All the above may be done with an electric beater.)
4. Fold in sugar with a spoon.
5. Preheat oven to 325°.
6. Sift flour into mixture. Fold over and over, with a spoon, until it is thoroughly mixed.
7. Pour into a large (10 x 4 inch) *ungreased* angel-cake pan and bake for 45 minutes.
8. Remove pan from oven. Invert pan and let cake hang in the pan for about ½ hour.
9. Remove cake from pan and place on cake plate.

SERVES 10.

BLARNEY STONES | *Mrs. Harry S. Truman*

6 egg whites
½ tsp. cream of tartar
1½ cups sugar
6 egg yolks, beaten well
1 cup cake flour, sifted before measuring

½ tsp. vanilla flavoring
½ tsp. lemon flavoring
¼ lb. butter (very soft)
2 cups confectioners' sugar, sifted
1 egg, beaten (for frosting)
1 cup finely ground jumbo peanuts

1. Beat egg whites and cream of tartar until stiff.
2. Fold in sugar which has been sifted twice.
3. Add egg yolks, flour and flavoring.
4. Bake in preheated oven (325° to 350°) in an ungreased pan (9 x 12 x 2 inches) for 45 minutes.

5. Hang upside down to cool (as for angel food cake).
6. Cut in strips any size.
7. In a medium-sized bowl, mix butter with sugar and egg until smooth (for icing). Makes 1½ cups of icing.
8. Spread all sides of strips with the icing.
9. Roll in peanuts.

MAKES about 36 (3 inch long) pieces.

BÛCHE DE NOËL | Mrs. Charles Lucet
The Embassy of France

This symbolic cake is served at Christmas time in France.

5 egg yolks
½ cup sugar
½ cup flour
5 egg whites, well beaten

3½ tbsps. melted butter
"Crème au Beurre" (p. 457)
"Meringues I" (p. 424)

Mix egg yolks with sugar. Add flour, egg whites and butter. Spread (½ inch thick) on buttered paper (or wax paper) on a 17 x 14-inch cookie tin. Bake in a preheated 400° oven for 12 minutes. Turn upside down on a kitchen towel and let cool.

Spread, on all the surface, a thin layer of "Crème au Beurre." Roll over into the shape of a log and let stand on its closing side. Using a pastry bag with a fluted nozzle, filled with the "Crème au Beurre," ice the cake in lengthwise strips resembling the bark of a log. Add small meringues to resemble mushrooms.

SERVES 10 to 12.

ALICE'S CHOCOLATE CAKE

½ cup butter
1½ cups sugar
4 egg yolks, well beaten
½ cup milk
1¾ cups (sifted) cake flour
2 tsps. baking powder

2 squares unsweetened chocolate
5 tbsps. water
2 tsps. vanilla
4 egg whites, beaten stiff
"Alice's Frosting" (p. 455)

1. Cream butter and sugar. Add egg yolks.
2. Add, alternately, milk and flour sifted with the baking powder.
3. Stir well and add chocolate and water which have been melted together in the top of a double boiler over boiling water.
4. Cool, add vanilla and fold in the egg whites.
5. Place in a flat, greased (15½ x 10¼ x ¾ inch) pan and bake in a 350° oven for about 20 to 25 minutes (or until a straw stuck in the center of the cake comes out dry).
6. Put "Alice's Frosting" on while cake is still in the pan.
7. Cut in 2 x 4-inch squares when cool (in the pan).
MAKES 20 pieces.
This is marvelous with a scoop of French vanilla ice cream on top of each serving.

BUTTERMILK CHOCOLATE CAKE | *Ethel Jackson*

Ethel Jackson was our friend and cook for many years. When she died she left, as a legacy, the recipe for this moist and superb flat-pan chocolate cake—for which we are eternally grateful.

Dry Ingredients:
2½ cups (sifted) cake flour
2 cups sugar
6 tbsps. cocoa *or* 2 squares unsweetened chocolate (melted over hot water in top of double boiler)
1 tsp. baking soda
1 tsp. baking powder
⅛ tsp. salt

Liquid Ingredients:
1 cup buttermilk
1 cup vegetable oil
2 eggs (whole), beaten
1 tsp. vanilla
1 cup hot water

1. Preheat oven to 350°.
2. In a large bowl mix dry ingredients and add buttermilk, oil, eggs and vanilla. Mix well. Add hot water.
3. Pour into flat (15½ x 10½ x 1 inch) pan greased with shortening and dusted with flour.
4. Bake for 25 minutes.
5. Frost with "Alice's Frosting" (p. 455).
MAKES 35 (2 inch) squares.

CHEESECAKE | *Margery Clifford Lanagan*

Crust:
16 graham crackers crushed
¼ cup melted butter

Filling:
3 (8 oz.) pkgs. cream cheese, softened
4 eggs, beaten
1 tsp. vanilla
½ cup sugar
1 pt. sour cream
7 tbsps. sugar (for sour cream)
1 (12 oz.) box frozen, mixed fruits and the juice
1 tsp. cornstarch

1. Line a spring form pan (9½ x 2¼ inches) with graham crackers and melted butter (mixed together).
2. In a bowl, mix cream cheese, eggs, vanilla and sugar. Pour into pan over graham cracker crust.
3. Bake in preheated 325° oven for 30 minutes. Remove from oven and let cool for 10 minutes.
4. Mix sour cream with sugar. Spread over cake. Return to oven for 10 minutes, then cool. Unmold.
5. Place the fruit juice in a small saucepan and stir in the cornstarch. Boil for 2 or 3 minutes until it thickens.
6. Add the fruits to the juice and pour over the cheesecake. Let it run down the sides of the cake.

SERVES 8 to 10.

SWEDISH CINNAMON CAKE

1 heaping tbsp. butter
1 cup sugar
1 egg, beaten
1 cup sifted cake flour
1 tsp. baking powder
1 tsp. cinnamon
½ cup milk
2 tbsps. sugar
¼ cup powdered sugar
½ pt. heavy cream, whipped

Cream butter and sugar. Add beaten egg. Sift together flour, baking powder and cinnamon. Add, alternately, to egg mixture with milk. Pour into buttered (8 x 8 x 2 inch) cake pan. Sprinkle top with granulated sugar. Bake in preheated 350° oven for 20 to 22 minutes.

When it is out of oven, sprinkle liberally with powdered sugar.

Serve hot, cut in large squares, with whipped cream for dessert, or cool and cut into small squares for tea.

SERVES 8 to 10.

MOTHER'S AUSTRIAN COFFEE CAKE

⅓ cup butter, softened
1 cup sugar
2 eggs, well beaten
½ cup milk
2½ cups flour
2½ tsps. baking powder
⅛ tsp. salt
1 tsp. vanilla

Topping:
¼ cup butter
⅔ cup sugar
1 tsp. flour

1. Cream softened butter with sugar; add eggs.
2. Add to this, alternately, the milk and the flour mixed with the baking powder.
3. Add salt and vanilla.
4. Pour into a buttered (8 x 8 x 2 inch) pan.
5. Mix the topping ingredients (butter, sugar and flour).
6. Spread this over the top of the coffee cake.
7. Bake in preheated 350° oven 30 to 40 minutes.

SERVES 8.

SOUR CREAM COFFEE CAKE | *Mrs. Henry Buhl*

1 cup butter or margarine
1½ cups sugar
2 eggs
2 cups flour, sifted before measuring
½ tsp. soda
1 tsp. baking powder
1 cup sour cream
1 tsp. vanilla

Filling:
6 tbsps. sugar (granulated)
1½ tsps. cinnamon
2 tsps. cocoa
½ cup nuts, chopped (reserve a little of this for topping)

1. Cream butter or margarine with sugar in a large bowl.
2. Add eggs, and the flour, soda and baking powder sifted together.
3. Add sour cream and vanilla.
4. Beat for 3 minutes.
5. Preheat oven to 325°.
6. Grease a 10-inch angel cake pan and dust with flour.
7. Put ½ of the batter in the pan and ⅔ of the filling.
8. Add remaining batter and top with rest of the filling mixture.
9. Bake for 1 hour. Do not open oven until it is done.

SERVES 12 to 14.

MOTHER'S DAFFODIL CAKE

White Part
6 egg whites
½ tsp. cream of tartar
⅛ tsp. salt
½ tsp. vanilla
¾ cup sugar, sifted
½ cup cake flour (sifted before measuring)

Yellow Part
6 egg yolks
¾ cup sugar
¼ cup boiling water
½ tsp. lemon extract
½ tsp. orange extract
¾ cup cake flour, sifted
1 tsp. baking powder

White Part

Beat egg whites until foamy. Add cream of tartar, salt and vanilla. Then beat until it stands in peaks, but is not dry. Fold in sugar with spoon. Then fold in flour (sifted again). Beat until thoroughly mixed. Pour into large (10 x 4 inch) angel-cake pan. (This can be made with an electric beater except for folding in sugar and flour with spoon.)

Yellow Part

Beat egg yolks well. Add sugar and beat. Add boiling water and flavorings. Beat well. Add flour with baking powder sifted into it. Mix well and *pour over white part*.

Bake for 45 to 50 minutes in preheated 325° oven. Invert pan and let cake hang in pan about ½ hour. Then take out of pan and place on cake plate.

SERVES 10 to 12.

EASY PINEAPPLE AND WALNUT UPSIDE DOWN CAKE

½ cup butter
1 cup brown sugar
6 pineapple slices (save juice)
½ cup chopped walnuts
6 Maraschino cherries
1 box gold cake mix
1 tsp. almond flavoring
"Foamy Sauce" (p. 460)

In heavy 10-inch ovenproof skillet, melt butter. Stir in brown sugar. Arrange pineapple slices, walnuts and cherries in a design and simmer until pineapple is golden on the bottom.

Follow directions on the box of gold cake mix, but use pineapple juice instead of milk. Add almond flavoring. Pour the mixture over the pineapple, walnuts and cherries.

Bake in same skillet in a preheated 350° oven for 25 to 30 minutes. Let stand for 15 minutes; then invert skillet onto a serving plate.

Serve with "Foamy Sauce."

SERVES 8 to 10.

GINGERBREAD

½ cup butter
½ cup brown sugar
2 egg yolks, beaten
1 tsp. cinnamon
1 tsp. ginger
½ tsp. cloves
¼ tsp. allspice
½ tsp. salt
2 cups sifted flour
1 tsp. baking soda dissolved in ½ cup boiling water
1 cup molasses
2 egg whites, beaten stiff
"Caramel Sauce" (p. 458) or ½ pt. heavy cream, whipped stiff
1 tsp. sugar

Cream butter and sugar in a large bowl. Add egg yolks. Mix spices with salt and flour and sift into egg mixture. Mix soda and water with the molasses, add to batter, and beat all together thoroughly. Fold in egg whites. Fill buttered and floured 12-section muffin pan a bit over ½ full and bake about 20 minutes in a preheated (350°) oven. Serve with "Caramel Sauce" or whipped cream with sugar added.

MAKES 12 individual gingerbread muffins.

GEORGE WASHINGTON COCOA ROLL

4 eggs
1 tsp. vanilla
¾ cup sugar
½ cup sifted cake flour
⅛ cup dry cocoa (not a mix)
1 tsp. baking powder
½ tsp. salt

⅛ cup confectioners' sugar
1 qt. ice cream
1 cup heavy cream
3 tbsps. instant cocoa mix
½ cup chopped pistachio nuts *or* chopped pecans *or* chopped toasted almonds

1. Grease a (15 x 10 inch) baking pan. Line with brown paper; grease paper.

2. Beat eggs with vanilla in large bowl of electric mixer at high speed until fluffy-thick and lemon-colored. Gradually beat in sugar until mixture is very thick.

3. Sift flour, cocoa, baking powder and salt over bowl. Fold in carefully until well blended. Spread batter evenly in prepared pan.

4. Bake in preheated 400° oven 10 to 12 minutes or until top springs back when lightly touched with fingertip.

5. Loosen cake around edges of pan with a sharp knife. Invert pan on a clean towel lightly dusted with confectioners' sugar; peel off wax paper. Cut off edges of cake if they are too crisp to roll. Starting at one end, roll up cake jelly-roll fashion; wrap in towel. Cool completely on a wire rack.

6. Soften ice cream slightly. Unroll cooled cake carefully. Spread evenly with softened ice cream and reroll. Place on cookie sheet (15 x 10 inches) and freeze at least 1 hour.

Frost with chocolate whipped cream made by beating cream and cocoa mix together until stiff (do not overbeat). Spread on cake roll at once. Sprinkle with chopped nuts.

MAKES 8 slices.

MOTHER'S SPONGE CAKE

6 egg yolks
¾ cup sugar
¼ cup boiling water
½ tsp. lemon extract

½ tsp. orange extract
¾ cup sifted cake flour
1 tsp. baking powder

Beat egg yolks well in a large bowl. Add sugar and beat again. Add boiling water and flavorings. Beat well. Add flour sifted with baking powder. Mix well. Place in square (8 x 8 x 2 inch) cake pan and bake in a preheated 325° oven for 40 to 45 minutes.

SERVES 8 to 10.

ICE CREAM ROLL

4 eggs
1 cup sugar
1 cup sifted cake flour
⅛ tsp. salt
1 tsp. baking powder
½ tsp. vanilla

⅛ cup confectioners' sugar
1 qt. vanilla ice cream
   "Chocolate Sauce I" (p. 459)
½ cup milk chocolate shavings *or*
   ½ cup chopped walnuts

1. Beat eggs until light in a large bowl.
2. Add sugar gradually.
3. Fold in flour sifted with salt and baking powder.
4. Add vanilla.
5. Spread the dough on a large cookie tin (17 x 14 inches) which has been buttered and lined with buttered brown paper.
6. Bake in preheated 400° oven for 12 minutes. Watch!
7. Trim edges and turn out on a towel lightly dusted with confectioners' sugar.
8. Roll in towel until ready to use. Keep at room temperature.
9. Spread cake out and cover with softened ice cream (about ½ inch thickness).
10. Roll up carefully.
11. Before serving, cover with hot "Chocolate Sauce I."
12. Sprinkle with shavings of milk chocolate or chopped walnuts.

SERVES 6 to 8.

SPONGE CAKE II

6 egg yolks	6 egg whites
1¼ cups sugar	1 rounded tsp. cream of tartar
6 tbsps. water	¼ tsp. lemon juice
1 heaping cup sifted cake flour	1 tsp. vanilla extract
⅛ tsp. salt	2 tsps. sifted confectioners' sugar

1. Beat yolks and sugar together in a large bowl until foamy and lemon-colored. Add water.
2. Sift the flour with the salt. Then add to first mixture. Stir in well.
3. Preheat oven to 325°.
4. Beat egg whites until foamy. Add cream of tartar and continue beating until it stands in peaks.
5. Fold into flour mixture. Add lemon juice and vanilla and mix completely.
6. Grease and lightly flour a 9-inch spring form pan (bottom only) and fill with cake mixture.
7. Bake for 40 to 45 minutes. Test center of cake with broom straw. If it comes out clean, cake is done.
8. Turn out on cake rack, put second cake rack on side that is up, and turn upside down so that top of cake is now up. Dust with confectioners' sugar.

SERVES 10 to 12.

ORANGE TORTE | *Bette Kovin*

¾ cup butter	1 tsp. baking soda
1 cup sugar	1 cup chopped dates
2 eggs	1 cup chopped walnuts
grated rind of 1 orange	1 cup orange juice
2½ cups sifted cake flour	1 cup confectioners' sugar
1 tsp. baking powder	½ pt. heavy cream, whipped
¼ tsp. salt	1 tbsp. sugar (for cream)
1 cup sour cream	

In a large bowl, soften butter, work in sugar until smooth, and add eggs one at a time, beating hard after each. Stir in grated rind. Sift flour with baking powder and salt and stir into mixture alternately with sour cream mixed with soda. Stir in dates and nuts. Spoon into oiled tube (10 x 4 inch) pan. Bake at 375° (preheated) for 1 hour.

Remove from oven and immediately pour over top mixture of orange juice and confectioners' sugar. Let stand until completely cold. Cut into wedges, and top with sweetened whipped cream.

SERVES 8 to 10.

UPSIDE-DOWN FRUIT AND RUM CAKE

¼ lb. butter
1 cup light brown sugar
1 (1 lb. 1 oz.) can mixed fruit, drained
4 eggs, separated
1 cup sugar
1 cup sifted flour
1 tsp. baking powder
⅛ cup rum
"Rum Sauce" (p. 463)

1. Over moderate heat, melt butter in 10-inch ovenproof skillet. Add brown sugar and, when dissolved, add the fruits in a design. Simmer until bottom of fruit is golden. Set aside.

2. In a large bowl, beat egg yolks until frothy and add sugar. Add, alternately, the flour, baking powder and stiffly beaten egg whites. Pour this mixture over the fruits in the skillet.

3. Place skillet in preheated 350° oven and bake for about 35 minutes.

4. When cool, unmold by turning skillet upside down. Sprinkle rum all over the top. Serve with "Rum Sauce."

SERVES 8 to 10.

GRANDMOTHER'S CARAMEL ICE CREAM

This used to be frozen by hand and if I was good, I could "lick the dasher."

1 cup sugar
1 qt. hot milk
4 eggs
1 tbsp. cornstarch
1 pt. light cream
1 tbsp. vanilla
⅛ tsp. salt

Caramelize 1 cup sugar in a small skillet until melted and golden. Add slowly to hot milk. Add eggs and cornstarch mixed together. Cook until thick. Cool and add cream and vanilla and salt.

Freeze in electric ice-cream freezer.

MAKES approximately 2 quarts.

MY GRANDMOTHER'S STRAWBERRY ICE CREAM

4 eggs
¾ cup sugar
1 tbsp. cornstarch
1 qt. hot milk

1 tbsp. vanilla
2 pt. boxes strawberries, washed, hulled and crushed
1 pt. heavy cream

Beat eggs, ½ cup sugar and cornstarch together in a bowl. Add to hot milk; cook until fairly thick. When cooled to room temperature, add vanilla, strawberries, remaining sugar and the cream.

Freeze in electric ice-cream freezer.

MAKES approximately 2 quarts.

CHOCOLATE MOUSSE

4 squares semisweet chocolate
2 squares unsweetened chocolate
6 eggs
¼ cup sugar

1½ cups heavy cream
2 tbsps. brandy
1 cup shaved semisweet chocolate

1. Melt chocolate in top of double boiler over hot water. Cool.

2. Separate eggs, putting whites in medium bowl and yolks in a large bowl. Beat whites with rotary beater until foamy and double in bulk. Add sugar slowly 1 tablespoon at a time, beating until whites stand in stiff peaks. Use same rotary beater (washed) to beat ½ cup of the cream in a small bowl until stiff.

3. Still using same beater (washed), beat egg yolks until thick and light; add cooled chocolate slowly and continue to beat until well blended. Add brandy gradually, beating until smooth.

4. Beat in about ¼ of the egg white mixture. Stir in remainder until no streaks of white remain. Fold in whipped cream. Spoon into crystal bowl or 8 wet (10 oz.) custard cups. Chill until firm (at least 1 hour).

5. Just before serving, beat remaining cream in small bowl until stiff. Put star tip on pastry bag. Fill bag with whipped cream. Press rosettes around edge of unmolded mousse or on top of individual unmolded cups and sprinkle with shaved semisweet chocolate.

SERVES 8.

STRAWBERRY MOUSSE

1 qt. strawberries, washed and hulled
½ cup sugar
½ cup white wine
2 envelopes (2 tbsps.) unflavored gelatin
½ cup cold water
½ cup boiling water
2 cups heavy cream
8 to 10 sprigs mint leaves
¼ cup water
¼ cup powdered sugar

1. Save 8 or 10 whole berries for decorating. Push the rest through a sieve. Add sugar and wine, stirring well. Chill.

2. Soften gelatin in cold water and add boiling water, stirring until dissolved.

3. Cool this mixture and add to strawberry mixture.

4. Beat until thick and fluffy.

5. Whip cream stiff (do not overwhip) and fold into above mixture.

6. Pour into a round 2-quart glass mold which has been rinsed in cold water.

7. Chill, covered, overnight.

8. Unmold and decorate with whole strawberries. Surround with fresh mint leaves—the edges dipped in water and then in powdered sugar to coat.

SERVES 8 to 10.

MERINGUES I

2 egg whites (room temperature)
½ tsp. vanilla
1/16 tsp. (tiny pinch) cream of tartar (optional)

½ cup confectioners' sugar
1½ tbsps. granulated sugar

1. Place egg whites in large bowl. Beat with an electric beater until they stand in peaks.
2. Beat in vanilla and cream of tartar (optional).
3. Sift sugar slowly into this mixture, beating steadily.
4. Preheat oven to 225°.
5. Place an exact size sheet of brown paper on a (15½ x 10¼ x ¾ inch) cookie sheet and with a spoon drop the size meringues you wish, not too close together. Sprinkle each meringue lightly with granulated sugar.
6. Bake for 1 hour; or more if your meringues are large.
7. Open the oven door when they are done and turn the heat off. Let stand for a few minutes in the oven. Then cool and "nudge" them off the paper with a spoon. Store in tightly covered tin, but only for 2 days as they dry out. It's better to serve them fresh.

MAKES about 6 (3 inch) meringues.

If used as topping on a cooked pie, bake in a preheated oven (425°) for 5 minutes.

MERINGUES II

This makes a whiter meringue than Meringue I.

4 egg whites
⅛ tsp. salt

4 tbsps. sugar

Beat egg whites stiff and add salt. Stir in sugar at once and drop from spoon on greased brown paper on a small cookie tin. Bake in preheated 225° oven for 1 hour. Break underside with spoon while hot.

MAKES about 7 (5 inch) meringues.

PASTRY (DOUBLE CRUST) | *Randall Clifford Wight*

2 cups sifted flour
1 tsp. salt
1 cup vegetable shortening
4 tbs. ice water *or* 4 tbsps. strained chilled orange juice (for berry pies)

1. Sift flour and salt. Cut into the shortening, in a large bowl, with a pastry blender until pieces are the size of tiny peas.
2. Sprinkle 1 tablespoon water (or juice) over part of the mixture. Toss gently with a fork. Push to one side of bowl and repeat until all is moistened. Gather up with your hands and form into a ball.
3. Divide ball in half. Use 2 sheets wax paper (one under the pastry, one over), flatten half ball slightly, smoothing the edges. Roll out ⅛ inch thick. Roll from center out to edges using a light stroke. Lift carefully and fit into 9-inch pie pan. Fill with pie filling.
4. Roll out remaining pastry, lift carefully and fit over the top of the pie, loosely, allowing ½ inch overhang around the rim of the pie pan.
5. Seal edges with a fork or flute with your fingers. Lightly pierce crust twice with a fork.

Pastry dough should be handled as little as possible to make tender and flaky pastry.

Pastry is better if it is made the day before using, and refrigerated, wrapped in wax paper.

MAKES 2 (9 inch) crusts.

CREAM PUFF PASTE | *Mrs. Joseph Charyk*

1 cup water
2 tbsps. butter
1 cup sifted flour
4 eggs

1. Place water in saucepan.
2. Add butter and bring to a gentle boil.
3. Add flour all at once, stirring in with a spatula. Turn off heat but keep the pan on the same burner. Stir briskly until mixture is completely smooth.
4. Put pan under hand electric mixer. Turn beaters on "slow" and add eggs,

one at a time. Use spatula to keep the mixture from climbing up the sides of the pan too far. Keep beating, for the raw eggs cook in the warm mixture.

5. After the fourth egg is smoothly added, scrape beaters and sides of pan to keep it all together.

6. Preheat oven to 350°.

7. Drop, in rows, by heaping teaspoonfuls onto buttered 17 x 14-inch cookie sheet.

8. Place in oven and bake until golden brown (about 25 minutes).

MAKES 24.

These "Puffs" may be frozen.

DEEP DISH BLUEBERRY PIE

1 double pie crust—see "Pastry (Double Crust)" above	1 tsp. grated lemon peel
2½ qts. fresh blueberries	1 tsp. lemon juice
2½ cups sugar	2½ tbsps. butter
7 tbsps. cornstarch	2 (8 oz.) pkgs. cream cheese *or* 2 qts. vanilla ice cream
¼ tsp. salt	

1. Make pie crusts and roll into one crust (14 x 9¼ inches). Wash and clean blueberries. Pat fairly dry with a paper towel.

2. Place berries in a large bowl. Add sugar, cornstarch, salt, lemon peel and lemon juice. Mix well.

3. Place mixture in an ovenproof (13½ x 8¾ x 1¾ inch) glass dish.

4. Dot the top with the butter.

5. Carefully lift the pie crust and place all over the berries (you will have ½ inch around the rim to spare).

6. With your fingers, pinch the ½ inch of crust all around the top edge of the dish.

7. Carefully pierce the crust with a fork in three places.

8. Preheat oven to 400°. Place pie on center shelf in oven. Bake at 400° for 10 minutes; then reduce heat to 350° and continue baking 35 to 45 more minutes.

9. Watch carefully and if the crust begins to get too brown, cover with a loose sheet of foil.

10. Serve *hot* with a side dish of ½-inch slices of cream cheese or a scoop of vanilla ice cream on top of each serving.

SERVES 16.

QUICK DEEP DISH BLUEBERRY PIE

1 pkg. frozen patty shells
1 (1 lb. 6 oz.) can blueberry pie filling
4 tbsps. butter (broken into "dots")
1 (3 oz.) pkg. cream cheese

1. Defrost patty shells and roll out together between sheets of wax paper to ⅛ inch thickness. Set aside in refrigerator until ready.
2. Preheat oven to 400°.
3. Grease 1-quart ovenproof dish with straight sides and add the blueberry mixture. Dot top with butter.
4. Place crust over the top with ½ inch overhang on the sides. Pinch all around with your fingers and poke six holes in the top with a fork.
5. Place in oven and bake at 400° for 10 minutes. Then reduce heat to 350° and continue to bake for about 20 minutes more or until crust is golden.
6. Serve hot with wedges of cream cheese on a side platter.
SERVES 6.

These frozen patty shells are made of very short pastry so the crust will be very short and very good. It is hard to cut so use a very sharp knife when serving it.

CHOCOLATE MARSHMALLOW PIE

Crust:
¼ cup melted butter
16 graham crackers, crushed
1 tbsp. sugar (optional)

1 square unsweetened chocolate
20 marshmallows (standard size)
⅔ cup milk
½ pt. heavy cream

Filling:
4 (4 oz.) sweet chocolate almond bars

Mix butter, crackers and sugar (optional) and line a 9½-inch pie pan. Bake in a preheated 275° oven for 20 to 25 minutes.

In top of double boiler over boiling water melt chocolate almond bars, unsweetened chocolate and marshmallows. Add milk and cook until thickened a bit. Cool, whip cream and fold into above mixture.

Put in pie shell in refrigerator for 3 hours.
SERVES 6 to 8.

COFFEE CHIFFON PIE

1½ cups graham cracker crumbs (about 17 or 18 crackers)
1 tbsp. sugar

½ tsp. salt
6 tbsps. melted butter
3 tbsps. water

Mix cracker crumbs, sugar, salt, butter and water together well. Press into a well-greased 9-inch pie pan. Bake in a preheated 350° oven for 15 minutes.

Filling:
1 envelope (1 tbsp.) plain gelatin
¾ cup cold strong coffee
4 egg yolks
1 scant cup sugar
½ tsp. salt

1 tbsp. lemon juice
4 egg whites
½ pt. heavy cream *or* ½ pt. Diet Whip (optional)
½ cup chopped pecans

1. Soak gelatin in ¼ cup cold coffee for 5 minutes. Then dissolve in remaining coffee heated.
2. Beat egg yolks slightly. Add ½ cup sugar and salt and cook in double boiler over boiling water until it looks like custard.
3. Add gelatin and coffee mixture and lemon juice. Cool slightly.
4. Beat egg whites until stiff and add remaining sugar. Fold this last mixture into the custard. Fill crust and chill. Serve spread with thin layer of whipped cream and chopped nuts. Diet Whip may be used for dieters.

SERVES 6 to 8.

COFFEE ICE CREAM PIE | *Randall Clifford Wight*

18 chocolate (filled) cookies
½ cup melted butter
1½ qts. coffee ice cream, softened
2 squares unsweetened chocolate
½ cup sugar

1 tbsp. butter
⅔ cup evaporated milk
1 cup heavy cream
½ cup chopped walnuts

1. Split chocolate cookies and remove the filling. Crush cookies with butter. Mix well together.
2. Line (9½ x 2¼ inch) spring form pan (bottom only) with this mixture. Push down with a fork. Chill.

3. Spread softened ice cream over the crust. Place in freezer.

4. Place chocolate in top of double boiler over hot water and stir in sugar, 1 tablespoon butter and, slowly, add evaporated milk. Stir constantly for about 7 minutes (it doesn't thicken).

5. Remove from stove and chill.

6. Remove mold from freezer and spread above mixture on top of the ice cream.

7. Freeze again.

8. Before taking pie from pan, whip cream until stiff and cover the pie. Unmold on chilled round platter to serve.

9. Top with chopped walnuts.

SERVES 6 to 8.

QUICK ICE CREAM PIE

18 graham crackers
¼ cup melted butter
2 qts. chocolate ice cream, slightly softened
½ pt. commercial marshmallow sauce
½ pt. heavy cream
½ cup shaved sweet chocolate

Make pie shell of cracker crumbs and butter and line a 10-inch pie pan. Bake 15 minutes in preheated 350° oven. Cool. Fill with ice cream and frost with marshmallow sauce ¼ inch thick. Place in refrigerator ice compartment or freezer until ready to serve. Then whip cream and put on top of marshmallow. Shave sweet chocolate all over the pie.

For Variations:
2 quarts peach ice cream and 1 cup fresh sliced peaches,
or
2 quarts strawberry ice cream and 1 cup sliced strawberries,
or
2 quarts coffee ice cream and 1 cup shaved chocolate
But be sure to use the thin layer of marshmallow on all the different combinations.

SERVES 7 to 8.

LEMON (OR LIME) CHIFFON PIE SUPREME | *John Lucas*

John Lucas has been a member of our household for eighteen years. This is his specialty and he is rightly famous for it. Even the most dedicated dieters can't resist it.

Crust:
2½ cups graham cracker crumbs
¼ lb. butter, melted
½ cup powdered sugar

Mix above well and press into pie plate with a large spoon.
Bake in preheated 275° oven for 20 minutes or until edges are slightly brown.
Set aside to cool completely.

Filling:
5 egg yolks, beaten to lemon color
½ cup fresh lemon juice (for lemon pie) *or* ½ cup fresh lime juice (for lime pie)
⅔ cup granulated sugar
1 envelope (1 tbsp.) plain gelatin
¼ cup cold water
5 egg whites, beaten stiff
½ pt. heavy cream
3 tbsps. sugar (for whipped cream)
½ tsp. vanilla
⅛ tsp. salt
1 tbsp. grated lemon peel (for lemon pie) *or* 1 tbsp. grated lime peel (for lime pie)

1. In top of double boiler over boiling water, cook the egg yolks, lemon juice or lime juice and sugar, stirring constantly until the consistency of thick custard.
2. In bowl, sprinkle cold water over gelatin until dissolved and add to above mixture. Stir. Remove from stove.
3. Fold in egg whites.
4. Fill the pie shell with the above.
5. Chill in refrigerator for 3 or 4 hours.
6. Just before serving, whip the cream, add the sugar, vanilla and salt and spread over top of the pie. Sprinkle grated lemon peel or lime peel on top.

SERVES 6 or 8.

PECAN PIE

Use half of recipe for "Pastry (Double Crust)" (p. 425).

⅛ cup butter or shortening
½ cup brown sugar
½ cup milk
1 cup chopped pecans
3 eggs, beaten
½ tsp. salt
1 cup dark corn syrup
½ tsp. vanilla

Cream butter and sugar in a large bowl. Add remaining ingredients and blend. Pour into unbaked (9 inch) pie shell. Bake in hot oven (425°) for 10 minutes. Then reduce oven heat to 350° and continue to bake for 25 more minutes or until firm.
SERVES 6 to 8.

PINEAPPLE MACADAMIA PIE

This recipe is very rich, very fattening, but *so* good. Use half of recipe for "Pastry (Double Crust)" (p. 425).

3 eggs
⅔ cup sugar
1 cup light corn syrup
¼ cup melted butter
1 tsp. vanilla
½ tsp. salt
1 can (13½ oz.) pineapple tidbits, drained
1 cup chopped macadamia nuts
½ pt. heavy cream (whipped)

1. Make pastry.
2. Beat together in a large bowl with rotary beater, until thoroughly mixed, the eggs, sugar, syrup, butter, vanilla and salt. Stir in pineapple and nuts.
3. Turn into pastry-lined 9-inch pie pan.
4. Bake in 350° oven for 45 minutes or until set.
5. Cool thoroughly on a rack before cutting.
6. Top with whipped cream.
SERVES 8.

PINEAPPLE ISLAND PIE

Use recipe for "Pastry (Double Crust)" (p. 425).

1 (1 lb. 4½ oz.) can crushed pineapple	2 tbsps. fresh lime juice
4 tbsps. sugar	3 tbsps. butter
3½ tbsps. cornstarch	½ cup light corn syrup
¼ tsp. salt	½ cup sliced almonds

1. Make pastry. Divide into halves. Roll out half on lightly floured board and fit into 9-inch pie plate.
2. Preheat oven to 425°.
3. Combine undrained pineapple, 2 tablespoons sugar, cornstarch and salt. Cook, stirring, over moderate heat about 5 minutes until mixture clears and thickens. Stir in lime juice and 2 tablespoons butter.
4. Turn into pastry-lined pie pan. Roll other half of pastry and fit over the filling. Seal and make high fluted rim. Prick top of pastry with a fork. Set pie plate on baking sheet (17 x 14 inches) and bake in 350° oven for 20 minutes or until crust begins to brown.
5. Meanwhile, combine remaining sugar, remaining butter and corn syrup in a saucepan. Cook, stirring, over low heat until mixture boils and sugar dissolves. This makes a glaze for top of pie.
6. Remove pie from oven. Sprinkle almonds on top of crust.
7. Spoon hot glaze topping evenly over all. Return pie to oven and bake 5 to 10 minutes longer, until topping is bubbly and lightly browned.
8. Cool completely before cutting.

SERVES 8.

MRS. RICHARD M. NIXON'S PUMPKIN PIE

1 10-inch pie crust	1 (1 lb.) can pumpkin
1¼ cups sugar	4 eggs
5 tbsps. plus 1 tsp. flour	3 cups milk
⅛ tsp. salt	1¼ tsps. vanilla
½ tsp. allspice	1 tbsp. molasses
⅛ tsp. ginger	2 tbsps. plus 2 tsps. melted butter

Line the unbaked pie crust with brown paper to come up above the sides. Fill the center with uncooked rice or beans (something to weight it down) and bake for 15 minutes in a preheated 375° oven.

Meanwhile, blend sugar, flour, salt, allspice and ginger. Stir in the pumpkin and beat in the eggs. Blend the milk and vanilla thoroughly into the mixture, then stir in the molasses and butter. Remove the paper and rice from pie shell and pour in the pumpkin filling. Bake in 375° oven for about 40 minutes, until custard is set.

SERVES 8.

PUMPKIN CHIFFON PIE

2 (9 in.) baked pie shells—"Pastry (Double Crust)" (p. 425). Pinch the edges of the pastry to ruffle it. Bake for 12 to 15 minutes (425° oven). Cool.

- 2½ envelopes plain gelatin
- 1½ cups sugar
- 1 tsp. salt
- 1 tsp. nutmeg
- 1 tsp. ginger
- ¼ tsp. powdered cloves
- 2 tsps. cinnamon
- 1⅓ cups evaporated milk
- 6 egg yolks, beaten until frothy
- 2½ cups pumpkin, canned or cooked
- 6 egg whites
- 1 pt. heavy cream
- ½ tsp. vanilla
- 4 tbsps. sugar (for topping)

To cook fresh pumpkin, see "Butternut Squash" (p. 236).

Mix together gelatin, ¾ cup sugar, salt and spices in saucepan. Stir in evaporated milk and egg yolks; blend well. Place over low heat and cook, stirring constantly, until gelatin dissolves and mixture thickens slightly (about 3 minutes). Remove from heat. Stir in pumpkin. Chill, stirring occasionally, until mixture mounds when dropped from a spoon (about 1 hour).

Beat egg whites until stiff but not dry. Gradually add remaining ¾ cup sugar and beat until very stiff. Fold in pumpkin mixture. Turn into pie shells and chill until firm (2 hours or overnight).

Top with cream, whipped with vanilla and sugar.

SERVES 16.

RUM PIE | The U.S. Senate Dining Room

- 1 graham cracker crust (follow "Coffee Chiffon Pie" crust recipe, p. 428)
- 1 pt. milk
- 9 tbsps. sugar
- 3 tbsps. cornstarch
- 5 egg yolks
- 1 envelope (1 tbsp.) plain gelatin
- ¼ cup cold water
- 2 cups heavy cream, whipped stiff
- ½ cup Jamaica rum (to your taste)
- 3 egg whites, beaten stiff
- ½ cup sweet chocolate shavings (optional)

1. Make and bake crust in a 9½-inch pie pan. Set aside to cool.
2. Heat milk in a saucepan and add 8 tablespoons sugar and the cornstarch mixed together. Cook, stirring, until thick.
3. In a bowl, beat egg yolks lightly and add a little of the hot milk mixture, beating constantly. Add to the above mixture. Cook and stir until thick.
4. Dissolve gelatin in cold water in the top of a double boiler over hot water. Add this to the milk and egg mixture. Add remaining sugar. When cool, fold in 1 cup whipped cream and add ¼ cup rum. Fold in egg whites and stir together.
5. Place in pie shell and chill in the refrigerator for 2 or 3 hours. Top with the rest of the whipped cream, slightly flavored with rum. Chocolate shavings may be sprinkled all over the top of the pie (optional).

SERVES 8.

RUM CREAM PIE | Mrs. Joseph Charyk

This is the most superb pie imaginable!

- 1 baked pie shell (p. 425; use half)
- 6 egg yolks
- 1 scant cup sugar
- 1 envelope (1 tbsp.) plain gelatin
- ½ cup cold water
- 1 pt. heavy cream
- ¼ cup Jamaica rum
- 1 cup bittersweet chocolate curls *or* 1 cup German sweet chocolate curls

1. Prepare pie shell in 9½-inch ovenproof glass pie dish. Cool.
2. Beat egg yolks in a large bowl until light.
3. Add sugar.
4. In a saucepan, place gelatin and cover with the cold water.

5. Place saucepan over low heat and let come *just* to a boil.

6. Add immediately to egg-sugar mixture, stirring briskly until it thickens (this cooks the eggs).

7. Whip cream until stiff and fold in the gelatin-egg mixture. Carefully fold in the rum. Cool.

8. Pour into pie shell and sprinkle chocolate curls, made by scraping chocolate with a sharp knife. Chill for 2 or 3 hours.

SERVES 8.

SWEDISH APPLE PUDDING

½ cup butter
1 cup brown sugar
1 cup sifted flour
½ tsp. baking powder
½ tsp. salt
1 cup chopped pecans

8 tart, firm apples, peeled and sliced
½ cup sugar
½ tsp. nutmeg
½ tsp. cinnamon
8 tbsps. butter (in dots)
1 pt. heavy cream

Cream ½ cup butter in a bowl and add brown sugar. Sift flour, baking powder and salt together. Add to creamed butter and sugar and add chopped nuts. Reserve.

Place a layer of apples in a buttered 2-quart round ovenproof dish. Sprinkle with part of sugar mixed with nutmeg and cinnamon. Dot with butter.

Repeat layers. Cover with the batter and bake 25 to 30 minutes in a preheated 375° oven. At 25 minutes, test apples, through the crust, with a fork. They must be cooked but still firm. Let stand away from the heat for 5 minutes to crisp crust. Serve hot with heavy cream, unwhipped.

SERVES 6 to 8.

PORTSMOUTH BROWN BETTY PUDDING

1 cup brown sugar, packed hard
1 cup water
⅛ tsp. salt
grated rind of 1 orange
¼ cup melted butter

3 cups day-old bread crumbs
3 cups sliced apples
1 tsp. lemon juice
1 pt. heavy cream

Combine sugar, water, salt and orange rind in a saucepan and simmer gently to form a syrup (about 10 minutes). Add melted butter to bread crumbs, in a bowl, and mix. Place a layer of this last mixture in 2-quart covered baking dish greased with butter. Cover with layer of apples. Alternate layers of crumbs and apples, finishing with crumbs. Add lemon juice to syrup mixture. Pour syrup over apples and bread crumbs. Cover and bake in a preheated moderate oven (350°) for 45 minutes. Uncover during last 15 minutes to brown. Serve hot with heavy cream, unwhipped.

SERVES 6 to 8.

CHOCOLATE PUDDING WITH MERINGUE

4 egg yolks
2 cups sugar
1 qt. milk
4 tbsps. flour
2½ squares unsweetened chocolate

2 tbsps. hot water
2 tsps. vanilla
4 egg whites
⅛ tsp. salt

Beat egg yolks and add 1½ cups sugar. Add milk gradually and stir in flour. Stir well until smooth. Put in 2-quart double boiler over hot water. Stir until thick.

In another smaller double boiler (1 quart), over hot water, put chocolate (cut up) and add 4 tablespoons sugar. Add the hot water. Stir constantly until dissolved. When custard is thick but still pourable, pass through a strainer, put back in double boiler, and add chocolate mixture. Stir and cook until it has thickened to pudding consistency (quite thick). Add vanilla. Put in 1-quart, buttered round casserole and cool.

To make meringue beat egg whites stiff. Add remaining sugar and the salt. Place meringue mixture on the top and seal with a knife so there are no air pockets. Bake in preheated 350° oven for 15 minutes to brown.

SERVES 4 to 6.

BAKED INDIAN PUDDING

1 qt. milk
¼ cup yellow cornmeal
1 cup molasses
½ tsp. ground ginger
½ tsp. ground cinnamon
1 tsp. salt
½ pt. heavy cream

In saucepan, scald milk. Stir in cornmeal. Cook until thickened. Add molasses, spices and salt. Pour into greased 1-quart round ovenproof glass baking dish. Set in larger pan of hot water (about 1 inch of water). Bake in preheated 325° oven for 2 hours. Add more water if it boils away. Stir once after first hour. Serve hot with whipped cream.

SERVES 6.

NEW ENGLAND LEMON PUDDING

2 cups fresh bread crumbs
4 cups milk
2 cups sugar
1 tbsp. butter (melted)
grated rind of 2 lemons
4 egg yolks, beaten until frothy
⅛ tsp. salt
juice of 2 lemons
4 egg whites
2 tbsps. sugar

1. Soak bread crumbs in milk, in a large bowl, and add 1 cup sugar, butter, grated lemon rind, egg yolks and salt.
2. Bake in 2-quart buttered round ovenproof baking dish in 325° preheated oven for 50 minutes.
3. Mix remaining sugar with lemon juice and let stand.
4. Take pudding from oven and poke holes in the top. Pour lemon juice mixture over top and into holes.
5. Make meringue by adding the 2 tablespoons sugar to stiffly beaten egg whites.
6. Spread over top of the pudding and put back in a 375° oven until meringue is golden.

SERVES 6 to 8.

CHRISTMAS PLUM PUDDING

4 egg yolks, beaten until frothy
1½ cups dark brown sugar
¼ cup lemon juice
   grated rind of 1 lemon
1½ cups finely diced suet
3¾ cups soft bread crumbs (no crusts)
3 tsps. baking powder
1½ tsps. salt
3 tsps. ground cinnamon
1½ tsps. grated nutmeg

1½ cups seedless raisins
8 oz. candied mixed fruits *or* 1½ cups
   cleaned currants
¾ cup coarsely chopped pecans
3 tbsps. flour
4 egg whites, beaten stiff
½ cup brandy
*2 tbsps. grain alcohol
fresh holly

1. In a large bowl, beat the egg yolks. Add the sugar and stir until smooth. Add lemon juice, lemon rind and the suet. Mix well. In another bowl, mix the bread crumbs, baking powder, salt and spices. Add these ingredients to the egg mixture.

2. Mix the raisins, candied fruits or currants, nuts and flour together. Add this to the previous mixture and stir well. Beat egg whites until stiff. Cut and fold them into the fruit-egg mixture.

3. Use a 2-quart covered pudding mold with a tube. In order that the pudding may be removed easily from the mold, cut a round of wax paper to fit the bottom of the mold. Grease the sides and paper-covered bottom of the mold with shortening. Lightly dust the inside of the mold with a little flour. Pour in the pudding. Cover and bake in a preheated oven (250°) for 3 hours. Remove from the oven, uncover the mold and allow pudding to cool. Then remove it from the mold and store it in a tightly covered tin cake box.

4. The pudding may be kept for several weeks. Before serving, pudding should be reheated. This may be done by replacing pudding in the mold in which it was baked and heating in a 350° oven. When quite hot, unmold again on a heated platter. Pour brandy and 2 tablespoons grain alcohol all over the pudding and light. Surround pudding with fresh holly as a garnish.

SERVES 18 to 20.

---

* Grain alcohol may be purchased at your pharmacy.

OLD-FASHIONED BLUEBERRY BREAD DESSERT

6 or 8 slices white bread
¼ cup butter
4 cups fresh cultivated blueberries, cleaned thoroughly
¾ cup sugar
1 cup water
½ pt. heavy cream *or* 1 qt. vanilla ice cream

Remove crusts from bread. Butter each slice on both sides. Combine blueberries, sugar and water in saucepan. Cook for 10 minutes—just until berries are soft. Dip the slices of buttered bread one at a time in the hot syrup. Line bottom of glass loaf pan (1½ qts.) with bread. Pour on ⅓ of the blueberry sauce. Repeat layers and pour remaining sauce over all. Cover with wax paper, foil or small dish and place a heavy weight directly on the dessert. Chill overnight in refrigerator. Serve cold with whipped cream or vanilla ice cream.
SERVES 6 to 8.

BUTTERSCOTCH ICEBOX CAKE

2 (3 oz.) pkgs. ladyfingers (12 whole ladyfingers)
½ cup sweet butter, softened
2 cups confectioners' sugar
⅛ tsp. salt
4 egg yolks, beaten
*2 tbsps. coffee flavoring *or* 2 tbsps. maple syrup
1½ pts. heavy cream
**¾ cup crushed butterscotch candy
½ cup grated nuts

Line sides and bottom of wet spring form mold (9½ x 2¼ inches) with split ladyfingers. Cream butter. Add sugar, salt, egg yolks and flavoring and fold in 1 pint cream, whipped stiff.

Cover ladyfingers with ⅓ of the mixture. Sprinkle with part of butterscotch and nuts and another layer of ladyfingers, egg mixture, etc., until all mixture, ladyfingers and nuts are used. Place in refrigerator overnight.

Unmold and top with remaining cream, whipped, and ¼ cup crushed butterscotch.
SERVES 8.

* Coffee flavoring may be purchased at your grocery.
** To crush butterscotch: Place candy in a clean dish towel and fold over. Place on cutting board and crush with a hammer.

CHOCOLATE ICEBOX DESSERT

1 (1 oz.) cake semisweet chocolate
4 tbsps. sugar
4 tbsps. water
4 egg yolks, well beaten
1 tsp. vanilla

4 egg whites, beaten stiff
2 (3 oz.) pkgs. ladyfingers (12 whole ladyfingers)
½ pt. heavy cream

Melt chocolate in top of double boiler, over hot water, with sugar and water. Add slowly, by teaspoonfuls, to beaten egg yolks, in a bowl, and add vanilla. Fold in whites. Mix well.

Line bottom of wet round 1-quart glass dish with ladyfingers. Stand up all around sides of dish. Pour in ½ mixture. Put more ladyfingers in the middle. Pour in the rest of the mixture. Trim ladyfingers to level of filling. Put in refrigerator overnight, covered, and when ready to serve, unmold and frost with whipped cream.

SERVES 4.

CHOCOLATE WAFERS ICEBOX CAKE

1½ pts. heavy cream
2 tbsps. sugar
⅛ tsp. salt
½ tsp. vanilla

1 box chocolate wafers (I use Famous Wafers)
1 cup crushed pistachio nuts

1. Whip cream; add sugar, salt and vanilla. (Reserve ⅓ for frosting.)
2. Place 1 chocolate wafer flat on small platter. Frost with ¼ inch whipped cream mixture and continue stacking the cookies with whipped cream between each one.
3. When stack gets "topply," carefully place it on its side on the platter and continue until all wafers are used.
4. Cover with wax paper and refrigerate overnight.
5. To serve, frost with the rest of whipped cream mixture on top and sides and sprinkle nuts all over it.

When you serve this, cut the roll, in slices, at an angle. Do not cut straight across.

Serves 6 to 8.

COFFEE ALMOND CRÈME

½ cup sugar for brittle
4 oz. almonds for brittle
2 cups heavy cream

½ cup sugar
3 tsps. instant coffee
1 cup "Chocolate Sauce" (p. 459)

1. Make "Almond Brittle" (p. 481).
2. Whip cream in a bowl and fold in sugar, coffee and crushed almond brittle mixed together.
3. Pour into a serving bowl (1-quart size).
4. Chill, covered, overnight in refrigerator.

Serve with "Chocolate Sauce" in a separate small serving bowl.

Serves 4 liberally.

MY GRANDMOTHER'S COFFEE CHARLOTTE RUSSE

I suggest the guests to whom you serve this dish be *very* thin.

2 (3 oz.) pkgs. ladyfingers (12 whole ladyfingers)
2½ envelopes plain gelatin (2½ tbsps.)
¼ cup cold water
1 cup strong coffee plus 1 tsp. freeze-dried coffee (to make very strong)

2 pts. heavy cream
⅓ cup sugar (or more)
1 tsp. vanilla
⅛ tsp. salt
1 (1 lb.) box peanut brittle, crushed
1 tbsp. sugar
½ pt. heavy cream (optional)

1. Line wet round 2-quart glass dish with ladyfingers split in half (round side toward the outside). Press in place and, on bottom of mold, place more split ladyfingers in wheel design.

2. Sprinkle gelatin with cold water in bowl.

3. Heat coffee and dissolve gelatin in this.

4. Set coffee and gelatin to cool in shallow pan as it cools more quickly than in a bowl. Watch carefully so it does not jell. It must be the consistency of syrup.

5. While coffee-gelatin mix is cooling, whip the 2 pints cream (do not overwhip or it will turn to butter). Add sugar, vanilla and salt.

6. When coffee mixture is syrupy, fold it into the whipped cream and stir until thoroughly mixed. Add more sugar if you like it sweeter.

7. Pour into mold and place more split ladyfingers on top in a wheel design.

8. If ladyfingers around the mold are higher than the contents of the mold, cut them off with a knife to the same level.

9. Cover and refrigerate overnight.

10. Unmold carefully on round platter and sprinkle crushed peanut brittle all over the top and sides.

SERVES about 10.

"Charlotte Russe" may be frosted with more whipped, sweetened cream before you add the peanut brittle.

COFFEE CRÈME

½ cup sugar
1 envelope (1 tbsp.) unflavored gelatin
⅛ tsp. salt

2 cups freshly brewed strong coffee
3 tbsps. coffee liqueur
¼ cup heavy cream, whipped
4 squares grated semisweet chocolate

Combine sugar, gelatin and salt in a bowl; add hot coffee, stirring until sugar and gelatin are dissolved. Cool slightly, stir in liqueur. Pour about ½ cup mixture into each of four (8 or 10 oz.) parfait glasses or dessert dishes; chill until set but not firm. Chill remaining mixture until slightly thickened. Blend in whipped cream. Spoon over first mixture in glasses. Chill overnight. Garnish with grated chocolate.

SERVES 4.

CREAM PRINCESSE

4 egg yolks
1 cup sugar
⅔ cup butter, softened
2 (1 oz.) squares unsweetened chocolate, melted over hot water in double boiler

½ tsp. vanilla
4 egg whites, beaten stiff

Beat egg yolks until frothy. Add sugar and mix well. Add butter and melted chocolate. Mix well. Add vanilla and fold into the egg whites. Pour into four dessert dishes. Chill in refrigerator for 4 hours or overnight.

SERVES 4.

This may be placed in a 1-quart dessert bowl instead of the individual dessert dishes. Serve in these same dishes or bowl.

FROSTED MINT DELIGHT | *Mrs. Dwight D. Eisenhower*

¾ cup mint-flavored apple jelly
2 (1 lb.) cans crushed pineapple, drained
1 envelope (1 tbsp.) unflavored gelatin

¼ cup cold water
1 cup juice from the pineapple cans
1 pt. heavy cream
2 tsps. confectioners' sugar

1. Melt the jelly in a saucepan. Add the pineapple and place in a large bowl or a 2-quart wet mold.
2. Place gelatin in a small bowl and sprinkle with cold water.

3. Heat pineapple juice in a small saucepan and pour over the gelatin to dissolve.

4. Add to jelly-pineapple mixture.

5. Whip cream stiff in another bowl. Add the sugar and fold into the above mixture.

6. Place in the freezer until firm. Do *not* freeze solid. Unmold and serve.
SERVES 10 to 12.

LIME FREEZE

3 tbsps. melted butter
1 cup fine graham cracker crumbs
2 egg yolks
1 can (15 oz.) sweetened condensed milk
1 tbsp. grated lime rind

2 tbsps. lime juice
3 drops green food coloring (optional)
2 egg whites
¼ cup sugar

Combine butter and cracker crumbs. Press ⅔ cup of crumb mixture on bottom and sides of lightly buttered refrigerator tray. Chill.

Beat egg yolks until thick; combine with condensed milk. Stir in lime rind and juice. Mix well. Tint pale green with food coloring if desired.

Beat egg whites until stiff, but not dry. Gradually add sugar and beat until very stiff. Fold into lime-milk mixture. Turn into chilled, lined refrigerator tray. Sprinkle top with remaining crumb mixture. Place in freezer compartment and chill at least 6 hours.
SERVES 6.

PARFAIT AMANDES | *Mrs. Jaimé Arguelles*
The Embassy of Spain

1½ cups sugar
½ cup water
6 egg yolks
2 tbsps. Crème de Noyau liqueur
2 cups whipped cream

1 can (5 oz.) toasted almonds, chopped fine
¼ cup chopped Maraschino cherries
12 Maraschino cherries with stems

1. Lightly butter an 8 cup (2-quart) mold. Line mold with foil, leaving a 2-inch overhang all around. Press foil smoothly against side of mold.

2. Combine sugar and water in a small saucepan; heat, stirring constantly, until sugar dissolves. Then cook rapidly, without stirring, to a 236° temperature on a candy thermometer. (A teaspoon of syrup will form a soft ball when dropped in cold water.)

3. Beat egg yolks in a medium-sized bowl until fluffy-light. Beating constantly, pour in hot syrup, in a thin steady stream. Continue beating until mixture is very light and thick; cool slightly. Beat in liqueur. Chill for about an hour until cold.

4. Beat cream in a medium-sized bowl until stiff. Fold into chilled egg mixture. Fold in almonds and chopped cherries. Spoon into prepared mold. Fold foil over top. Freeze several hours or overnight until very firm.

5. When ready to serve, pull back foil from top of mold. Pull up on foil to loosen around edge. Invert onto a chilled serving plate; peel off foil. Garnish plate with whole Maraschino cherries with stems. Cut into slices with sharp knife.

SERVES 8.

MARY ELLEN MONRONEY'S FROZEN RICE

½ cup rice
1 qt. cold water
1 qt. milk
1¾ cups of sugar

¼ tsp. salt
1 pt. heavy cream, whipped
1 tsp. vanilla
"Brandy Sauce" (p. 458)

Bring rice and water to a boil. Drain off liquid, add milk and cook in double boiler over boiling water for 1 hour. Add sugar and cook ½ hour more. Add salt and cool. Add cream, flavor with vanilla and freeze in two refrigerator trays.

Serve with "Brandy Sauce."

SERVES 12.

STRAWBERRY DELIGHT

1 envelope (1 tbsp.) plain gelatin
4 tbsps. cold water
1 cup crushed strawberries
3 tbsps. confectioners' sugar
½ cup sugar
2 egg whites, beaten stiff
¼ cup heavy cream, whipped
12 large fresh strawberries, whole
6 sprigs fresh mint

1. Soften gelatin in water in top of double boiler over hot water and stir until gelatin is dissolved. Remove from stove.
2. Add the crushed berries and chill until mixture just begins to set.
3. Fold in the sugar (both kinds), egg whites and whipped cream.
4. Pour into 1-quart mold which has been rinsed in cold water. Cover.
5. Chill in refrigerator overnight.
6. Unmold carefully and garnish with whole strawberries and mint leaves.

SERVES 4.

SHERBET BALLS WITH LOGANBERRY JUICE AND COINTREAU

1 qt. raspberry sherbet
1 qt. lime sherbet
1 qt. orange sherbet
*4½ cups loganberry or boysenberry juice
⅛ cup Cointreau (more if you like it stronger)
1 sprig of fresh mint

Using ice cream scoop, make balls of all the sherbets and pile in silver or crystal bowl. Keep frozen in freezer. Take out 15 to 20 minutes before serving. Add Cointreau to loganberry juice (or boysenberry juice) and pour this over the sherbet balls. Place sprig of fresh mint in center of bowl. Serve with "Sponge Cake."

SERVES 20 to 22.

* May be purchased in a specialty store.

CRANBERRY SHERBET

This is different, pretty and good to serve with turkey on Thanksgiving or Christmas.

2 lbs. cranberries
3 cups water
2 cups granulated sugar

36 marshmallows (regular size)
½ cup orange juice
4 tsps. lemon juice

Bring cranberries to a boil in water in a large saucepan. Then turn down to simmer and cook until berries are soft. Put through a food mill into another large saucepan and add the sugar. Stir well. Take out 1 cup of the cranberries and sugar and place in top of your largest double boiler over boiling water. Add the marshmallows. Stir, cover and cook until marshmallows are melted. Add to remaining cranberry-sugar mixture and stir well. Add orange juice and lemon juice.

Place in refrigerator trays, rinsed in cold water, and when cool, cover and place in freezer compartment overnight. Stir several times as it freezes. Scoop with a large spoon or ice-cream scoop into sherbet glasses (2 scoops per person).
SERVES 16 to 18.

PINEAPPLE SHERBET WITH BLACK BING CHERRIES IN BRANDY

2 qts. pineapple sherbet
2 (1 lb. 1 oz.) jars brandied black Bing cherries

¼ cup brandy
*1 to 2 tbsps. grain alcohol
24 macaroons (see p. 473)

1. Place sherbet in silver bowl.
2. Pour over cherries and juice.
3. Sprinkle brandy and grain alcohol over just before serving.
4. Light and serve flaming.

Serve with macaroons.
SERVES 12 to 14.

* Grain alcohol may be purchased at your pharmacy.

CREAMY LIME SHERBET

2 cups crushed ice	1½ tsps. grated lime rind
1 (14 oz.) can sweetened condensed milk	1½ tsps. vanilla extract
	2 to 3 drops green food coloring
1 (6 oz.) can frozen concentrate for limeade	16 fresh strawberries *or* 1 pt. box of raspberries
1 cup heavy cream	4 tbsps. sugar
1 egg	8 sprigs of fresh mint

In blender, combine crushed ice, condensed milk, frozen undiluted limeade concentrate, cream, egg, lime rind, vanilla extract and food coloring. Blend at high speed 1 minute or until smooth. Place in 1½-quart mold, rinsed out with cold water. Cover completely and put in freezer overnight.

Unmold on round chilled silver platter by dipping mold for a few seconds in a larger pan of very hot water. (Be careful so that mold will be intact.) Surround mold with fresh sugared strawberries or sugared raspberries and fresh mint leaves.

SERVES 6.

APRICOT SOUFFLÉ | *Josephine Alston*

1 (8 oz.) pkg. dried apricots	1 cup juice from the apricots
2 tsps. lemon juice	8 egg whites
1 cup boiling water	1½ cups "Chantilly Cream" (p. 459)
1 cup sugar	

1. Place apricots and lemon juice in a saucepan and cover with boiling water. Cook until apricots are very soft.
2. Add sugar and mix well.
3. Pour off the juice *reserving* 1 cup.
4. Place apricot mixture, with the cup of reserved juice, in an electric blender on "Purée" for about 1 minute.
5. Remove from blender and measure 1½ cups of the puréed apricots. Cool completely.
6. Preheat oven to 400°.

7. Beat egg whites stiff in a large bowl and add the apricot purée. Mix completely.

8. Pour into a buttered ovenproof 2½-quart soufflé dish. Attach soufflé collar (see below).

9. Place dish in a larger ovenproof pan and pour boiling water around the dish to the depth of 2 inches.

10. Place in oven and bake for 25 to 30 minutes.

11. Serve at once with a sauce dish of "Chantilly Cream."

SERVES 6.

How to make a Soufflé "Collar"

Cut a 7-inch wide strip of double brown paper measured to fit the soufflé dish. Butter one side of the paper. Place around dish 2 inches from the top so that the other 5 inches rise around the soufflé dish. Secure firmly with wet twine. This allows the soufflé to rise far above the soufflé dish. Before serving, *gently* remove the "collar."

CHOCOLATE SOUFFLÉ I

1 cup milk	6 egg whites (10 may be used)
½ cup sugar	4 egg yolks (6 may be used)
2 squares unsweetened chocolate	3 cups "Foamy Sauce" (p. 460) *or*
1 tsp. vanilla	½ pt. whipping cream
2 tbsps. butter or margarine	1 tbsp. sugar
3 tbsps. flour	⅛ tsp. salt
¼ tsp. salt	1 tsp. vanilla

1. Coat a round 2-quart (3¾ x 7¼ inch) soufflé dish well with melted butter. Dust evenly with sugar, tapping out excess.

2. Combine milk and ⅓ cup sugar in small saucepan. Heat slowly until bubbles appear around the edge. Place over hot water and add chocolate; continue heating, stirring constantly, until chocolate is melted. Remove from heat and stir in vanilla.

3. Melt 2 tablespoons butter or margarine in a medium-sized saucepan; blend in flour and salt and slowly stir in chocolate mixture. Cook over low heat, stirring constantly until mixture thickens and bubbles for 1 minute. Cool slightly while you beat the eggs.

4. Beat egg whites in medium-sized bowl until soft peaks form.

5. Beat egg yolks in large bowl, slowly stirring in thickened chocolate mixture. Fold in beaten egg whites until no streaks of white remain. Carefully spoon mixture into prepared soufflé dish. Place dish in a large baking pan on oven rack; pour boiling water into pan to depth of 1 inch.

6. Bake in preheated 350° oven 50 minutes. Do not open oven until done. If using 10 egg whites and 6 yolks, make a buttered, sugared collar of brown paper standing up 4 to 5 inches and wrap around soufflé dish. Secure with wet twine. After soufflé mixture is in soufflé dish, run a knife 1½ inches in from edge of pan. This will make a double top to soufflé. When done, carefully remove the paper collar.

Serve with "Foamy Sauce" or whipped cream with sugar, salt and vanilla added.

SERVES 6.

To keep soufflé for a few minutes, if necessary, before serving, place pan of hot water in oven on oven rack directly above soufflé. However, if possible, serve the soufflé at once.

CHOCOLATE SOUFFLÉ II

- 2 tbsps. butter
- 2 tbsps. flour
- ¾ cup milk
- 3 egg yolks, well beaten
- ⅓ cup sugar
- 1½ squares unsweetened chocolate
- 3 tbsps. hot water
- 3 egg whites, beaten stiff
- ½ tsp. vanilla
- 2 cups "Foamy Sauce" (p. 460)

Melt butter in a saucepan and add flour. Add milk gradually while stirring constantly. Cook to boiling point. Stir until smooth. Cool a bit. Add egg yolks, sugar and chocolate which has been melted with 3 tablespoons of hot water in top of double boiler over hot water. Cool. Fold in egg whites and add vanilla. Bake in an ovenproof (1 quart) soufflé dish set in a larger pan of hot water (about 1 inch high).

If desired firm, bake 40 to 50 minutes in a moderately slow preheated oven (325°).

If desired soft (French method), bake 20 minutes in a moderately hot oven (375°).

Serve as soon as it is baked.
Serve with "Foamy Sauce."
SERVES 4.

ORANGE MARMALADE FLUFF SOUFFLÉ

6 tbsps. sugar
4 tbsps. orange marmalade

6 egg whites, beaten stiff
"Foamy Sauce" (p. 460)

Fold sugar and marmalade into egg whites. Pour into top of buttered 2-quart double boiler and cook over water that is just barely boiling. The water must *not* touch the upper pan. Cover, but watch carefully, and cook slowly 1 hour. If water boils away add more boiling water from time to time. Turn out carefully into a heated serving bowl and serve with "Foamy Sauce" in a separate dish.
SERVES 4 to 6.

RASPBERRY OR STRAWBERRY SOUFFLÉ
Mrs. Charles Lucet
The Embassy of France

1 lb. fresh raspberries *or* 1 lb. fresh strawberries

1¼ cups sugar
6 egg whites

Cook crushed raspberries or strawberries for 20 minutes over medium heat and pass them through a very fine sieve. Add the sugar. Let the mixture boil down to half its original volume (about 7 minutes). You will have a little less than a cup. Cool.

Beat egg whites until they are snowy and mix them with the berries, folding them in carefully. Put the mixture in an ovenproof (9½ x 3½ inch) round buttered soufflé dish and cook 20 minutes in a preheated 250° oven. Serve at once.
SERVES 6.

FROSTINGS, ICINGS AND DESSERT SAUCES

ALICE'S FROSTING

4 cups powdered sugar
1 cup cocoa
10 tbsps. boiling water

4 tbsps. melted butter
1 tsp. vanilla
¼ tsp. salt

Mix sugar and cocoa in a bowl. Stir in water, butter and vanilla and add salt.

MAKES 2 cups (enough to frost an 8-inch layer cake).

BOILED FROSTING

2 cups granulated sugar
⅔ cup water
2 tbsps. cider vinegar

3 egg whites, beaten stiff
½ tsp. vanilla

Boil sugar, water and vinegar in a saucepan, until mixture becomes brittle when pressed between fingers (in iced water). Add very gradually to egg whites in a bowl. Continue beating and stir in vanilla.

MAKES 5 cups (enough to frost two 9-inch layer cakes).

BUTTER CREAM FROSTING

4 cups confectioners' sugar
1 cup soft butter
¼ tsp. salt

2 tsps. vanilla
8 tbsps. milk

Cream ⅓ of the sugar with butter and salt in large bowl. Blend in vanilla, 1 teaspoon milk and the rest of the sugar. Gradually stir in remaining milk until desired spreading consistency is reached.

MAKES about 1½ cups frosting. Double recipe for 9-inch layer cake.

CARAMEL ALMOND FROSTING

1¼ cups light brown sugar
¼ cup cold water

2 egg whites, beaten stiff
1 tsp. almond extract

In a saucepan, melt sugar with the water, stirring constantly, and cook until it makes a ball when a little is dropped in a cup of cold water. Do not boil. Cool a little.

Gradually pour syrup into egg whites and continue beating until frosting is thick. Add the almond extract. Set bowl in a larger bowl of cold water for about 15 to 20 minutes or until you think the frosting will spread on the cake without running. Will frost single layer cake.

MAKES 1½ cups.

CHOCOLATE CREAM CHEESE ICING

1 (3 oz.) pkg. cream cheese
2 tbsps. milk
8 oz. (half 1 lb. box) confectioners' sugar

1 (1 oz.) square chocolate, melted
1 tsp. vanilla

Soften cream cheese with milk.

Gradually add sugar, then chocolate (melted in top of double boiler over hot water), and vanilla.

Makes enough to ice 1 single layer cake.

CRÈME AU BEURRE | *Mrs. Charles Lucet*
The Embassy of France

4 (1 oz.) squares semisweet chocolate
1 cup sugar
8 egg yolks, beaten well

1 pt. milk
1 lb. sweet butter, softened
1 tsp. vanilla (optional)
⅛ tsp. salt (optional)

Melt the chocolate in the top of a double boiler over hot water. Mix, in a bowl, the sugar with egg yolks. Heat milk in a saucepan to boiling and then cool a bit. Add to sugar mixture. Cook in a saucepan on top of the stove, without boiling, until thickened. Add the chocolate. When almost cold, mix thoroughly with the softened butter. Flavor to taste.

Makes 2 cups. Frosts one "Bûche de Noël."

MOCHA ICING

½ cup sweet butter
2½ cups confectioners' sugar (more if needed)

2 tbsps. cocoa
2 tbsps. hot coffee
½ tsp. vanilla

Cream butter until soft and pliable. Add sugar gradually, beating well. As mixture thickens, add cocoa, mixed with coffee and vanilla. Continue to beat and add more sugar until light and fluffy and thick enough to spread.

Frosts tops and sides of single layer 9-inch cake. Double recipe for 9-inch 2-layer cake.

SAUCE ANGLAISE

1 cup milk
1 cup cream (light)
4 or 5 egg yolks
½ cup sugar

½ tsp. flour
1 tsp. vanilla
¼ cup whipping cream

In saucepan scald milk and cream. Whip yolks in a bowl with sugar and flour until light yellow; add hot milk and cream mixture. Place in a double boiler and cook, stirring, until thick. Cool.

Add vanilla and fold in whipped cream. May be kept in refrigerator. Sprinkle a little sugar on top to prevent skim.

MAKES about 3 cups.

MARY ELLEN MONRONEY'S BRANDY SAUCE

¼ lb. butter
¼ lb. brown sugar
2 egg yolks, beaten well

2 tbsps. brandy
⅛ tsp. nutmeg

Cream butter in bowl; add sugar and stir. Transfer to top of 1-quart double boiler over hot water.

Remove from stove, cool a bit and add egg yolks. Stir, again over hot water, until thickened. Add brandy and nutmeg.

SERVES 4.

CARAMEL SAUCE

1 cup granulated sugar

1 cup boiling water

Melt sugar, stirring constantly, in a 10-inch skillet over high heat. Cook until it is the color of honey.

Add boiling water slowly.

Reduce heat to medium and boil, gently, for ten minutes or until the mixture thickens.

Makes ⅔ cup.

EASY CARAMEL SAUCE

½ lb. caramels
2 tsps. butter

¼ cup cream (light)
⅛ tsp. salt

In top of double boiler, melt caramels. When melted, add butter and cream. Stir and add salt. Serve hot or cold.

Makes about 1 cup.

CHANTILLY CREAM

1 cup heavy cream, whipped stiff
4 tbsps. confectioners' sugar

3 drops almond extract

Add sugar and almond extract to cream in small bowl. Chill.

Makes 1¼ cups.

CHOCOLATE SAUCE I

2 squares unsweetened grated chocolate
⅔ cup sugar

1 cup heavy cream
1 heaping tsp. butter
⅛ tsp. salt

Place chocolate, sugar, cream and butter in top of 1-quart double boiler over hot water.

Cook slowly, until chocolate is melted.

Add salt and cook for 10 minutes longer or until fairly thick, stirring occasionally.

Makes about 1½ cups sauce.

CHOCOLATE SAUCE II

1 cup sugar
4 heaping tsps. cocoa
½ cup light cream

1 tbsp. butter
⅛ tsp. salt

In a quart saucepan, place the sugar mixed with the cocoa. Add the cream. Over high heat boil, stirring constantly, for about 5 minutes or until the mixture thickens.

Remove from stove and stir in the butter. Add the salt.

Serve hot or cold.

MAKES 1 cup.

EASY CHOCOLATE SAUCE

1 (4 oz.) bar of sweet chocolate
6 tbsps. light cream

1 tbsp. butter
⅛ tsp. salt

1. Melt the chocolate in the top of a 1-quart double boiler over very hot water.
2. When melted, add the cream and stir in the butter.
3. Add the salt.
4. Keep hot over the hot water.

MAKES ½ cup.

FOAMY SAUCE

6 egg yolks
3 cups powdered sugar
½ tsp. vanilla

⅛ tsp. salt
1½ pts. whipping cream
3 tbsps. rum or sherry (optional)

1. Beat egg yolks lightly.
2. Add powdered sugar, vanilla and salt.

3. Whip the cream stiff and add the egg yolk mixture.
4. Add the sherry or rum if you desire either of these flavors.

Makes about 4½ cups.

HARD SAUCE FOR PLUM PUDDING

½ cup butter, softened
3 cups powdered sugar
4 tsps. vanilla

⅛ tsp. salt
8 tbsps. brandy

Cream butter and sugar. Add vanilla, salt and brandy (a tiny bit at a time). Use hand or electric beater for this. Be careful it doesn't separate.

Makes 2 cups.

HONEY SCOTCH SAUCE

¾ cup honey
1 (5⅓ oz.) can evaporated milk
½ cup sugar

¼ cup butter
¼ tsp. salt

Combine honey, ⅓ cup evaporated milk, sugar, butter and salt in pan.

Cook over medium heat, stirring occasionally. until it forms a soft ball when dropped in glass of cold water. (If using candy thermometer—234°.)

Stir in remaining evaporated milk, stirring constantly, until thick and smooth (about 3 minutes longer).

Makes about 2 cups of sauce.

Serve over French vanilla or coffee ice cream and sprinkle with chopped pecans or chopped toasted almonds.

GRAND MARNIER SAUCE

4 egg yolks
½ cup sugar
¾ cup heavy cream

½ cup milk
2 tbsps. vanilla
4 tbsps. Grand Marnier liqueur

Beat egg yolks in a medium bowl with the sugar until very light. Add cream and milk. Mix thoroughly. Place mixture in the top of a 1-quart double boiler, *over direct low heat;* stir and cook. Be careful as too much heat will curdle the mixture. Stir constantly until thickened. Add vanilla and Grand Marnier and strain through a sieve. Set back in double boiler on stove over hot water.

MAKES about 2 cups.

LEMON SAUCE

juice of 2 lemons
2 eggs, beaten
1 cup sugar

2 tbsps. water
2 tbsps. butter, melted

Beat all together in a medium bowl. Transfer to saucepan and let boil 2 minutes, stirring constantly.

MAKES 1½ cups. SERVES 4.

PEACH SAUCE

1 (1 lb. 13 oz.) can peach halves
  and juice from the can
¼ cup sugar

juice of ½ lemon
¼ cup Cointreau liqueur *or* ¼ cup
  Curaçao liqueur

Place drained peach halves in an ovenproof glass dish (11¾ x 7½ x 1¾ inches) and broil (in a preheated oven). When they are more golden, remove from oven and keep warm.

Put peach juice in top of 2-quart double boiler. Add sugar and lemon juice and cook over medium heat for 7 minutes until it thickens a little. Stir.

Add Cointreau or Curaçao liqueur and peaches. Keep hot in top of double boiler over hot water.

MAKES 2 cups. SERVES 6.

This may also be made with apricots.

Serve as a sauce over French vanilla ice cream.

SAUCE FOR LEMON SNOW | Mrs. Michael de V. Flinn

½ cup whipping cream
3 egg yolks
¼ cup sugar
⅛ cup melted butter

3 tbsps. lemon juice
3 tbsps. Grand Marnier
1 tsp. finely minced lemon peel

Whip cream stiff in a large bowl.

Beat egg yolks thoroughly in another bowl. Add sugar, butter, lemon juice, Grand Marnier and lemon peel.

Add this mixture to the whipped cream. Mix well.

SERVES 4 to 6.

RUM SAUCE

2 egg yolks
1 cup powdered sugar
½ pt. heavy cream, whipped stiff

⅛ tsp. salt
1 tbsp. white rum (or more if you want stronger flavor)

Beat egg yolks and sugar. Fold in whipped cream and salt. Add rum. Put in refrigerator.

MAKES about 1½ cups.

COOKIES

When you are making any of these cookies, grease the cookie sheet with shortening instead of butter. This makes it easier to remove the cookies from the cookie sheet. Use a wide spatula, face down, and press down on the pan as you lift off the cookies. Place them on waxed paper to cool.

Be sure to leave ample space between cookies dropped by spoon on a cookie sheet. Otherwise they will run together.

BUTTERSCOTCH SQUARES

¼ cup butter
1½ cups brown sugar
2 eggs
1½ cups flour

½ tsp. salt
⅓ cup heavy cream
½ cup chopped pecans

Cream butter and add ¾ cup sugar. Cream together thoroughly. Add 1 egg, beat well; mix flour and salt and add to first mixture alternately with cream.

Spread ⅛ inch thick on greased cookie sheet (15½ x 10¼ x ¾ inches). Brush with remaining egg, well beaten. Sprinkle with remaining ¾ cup sugar mixed with pecans.

Bake in moderate preheated oven (350°) for 14 to 20 minutes. Cut into 2-inch squares while still hot.

MAKES about 35 squares.

CHOCOLATE CRISPIES

2 squares unsweetened
    chocolate
½ cup butter
1 cup sugar

2 eggs, beaten
½ cup sifted flour
½ tsp. vanilla
½ cup finely chopped pecans

Melt chocolate in top of double boiler over hot water.

Pour melted chocolate into a bowl. Add butter, sugar, eggs, flour and vanilla, beating well.

Spread mixture with spatula on greased baking sheet (15½ x 10½ x ¾ inches).

Sprinkle nuts on top. Bake in 350° preheated oven for 15 minutes. While still warm, cut into 2-inch squares. Cool.

MAKES about 35 squares.

CHOCOLATE NUT COOKIES

- 2 squares unsweetened or semisweet chocolate
- ½ cup butter
- 1 cup sugar
- 2 eggs, well beaten
- ⅔ cup flour
- ⅛ tsp. salt
- 1 tsp. vanilla
- ¾ cup chopped pecans

1. Melt chocolate in top of double boiler over hot water.
2. Cream butter with sugar in a bowl. Add eggs.
3. Then add melted chocolate, flour, salt and vanilla.
4. Lastly add nuts. Drop by teaspoon onto greased (15½ x 10½ x ¾ inch) cookie tin. Bake about 15 minutes in preheated 350° oven. Watch carefully because chocolate burns easily. If you like cookies "chewy," don't bake quite so long.

MAKES 60 cookies.

CHRISTMAS COOKIES (HALF MOON SHAPE)

- ½ lb. butter
- 5 tbsps. confectioners' sugar
- 2½ cups sifted flour
- 1 tsp. cold water
- 2 tsps. vanilla
- 1 cup chopped pecans
- 1 cup confectioners' sugar (for rolling)

Cream butter with 5 tablespoons sugar. Add flour, water, vanilla and pecans. Shape into half-moon shape. On 2 flat greased cookie tins (17 x 14 inches), bake in slow (preheated) oven (325°) for 30 minutes or until light brown. Roll in confectioners' sugar while still hot. Be sure to watch carefully while baking so cookies do not brown too much.

MAKES 60 cookies (1½ inches long and ½ inch high).

DATE NUT STICKS

3 eggs
1¼ cups sugar
2 tsps. vanilla
1 cup finely chopped dates

1 cup finely chopped nuts
1 cup flour
2 tsps. baking powder
¼ cup confectioners' sugar

1. Beat eggs thoroughly. Add sugar and vanilla. Beat 3 minutes.
2. Add dates and nuts.
3. Sift flour with baking powder and add to first mixture.
4. Spread in a shallow greased (15½ x 10½ x ¾ inch) pan, and bake in preheated moderate oven (350°) for 15 minutes. While still hot, sprinkle with confectioners' sugar. Cool and cut in 2-inch squares.

MAKES about 35 squares.

FLORENTINES I

1 cup sliced almonds
½ cup candied orange peel, chopped
¼ cup diced candied red cherries
1 tsp. grated lemon rind
¼ cup sifted all-purpose flour
¼ cup (½ stick) butter or margarine

¼ cup sugar
¼ cup honey
¼ cup heavy cream
6 squares semisweet chocolate
1½ tbsps. butter or margarine (for coating)
1½ cups "Butter Cream Frosting" (p. 456; optional)

1. Combine almonds, orange peel, cherries, lemon rind and flour in a small bowl. Toss to coat thoroughly.
2. Combine the ¼ cup butter, sugar, honey and cream in a small saucepan. Heat slowly, stirring constantly, just to boiling. Remove from heat; carefully stir in almond mixture just until well coated.
3. Drop by slightly rounded teaspoonfuls onto two 17 x 14-inch greased cookie sheets. Flatten with spatula to thin cookies to about 1½ inches in diameter.
4. Bake in preheated 350° oven for 10 minutes or until golden. Cool on cookie sheets about 1 minute or until firm. Lift with spatula and turn over, flat side up, onto a wire rack to cool completely.

5. Melt chocolate and 1½ tablespoons butter or margarine in top of double boiler over hot water. Stir to blend.

6. Spread thinly on flat sides of cookies almost to the edges. Set in cool place until firm.

These can be made into cookie sandwiches by filling with "Butter Cream Frosting."

To store for a few days, arrange cookies in layers in a pan with wax paper between. Cover and keep in a cool place.

MAKES about 4 dozen single cookies or 2 dozen sandwich cookies.

FLORENTINES II

½ cup heavy cream
3 tbsps. butter
½ cup sugar
⅛ tsp. salt
1¼ cups very finely chopped almonds

⅓ cup sifted enriched flour
¾ cup finely chopped candied orange peel

1. Preheat oven to 350°.
2. In saucepan combine cream, butter and sugar; add salt and bring to a boil. Remove from heat and add almonds, flour and peel.
3. Drop the batter from a teaspoon onto a (17 x 14 inch) greased cookie sheet, leaving at least 2 inches between cookies. Bake only 4 to 6 at a time. Bake 8 to 10 minutes and watch to make certain that they don't burn.
4. Using a buttered knife, remove the cookies from baking sheet while they are hot. Leave them flat or bend them slightly around the greased handle of a wooden spoon. Cool on a cake rack.

MAKES about 30 cookies.

FUDGE CRISPS

½ lb. sweet chocolate
½ tsp. vanilla

½ cup chopped pecans
2 cups corn flakes

Melt chocolate over lukewarm water in a double boiler.

Add vanilla, chopped pecans and corn flakes. Toss together until flakes and nuts are well coated.

Drop by teaspoonfuls onto wax paper on cookie tin (17 x 14 inches) and set in refrigerator to crisp.

MAKES 34 "Fudge Crisps."

ICEBOX COOKIES

For a large tea party!

- 2 eggs
- 2 cups brown sugar
- 1 cup melted butter
- ⅛ tsp. salt
- ½ tsp. vanilla
- 3¼ cups sifted flour
- 1 tsp. baking soda
- 1 cup chopped walnut meats
- 2 squares semisweet chocolate (optional)

Beat the eggs in a large bowl. Add sugar and butter. Add salt and vanilla. Sift flour and soda together; add slowly to first mixture. When thoroughly mixed, add walnut meats. Make into a roll 1½ inches in diameter and let stand in refrigerator wrapped in waxed paper until thoroughly chilled. When ready to use, slice thin (as much as you wish to make) and bake in a preheated moderate oven (350°) on a greased (17 x 14 inch) cookie sheet until slightly golden (about 8 minutes). If you want chocolate cookies, melt chocolate over hot water in top of double boiler and add to batter.

MAKES 344 ⅛-inch thick cookies or 172 ¼-inch thick cookies.

MACAROONS

- ½ lb. almond paste
- 1 cup sugar
- 3 egg whites, not beaten
- ⅓ cup powdered sugar
- 2 tbsps. cake flour
- ⅛ tsp. salt

1. Mix, in a bowl, the almond paste with sugar and egg whites, added gradually. Mix with your hands.
2. Sift in sugar, flour and salt. Mix well.
3. Cover two (17 x 14 inch) cookie pans with brown paper and drop the

above mixture by the teaspoonful. Wet your finger and flatten each macaroon. Let stand for 3 hours.

4. Bake in a preheated 350° oven for 30 minutes. Put the paper on a damp cloth and remove the macaroons.

MAKES 36 macaroons.

Store macaroons in cookie jar with a tight lid and put one apple (quartered) on top to keep them moist.

NUT LACE WAFERS

½ cup butter, softened
1 cup light brown sugar
3 tbsps. flour
1 tsp. baking powder

1 cup chopped pecans
1 egg, beaten
1 tsp. vanilla

Cream the butter and sugar until very light. Sift the flour and baking powder. Add this to the chopped nuts. Add softened butter and sugar, egg and vanilla. Mix thoroughly and drop from the tip of a teaspoon onto a greased cookie pan (17 x 14 inches) about 2 inches apart.

Bake in preheated moderate (350°) oven about 5 minutes. Remove from pan while still hot.

MAKES 52 wafers.

CHRISTMAS GINGER SNAPS | *Mrs. Hubert de Besche*
(*Pepparkakor*) | The Royal Embassy of Sweden

These cookies belong to the Swedish Christmas tradition and are a "must" in every Swedish home.

⅔ cup shortening
¾ cup sifted light brown sugar, firmly packed
2 tbsps. molasses
3 tbsps. boiled, cooled water
1 tsp. grated lemon rind

2¼ cups sifted all-purpose flour
1 tsp. baking soda
1 tbsp. cinnamon
1½ tsps. cloves
1 tsp. pulverized or ground cardamom seeds

Cream shortening and sugar thoroughly in a bowl. Add molasses, water and lemon rind. Sift flour with baking soda and spices. Add to creamed mixture a little at a time. Blend well. Flour hands, toss dough quickly on floured surface, wrap in waxed paper and place in refrigerator to chill overnight.

Turn dough onto floured surface. Roll out very thin and cut in desired shapes with floured cookie cutters. Bake on two greased (17 x 14 inch) cookie sheets in moderate oven (350°) for 8 to 10 minutes. Cool on cookie sheet.

MAKES about 60 cookies.

Will keep for about 2 to 3 weeks in a tin box with a tight lid, but better eaten fresh.

CRISP OATMEAL COOKIES

½ cup melted butter
1 cup sugar
1 egg, beaten
1 cup oatmeal

5 tbsps. flour
¼ tsp. baking powder
½ tsp. vanilla

To melted butter, add sugar, then egg and oatmeal, then flour and baking powder that have been mixed and sifted. Add vanilla. Drop by the tablespoon onto a cookie sheet (17 x 14 inches) and bake in a slow oven (325°) until cookies are faintly golden (8 minutes).

MAKES 52 cookies.

RUM BALLS

30 vanilla wafers, crushed
2 tbsps. cocoa
2 tbsps. corn syrup

1 cup pecans, chopped fine
1 jigger (¼ cup) rum
½ cup powdered sugar

Mix first five ingredients well, then roll in balls the size of a marble. Roll in powdered sugar and store in an airtight container in refrigerator. The longer they stand, the better they are.

MAKES 38 "Rum Balls."

BROWN SUGAR COOKIES

2 eggs
2 cups brown sugar
10 tbsps. flour
⅛ tsp. salt

⅛ tsp. baking soda
2 cups broken pecans
¼ cup confectioners' sugar

Beat eggs. Add sugar, flour, salt, soda and nutmeats. Spread in greased pan (15½ x 10¼ x ¾ inches). Pan must have sides. Bake in preheated 350° oven exactly 20 minutes. Let cool thoroughly before cutting into 2-inch squares. Sprinkle confectioners' sugar on top.

MAKES about 35 squares.

VANILLA WAFERS

1 scant cup of sugar
¼ lb. butter (½ cup)
2 eggs, not beaten
1¼ cups sifted flour

1 tsp. vanilla
½ tsp. lemon extract
40 walnut halves

Cream sugar and butter together in a bowl. Add eggs. Then add sifted flour, vanilla and lemon flavorings. Drop by half-teaspoonfuls on 3 well-greased cookie tins (17 x 14 inches). (Spread far apart—about 14 to a cookie sheet.) Place a walnut meat on top of each. Bake in preheated 350° oven until the edges are slightly golden (5 minutes). Watch carefully. Cool and lift off the pans with a spatula.

MAKES 40 wafers.

A candy is a candy is a candy . . . except in the case of Lindy Boggs' "New Orleans Pralines" when "candy" is like biting off a chunk of heaven!

ALMOND BRITTLE

2 cups sugar 12 coarsely crushed almonds

Melt sugar in a skillet over a low fire. When dissolved, add coarsely crushed almonds and stir until they are coated well and turning golden brown. Pour into an oiled (8 x 8 x 2 inch) pan. Chill and when brittle is cold, break into bite-sized pieces.

MAKES about ¾ lb.

MARY ELLEN MONRONEY'S BUTTERSCOTCH CANDY

¾ cup butter 1½ cups whole pecans
2 cups fine light brown sugar

1. In 10-inch iron skillet melt butter with the sugar. Cook mixture slowly, testing in ice water, several drops at a time until it is clear and glassy.
2. Keep mixture hot in top of double boiler over hot water.
3. In the bottom of 2 metal pans (8 x 8 x 2 inches), place the pecans.
4. Spread the butterscotch mixture thinly over the pecans in each pan.
5. Let cool completely.
6. To loosen from pans, press up under each pan and candy will crack loose. The secret of this is cooking the butter and sugar slowly and long enough.

MAKES 1¼ lbs.

This candy is very buttery to the touch. After you remove it from the pan, broken up, place on brown paper to absorb some of the butter. Pat the top with paper toweling.

FUDGE I

This is called "Heavenly Fudge" and it is.

1 (14 oz.) can condensed milk ⅛ tsp. salt
2 (6 oz.) pkgs. chocolate chips

Heat milk, chocolate chips and salt together in double boiler over hot water until chips melt.

Place to cool in square cake pan (8 x 8 x 2 inches). Cut while soft.
Variations:
1. Add ½ cup chopped pecans.
2. Place 49 marshmallows in rows (7 to a row) and carefully pour fudge mixture over them. If you do this, cut between rows of marshmallows (1 marshmallow per square).

MAKES 64 (1 inch) squares of fudge, or 49 squares with marshmallows.

FUDGE II

4½ cups sugar ½ cup butter
1 (13 oz.) can evaporated milk ⅛ tsp. salt
3 (6 oz.) pkgs. chocolate chips 1 lb. chopped pecans
1 (7 oz.) jar marshmallow fluff

Melt sugar in a saucepan with the milk. Cook over medium heat for 8 to 10 minutes until it forms a soft ball in ice water.

Place mixture in top of double boiler over very hot water, and add the chocolate chips, marshmallow fluff, butter, salt and chopped pecans.

When all is melted and stirred together, pour into buttered oblong (11¾ x 7½ x 1¾ inch) glass pan. When almost cool, cut in 1-inch squares.

MAKES about 77 squares of fudge.

NEW ORLEANS PRALINES | *Mrs. Hale Boggs*

4 cups brown sugar
2 cups white sugar
3 cups water
1 tsp. vanilla

4 cups whole pecans
½ tsp. salt
2 tbsps. butter

Place both kinds of sugar in a large saucepan. Stir in water and vanilla until well mixed. Bring to a boil and add pecans and salt. Cook until a teaspoon of the mixture forms a soft ball in cold water (236° on a candy thermometer). Add butter and beat until creamy. Drop by tablespoonfuls on wax paper on table top.

MAKES 40 three-inch round pralines.

I may be a simple soul, for I find great satisfaction in making my own pickles, relishes, jams and jellies. I put aside two or three days in the fall to undertake this nostalgic task.

When I make "Chili Sauce," the wonderful spicy smell permeates the house and my thoughts instantly return to the many autumns of my childhood when life was so much simpler and a big event was "Chili Sauce" time. First came the picking, then the slicing and peeling, the cooking and stirring (this was my contribution) and then the filling of the jars and the labeling. They went, finally, into the storage closet in our old brick cellar.

At apple-picking time—not before—I was allowed to gorge on the red, glossy Northern Spy and fragrant McIntosh apples. Another memorable day for me was when the asparagus was ready for cutting and later, the new corn. We would abandon all other food and simply have platters of these heavenly vegetables fresh from our garden.

And what all this has to do with pickles, et cetera? I couldn't possibly tell you!

Warning: When using recipes with vinegar for pickles, *do not* use an iron kettle as vinegar draws the taste of the iron from the pot.

QUICK KOSHER AND DILL PICKLES

10 large kosher pickles
6 large sour dill pickles
2 cups white sugar
2 tbsps. mustard seed

Peel and slice the pickles.

Let stand one hour in a large bowl with sugar and mustard seed sprinkled on. Stir well to mix.

Put in 1-quart jar in refrigerator for 2 days and then turn upside down and leave in for 2 more days. The pickles are then ready to serve. Keep pickles in same jar in refrigerator while using.

MAKES 1 quart.

When pickles are gone I strain the juice and keep it in refrigerator to use in French dressings instead of vinegar.

MARYLAND WINTER PICKLES

12 cucumbers, sliced
3 Bermuda onions, sliced
⅓ cup salt
2 tbsps. mustard seed
2 tsps. celery seed
3 cups brown sugar
1 clove garlic, peeled and cut in half
cider vinegar to cover

Put cucumbers and onions in large bowl with the salt. Let stand for 3 hours. Drain in a large colander through running cold water. Place in large kettle (not iron) and add mustard seed, celery seed, sugar and garlic. Just cover with vinegar. Bring to a boil and then lower heat to simmer. Cook for about 40 minutes or until cucumbers are transparent. Do not overcook or cucumbers will be limp. Place in sterilized jars (you will need three 1-quart jars and one 1-pint jar) and seal.

Makes 3½ quarts.

Use jars with self-sealing tops. If you have any other type of jar, use two layers of paraffin to seal them.

MADAME AUGUSTE CHOUTEAU'S SPANISH PICKLE

This recipe dates back to the 1700's and was given to me by Mrs. Richard S. Bull of St. Louis who is the fourth-generation granddaughter of Auguste Chouteau, the co-founder, with Pierre Laclede, of St. Louis. Before the French came, the territory belonged to Spain—hence, the name "Spanish Pickle." In those days nothing was wasted. In the late fall, using the onions left in the ground, the peppers which had turned red, and the green tomatoes which would never ripen, the settlers made this pickle. I have modernized Madame Chouteau's original recipe to the extent of explaining the cooking method.

½ peck green tomatoes (cleaned and sliced thin)
5 large Bermuda onions *or* 12 smaller white onions (sliced thin)
12 sweet red peppers (seeded and cut in ⅛-in. strips)
2 cups salt
2 tbsps. turmeric
3 tbsps. mustard seed
2 tbsps. dry mustard
1 tbsp. allspice
1 tbsp. powdered ginger
2 lbs. dark brown sugar
½ gallon apple cider vinegar

Place tomato, onions and red pepper in your largest kettle (a canning kettle will do). Salt each layer as you fill up the kettle. When all are in, take a large spoon and mix all together. Cover and let stand for 24 hours in your kitchen.

At the end of the time, wash the salt completely away with running cold water. Do this little by little in a large colander. Drain vegetables thoroughly and put back in large kettle. Add spices, sugar and vinegar. Stir well and place on high heat. When mixture begins to boil, turn down to simmer and continue cooking, covered, for 2 hours or until liquid clears and onions are opaque.

In the meantime, sterilize eight 1-quart jars and their tops by placing them, upside down, in about 4 inches of boiling water for 5 minutes. Sterilize kitchen tongs at the same time. When pickle is done, have jars ready. Fill each jar with the pickle and juice to within ½ inch of the top. With the sterile tongs, place the lids on the jars and screw them on tightly.

Makes 8 quarts.

WINTER SPICED SWEET PICKLE

1 jar (1 qt.) dill pickles
¾ cup sugar per cup of sliced pickles
vinegar to cover
1 (1¼ oz.) box mixed pickle spices

Cut dill pickles in slices about ½ inch thick. To each cup of sliced pickle, add ¾ cup sugar and let stand in a medium bowl (covered) for 24 hours. Then add enough vinegar to cover and stir in mixed pickle spices. Put in a 1-quart jar and let stand for 10 days in refrigerator.

MAKES 1 quart.

GREEN TOMATO PICKLE

5 lbs. green tomatoes, sliced
10 large onions, peeled and sliced
1 cup salt
3 cups cider vinegar
3 green peppers, seeded and sliced
3 red peppers, seeded and sliced
3 cloves garlic, crushed
1 lb. dark brown sugar
1½ tsps. dry mustard
12 whole cloves (in a cheesecloth bag)
1 tsp. ground cinnamon
2 tsps. ground ginger
1 tsp. salt
1 tsp. celery seed

1. Mix tomatoes and onions with salt and let stand 12 hours in 8- or 10-quart bowl (covered).
2. Drain and rinse under cold water.
3. In a 10- or 12-quart kettle combine tomatoes and onions with the remaining ingredients and simmer for 2 hours or until tomatoes are transparent. Stir frequently. Remove clove bag.
4. Pour into sterilized jars and seal carefully with two layers of melted paraffin. Pour one layer paraffin. Let cool and pour on another layer.

MAKES 4 quarts.

CHILI SAUCE

- 30 firm red tomatoes, chopped and peeled
- 12 onions, chopped
- 5 cups vinegar
- 3 cups brown sugar
- 2 cups white sugar
- 8 green peppers, deseeded and chopped
- 2 red peppers, deseeded and chopped
- 2 tbsps. fresh ground horseradish
- ⅛ tsp. turmeric
- 1 tbsp. cloves
- 1 tbsp. cinnamon
- 1 tbsp. ginger
- ¼ cup salt
- 1 (1 lb.) box paraffin

1. Place first nine ingredients in largest (10 quart) kettle with cover.
2. Tie in a bag: cloves, cinnamon, ginger and salt. Add to kettle.
3. Bring to a boil with cover on; then reduce heat to simmer and cook slowly for 6 to 7 hours, uncovered.
4. Remove spice bag and cool.
5. Pour in sterilized jars and cover the "Chili Sauce" with two ¼-inch layers of paraffin, letting first cool before adding second.

Melt cakes of paraffin in top of double boiler over boiling water. Be careful as paraffin is flammable.

To peel tomatoes easily, cover with boiling water, let stand 2 minutes, pour off water and peel will come right off. This applies to fresh peaches too.

Makes 7 quarts.

APPLE CHUTNEY

- 5 cups sliced tart apples, peeled and cored
- 1 cup apple cider vinegar
- 1 tsp. finely chopped garlic
- 1 heaping tsp. salt
- 3 roots of whole ginger, scraped and cut into small pieces
- 1 cup brown sugar
- 1 cup white sugar
- ½ cup raisins

Bring the first five ingredients to a boil in a heavy (5 quart, 1 pint) saucepan.
Add brown sugar, white sugar and raisins.
Simmer for 1½ hours.

This chutney will keep indefinitely in covered sterilized jars and in the refrigerator.

Makes 4 (8 oz.) jars.

SAUCE BALI

- 1 cup catsup
- ½ cup strained honey
- 5 tbsps. soy sauce
- 8 dashes Tabasco sauce
- small clove garlic, finely minced
- 5 tsps. curry powder
- ½ cup preserves (strawberry, damson plum, apricot or pineapple)
- ½ cup chutney, chopped

Combine all ingredients, mix well, set aside in refrigerator.

Makes 2½ cups.

This sauce is sensational with cold beef, lamb and, especially, pork.

RHUBARB CONSERVE

- 6 cups rhubarb (cut in 1-in. pieces and washed)
- 2 cups strawberries (washed and cut in half)
- 2 oranges (put through meat grinder, juice, peel and all, but take out seeds)
- 4 tbsps. lemon juice
- 2 lemon rinds put through grinder
- 1 cup raisins
- 2½ cups sugar
- 2 cups corn syrup
- 1 tsp. salt

Cook above together at slow boil for 2 hours and 10 minutes or until thick. Seal in sterile jars with two layers of paraffin.

Makes 9 (8 oz.) jars.

SPICED BLUEBERRY PRESERVES

1 qt. washed and cleaned blueberries
¼ cup cider vinegar
2 cups sugar
¼ tsp. allspice
¼ tsp. cinnamon
¼ tsp. nutmeg
¼ tsp. cloves (powdered)

Combine ingredients and simmer until blueberries are tender and preserve is thick. (After it starts to boil, boil for about 13 to 15 minutes.) Pour into two sterilized pint jars and after it has cooled for 20 minutes, seal with paraffin.

MAKES 1 quart.

LIME MARMALADE

12 large or 18 medium-sized limes, washed and seeded
water
¾ cup sugar (per cup of lime mixture)

1. Put the washed limes through a food chopper. Measure the resulting pulp and add 3 times as much water. Set aside overnight in a pottery or ceramic bowl.

2. Transfer the mixture to a 3-quart enamelware kettle and bring to a boil. Simmer gently 20 minutes; let stand overnight again in the pottery bowl.

3. Measure the mixture into a large 4-quart kettle and add 1 cup of sugar for each cup of lime mixture. Bring to a boil, stirring, until the sugar dissolves. Boil rapidly, stirring to prevent sticking (approximately 28 minutes), until the marmalade sheets on the spoon, a drop chilled on a plate leaves a track when pushed by the finger or candy thermometer registers 220°. Skim foam impurities from the top with a spoon.

4. Let cool in the kettle for 20 minutes and then put in sterilized jars. Top with two layers of melted paraffin. Store in a cool dry dark place.

MAKES 14 (6 oz.) jars.

BEACH PLUM JELLY | *Mrs. James Crowley*

1 peck beach plums (⅓ ripe, plum color, ⅔ green color)
water to cover
3 cups sugar to each 4 cups juice

1. Pick beach plums before they have fully ripened. Remove stems and place in very large kettle and cover with water.
2. Boil until the fruit is soft and separates from the pits.
3. Strain through several thicknesses of cheesecloth hung from any available hook or knob in your kitchen. Place pans to catch the juice under each cheesecloth bag.
4. Let drip overnight.
5. In large kettle place the strained juice and add the sugar.
6. Boil rapidly until the jelly coats a spoon and a sheet of jelly hangs off the spoon (about 220° on a candy thermometer).
7. Sterilize 24 (6 oz.) jars, upside down, in boiling water for 5 minutes. Fill them, cool, and cover them with two layers of paraffin.

MAKES approximately 24 jars.

When picking beach plums you will find some fully ripe and plum colored and others still green.

SPICED CRAB-APPLE JELLY | *Sally Dingwall*

1 peck crab apples (dark ones)
water to cover
1 cup vinegar
1 oz. allspice (powdered)
1 oz. whole cloves
1⅛ oz. stick cinnamon, cut up
sugar (1 cup per cup of crab-apple juice *or* ¾ cup per cup of crab-apple juice for less sweet jelly)

Cover crab apples with water. Add vinegar. Cook until soft but not mushy. Strain through cheesecloth. Don't squeeze. Let crab apples drip a few hours or overnight into a large bowl or bowls.

Make a bag (not porous). Put in it: allspice, cloves and cinnamon. Tie up bag and pound all spices. Put bag in juice. Let cook slowly until well spiced (1½ hours to 2 hours at least).

Take out spice bag. Measure juice and add equal amount of sugar or ¾ cup sugar to one cup juice. Cook until it jells (45 minutes to 1 hour boiling time).

This all depends on the pectin in the apples. To test jelling stage, drop from wooden spoon. When two drops merge into one drop and make a slow dripping thread, jelly is done (220° on a candy thermometer). Put in sterilized jars and cover with two layers of paraffin.

Makes approximately 18 to 24 (6 oz.) jelly jars.

Suffice it to say that any one of the following recipes for "spirits" warms the heart, releases the subconscious, bolsters the timid, ends a day with grace and generally improves the appetite (unfortunately). A warning "Go Slow," even though ungrammatical, should be pasted on each of Clark's julep cups—but how refreshing they are on a hot summer day!

One of our Presidents, who must remain nameless, when offered a drink at eleven o'clock in the morning, said, "Well, why not? The sun must be over the yardarm someplace!"

CAFÉ BRÛLOT

2 oranges (use only the peel)
2 lemons (use only the peel)
12 lumps of sugar
1 (4 in.) piece of stick cinnamon (broken)
4 whole allspice
4 whole cloves
1 cup brandy
¼ cup bourbon
4 cups hot strong black coffee

1. Cut peel thinly (bright part only) from oranges and lemons in a continuous spiral. Place in deep chafing dish with sugar, cinnamon, allspice and cloves. Mash sugar against peel with the back of a wooden spoon.
2. Add brandy and bourbon; allow to stand 10 minutes.
3. Heat chafing dish until liquid begins to bubble. Dip out part of the liquid with a long-handled ladle and carefully ignite.
4. Swirl over chafing dish to ignite contents. Slowly pour in coffee and continue to stir until flames die out.
5. Pour through fine strainer into demitasse cups. If you have no chafing dish, prepare in a 10-inch enamel skillet and transfer to silver coffeepot.
SERVES 8 (4 ounce) servings.

EGG NOG

1 pt. fine bourbon
1 cup sugar
6 egg yolks
2 pts. heavy cream
6 egg whites (beaten fairly stiff)
¼ cup rum

1. Mix bourbon with the sugar 24 hours before planning to serve.
2. Beat egg yolks until light.

3. Add bourbon and sugar mixture to the yolks slowly.
4. Whip cream, beat egg whites and add to bourbon mixture.
5. Add rum.

Makes about 8 cups.

RAMOS' GIN FIZZ

This is the original recipe given to my father by Ramos in New Orleans. It was our annual Christmas Open House drink. My father spent most of Christmas morning shaking this up in the kitchen with a few helpful friends. Nowadays, all of the recipe can be done in seconds in an electric blender. It looks and tastes innocuous, but *watch out!*

1 pt. cream
½ pt. gin
3 heaping tsps. powdered sugar
2 egg whites

*1 tsp. Orange Flower Water
1 (1 oz.) jigger lemon juice
ice

In a cocktail shaker (or electric blender), put cream and gin. Add powdered sugar, the egg whites and the Orange Flower Water. Add, at the last, the lemon juice and ice. Shake hard or, if using blender, blend for 10 seconds in two steps or it will overflow.

Serves 6 or 7 (4 oz.) drinks.

STRONG ICED COFFEE

4 cups fresh, cold coffee (for ice tray)   4 cups fresh, cold coffee

Freeze 4 cups strong cold coffee in refrigerator ice-cube trays overnight.
Add cubes to cold strong coffee in four tall glasses.
Serves 4.

* Orange Flower Water may be purchased in your drugstore. It comes in 2-ounce and 7-ounce bottles.

HAWAIIAN MAI TAI

2 tsps. sugar
2 tsps. cold water
2 cups finely crushed ice
2 jiggers dark rum

2 jiggers golden rum
2 jiggers light rum
juice of 1 lime

In two double old-fashioned glasses, put granulated sugar diluted with cold water. Add ice to the top of the glass. Pour in each 1 jigger dark rum, golden rum, light rum plus ½ of the lime juice. Stir well and serve.

Makes 2 drinks.

CLARK'S MINT JULEP

2 large bunches fresh mint leaves washed and stemmed
2 cups boiling water
8 tsps. sugar
10 lbs. crushed ice

1 pt. fine bourbon (approximately— you may need more)
¼ cup powdered sugar
8 sprigs of fresh mint

The Mash
1. In bowl, place mint leaves.
2. Pound and crush mint leaves thoroughly.
3. Add boiling water.
4. Let stand for 1 hour.

Use this as a base for the juleps.

The Julep
1. In bottom of each julep cup, put 2 tablespoons of the above mash mixed with 1 teaspoon sugar. Stir well.
2. Add layer of finely crushed ice, then bourbon, then ice, then bourbon, etc. (2 ounces bourbon per julep). Stir well.
3. Place cups in ice compartment of refrigerator for about ½ hour to frost.
4. Before serving, wrap around each julep cup a small napkin held in place by an elastic band. (This is *not* very fancy but keeps our friends from freezing their hands.)

5. Dip a sprig of mint (slightly dampened) in powdered sugar and place 1 on top of each julep cup.

By this method juleps may be prepared ahead and frosted beautifully.

MAKES 8 juleps and a good deal of animated conversation.

BEN RUSSELL'S NANTUCKET BREW

Something tells me that, after several swigs of this brew, you can fly to the mainland without benefit of airplane.

1 qt. Scotch whisky
4 cups sugar
1 qt. ripe beach plums

6 whole cloves
1-in. stick of cinnamon

Mix all ingredients together and let stand in covered, 2-quart crockery jar for 1 week.

Strain and serve.

MAKES 1½ to 2 qts.

LOUISE JACKSON'S RUM AND BEACH PLUMS

1 scant qt. of dark beach plums

3 cups dark or light rum (or enough to cover the plums)

1. Fill a 1-quart crockery jar (with lid) almost to the top with dark beach plums.
2. Pour rum in jar to cover the plums.
3. Let stand covered for one week.
4. Strain and serve.

MAKES about 1 quart.

After several swigs of this you can fly *back* from the mainland without benefit of airplane.

SALTY JOE COCKTAIL

juice of ½ lemon
1 tsp. salt
3 oz. vodka

6 ice cubes (crushed)
1 cup fresh-squeezed and strained grapefruit juice

Ice 2 glasses ("old-fashioned" size) in refrigerator.
Dip rims in lemon juice and then in salt.
Add vodka, ice cubes and fill with grapefruit juice.
MAKES 2 drinks.

SANGRÍA I

1 bottle dry red wine (24½ oz.)
juice of ½ lemon
juice and peel of 1 orange

10 or 12 ice cubes
1 (10 oz.) bottle club soda (or more to fill the pitcher)

1. Combine in tall (2 quart) pitcher the wine, lemon juice and orange juice.
2. Add the orange peel.
3. Add ice cubes.
4. Fill pitcher with chilled club soda.

MAKES about 1½ quarts. SERVES 6.

SANGRÍA II

3 (25.6 oz.) bottles of Burgundy wine
½ cup sugar
1½ cups orange juice

1½ cups Cointreau
1½ cups Cognac
6 lemon slices
6 lime slices

Mix together a few hours before serving. Then pour over 18 or 20 ice cubes in 1-gallon pitcher.
MAKES about 3½ quarts.

BARONESS SILVERCRUYS' "TIGER'S MILK"

1 qt. milk
1 tsp. yeast
¼ to ½ cups powdered nonfat milk

2 tbsps. wheat germ
1 tbsp. molasses *or* ½ (11 oz.) can apricot nectar

1. Pour 2 cups milk into blender.
2. Start the motor and add the dry ingredients.
3. Add the molasses diluted with ½ glass of the milk.
4. Blend for 1 minute.
5. Pour into 2 quart bottles containing the rest of the milk.
6. Keep covered and cold in refrigerator. Shake well before serving.

A number of health-building ingredients may be added to the above such as:

1 tsp. powdered bone
1 tsp. calcium gluconate
1 tbsp. powdered lecithin

½ tsp. rose hips
20 drops ascorbic acid (vitamin C)

Go to a health store for these ingredients.
MAKES about 1¼ quarts.

CHRISTMAS WINE | Mrs. Hubert de Besche
(*Julglögg*) | The Royal Embassy of Sweden

There are many ways of preparing this favorite Swedish Christmas drink, but I have found this one the easiest and most popular among my American friends.

1 bottle Swedish aquavit or gin
2 bottles Burgundy
¾ cup raisins
½ cup sugar
1 small piece lemon peel

1 tbsp. cardamom seeds
½ tsp. whole cloves
3 (½ in.) pieces cinnamon stick
1 cup blanched almonds

Pour ½ of aquavit or gin and all of Burgundy into large saucepan. Add raisins, sugar and lemon peel. Tie spices in cheesecloth and drop into wine mixture. Cover pan, bring very slowly to the boiling point, let simmer 30 minutes. Add remaining gin or aquavit. Remove from heat and remove spice bag. Put a match to "glogg" in saucepan. Using a long-handled ladle, pour hot into punch glasses over a few almonds in each glass.

To serve more dramatically, before lighting, pour "glogg" into a chafing dish (a good way of keeping "glogg" hot for a second serving) and turn off the lights in the room before igniting "glogg."

USEFUL INFORMATION

HERB CHART

	APPETIZERS	FISH	MEAT	VEGETABLES
BASIL	in vegetable, shrimp or fish cocktails and in stuffed celery	with shrimp and fish stuffings	add to stew, hash, meat loaf and braised meat	always with tomatoes; very good with peas, beans, cucumbers
CHERVIL	with cold vegetable in a sauce	in seafood salads	veal or chicken	with asparagus or endive
CHIVES	in vegetable cocktails and cheese spreads	especially good in seafood salads	with sour cream in hamburgers and meat loaf	in mashed potatoes
DILL	in cottage cheese and cream cheese	in sauces or in melted butter on fish	sprinkle over lamb chops after broiling	use seed in spiced beets
MARJORAM	roast beef	sprinkle over broiled fish	sprinkle over roasts before cooking, add to stews, meat loaf	sprinkle over spinach, zucchini, mushrooms and potatoes
MINT	in fruit cocktail	—	in sauce or jelly with lamb	on carrots or peas and chopped cabbage
OREGANO	tomato juice	stuffing	ravioli pizza spaghetti	broccoli tomatoes lentils

	APPETIZERS	FISH	MEAT	VEGETABLES
PARSLEY	as garnish, also good in vegetable cocktails	sprinkle over all seafood, and put in stuffing	mix in hash, meat loaf; sprinkle over broiled meat	on buttered potatoes and creamed vegetables
ROSEMARY	seafood cocktails	with boiled fish and shell fish	with braised stewed meat, game, kidneys and roasts	use small amounts with vegetables, mushrooms
SAGE	in soft cheese	on broiled fish	in stews, meat puddings, and with game, pork and sausage	stuffings and dressings
SAVORY	veal roast	good with any fish	good in all meat dishes, game and stuffing	excellent with beans, good with cabbage
TARRAGON	with pickled fish or with vegetable cocktail	in sauces with boiled and stewed fish and shell fish	serve on meat and game	with peas and tomatoes and in creamed mushrooms
THYME	in vegetable cocktail	good in stuffing	in croquettes, stuffing, loaves and on pork and veal	with peas, carrots, onions

EQUIVALENTS

pinch (dry)	=	⅛ teaspoon
dash (liquid)	=	2 drops
3 teaspoons	=	1 tablespoon
4 tablespoons	=	¼ cup
8 tablespoons	=	½ cup
16 tablespoons	=	1 cup
2 cups	=	1 pint
2 pints	=	1 quart
4 quarts (liquid)	=	1 gallon
8 quarts (dry)	=	1 peck
4 pecks (dry)	=	1 bushel
1 ounce	=	28 grams (approximately)
1 pound	=	454 grams "
1 kilogram	=	2$\frac{1}{10}$ pounds "
1 liter	=	1 quart "
1 jigger	=	3 tablespoons
1 large jigger	=	¼ cup
1 tablespoon cornstarch	=	2 tablespoons flour

OVEN HEATS

Very Slow	—	250°
Slow	—	300°
Moderately Slow	—	325°
Moderate	—	350°
Moderately Hot	—	375°
Hot	—	400°
Very Hot	—	450° to 500°

KITCHEN EQUIPMENT

Baking Dishes and Cooking Pans

12 (8 oz. or 10 oz.) ovenproof custard cups
2-qt. ovenproof glass baking dish (11¾ x 7½ x 1¾ in.)
3-qt. ovenproof glass baking dish (13½ x 8¾ x 1¾ in.)
round ovenproof baking dishes (1 qt., 2 qts., 3 qts.)
square ovenproof baking dish (8 x 8 x 2 in.)
2 white porcelain ovenproof soufflé dishes (1 qt., 2 qts.)
plum pudding mold with cone in center and cover (2 qts., 3 qts.)
ring molds (1 qt., 1½ qts., 2 qts., 3 qts.)
angel-cake pan (10 x 4 in.)
2 round cake pans (9 x 1½ in.)
2 square cake pans (8 x 8 x 2 in.)
2 iron cornstick pans
8 escargot pans
lasagne pan (10 x 14 x 2 in.)
loaf pan (8½ x 4½ x 2 in.)
loaf pan (9½ x 5¼ x 2¾ in.)
muffin tin (12 sections)
muffin pan (iron—11 sections)
paella pan (3 qts., 6 qts.)
12 (8 oz.) ramekins
1 small roasting pan with cover
1 large roasting pan with cover
1 large open roasting pan (18¾ x 12½ x 5 in.)
spring form pan (9½ x 2¼ in.)
bean pots with covers (2½ qts., 3½ qts.)
open-mouth heatproof earthenware pots with covers (2 qts., 4 qts., 6 qts., 8 qts.)
2 cookie sheets (15½ x 10¼ x ¾ in.)
2 cookie sheets (17 x 14 in.)
12 medium scallop shells
12 large scallop shells

Electrical Equipment

blender
can opener
carving knife

chafing dish
10-cup percolator
50-cup percolator
large skillet (10 or 12 in.)
deep-fat frying kettle with basket (9½ x 4½ in.)
knife sharpener
smokeless open grill with a rotisserie
meat grinder
hand mixer with bowl
orange juice squeezer
roasting pan (large, for 12- to 14-lb. turkey—17½ x 12 x 5½ in.)
toaster
vegetable juicer
fondue pan

Pans and Kettles

oval asparagus pan with lid
asparagus steamer
double boiler (1 qt., 2 qts., 3 qts., 6 qts.)
porcelain and copper double boiler (2 qt.) for sauces
clam or lobster steamer (20 qt.)
crepe pan (about 6 in.)
French omelet pan (9½ in.)
iron griddle (11 in.)
aluminum covered kettles (4 qts., 6 qts., 8 qts., 10 qts., 12 qts., 16 qts.)
largest size canning kettle (holds 7 jars) with rack and cover
large tea kettle (4 qts.)
Dutch oven with cover (2 qts., 4 qts., 10 qts.)
stainless-steel ovenproof oval deep dish with cover
fish-poaching pan (oval with cover—3 qts., 6 qts.)
large stainless-steel ovenproof platter
iron, aluminum or Teflon skillets (5 in., 8 in., 9 in., 10 in., 12 in.)
large vegetable steamer
medium-sized Chinese wok, cover and rim stand
large Chinese wok, cover and rim stand

Miscellaneous Equipment

8 small and 8 large apothecary jars (for flour, salt, coffee, etc.)
fruit and butter baller

KITCHEN EQUIPMENT | 515

"Bird's Nest" double deep-fat frying basket with long handles (found in specialty cooking equipment stores)
rotary egg beater
chopping block
cutting board
steel bowl (6 qts.)
nest of steel bowls
open-fire broiler with long handles
dustpan and brush
pastry brush
vegetable brush
broom
push broom with long handle
butter dish
nut chopper
small colander
large colander
apple corer
corkscrew
heatproof glass measuring cups (1 cup, 2 cup, 4 cup)
nest of cookie cutters
8 escargot forks
12 fondue forks
2 heavy lifting forks (for roasts)
2 long-handled meat forks
set of special fork, spoon and spatula for use with Teflon (white)
small funnel
large funnel
stainless-steel grater
cheese grinder
hand food grinder (meat)
nut grinder
pepper grinder
set of really fine steel knives
bread knife (serrated edge)
heavy chopping knife
large Chinese chopping knife
grapefruit knife
soup ladle (½ cup)
food mill
dry mop

wet mop
wooden mortar and pestle (for herbs)
wooden meat tenderizer mallet
potato masher
bottle opener
can opener
wine bottle opener
pastry cloth
pastry tube
rolling pin (wooden)
egg poacher (4 sections)
garlic press
onion press
2 cake racks
Lucite cookbook rack
potato ricer
set of refrigerator dishes
kitchen scales
ice-cream scoops
sugar, flour, coffee scoops
pepper shaker
salt shaker
kitchen shears
sieves: small, medium, large
flour sifter
16 small steel skewers
16 long steel skewers
16 extra long skewers (for outside grill)
steel-wool pads
skimmer (for jellies, etc.)
marble slab (for pastry, candy, etc.)
cheese slicer
egg slicer
string-bean slicer
vegetable slicer
spatulas (wide and narrow—metal)
wide metal pancake spatula
rubber bowl spatula
2 long-handled kitchen spoons
sets of measuring spoons
small wooden spoon

large wooden spoon
long-handled Chinese wok spoon
lemon squeezer (glass)
basting syringe
thermometers: candy, deep-fat frying, meat
egg timer
2 pair kitchen tongs (short- and long-handled)
small wire whisk
large wire whisk
12 dish towels
6 hot pads
6 dish cloths
paper towels and rack
foil—small and large rolls
refrigerator wrap
wax paper
cheesecloth
various soaps and cleansers
plate scraper (sponge rubber)
sink scraper
tube of salve for burns
sponges (small and large)
pair rubber gloves
pair oven mitts

As a parting thought it might prove helpful to have a stove, disposal, dishwasher and refrigerator.

INDEX

INDEX

African Lobster Tails Salad, 270
Alaskan King Crab Remoulade, 263
Alice's Chocolate Cake, 412
Alice's Frosting, 455
Almond, Almonds
  Brittle, 481
  and Chicken, Casserole of, 307
  Macaroons, 473
  Parfait Amandes, 444
Alsatian Cake, 410
Alston, Josephine, 19, 448
Altemus, Edna, 274
Anchovies and Potatoes, Baked (Jansson's Temptation), 165
Andalusian Soup, Cold, 47
Angel Cake, Grandmother's, 411
Anglaise Sauce, 458
Anticuchos (Peruvian Barbecued Beef Heart), 114
Appetizers
  Alaskan King Crab Remoulade, 263
  Avocado Mousse, 283
  Caviar, Domestic, and Cream Cheese, 25
  Caviar, Sour Cream and Almonds, 25
  Celery Root Remoulade, 259
  Cheese
    and Chutney, Hot, 26
    Cubes, Hot, 27
    Hors d'Oeuvre, Hot, 26
    Hors d'Oeuvre, Small, Resembling Poached Eggs, 28
    Hot, with Bacon, 26
    Puffs, 27
    Wafers, 28
  Chicken Livers in a Blanket, 29
  Crabmeat Canapé, Hot, 30
  Crabmeat with Capers, Hot, 184
  Dates, Stuffed, in a Blanket, 29
  Dill Pickle, Stuffed, 38
  Eggplant, Sour Cream and Caviar, 220
  Egg Rolls, 83
  Eggs, Stuffed, Sesame, 30
  Endive (Raw) Canapé, 31
  Giblet Paté, 35
  Guacamole, Mexican, 268
  Ham, Deviled, with Chutney Canapé, 31
  Herring, Salt, Pickled *(inlagd sill)*, 32
  Latvian Paté, 36
  Lobster Canapé with Mustard Mayonnaise, 33
  Meatballs, Small *(små köttbullar)*, 33
  Mushroom Canapés, Hot, 34
  Pâté de Foie Gras in Aspic with Chicken, 294
  Pâté en Gelée, 34
  Paté with Scallions and Brandy, 36
  Pirogi, 41
  Quiche, Easy, 43
  Roquefort Mousse, 295
  Salami Rolls, 41
  Sardines, Broiled, 37
  Seafood Quiche, 44
  Shad Roe Dip, 38
  Shrimp Quiche, 43
  Smoked Salmon with Capers, Bette Kovin's, 37
  Smoked Salmon Mousse, 295
  Smoked Turkey Paté, 38
  Steak Tartare, 39
  Tamales, Hot, in a Blanket, 30
  Vegetable (Raw) Canapés, 40
  Vinaigrette (for Cold *Zakuski*), 40
  Watermelon Pickle in a Blanket, 29
  Zakuski, 40
Apple, Apples
  Baked, 399
  Brown Betty Pudding, Portsmouth, 435
  Chutney, 492
  Pudding, Swedish, 435
Apricot Soufflé, 448
Archiduc Sauce, Ambassador David K. E. Bruce's, 333

Arden, Elizabeth, 251, 363
Arguelles, Mrs. Jaimé, 18, 444
Arroz con Pollo, Puerto Rican, 127
Artichoke, Artichokes
    Bottoms with Capers, 208
    How to Cook, 207
    Sevilla, 208
Asian Style Broiled Chicken, 128
Asparagus, Curried, 209
Asparagus, Fresh, 209
Aspic Dishes
    Avocado Mousse, 283
    Avocado Salad, Molded, 283
    Avocado Stuffed with Tomato Aspic Salad, 254
    Chicken Aspic, 285
    Chicken and Cucumber Mousse, 286
    Chicken Curry Mousse, 288
    Chicken Mousse Supreme, 287
    Chicken Salad Mold, Jellied, 285
    Corned Beef Mousse, 289
    Crabmeat Mousse, 290
    Cream Cheese and Pineapple Salad, Jellied, 290
    Egg Curry Mousse, 291
    Eggs en Gelée, 77
    Ham Mousse I, 291; II, 292
    Lamb Mousse with Vegetable Salad, 292
    Mushroom Ring Mold, 294
    Pâté de Foie Gras in Aspic with Chicken, 294
    Pâté en Gelée, 34
    Paté with Scallions and Brandy, 36
    Roquefort Mousse, 295
    Shrimp Mousse for Salad, 296
    Shrimp Ring, 277
    Tomato Aspic, 297
    Tunafish Mousse, 298
Austrian Coffee Cake, Mother's, 415
Avocado, Avocados
    with Chutney Salad, 253
    and Grapefruit Salad, 254
    Guacamole, Mexican, 268
    Mousse, 283
    Salad, Molded, 283
    Sauce for Tomato Aspic, 333
    Stuffed with Fresh Crabmeat Salad, 253
    Stuffed, Salad, 255
    Stuffed with Tomato Aspic Salad, 254

Bacon and Pea Sauce, 339

Bacon, Canadian, Baked, Betty Bruce Bowersock's, 107
Bali Sauce, 493
Barbecue, Barbecued Dishes
    Beef Heart, Peruvian *(anticuchos),* 114
    Charcoal Steaks, 100
    Fish Casserole, 313
    Mint Lamb, 100
    Ribs (spareribs), 113
    Sauce I, 339; II, 340
    Sauce (for) Chicken I and II, 341
    Sauce, Special, 340
Barkley, Mrs. Alben, 131, 365
Barley Ring, 243
Basil, uses, 510
Bay Ranch Salad, 256
Beach Plum Jelly, 495
Beach Plums and Rum, Louise Jackson's, 504
Beans, Green or String
    French, with Chicken Gizzards, Fried, 116
    Fresh, 210
    (and) Mushroom Soup and French Fried Onion Casserole, 303
Beans, Lima, Supreme, 221
Béarnaise Sauce, 341
Béchamel Sauce I and II, 342
Beef
    Brisket of, Betty Bruce Bowersock's, 91
    Chili con Carne, 96
    Chow Mein Casserole, 310
    Corned Beef Mousse, 289
    Cornish Pasties, 97
    and Eggplant Casserole, Joyce Clifford Burland's, 303
    Filet of, Shish Kabob, 92
    Heart, Barbecued, Peruvian *(anticuchos),* 114
    and Kidney Pie, London, 304
    Meat Loaf, German, 97
    Poule au Pot, La, 143
    Roast, Leftover, Open Sandwich with Gravy, 391
    Sailors' *(sjömansbiff),* 98
    Sauerbraten, German, 99
    Soup, Mrs. Hubert H. Humphrey's, 48
    Steak, Charcoal Steaks, 100
    Steak Tartare, 39
    Stroganoff, 92
    Stroganoff, Quick, 94

Beef (*continued*)
　Tongue, 121
　Wellington (adapted from the Foxcroft cookbook), 94
Beets, 211
　Borsch, Cold (Blender), 48
　Borsch, Iced, 49
　Borsch, Latvian, 49
Benchley, Nathaniel, 9, 166
Berckemeyer, Mrs. Fernando, 18, 114
Beverages
　Coffee, Iced, Strong, 502
　Tiger's Milk, Baroness Silvercruys', 506
Beverages, Alcoholic
　Café Brûlot, 501
　Christmas Wine *(Julglögg),* 506
　Eggnog, 501
　Hawaiian Mai Tai, 503
　Mint Julep, Clark's, 503
　Nantucket Brew, Ben Russell's, 504
　Ramos' Gin Fizz, 502
　Rum and Beach Plums, Louise Jackson's, 504
　Salty Joe Cocktail, 505
　Sangría I and II, 505
Biscuits, Baking Powder, Mother's, 375
Blake, Maria, 336
Blake, Tom, 56, 279
Blarney Stones, 411
Blintzes, 383
Blueberry
　Bread Dessert, Old-Fashioned, 439
　Muffins, Mother's, 375
　Pie, Deep Dish, 426
　Pie, Deep Dish, Quick, 427
　Preserves, Spiced, 494
Bluefish, Broiled with Gin, Nantucket, Nat Benchley's, 166
Bluefish Salad, Nantucket, 256
Boggs, Mrs. Hale (Lindy), 18, 479, 483
Boiled Dressing I, 363; II, 364
Boiled Frosting, 455
Borsch, *see* Beets; Soup
Bourbon, Mint Julep, Clark's, 503
Bowersock, Betty Bruce, 91, 107, 378
Bran Muffins, My Father's, 376
Brandied Chicken with Garlic in Casserole, 308
Brandy Sauce, Mary Ellen Monroney's, 458
Breads
　Biscuits, Baking Powder, Mother's, 375

Bread
　Arab or Greek, *see* note, 251
　Brown, New England, Old-Fashioned, 376
　Cinnamon Sugar Loaf for Tea, My Mother's, 377
　Lettuce Loaf, 379
　Nut, 379
　Orange, 380
　Corn Dodgers, Betty Bruce Bowersock's, 378
　Muffins
　　Blueberry, Mother's, 375
　　Bran, My Father's, 376
　　Cornbread, 377
　Popovers, 380
　Popovers, Cheese, 381
　Rolls, Icebox, 381
　Rolls, Parker House, Mother's, 382
　Yorkshire Pudding, 383
Broccoli, 212
Broccoli Salad, 257
Brown Betty Pudding, Portsmouth, 435
Brown Bread, New England, Old-Fashioned, 376
Brown Sugar Cookies, 476
Bruce, Ambassador David K. E., 9, 18, 331, 333
Bûche de Noël, 412
Buhl, Mrs. Henry, 156, 415
Bull, Mrs. Richard S., 490
Burland, Joyce Clifford, 129, 303, 350
Burland, Katya, 40
Burland, Sascha, 103
Butter Cream Frosting, 456
Buttermilk Chocolate Cake, 413
Butters, Compound
　Garlic, for Steak, 343
　(for) Steak, 343
　Tarragon, for Steak or Broiled Fish, 344
Butterscotch
　Candy, Mary Ellen Monroney's, 481
　Icebox Cake, 439
　Squares, 469

Cabbage
　Baked with Consommé, 213
　Casserole, 305
　Cole Slaw, Garden, 263
　Cole Slaw, Nora's, 263

Cabbage (*continued*)
  Green, Rolls, Stuffed, 215
  Red, with Apples, 214
  Red, German, Ruth Hayden's, 214
  Red, Salad, 248
  Salad, East India, 257
  Sweet and Sour, Chinese, 216
Caesar Salad, 258
Café Brûlot, 501
Cakes and Torten
  Angel Cake, Grandmother's 411
  Bûche de Noël, 412
  Buttermilk Chocolate Cake, 413
  Cheesecake, 414
  Chocolate Cake, Alice's, 412
  Cinnamon Cake, Swedish, 414
  Cocoa Roll, George Washington, 418
  Coffee Cake, Austrian, Mother's, 415
  Coffee Cake, Sour Cream, 415
  Daffodil Cake, Mother's, 416
  Icebox Cake, Butterscotch, 439
  Icebox Cake, Chocolate Wafers, 440
  Icebox Dessert, Chocolate, 440
  Ice Cream Roll, 419
  Orange Torte, 420
  Sponge Cake, Mother's, 418
  Sponge Cake II, 420
  Upside Down Cake, Fruit and Rum, 421
  Upside Down Cake, Pineapple and Walnut, Easy, 417
Calf's Liver, *see* Liver; Veal
Canadian Bacon, Baked, Betty Bruce Bowersock's, 107
Candy
  Almond Brittle, 481
  Butterscotch, Mary Ellen Monroney's, 481
  Fudge I, 482; II (with pecans), 482
  Pralines, New Orleans, 483
Cannelloni, 65
Cantaloupe Chicken Salad, Polynesian, 273
Caramel
  Almond Frosting, 456
  Coconut Caramel Crunch Ring, 401
  Custard (*krema karamela*), 402
  Flan I, 402; II, 403
  Ice Cream, Grandmother's, 421
  Sauce, 458
  Sauce, Easy, 459
Carrot, Carrots
  Casserole, 306
  Ring, 216
  with Sour Cream, 217
  Whiskey, Lansing, 217
Castle, Mrs. Nancy, 19
Carusi, Mrs. Eugene C., 183
Cauliflower, How to Cook, 218
Caviar
  Domestic, with Cream Cheese, 25
  (with) Sour Cream and Almonds, 25
  and Sour Cream Omelets, 79
Celery, 218
  and Mushroom Salad, 259
  and Nuts (sandwich filling), 387
  Sauterne, 219
Celery Cabbage
  with Ginger, 213
  Monk's Dish, 222
  Sweet and Sour, Chinese, 216
Celery Root Remoulade, 259
Chafing Dish Eggs, 75
Chantilly Cream, 459
Charlotte Russe, Coffee, My Grandmother's, 441
Charyk, Mrs. Joseph, 407, 425, 434
Cheese, Cheese Dishes
  Cheddar
    and Chutney, Hot, 26
    Cubes, Hot, 27
    Hors d'Oeuvre, Hot, 26
    Hot, with Bacon, 26
    Never Fail Cheese Dish, 85
    Popovers, 381
    Puffs, 27
    Sauce, 344
    Sharp Cheese and Bacon (sandwich filling), 387
    Shrimp Casserole, 321
    Soufflé, 326
    Soufflé Ring, 326
    Tomato and Bacon Sandwich, Hot, 391
  Cream
    and Bar-le-Duc Salad, Mother's, 255
    Chocolate Icing, 456
    and Guava Jelly (sandwich filling), 387
    and Olive (sandwich filling), 387
    and Pineapple Salad, Jellied, 290
    Strawberries with Cream Cheese, 409
  Eggs Mornay, 79
  Hors d'Oeuvre, Small, Resembling Poached Eggs, 28
  Roquefort Dressing I and II, 369
  Roquefort Mousse, 295

Cheese, Cheese Dishes (*continued*)
  Swiss, and Egg Salad, 265
  Swiss, Nantucket Sandwich, 392
  Tomato, Toast, Cheese Dish, 86
  Wafers, 28
Cheesecake, 414
Chef Salad, 260
Chervil, uses, 510
Chesapeake Crabcakes, 185
Chicken, *see also* Chicken Giblet; Chicken Gizzards; Chicken Livers and Almonds, Casserole of
  Arroz con Pollo, Puerto Rican, 127
  Aspic, 285
  Brandied, with Garlic in Casserole, 308
  Broiled, Asian Style, 128
  with Burgundy, 129
  Cacciatore, Quick, 129
  (and) Cantaloupe Salad, Polynesian, 273
  Casserole, 306
  Celery and Noodles, Grandmother's, 131
  Chambord, 131
  with Cointreau or Grand Marnier, 132
  Croquettes, 132
  and Cucumber Mousse, 286
  Curry, 134
    Kapitan, 135
    Mousse, 288
    with Rice Pilaf, 136
    with Saffron Rice, 135
  Divan, 137
  Florentine, Casserole of, 307
  Fricassee of, 137
  Fried, 138
  with Garlic and Ginger, 138
  Hash Deluxe, 139
  Hashed in Cream, 133
  Leftover, Open Sandwich with Gravy, 391
  Loaf, 140
  Mousse, Imperial (hot), 325
  Mousse Supreme (cold), 287
  and Mushroom Filling (for pancakes), 386
  Normandie Casserole, 309
  Paprika (with) Sour Cream, 146
  Pâté de Foie Gras in Aspic with Chicken, 294
  Polynesian, 142
  Poule au Pot, La, 143
  Rice Casserole, 319
  and Rice Salad, 262
  Ring, Mother's, 146
  Rolls, Sautéed, 147
  Salad I, 260; II, 261
    with Celery (sandwich filling), 388
    Hot, 262
    Mold, Jellied, 285
  Sauce, Mother's, 345
  Shirin Polo, Iranian, 142
  Sliced (sandwich filling), 390
  Soufflé (baked), 327
  Soufflé, Cold, 327
  Soup, 50
  Stock, How to Make, 344
  (and) Sweetbread Ragout in Shells or Ramekins, 323
  and Vegetables, Chinese, 140
  and Vegetables in Wine, 148
  with Wine, French, 141
Chicken Giblet Paté, 35
Chicken Gizzards with French Beans, Fried, 116
Chicken Gizzards in Sauce, 116
Chicken Liver, Livers
  in a Blanket, 29
  with Brandy, 117
  Casserole, 309
  with Hominy Grits, Ruth Coburn's, 315
  Latvian Paté, 36
  Sautéed, 117
  Shirred Eggs with, 82
Chili con Carne, 96
Chili Sauce, 492
Chinese Chicken and Vegetables, 140
Chinese Fried Parsley, 226
Chinese Scallops and Mushrooms, 194
Chinese Shrimp with Hot Soy Sauce, 198
Chinese Shrimp and Zucchini Casserole, Easy, 322
Chinese Style Duck, Crisp, 148
Chinese Sweet and Sour Cabbage, 216
Chives, uses, 510
Chocolate
  Buttermilk Cake, 413
  Cake, Alice's, 412
  Cream Cheese Icing, 456
  Cream Princesse, 443
  Crème au Beurre, 457
  Crispies, 469
  Fudge Crisps, 472
  Icebox Dessert, 440
  Marshmallow Pie, 427

Chocolate (*continued*)
  Mousse, 422
  Nut Cookies, 470
  Pudding with Meringue, 436
  and Rice Krispies Ring, 401
  Sauce I, 459; II, 460
  Sauce, Easy, 460
  Soufflé I, 449; II, 450
  Wafers Icebox Cake, 440
Chouteau, Auguste, 490
Chouteau, Madame Auguste, 490
Chowder, *see* Soup
Chow Mein Casserole, 310
Christmas Cookies (Half-Moon Shape), 470
Christmas Ginger Snaps (*pepparkakor*), 474
Christmas Plum Pudding, 438
Christmas Wine (*Julglögg*), 506
Cinnamon Cake, Swedish, 414
Cinnamon Sugar Loaf for Tea, My Mother's, 377
Chutney, Apple, 492
Clam, Clams
  Bouillon, My Grandmother's, 50
  Chowder, Maine, 51
  Steamed, 183
Clark's Favorite Sautéed Slivered Potatoes, 232
Clark's Mint Julep, 503
Clifford, Clark, 9, 11, 12, 14, 93
Coburn, Ruth, 315, 407, 409
Cocoa, Alice's Frosting, 455
Cocoa Roll, George Washington, 418
Coconut Caramel Crunch Ring, 401
Coffee
  Almond Crème, 441
  Café Brûlot, 501
  Charlotte Russe, My Grandmother's, 441
  Chiffon Pie, 428
  Crème, 442
  Custard, Baked, 400
  Ice Cream Pie, 428
  Iced, Strong, 502
Coffee Cake, *see* Cakes and Torten
Cole Slaw, *see* Cabbage; Salad
Congress of the United States, 208
Consommé, *see* Soup
Cookies and Small Cakes
  Blarney Stones, 411
  Brown Sugar Cookies, 476
  Butterscotch Squares, 469
  Chocolate Crispies, 469

Chocolate Nut Cookies, 470
Christmas Cookies (Half-Moon Shape), 470
Christmas Ginger Snaps (*pepparkakor*), 474
Date Nut Sticks, 471
Florentines I, 471; II, 472
Fudge Crisps, 472
Gingerbread, 417
Icebox Cookies, 473
Macaroons, 473
Nut Lace Wafers, 474
Oatmeal Cookies, Crisp, 475
Rum Balls, 475
Vanilla Wafers, 476
Corn, Cornmeal
  Chowder, New England, 52
  Cornbread and Herb Stuffing, for Turkey, 158
  Cornbread Muffins, 377
  Dodgers, Betty Bruce Bowersock's, 378
  Pudding, 219
  Pudding, Easy, 220
  Soufflé, Lansing, 328
Cornish Pasties, 97
Country Gravy for Fried Chicken, 348
Country Ham (Mrs. Westmoreland's), 108
Country Ham, To Cook, 109
Crab Apple Jelly, Spiced, 495
Crab, Crabmeat
  Avocado Stuffed with Fresh Crabmeat Salad, 253
  Bay Ranch Salad, 256
  Canapé, Hot, 30
  with Capers, Hot, 184
  Crabcakes Chesapeake, 185
  Curry, Hawaiian, 186
  Fresh or Canned (sandwich filling), 388
  King Crab, Alaskan, Casserole, 311
  King Crab, Alaskan, Remoulade, 263
  Mousse, 290
  Royale, 186
  Salad, 264
  in Scallop Shells, Baked, 183
Cranberry Sherbet, 447
Cream, Chantilly, 459
Cream Desserts
  Coffee Almond Crème, 441
  Coffee Crème, 442
  Cream Princesse, 443
  Parfait Amandes, 444

INDEX | 527

Cream Puffs, 425
Crème au Beurre (chocolate), 457
Crème Brûlée I, 399; II, 400
Crème Vichyssoise, 64
Creole Sauce, 345
Creole Shrimp, 199
Creole Shrimp in Remoulade Sauce, 275
Cromer, Countess of, 18, 97, 405
Croquettes, Chicken, 132
Cucumber, Cucumbers
  Kosher and Dill Pickles, Quick, 489
  Salad, 264
  (sandwich filling), 388
  Sauce, 346
  Spiced Sweet Pickle, Winter, 491
  Vinaigrette, 265
  Winter Pickles, Maryland, 489
Curry, Curried
  Asparagus, 209
  Blender Mayonnaise, 367
  Chicken, 134
  Chicken Mousse, 288
  Chicken, with Rice Pilaf, 136
  Chicken, with Saffron Rice, 135
  Consommé and Cream, 55
  Crab, Hawaiian, 186
  Deviled Eggs in Casserole, 312
  Egg Mousse, 291
  Eggs Goldenrod, 78
  Kapitan (chicken), 135
  Lamb, with Rice Pilaf, 136
  Lamb, with Saffron Rice, 135
  Lobster, with Rice Pilaf, 136
  Lobster, with Saffron Rice, 135
  Sauce I, 346; II, 347
  Sauce, Cold, for Vegetable Dip, 334
  Sauce, Hot, 347
  Shrimp, with Rice Pilaf, 136
  Shrimp, with Saffron Rice, 135
  Soup, Cold, 54
Custards, Dessert
  Caramel Custard (krema karamela), 402
  Caramel Flan I, 402; II, 403
  Coffee Custard, Baked, 400
  Crème Brûlée I, 399; II, 400
  Grand Marnier Sauce, 462
  Sauce Anglaise, 458

Daffodil Cake, Mother's, 416
Dandelion Greens, 239
Date Nut Sticks, 471

Dates, Stuffed, in a Blanket, 29
de Besche, Mrs. Hubert, 18, 32, 33, 98, 165, 474, 506
de Olliqui, Mrs., 18, 403
Desserts, see Cakes and Torten; Cookies and Small Cakes; Cream Desserts; Custards, Dessert; Frozen Desserts; Ice Cream; Jellied Desserts; Ladyfinger Desserts; Meringue Desserts; Mousse, Dessert, Cold; Pie, Dessert; Pudding, Dessert; Sherbet; Soufflé, Dessert, Baked; see also Fruit and names of fruits; for dessert omelet see Eggs; for dessert sauces see Sauce, Dessert
Deviled Curried Eggs in Casserole, 312
Devron, Howard, 93
Dill
  Pickle, Stuffed, 38
  Sauce I, 334; II, for Cold Salmon, 334
  Sauce for Poached Filet of Sole, 348
  uses, 510
Dingwall, Sally, 111, 495
Douglas, Justice William O., 18, 100
Dove with Mushrooms (from Mexico), 156
Dove, Wild, Breast of, 152
Duchess Potatoes, 229
Duck, Crisp, Chinese Style, 148
Duck, Wild, I, in Foil, 152; II, with Sauerkraut Stuffing, 153
Duckling, Roast, with Orange and Wine, 149

East India Cabbage Salad, 257
East Indian Fish Salad, 267
Ecuadorian Salad Soup, 60
Egg, Eggs
  Hard-Boiled
    Curry Mousse, 291
    Deviled Curried, in Casserole, 312
    Dressing Sauce, 335
    Goldenrod, 78
    Goldenrod Curry, 78
    Mornay, 79
    and Onion (sandwich filling), 388
    and Potato Salad, 274
    Salad with Stuffed Olives (sandwich filling), 388
    Sauce for Boiled Salmon, 347
    Stuffed, Sesame, 30
    and Swiss Cheese Salad, 265

Egg, Eggs (*continued*)
  Luncheon Dish, Florentine, 76
  Omelet, Omelets
    Caviar and Sour Cream, 79
    Fluffy, 80
    French, Plain, 80
    Soufflé, with Strawberries, 81
  Poached
    Benedict, 75
    Chafing Dish, 75
    Florentine, *en Croûte*, 76
    en Gelée, 77
  Scrambled, 81
    with Broiled Veal or Lamb Kidneys and Broiled Tomatoes, 118
    with Onions and Smoked Oysters, 82
    Shirred, with Chicken Livers, 82
    and Spinach Casserole, Baked, 311
    in Tomatoes, 85
Eggnog, 501
Eggplant
  and Beef Casserole, Joyce Clifford Burland's, 303
  Khorake Bademjan, Iranian, 316
  Moussaka, 317
  (with) Sour Cream and Caviar, 220
  Stuffed, Greek, 221
  Tomato (and) Onion, 238
Egg Rolls, 83
Eisenhower, President Dwight David, 12
Eisenhower, Mrs. Dwight D., 9, 12, 18, 443
Ellis, Clarence, 14
Enchiladas, Mrs. Lyndon B. Johnson's, 313
Endive
  Canapé, Raw, 31
  with Cream, 221
  (and) Mushroom and Watercress Salad, 266

Falter, John, 18
Father's Bran Muffins, 376
Fennel Salad, 266
Fennel Villa la Massa, 222
Filling, *see also* Stuffing
  Chicken and Mushroom (for pancakes), 386
  I (sirloin and hard-boiled egg, for *pirogi*), 42
  II (cabbage, for *pirogi*), 42
Finnan Haddie, Baked, 168
Finnan Haddie, Creamed, 168

Fish, *see also* names of individual fishes
  Barbecued, Casserole, 313
  Chowder, 52
  Chowder, Mother's, 53
  Mold, 165
  Mousse with Lobster Sauce, 325
  Salad, East Indian, 267
  in Sour Cream, 166
Flan, Caramel, I, 402; II, 403
Flinn, Mrs. Michael de V., 406, 463
Florentine Eggs *en Croûte*, 76
Florentines I, 471; II, 472
Foamy Sauce, 460
France, Embassy of, 143, 412, 451, 457
Frankfurter and Noodle Casserole, Yankee, 314
French Chicken with Wine, 141
French Crepes or Pancakes, 384
French Dressing, Basic, I and II, 364; III and IV, 365
French Dressing, Pink, 366
French Omelet, Plain, 80
Frogs' Legs, Sautéed, in Lemon Butter, 167
Frostings and Icings
  Alice's Frosting, 455
  Boiled Frosting, 455
  Butter Cream Frosting, 456
  Caramel Almond Frosting, 456
  Chocolate Cream Cheese Icing, 456
  Crème au Beurre (chocolate), 457
  Mocha Icing, 457
Frozen Desserts, *see also* Ice Cream; Sherbet
  Frozen Rice, Mary Ellen Monroney's, 445
  Lime Freeze, 444
  Parfait Amandes, 444
Fruit, Fruits, *see also* names of individual fruits
  Cup with Candied Ginger, 404
  Dessert, Hot, 404
  with Kirsch Liqueur, 405
  and Rum Upside Down Cake, 421
  Salad, 267
  Salad, Molded, 293
Fudge I, 482; II (with pecans), 482
Fudge Crisps, 472

Garden Cole Slaw, 263
Garden, Mary, 11, 12
Garlic Butter for Steak, 343
Gaspacho (Cold), 55

INDEX | 529

Gaspacho, Mock, Cold, I and II, 56
Gelatin dishes for appetizers and entrées, see Aspic Dishes
Gelatin dishes for desserts, see Jellied Desserts
George Washington Cocoa Roll, 418
Georgia Ham (Pidcock Ham), 110
German Meat Loaf, 97
German Pancake, 384
German Potato Pancakes, 230
German Red Cabbage, Ruth Hayden's, 214
German Sauerbraten, 99
"German" Spaghetti, 71
Giblet Gravy (turkey), 349
Giblet Paté (chicken), 35
Gin Fizz, Ramos', 502
Gingerbread, 417
Ginger Snaps, Christmas (pepparkakor), 474
Gizzards, see Chicken Gizzards
Gnocchi I and II, 67
Golden Marinade, 352
Grand Marnier Sauce, 462
Grandmother's Recipes
 Angel Cake, 411
 Caramel Ice Cream, 421
 Chicken, Celery and Noodles, 131
 Clam Bouillon, 50
 Coffee Charlotte Russe, 441
 Mushrooms, Baked, 224
 Strawberry Ice Cream, 422
 Sweet Potato Delight, 232
Grape, White, and Mandarin Orange Salad, 271
Grapefruit and Avocado Salad, 254
Grapefruit, Salty Joe Cocktail, 505
Gravy, see also Sauce
 Country, for Fried Chicken, 348
 Pork Roast, 349
 Turkey Giblet, 349
Great Britain, Embassy of, 97, 405
Greece, Embassy of, 235, 317, 402
Greek Stuffed Eggplant, 221
Green Rice, 247
Green Salad, Crispy, 268
Grennan, Dr. H. Arthur, 173
Guacamole, Mexican, 268
Gunneng, Mrs. Arne, 18, 155

Haddock, see Finnan Haddie
Halibut, Fish Mold, 165
Halibut "Point Shirley" with Clams, 169

Ham
 Boned Cooked, 109
 Country (Mrs. Westmoreland's), 108
 Country, To Cook, 109
 Deviled, with Chutney Canapé, 31
 Deviled, and Chutney (sandwich filling), 389
 Mousse I, 291; II, 292
 Nantucket Sandwich, 392
 Pidcock (Georgia), 110
 Ring with Turnips, 110
 Salad (sandwich filling), 389
 Slice, 111
 Virginia, To Cook, 109
Hard Sauce for Plum Pudding, 461
Hash, Chicken or Turkey, in Cream, 133
Hash, Chicken or Turkey, Deluxe, 139
Hawaii Pineapple-Glazed Luau Pork, 111
Hawaiian Crab Curry, 186
Hawaiian Mai Tai, 503
Hawaiian Shrimp Salad in Papaya, 276
Hayden, Loret, 278, 366
Hayden, Ruth, 214
Health Salad, 269
Henry IV (of Navarre), King of France, 143
Herb Chart, 510-511
Herring, Salt, Pickled (inlagd sill), 32
Hollandaise Sauce, 350
 Blender, Joyce Burland's, 350
 Freezer, 351
 Mock, 351
Hominy Grits with Chicken Livers, Ruth Coburn's, 315
Honey Ginger Glaze Marinade, 353
Honey Scotch Sauce, 461
Horseradish Sauce, 335
Hot Sauce for Avocados, 353
Hotel King Alfonso XIII, Sevilla, Spain, 208
Howard, Mary, 19
Humphrey, Mrs. Hubert H., 9, 18, 48

Icebox Cookies, 473
Icebox Rolls, 381
Ice Cream, Ice Cream Desserts
 Caramel, Grandmother's, 421
 Coffee Ice Cream Pie, 428
 Pie, Quick, 429
 Roll, 419
 Strawberry Bavarian, 409
 Strawberry, My Grandmother's, 422

Imperial Saffron Sauce, 356
Indian Pudding, Baked, 437
Indonesian Sole, 173
Inlagd sill (pickled salt herring), 32
Iranian *Khorake Bademjan*, 316
Iranian *Shirin Polo*, 142
Israel, Embassy of, 383
Italy, Embassy of, 65
Jackson, Ethel, 413
Jackson, Louise, 504
Jansson's Temptation (baked anchovies and potato), 165
Jellied Desserts
  Coffee Charlotte Russe, My Grandmother's, 441
  Coffee Crème, 442
  Frosted Mint Delight, 443
  Lancashire Stone Cream, 405
  Lemon Snow, 406
  Pumpkin Chiffon Pie, 433
  Rum Pie, 434
  Strawberry Delight, 446
  Strawberry Mousse, 423
Jelly, Beach Plum, 495
Jelly, Crab Apple, Spiced, 495
Johnson, Mrs. Lyndon B., 9, 14, 18, 201, 313
Johnson, President Lyndon B., 12, 14, 201
Julglögg (Christmas Wine), 506

Kale, 239
Kennedy, Mrs. Edward M., 18, 399
Kennedy, President John F., 10, 12
Khorake Bademjan, Iranian, 316
Kidney, Kidneys
  Lamb, and Beef Pie, London, 304
  Lamb or Veal, Broiled, with Broiled Tomatoes and Scrambled Eggs, 118
  Lamb or Veal, Mixed Grill, 102
  Veal, Stew, 118
Kimball, Marny (Mrs. Clark Clifford), 9-15
King Crab, Alaskan, Casserole, 311
King Crab, Alaskan, Remoulade, 263
Kitchen Equipment, 513
Kosher and Dill Pickles, Quick, 489
Kovin, Bette, 37, 43, 68, 420
Krema Karamela (Caramel Custard), 402
Kumquat, Strawberry and Almond Supreme, 410

Ladyfinger Desserts
  Alsatian Cake, 410
  Butterscotch Icebox Cake, 439
  Chocolate Icebox Dessert, 440
  Coffee Charlotte Russe, My Grandmother's, 441
Laclede, Pierre, 490
Lamb
  Chops Orientale, 105
  Chops, Stuffed, 101
  Curry with Rice Pilaf, 136
  Curry with Saffron Rice, 135
  Kidney and Beef Pie, London, 304
  Kidneys, Broiled, with Broiled Tomatoes and Scrambled Eggs, 118
  Mint Lamb for Barbecue, 100
  Mixed Grill, 102
  Mousse with Vegetable Salad, 292
  Roast, Leftover, Open Sandwich with Gravy, 391
  Roast with Lemon Pepper Marinade, 102
  Shashlik, Russian, Sascha Burland's, 103
Lanagan, Margery Clifford, 69, 70, 92, 414
Lancashire Stone Cream, 405
Lansing Whiskey Carrots, 217
Lasagne, 68
Latvian Borsch, 49
Latvian Pâté, 36
Lemon
  Chiffon Pie Supreme, 430
  Pudding, New England, 437
  Sauce, 462
  Snow, 406
Lettuce Loaf, 379
Lime
  Chiffon Pie Supreme, 430
  Freeze, 444
  Marmalade, 494
  Sherbet, Creamy, 448
Liver, Livers
  Calf's, and Bacon, 115
  Calf's, Loaf, 119
  Chicken
    in a Blanket, 29
    with Brandy, 117
    Casserole, 309
    with Hominy Grits, Ruth Coburn's, 315
    Latvian Paté, 36
    Sautéed, 117
    Shirred Eggs with, 82

Lobster, Lobsters
  Canapé with Mustard Mayonnaise, 33
  Curry with Rice Pilaf, 136
  Curry with Saffron Rice, 135
  Live, How to Boil, 187
  Live, How to Steam, 187
  Salad, 269
  (sandwich filling), 389
  Sauce, 352
  Stew, 58
  Tails, African, Salad, 270
  Thermidor, 188
London Beef and Kidney Pie, 304
Louis Sauce, 336
Lucas, John, 19, 430
Lucet, Mrs. Charles, 18, 143, 412, 451, 457
Luncheon Egg Dish Florentine, 76

McConnell, General John P., U. S. A. F. Ret., 18, 157, 171
Macrae, John, Jr., 163
Macadamia Pineapple Pie, 431
Macaroni and Cheese Supreme, 69
Macaroon Ring with Ice Cream and Caramel Sauce, 406
Macaroons, 473
Mack, Lois, 201
Maffitt, Mrs. Edward P., 326
Maine Clam Chowder, 51
Mai Tai, Hawaiian, 503
Malaysia, Embassy of, 83, 116, 128, 135, 222, 245, 265, 357
Mandarin Orange and White Grape Salad, 271
Manicotti, 70
Marinade
  Golden, 352
  Honey Ginger Glaze, 353
  Oriental, 353
Marjoram, uses, 510
Marmalade, Lime, 494
Marshmallow
  Chocolate Pie, 427
  Dressing for Fruit Salad, 367
  Muscatel Fluff, 407
Martinelli, Giovanni, 11
Maryland Winter Pickles, 489
Maurice Salad, 270
Mayonnaise
  Blender, 367
  Blender, Curried, 367
  Mustard, 368
  Never Fail, 368
Meat, see Meatballs; Meat Loaf; see also Beef; Ham; Lamb; Pork; Veal; Venison
Meatballs, Small (små köttbullar), 33
Meat Loaf
  Chicken, 140
  German, 97
  Liver (calf's), 119
Menus (listed by main dish or occasion)
  Anticuchos, 115
  Beef Stroganoff, 92
  Beef Wellington, 96
  Canadian Bacon, Baked, 108
  Cannelloni, 66
  Chicken with Burgundy, 130
  Chicken with Cointreau or Grand Marnier, 132
  Chicken Hash Deluxe, 119
  Chicken Mousse Supreme, 288
  Chicken Salad Mold, Jellied, 286
  Chicken or Turkey Ring, Mother's, 146
  Chinese Shrimp with Hot Soy Sauce, 199
  Christmas Dinner, 150-151
  Crabmeat with Capers, Hot, 185
  Enchiladas, Mrs. Lyndon B. Johnson's, 313
  Filet of Sole with Shrimp Mousse, 175
  Fish Chowder, Mother's, 53
  French Chicken with Wine, 141
  Fricassee of Chicken, 138
  Fruit Salad, Molded, 293
  Kidney Stew (Winter Sunday Breakfast), 119
  Lamb Chops, Stuffed, 102
  Lobsters, Steamed, 188
  Lobster Stew, 57
  Malaysian, 128
  Maurice Salad, 271
  Mint Lamb, 101
  New Year's Day Party, 92
  Osso Buco Milanese, 106
  Polynesian Chicken, 142
  Poule au Pot, La, 145
  Quail or Dove with Mushrooms, 156
  Sailors' Beef, 98
  Scallops with Mushrooms and Wine, Party, 197
  Scrambled Eggs with Onions and Smoked Oysters, 82

Menus (*continued*)
  Seafood au Gratin with Madeira Wine, 321
  Shrimp Salad in Papaya, Hawaiian, 276
  Shrimp with Wild Rice, 201
  Spanish Paella, 193
  Swordfish Nantucket, Broiled, 178
  Thanksgiving Dinner, 150-151
  Venison Ribs, 157
Meringue Desserts
  Chocolate Pudding with Meringue, 436
  Lemon Pudding, New England, 437
  Macaroon Ring with Ice Cream and Caramel Sauce, 406
  Meringues (baked) I and II, 424
Mexican Guacamole, 268
Mexican Quail or Dove with Mushrooms, 156
Mexico, Embassy of, 403
Mint
  Frosted Mint Delight, 443
  Julep, Clark's, 503
  uses, 510
Mixed Grill, 102
Mocha Icing, 457
Monk's Dish, 222
Monroney, Mary Ellen, 445, 458, 481
Morgan, Mrs. Edward P., 148
Mornay Sauce, 354
Mother's Recipes
  Austrian Coffee Cake, 415
  Baking Powder Biscuits, 375
  Bar-le-Duc and Cream Cheese Salad, 255
  Blueberry Muffins, 375
  Chicken or Turkey Ring, 146
  Chicken or Turkey Sauce, 345
  Cinnamon Sugar Loaf for Tea, 377
  Daffodil Cake, 416
  Fish Chowder, 53
  Parker House Rolls, 382
  Scalloped Potatoes, 231
  Sponge Cake, 418
Moules Marinière, 189
Moussaka, 317
Mousse, Dessert, Cold
  Chocolate, 422
  Strawberry, 423
Mousse, Entrée
  Avocado (cold), 283
  Chicken and Cucumber (cold), 286

Chicken Curry (cold), 288
Chicken, Imperial (hot), 325
Chicken, Supreme (cold), 287
Corned Beef (cold), 289
Crabmeat (cold), 290
Egg Curry (cold), 291
Fish, with Lobster Sauce (hot), 325
Ham (cold), I, 291; II, 292
Lamb, with Vegetable Salad (cold), 292
Roquefort (cold), 295
Shrimp (hot), 175
Shrimp, for Salad (cold), 296
Smoked Salmon (cold), 295
Tunafish (cold), 298
Mousseline Sauce, 354
Muffins, *see* Breads
Muscatel Marshmallow Fluff, 407
Mushroom, Mushrooms
  Baked, My Grandmother's, 224
  Benedict, 223
  Canapés, Hot, 34
  Creamed, 224
  (and) Endive and Watercress Salad, 266
  with Madeira Wine, 225
  Ring, 225
  Ring Mold, 294
  Sandwiches, Toasted, 392
  Sauce, 354
  Soup, 57
  Soup, Cold, 57
Muskie, Mrs. Edmund S., 18, 51
Mussels, *Moules Marinière*, 189
Mussels Nantucket, in Wine, 189
Mustard
  Mayonnaise, 368
  Sauce, Creamy, 336
  Sauce for Spinach Salad, Maria Blake's, 336
Mustard Greens, 239
My Father's Recipe, *see* Father's Bran Muffins
My Grandmother's Recipes, *see* Grandmother's Recipes
My Mother's Recipes, *see* Mother's Recipes

Nantucket Bluefish Broiled with Gin, Nat Benchley's, 166
Nantucket Bluefish Salad, 256
Nantucket Brew, Ben Russell's, 504
Nantucket Broiled Swordfish, 178
Nantucket Mussels in Wine, 189

Nantucket Sandwich (ham and Swiss cheese), 392
Never Fail Cheese Dish, 85
Never Fail Mayonnaise, 368
New England Brown Bread, Old-Fashioned, 376
New England Corn Chowder, 52
New England Lemon Pudding, 437
New Orleans Pralines, 483
Niçoise Salad, 271
Nixon, Mrs. Richard M., 9, 18, 432
Nora's Cole Slaw, 263
Norway, Embassy of, 155
Nut, *see also* names of individual nuts
    Bread, 379
    Date Nut Sticks, 471
    Lace Wafers, 474

Oatmeal Cookies, Crisp, 475
Omelets, *see* Egg, Eggs
Onassis, Jacqueline Kennedy, 10, 18, 52
Onion Dressing for Duck, 159
Onions, Creamed, with Slivered Almonds, 226
Orange, Oranges
    Bread, 380
    Cointreau, Frosted, 407
    Madrilene, Cold Soup, Tom Blake's, 56
    Mandarin, and White Grape Salad, 271
    Marmalade Fluff Soufflé, 451
    Torte, 420
Oregano, uses, 510
Oriental Marinade, 353
Ortona, Mrs. Egidio, 18, 65
Osso Buco Milanese, 106
Oven Heat, 512
Oyster, Oysters
    Fried, 190
    Rockefeller, 192
    Scalloped, I, 190; II, 191
    Stew, 57
    Stuffing, for Turkey, 159

Paella, Spanish, 192
Pancakes and Crepes
    Blintzes, 383
    French Crepes or Pancakes, 384
    German Pancakes, 384
    Potato Pancake, German, 230
    Thin Quick Pancakes with Brandy, 385

Pandemonium Tunafish with Mushrooms, 324
Parfait Amandes, 444
Parker House Rolls, Mother's, 382
Parsley, Chinese Fried, 226
Parsley, uses, 511
Parsnips, 227
Partridge with Brandy Sauce, 156
Partridge with Crouton Dressing, 153
Pasta
    Cannelloni, 65
    Gnocchi I and II, 67
    Lasagne, 68
    Macaroni and Cheese Supreme, 69
    Manicotti, 70
    Spaghetti, "German," 71
    Spaghetti with Sauce, 72
Pastry, *see also* Pie
    Crust for Quiche, 42
    Cheese Puffs, 27
    Cornish Pasties, 97
    Cream Puffs, 425
    Double-Crust, 425
    Pirogi, 41
    Spinach Squares (*spanakopeta*), 235
Paté
    de Foie Gras in Aspic with Chicken, 294
    en Gelée, 34
    Giblet, 35
    Latvian, 36
    with Scallions and Brandy, 36
    Smoked Turkey, 38
Pea, Peas, 227
    Puréed, in Onion Shells, 228
    Split Pea Soup, 61
Peach, Peaches
    Fresh Peach Brûlée, 407
    Sauce, 462
    and Strawberries Flambé, 408
Peanut Butter and Bacon (sandwich filling), 389
Pear, Pears
    in Cointreau with Frozen Cream, Mrs. Woodrow Wilson's, 408
    Frozen Pear Salad, 272
    Stuffed with Cream Cheese and Grape Jelly Salad, 273
Pecan, Pecans
    Brown Sugar Cookies, 476
    Celery and Nuts (sandwich filling), 387
    Chocolate Nut Cookies, 470

Pecan, Pecans (*continued*)
  Fudge II, 482
  Macaroon Ring with Ice Cream and Caramel Sauce, 406
  New Orleans Pralines, 483
  Nut Lace Wafers, 474
  Pie, 431
  Rum Balls, 475
Pepparkakor (Christmas Ginger Snaps), 474
Peru, Embassy of, 114
Peruvian Barbecued Beef Heart *(anticuchos)*, 114
Pheasant, Roast, 154
Pickles and Relishes, *see also* Preserves
  Apple Chutney, 492
  Chili Sauce, 492
  Green Tomato Pickle, 491
  Kosher and Dill Pickles, Quick, 489
  Maryland Winter Pickles, 489
  Sauce Bali, 493
  Spanish Pickle, Madame Auguste Chouteau's, 490
  Winter Spiced Sweet Pickle, 491
Pidcock Ham (Georgia Ham), 110
Pie, Dessert
  Blueberry, Deep Dish, 426
  Blueberry, Deep Dish, Quick, 427
  Chocolate Marshmallow, 427
  Coffee Chiffon, 428
  Coffee Ice Cream, 428
  Ice Cream, Quick, 429
  Lemon Chiffon, Supreme, 430
  Lime Chiffon, Supreme, 430
  Pecan, 431
  Pineapple Island, 432
  Pineapple Macadamia, 431
  Pumpkin Chiffon, 433
  Pumpkin, Mrs. Richard M. Nixon's, 432
  Rum, 434
  Rum Cream, 434
Pie, Entrée and Appetizer
  Beef and Kidney Pie, London, 304
  Quiche, Easy, 43
  Seafood Quiche, 44
  Shrimp Quiche, 43
Pillsbury, Mrs. H. Bourne, 100
Pineapple
  Frosted Mint Delight, 443
  Island Pie, 432
  Macadamia Pie, 431

Oriental Sauce, Sweet and Sour, 355
Sherbet with Black Bing Cherries in Brandy, 447
and Walnut Upside Down Cake, Easy, 417
Pink Sauce for Shrimp, 337
Pirogi, 41
Plum Pudding, Christmas, 438
Polynesian Chicken, 142
Polynesian Chicken Cantaloupe Salad, 273
Polynesian Sauce, 355
Popovers, 380
Popovers, Cheese, 381
Pork, *see also* Bacon; Ham
  Casserole, 318
  Luau, Pineapple Glazed, from Hawaii, 111
  Rice Casserole, 319
  Roast, 112
  Roast Gravy, 349
  Roast, Leftover, Open Sandwich with Gravy, 391
  Spareribs, Barbecued Ribs, 113
  Spareribs and Sauerkraut, 113
  Sweet-Sour, 112
Portsmouth Brown Betty Pudding, 435
Potato, Potatoes
  Duchess, 229
  and Egg Salad, 274
  Hashed Brown, 229
  O'Brien, 230
  Pancakes, German, 230
  Salad, Edna Altemus, 274
  Sautéed Slivered, Clark's Favorite, 232
  Scalloped, Mother's, 231
  Straw, 231
Poule au Pot, La, 143
Poultry, *see* names of individual birds and game birds
Pralines, New Orleans, 483
Preserves, *see also* Pickles and Relishes
  Beach Plum Jelly, 495
  Blueberry Preserves, Spiced, 494
  Crab Apple Jelly, Spiced, 495
  Lime Marmalade, 494
  Rhubarb Conserve, 493
Ptarmigan, 155
Pudding, Dessert
  Apple, Swedish, 435
  Blueberry Bread Dessert, Old-Fashioned, 439

Pudding, Dessert (*continued*)
  Brown Betty, Portsmouth, 435
  Chocolate, with Meringue, 436
  Frozen Rice, Mary Ellen Monroney's, 445
  Indian, Baked, 437
  Lemon, New England, 437
  Plum, Christmas, 438
Pudding, Entrée
  Corn, 219
  Corn, Easy, 220
  Never Fail Cheese Dish, 85
  Tomato, Toast, Cheese Dish, 86
  Yorkshire, 383
Puerto Rican *Arroz con Pollo*, 127
Puerto Rican Shrimp *Asopao*, 199
Pumpkin Chiffon Pie, 433
Pumpkin Pie, Mrs. Richard M. Nixon's, 432

Quail
  with Brandy Sauce, 156
  in Casserole, 318
  with Mushrooms (from Mexico), 156
Quiche
  Crust for, 42
  Easy, 43
  Seafood, 44
  Shrimp, 43

Rabin, Mrs. Yitzhak, 18, 383
Radish and Butter (sandwich filling), 359
Rail in Casserole, 315
Raisin Sauce, 356
Ramos' Gin Fizz, 502
Raspberry Soufflé, 451
Ratatouille, 233
Remoulade Sauce, 337
Rhubarb Conserve, 493
Rice, *see also* Wild Rice
  Baked in Chicken Consommé, 245
  Chicken or Pork Casserole, 319
  Chicken and Rice Salad, 262
  Fried, 245
  Fried, Quick, 246
  Frozen, Mary Ellen Monroney's, 445
  Green, 247
  Pilaf, 248
Roquefort Dressing I and II, 369
Roquefort Mousse, 295
Rosemary, uses, 511

Rum
  Balls, 475
  and Beach Plums, Louise Jackson's, 504
  Cream Pie, 434
  Hawaiian Mai Tai, 503
  Pie, 434
  Sauce, 463
Russell, Ben, 504
Russian Shashlik, Sascha Burland's, 103

Saffron Rice Pilaf, *see* Rice Pilaf, 248
Saffron Sauce, Imperial, 356
Sage, uses, 511
Sailors' Beef (*sjömansbiff*), 98
St. Jacques Casserole, 320
Salad
  Alaskan King Crab Remoulade, 263
  Avocado with Chutney, 253
  Avocado and Grapefruit, 254
  Avocado, Molded, 283
  Avocado Mousse, 283
  Avocado, Stuffed, 255
    with Fresh Crabmeat, 253
    with Tomato Aspic, 254
  Bar-le-Duc and Cream Cheese, Mother's, 255
  Bay Ranch (crabmeat), 256
  Bluefish, Nantucket, 256
  Broccoli, 257
  Cabbage, East India, 257
  Cabbage, Red, 258
  Caesar, 258
  Celery and Mushroom, 259
  Celery Root Remoulade, 259
  Chef, 260
  Chicken, I, 260; II, 261
  Chicken Aspic, 285
  Chicken Cantaloupe, Polynesian, 273
  Chicken and Cucumber Mousse, 286
  Chicken, Hot, 262
  Chicken Mold, Jellied, 285
  Chicken Mousse Supreme, 287
  Chicken and Rice, 262
  Cole Slaw, Garden, 263
  Cole Slaw, Nora's, 263
  Corned Beef Mousse, 289
  Crabmeat, 264
  Crabmeat Mousse, 290
  Cream Cheese and Pineapple, Jellied, 290
  Crispy Green, 268
  Cucumber, 264

536 | INDEX

Salad (*continued*)
  Cucumber Vinaigrette, 265
  Egg Curry Mousse, 291
  Egg and Swiss Cheese, 265
  Endive, Mushroom and Watercress, 266
  Fennel, 266
  Fish, East Indian, 267
  Frozen Pear, 272
  Fruit, 267
  Fruit, Molded, 293
  Guacamole, Mexican, 268
  Ham Mousse II, 292
  Health, 269
  Lamb Mousse with Vegetable, 292
  Lobster, 269
  Lobster Tails, African, 270
  Mandarin Orange and White Grape, 271
  Maurice, 270
  Mushroom Ring Mold, 294
  Niçoise, 271
  Pear Stuffed with Cream Cheese and Grape Jelly, 273
  Potato, Edna Altemus, 274
  Potato and Egg, 274
  Shrimp, 264
  Shrimp, Creole, in Remoulade Sauce, 275
  Shrimp, Marinated, 275
  Shrimp, Mousse, 296
  Shrimp, in Papaya, Hawaiian, 276
  Shrimp Ring, 277
  Special, Loret Hayden's, 278
  Spinach, 277
  Sweetbread and Cucumber, 278
  Tomato Aspic, 297
  Tomato Stuffed with Pineapple, Red Onion and Cucumber, 279
  Tunafish Mousse, 298
  Vegetable, Leftover, Tom Blake, 279
Salad Dressing
  Boiled, I, 363; II, 364
  French, Basic, I and II, 364; III and IV, 365
  French, Pink, 366
  for Fruit Salad, 366
  Loret Hayden's, 366
  Marshmallow, for Fruit Salad, 367
  Mayonnaise
    Blender, 367
    Blender, Curried, 367
    Mustard, 368
    Never Fail, 368
  Roquefort, I and II, 369
  Sesame, 369
  Sour Cream, 370
  Special, Elizabeth Arden's, 363
Salami Rolls, 41
Salmon
  Boiled, with Egg Sauce, 169
  Broiled, 170
  Chowder, see New England Corn Chowder, 52
  Cold, 170
  Steak, Baked, 171
Salmon, Smoked
  with Capers, Bette Kovin's, 37
  Mousse, 295
Salty Joe Cocktail, 505
Sandwiches, Sandwich Fillings
  Beef, Leftover Roast, Open, with Gravy, 391
  Celery and Nuts, 387
  Cheese, Sharp, and Bacon, 387
  Cheese, Tomato and Bacon, Hot, 391
  Chicken, Leftover, Open, with Gravy, 391
  Crabmeat, Fresh or Canned, 388
  Chicken (sliced), 390
  Chicken Salad with Celery, 388
  Cream Cheese and Guava Jelly, 387
  Cream Cheese and Olive, 387
  Cucumber, 388
  Deviled Ham and Chutney, 389
  Egg and Onion, 388
  Egg Salad with Stuffed Olives, 388
  Ham Salad, 389
  Lamb, Leftover Roast, Open, with Gravy, 391
  Lobster, 389
  Mushroom, Toasted, 392
  Nantucket (ham and Swiss cheese), 392
  Peanut Butter and Bacon, 389
  Pork, Leftover Roast, Open, with Gravy, 391
  Radish and Butter, 389
  Sardine, 390
  Shrimp Hollandaise, on Toast, Open, 393
  Tunafish, 390
  Turkey, 390
  Turkey with Caviar, 390
  Turkey, Leftover, Open, with Gravy, 391
  Watercress, 390
Sangría I and II, 505

Sardine (sandwich filling), 390
Sardines, Broiled, 37
Sauce, *see also* Gravy; Sauce, Dessert; Salad Dressing
   Archiduc, Ambassador David K. E. Bruce's, 333
   Avocado, for Tomato Aspic, 333
   Bacon and Pea, 339
   Bali, 493
   Barbecue, I, 339; II, 340
   Barbecue, (for) Chicken, I and II, 341
   Barbecue, Special, 340
   Béarnaise, 341
   Béchamel, I and II, 342
   Cheddar Chesse, 344
   Chicken, Mother's, 345
   Creole, 345
   Cucumber, 346
   Curry, I, 346; II, 347
   Curry, Cold, for Vegetable Dip, 334
   Curry, Hot, 347
   Dill, I, 334; II, for Cold Salmon, 334
   Dill, for Poached Filet of Sole, 348
   Egg, for Boiled Salmon, 347
   Egg Dressing, 335
   for German Sauerbraten, 357
   Hollandaise, 350
      Blender, Joyce Burland's, 350
      Freezer, 351
      Mock, 351
   Horseradish, 335
   Hot, for Avocados, 353
   Lobster, 352
   Louis, 336
   Mornay, 354
   Mousseline, 354
   Mushroom, 354
   Mustard, Creamy, 336
   Mustard, for Spinach Salad, Maria Blake's, 336
   Pineapple Oriental, Sweet and Sour, 355
   Pink, for Shrimp, 337
   Polynesian, 355
   Raisin, 356
   Remoulade, 337
   Saffron, Imperial, 356
   (for) Shrimp Mousse, 176
   Sour Cream, for Tunafish Mousse, 337
   Special, for Fish Mold, 358
   for Sweet-Sour Pork, 357
   Tarragon, 338
   Tartar, 338
   Tomato, 358
   Turkey, Mother's, 345
   Vinaigrette I, 338; II, 339
   White, I (thin), 358; II (thick), 359; III (thickest), 359
Sauce, Dessert
   Anglaise, 458
   Brandy, Mary Ellen Monroney's, 458
   Caramel, 458
   Caramel, Easy, 459
   Chantilly Cream, 459
   Chocolate, I, 459; II, 460
   Chocolate, Easy, 460
   Foamy, 460
   Grand Marnier, 462
   Hard, for Plum Pudding, 461
   Honey Scotch, 461
   Lemon, 462
   for Lemon Snow, 463
   Peach, 462
   Rum, 463
Sauerbraten, German, 99
Sausage Stuffing, for Turkey, 159
Sauterne Celery, 219
Savage, Katrine, 233
Savory, uses, 511
Scallop, Scallops
   en Brochette, 193
   Casserole St. Jacques, 320
   in Cheddar Cream Sauce, 194
   Chowder, 60
   Creamed, 195
   and Mushrooms, Chinese, 194
   with Mushrooms and Wine, My Special Party, 196
   with Shrimp, Quick, 196
Seafood
   Casserole, Baked, 320
   Casserole St. Jacques, 320
   Continental (sole and shrimp), 197
   au Gratin with Madeira Wine, 321
   Quiche, 44
Senegalese Soup, 62
Senegalese Soup, Quick, 62
Sesame Dressing, 369
Shad and Roe, Fresh, 171
Shad Roe Dip, 38
Shashlik, Russian, Sascha Burland's, 103
Shellfish, *see* Clams, Crab, Lobster, Mussels, Oysters, Scallops, Shrimp

Sherbet
  Balls with Loganberry Juice and Cointreau, 446
  Cranberry, 447
  Lime, Creamy, 448
  Pineapple, with Black Bing Cherries in Brandy, 447
Shirin Polo, Iranian, 142
Shish Kabob, Filet of Beef, 92
Shrimp
  Asopao, Puerto Rican, 199
  Bisque, 61
  Cheese Casserole, 321
  Creole, 199
  Creole, in Remoulade Sauce, 275
  Curry with Rice Pilaf, 136
  Curry with Saffron Rice, 135
  Hollandaise Open Sandwich on Toast, 393
  with Hot Soy Sauce, Chinese, 198
  Marinated, Salad, 275
  Mousse, 175; Sauce, 176
  Mousse for Salad, 296
  Quiche, 43
  Ring, 277
  Salad, 264
  Salad in Papaya, Hawaiian, 276
  Sukiyaki, 200
  To Cook, 198
  with Wild Rice, 201
  and Zucchini Casserole, Chinese, Easy, 322
Silvercruys, Baron, 12
Silvercruys, Baroness, 243, 506
Sjömansbiff (Sailors' Beef), 98
Skewered Dishes
  Beef Heart, Barbecued, Peruvian *(anticuchos)*, 114
  Filet of Beef Shish Kabob, 92
  Scallops *en Brochette*, 193
  Shashlik, Russian, Sascha Burland's, 103
Små köttbullar (small meatballs), 33
Sole, Filets of Sole
  Florentine, 172
  Indonesian, 173
  Poached, 173
  with Shrimp Mousse (adapted from McCall's Cooking School), 175
  with Shrimp Sauce, 177
  Stuffed with Shrimp, 174
  Véronique, 177

Soufflé, Dessert, Baked
  Apricot, 448
  Chocolate, I, 449; II, 450
  Orange Marmalade Fluff, 451
  Raspberry, 451
  Strawberry, 451
Soufflé, Entrée
  Cheese (Cheddar, baked), 326
  Cheese, Ring (Cheddar, baked), 326
  Chicken (baked), 327
  Chicken (jellied, cold), 327
  Corn (baked), Lansing, 328
Soup
  Andalusian, Cold, 47
  Beef, Mrs. Hubert H. Humphrey's, 48
  Borsch, Cold (Blender), 48
  Borsch, Iced, 49
  Borsch, Latvian, 49
  Butternut Squash, 62
  Chicken, 50
  Chowder
    Clam, Maine, 51
    Corn, New England, 52
    Fish, 52
    Fish, Mother's, 53
    Salmon, *see* New England Corn Chowder, 52
    Scallop, 60
  Clam Bouillon, My Grandmother's, 50
  Consommé, Cold, with Caviar, 54
  Consommé and Cream Curry, 55
  Crème Vichyssoise, 64
  Curry, Cold, 54
  Ecuadorian Salad, 60
  Gaspacho, (Cold), 55
  Gaspacho, Mock, Cold, I and II, 56
  Hors d'Oeuvre, Cold, 58
  Hubbard Squash, 62
  Lobster Stew, 58
  Mushroom, 57
  Mushroom, Cold, 57
  Orange Madrilene, Cold, Tom Blake's, 56
  Oyster Stew, 57
  Senegalese, 62
  Senegalese, Quick, 62
  Shrimp Bisque, 61
  Split Pea, 61
  Tomato, Jellied, 63
  Turkey, 50
  Vegetable, 63

Soup (*continued*)
    Vichyssoise, Iced, Quick, 65; *see also* Crème Vichyssoise, 64
    Watercress, Cold, 64
Sour Cream
    Chicken Paprika, 146
    Coffee Cake, 415
    Dressing, 370
    Sauce for German Sauerbraten, 357
    Sauce for Tunafish Mousse, 337
Spaghetti, "German," 71
Spaghetti with Sauce, 72
Spain, Embassy of, 444
Spanakopeta (Spinach Squares), 235
Spanish Paella, 192
Spanish Pickle, Madame Auguste Chouteau's, 490
Spareribs, *see* Pork
Spinach
    Divine, Easy, 233
    and Eggs Casserole, Baked, 311
    with Mushrooms, 234
    Ring, 234
    Salad, 277
    Squares (*spanakopeta*), 235
Sponge Cake, Mother's, 418
Sponge Cake II, 420
Squash, *see also* Zucchini
    Butternut, 236
    Butternut, Soup, 62
    Hubbard, Soup, 62
    Yellow Summer, and Zucchini, 236
Sri Ong, Puan, 13, 18, 83, 128, 135, 222, 245, 265, 357
Steak, *see* Beef
Stew
    Fricassee of Chicken, 137
    Kidney (veal), 118
    Lobster, 58
    Oyster, 57
    Veal, 107
    Venison, 157
Stock, Chicken or Turkey, How to Make, 344
Strawberry, Strawberries
    Bavarian, 409
    with Cream Cheese, 409
    Delight, 446
    Ice Cream, My Grandmother's, 422
    (and) Kumquat and Almond Supreme, 410
    Mousse, 423
    and Peaches Flambé, 408
    Puffy Soufflé Omelet with Strawberries, 81
Soufflé, 451
Straw Potatoes, 231
Stuffing, *see also* Filling
    Cornbread and Herb, for Turkey, 158
    Onion Dressing for Duck, 159
    Oyster, for Turkey, 159
    Sausage, for Turkey, 159
Sukiyaki, Shrimp, 200
Sully, Maximilien de Béthune, minister of finance to Henry IV (King of France), 143
Sweden, Royal Embassy of, 32, 33, 98, 165, 474, 506
Swedish Apple Pudding, 435
Swedish Cinnamon Cake, 414
Sweet and Sour, Sweet-Sour
    Cabbage (or Celery Cabbage), Chinese, 216
    Pineapple Oriental Sauce, 355
    Pork, 112
Sweetbreads
    Broiled, 120
    (and) Chicken Ragout in Shells or Ramekins, 323
    Creamed, with Ginger, 120
    Creamed, with Sherry Casserole, 324
    and Cucumber Salad, 278
    How to Cook, 120
Sweet Potato Delight, Grandmother's, 232
Swordfish, Nantucket, Broiled, 178
Symington, Mrs. Stuart, 18, 77

Tamales, Hot, in a Blanket, 30
Tarragon
    Butter for Steak or Broiled Fish, 344
    Sauce, 338
    uses, 511
Tartar Sauce, 338
Thayer, Mary Van Rensselaer, 18
Thyme, uses, 511
Tiger's Milk, Baroness Silvercruy's, 506
Tomato, Tomatoes
    Aspic, 297
    Broiled, I and II, 237
    Chili Sauce, 492
    Eggs in Tomatoes, 85
    Green Tomato Pickle, 491

540 | INDEX

Tomato, Tomatoes (continued)
  (and) Onion and Eggplant, 238
  Sauce, 358
  Soup, Jellied, 63
  Stuffed with Pineapple, Red Onion and Cucumber, 279
  Toast, Cheese Dish, 86
Tongue, Beef, 121
Trout, Brook Trout
  Baked, 178
  Baked with Stuffing, 179
  Fresh (sautéed), 179
Truman, Mrs. Harry S., 9, 12, 18, 411
Truman, President Harry S., 12, 163
Tunafish
  Mousse, 298
  with Mushrooms, Pandemonium, 324
  (sandwich filling), 390
Turkey
  with Caviar (sandwich filling), 390
  Florentine, Casserole of, 307
  Giblet Gravy, 349
  Hash Deluxe, 139
  Hashed in Cream, 133
  Leftover, Open Sandwich with Gravy, 391
  Ring, Mother's 146
  (sandwich filling), 390
  Sauce, Mother's, 345
  Soup, 50
  Stock, How to Make, 344
  22 to 24 pounds, How to Cook, 150 II, 151
Turkey, Smoked, Paté, 38
Turnip Greens, 239
Turnips, 238

U. S. Senate Dining Room, 434

Vanilla Wafers, 476
Vaughan, General Harry, 163
Veal
  Calf's Liver and Bacon, 115
  Calf's Liver Loaf, 119
  in Consommé, 104
  Kidneys, Broiled, with Broiled Tomatoes and Scrambled Eggs, 118
  Kidneys, Mixed Grill, 102
  Kidney Stew, 118
  Milanesa, 105
  Osso Buco Milanese, 106
  Stew, 107
Sweetbreads
  Broiled, 120
  (and) Chicken Ragout in Shells or Ramekins, 323
  Creamed, with Ginger, 120
  Creamed, with Sherry Casserole, 324
  and Cucumber Salad, 278
  How to Cook, 120
Vegetable, Vegetables, see also names of individual vegetables
  Andalusian Soup, Cold, 47
  Canapés, Raw, 40
  and Chicken, Chinese, 140
  Crispy Green Salad, 268
  Health Salad, 269
  Leftover Salad, Tom Blake, 279
  Methods for Cooking, 207
  Ratatouille, 233
  Soup, 63
Venison
  German Meat Loaf, 97
  Ribs, 157
  Stew, 157
Vichyssoise, Iced, Quick, 65; see also Crème Vichyssoise, 64
Villa la Massa Fennel, 222
Villa Papiano, Florence, Italy, 67
Vinaigrette (for Cold Zakuski), 40
Vinaigrette Sauce I, 338; II, 339
Virginia Ham, To Cook, 109
Vitsaxis, Mrs. Basil George, 18, 235, 317, 402

Walnut, Walnuts
  Icebox Cookies, 473
  Nut Bread, 379
  and Pineapple Upside Down Cake, Easy, 417
Warfield, Kitty, 56
Watercress
  (and) Endive and Mushroom Salad, 266
  (sandwich filling), 390
  Soup, Cold, 64
Watermelon Pickle in a Blanket, 29
Weights and Measures, 512
Westmoreland, Mrs. William C., 18, 108
White Sauce I (thin), 358; II (thick), 359; III (thickest), 359
Wight, Randall Clifford, 425

Wild Dove, Breast of, 152
Wild Duck I (in Foil), 152; II (with Sauerkraut Stuffing), 153
Wild Rice, Baked, 246
Wild Rice Casserole, 319
Wilson, Mrs. Woodrow, 9, 408
Winter Spiced Sweet Pickle, 491
Wok (Chinese cooking pot), 136
Woodcock in Casserole, 318

Yankee Frankfurter and Noodle Casserole, 314
Yorkshire Pudding, 383

Zakuski, 40; Cold, 40; Hot, 41
Zucchini
    Parmesan, 239
    and Shrimp Casserole, Chinese, Easy, 322
    and Yellow Summer Squash, 236

MARNY CLIFFORD was reared in New England; Clark Clifford in St. Louis. They met in Germany, married, and, after living in St. Louis for thirteen years, moved to Washington in 1946. They have three daughters and twelve grandchildren.